Contents

04 Sixty years of Excellence
Always staying a step ahead of the opposition

08 In profile...
The man behind Corgi, Marcel Van Cleemput

10 The Early Years
Where it all started...

14 Corgi in the 1960s
The models produced during the Swinging Sixties

18 TV & Film during the 50s and 60s
A look at early successes

23 Corgi in the 1970s and 1980s
"Living in the Eighties"

29 TV & Film models during the 70s and 80s

32 In profile...
We meet product designer Terry Fox

34 Corgi Castings
One cast, two models

38 60th Anniversary Range
Models to celebrate such a special birthday

42 Corgi in the 90s
The new golden age

46 Corgi in the 00s
Millennium models

51 TV & Film 1990s onward
Corgi culture at its best

54 In profile...
Susan Pownall, the force behind the Collectors Club

56 In Profile...
It's a family affair with Don & Adrienne Fuller

58 Best Sellers
GIft sets combining classic models and new releases

62 Accessories & Figures
The finishing touches

67 In the Spotlight...
A closer look at the Simon Snorkel Fire Engine

69 In the Spotlight...
Commer Constructor

70 Nevva Wazzas
The models that were planned but never built

74 Corgi Catalogues
Marketing which is as collectable as the models

78 Corgi boxes
Packaging stretching back over six decades

80 The Great Book of Corgi

83 In the Spotlight...
007's Moon Buggy

84 Vanguards
A unique look into the story behind range

88 Aviation Archives
We chart the history of these popular aircraft

92 Road Haulage
Transportation and the models that came along

96 Trackside
Emerging from the shadow of Days Gone

98 In the Spotlight...
John Player Special Lotus 72 Formula 1

99 Price Guide
Value your collection

Welcome

Let us take you on a trip down memory lane. To be specific let us take you back to your childhood when amongst your many boxes of toys were Corgi models of all shapes and sizes. Over the last 60 years, since the Corgi name first came into existance, most of us have loved something made by this very British of brands.

So, to celebrate that landmark, we have pulled together this special 132-page anniversary issue looking at the origins of the firm, its development over the decades, the highs and lows, but most importantly the key models and ranges Corgi has produced.

Perhaps you loved the commercial vehicles, or the aviation models? Maybe the many fantastic cars or buses produced were your particular favourite? Or, like many, it was the models inspired by classic TV and film characters that excited you most. These pages are packed with memories of all of those.

Of course, to this day, many people (adults!) still collect vintage and new Corgi models and they are always on the lookout for that rare piece missing from their private collection. Maybe you've got it?

If you want to know just how much your models are worth we also have a 32-page section valuing all Corgi models at the back of this magazine. Why not value yours...you might be in for a very plesasant surprise!

CONTACT US...

EDITORIAL
PRODUCTION EDITOR
Cathy Herron
Contributors: David Boxall, Gijs Noordam, Paul Lumsdon, Rick Wilson

HEAD OF DESIGN & PRODUCTION
Lynn Wright

DESIGNER **Cathy Herron**

ADVERTISING
GROUP KEY ACCOUNT MANAGER
Claire Morris 01778 391179
clairem@warnersgroup.co.uk

ADVERTISING PRODUCTION
Danielle Tempest 01778 392420

PUBLISHED BY
PUBLISHER **Rob McDonnell**
Warners Group Publications PLC
The Maltings, West Street, Bourne,
Lincolnshire PE10 9PH
01778 391000
www.warnersgroup.co.uk

NEWSTRADE DISTRIBUTION
Warners Group Publications PLC
01778 391150

PRINTING

This publication is printed by Warners
01778 395111

Keeping ahead of the game!

Paul Lumsdon looks at 60 years of Corgi innovation

From top down:
Sights and sounds ME109 prototype; Sights and sounds Dambuster Lancaster; Sights and Sounds Spitfire

What makes a brand distinctive? To me it's a lot more than just a flashy pack or a colourful picture in a catalogue. Don't get me wrong, packaging and presentation are important in their own right but with a product like Corgi diecast there is something else that is harder to define – it has a 'Corginess' about it that has been born out of decades of culture from a dedicated, passionate workforce, instilled with an ethos of excellence and innovation.

When I joined Corgi in the late 1990s the brand was already over 40 years old, but I was immediately very aware that maintaining a position as market leader is not down to luck, but rather hard work and the skill and innovation of some of the industry's top professionals. The ethos was still present!

And at Corgi it was ever thus. Back in 1956, when Marcel Van Cleemput and his team of designers were about to unleash the first Corgi models upon the toy world, the instant impact of diecast models with clear plastic moulded windows was a major innovation of the day. It may seem insignificant, even trivial in today's high-tech world, but 'The Ones With Windows' was a major selling point over rivals Dinky, to the point where the phrase stuck as a key selling slogan and is remembered with affection to this day.

Including windows in models was a great start for Corgi, but in order to keep ahead of the competition, there was always a desire and drive to come up with something better, something unique. Corgi became very good at it and throughout the heyday of diecast in the 60s and 70s, right through to the current ranges, there are examples of truly excellent design and great innovation. Let's look at just a few examples from different eras.

1965 – JAMES BOND ASTON MARTIN (261)

Probably one of the finest toys ever produced, and certainly one of the most popular – even today it is in the

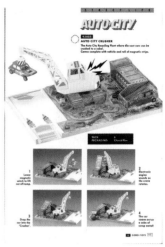

> Yet its original launch was rushed, its design was somewhat shambolic and the fact it all came together and worked, a minor miracle

Corgi range – yet its original launch was rushed, its design was somewhat shambolic and the fact it all came together and worked, a minor miracle. It was only after the success of the James Bond film Goldfinger, which premiered in London in September, 1964, that Corgi decided to make a model of the car that featured in the film. In fact it was early into 1965 before that decision was finally made and the target was to have the completed Aston Martin DB5 model available for Christmas 1965. The tooling lead time for a normal diecast car product was around 12 months, whereas this model was to be laden with working features just like the version in the film. So the challenge was set and there was no

time to lose, in fact it had already been lost! The only way the deadline could possibly be met was by having the car worked on by various designers at the same time. It was quickly determined that the key features would be an opening roof with ejection seat, a ping-up rear bullet proof shield and flick-out over-riders with machine guns. A designer was assigned to each feature and each was charged with keeping in close communication with the rest of the team. This was not ideal by any stretch of the imagination, particularly as each feature had to fit into a modified version of the existing Corgi Aston Martin body mould (model 218). The margins for error were huge but despite much tearing

Top down: 50th Anniversary Aston Martin DB5 from the James Bond film, Thunderball; James Bond original Aston Martin DB5, Corgi model 261

around with no small amount of panic thrown in, the Corgi team managed to pull it all together in time. Production then took over and the model had to be manufactured in time for Christmas sales. Incredibly they made it with seven weeks to spare but were then swamped by the demand. This was to become the big Christmas 1965 hit and retailers were selling out of DB5s within hours of receiving them. In the lead up to Christmas around 750,000 were sold, and there were still disappointed children that Santa could not supply. Since then there has hardly been a year pass, when the DB5, complete with all the original features, has not been in the Corgi range. In fact even recently the furore

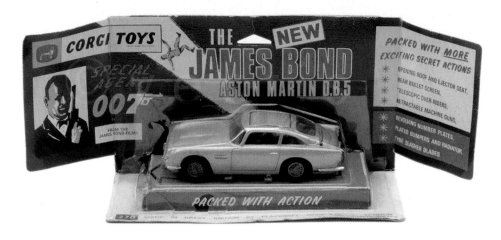

over the latest Corgi release to mark the 50th anniversary of Thunderball, continues as collectors try to obtain a highly limited 'gold' painted version of the DB5.

I doubt Marcel van Cleemput and his design team could have had even the slightest inkling that their somewhat rushed together design would still be enchanting children and collectors alike some 50 years later!

1991 – 1995 CORGI AUTO CITY

With our current day collector hats on it is quite easy to forget that Corgi Toys were for many years just that – Toys. During the 1970s and early 1980s there was intense competition between Corgi, with its 'Juniors' and 'Whizzwheels' brands and Mattel with its 'Hotwheels'. Many believe that when Mattel took over Corgi in 1989, it was primarily to take over the 'Juniors' toy ranges and to remove a major competitor. However, with Corgi as part of the 'team', the designers got to work on some exceptional toys which were marketed under the Corgi brand as 'Auto City'. What the development and tooling costs must have been is beyond me. These fantastic play sets featured a 'Juniors' vehicles combined with electronics for maximum realism and some fantastic feature packed buildings according to the set purchased. The 'Electronic Garage' as an example was a complete multi-storey car park plus a garage repair centre with ramp, car showroom plus roadway playmat with road signs. On the electronics side there were screeching tyre sounds, an electronic welding unit and the showroom had a revolving turntable and spotlights. Even when I flick through my old Corgi catalogue now I think – 'I wish I could have had one of them'. I have never seen an example of the Auto City Car Crusher but I would love one. A magnetic winch lifts the car from its ramp. There are electronic engine sounds as the crane rotates, the car is dropped into the crusher and a cube of scrap metal exits the other end – fantastic! Other sets had different features but all were designed with one thing in mind – having fun!

Sadly the Auto City brand was lost

> " With our current day collector hats on it is quite easy to forget that Corgi Toys were for many years just that – toys

to Corgi in 1995 when the Management Buyout took the Corgi collectable business over. It did however survive as Mattel Auto City until around 2003.

2005 – SIGHTS AND SOUNDS

The digital sound revolution, combined with advances in the miniaturisation of speakers, led to the development of 'Sight's and Sounds' technology from Corgi, offering new levels of realism, both visually and audibly, in collector products for the adult market. Although it was applied across various 'collector' ranges let's look at its application within Aviation Archive. As the models grew in size with the launch of 1/32nd scale aircraft, so did the detail and accuracy, to the point where it was felt –'What if the propeller rotated and the undercarriage could deploy and retract automatically?' Fast forward a few months and a mock-up for the 1/32nd scale Spitfire was underway. To encapsulate all the electronics in the model itself was not possible so the decision was taken to use the stand instead and to feed the wiring into the model via a connector on the underside of the model/top of the stand

From the top down:
Corgi 270 DB5 with tyre slashers. Image courtesey of Vectis; Corgi 261 DB5. Image courtesey of Vectis; Corgi 261 DB5 with original ejector seat.

cradle. With the extra space available in the stand base a sound chip and speaker could also be incorporated for extra realism. The development team bought some special outdoor microphones and arrangements were made to go and digitally record a real Spitfire. Meanwhile the new internal components were designed and electric motors were incorporated to drive the propeller and the undercarriage mechanism. For good measure small green and red LEDs were fed out to the wingtip navigation lamps and the stand base itself was designed to look like the internal controls of the Spitfire, with working switches for the engine start-up and other features. The technology went on to be used on other aircraft, including the 1/72nd scale Lancaster and Heinkel III, both of which were presented as bombers on sorties with sirens and spotlights to bring the scenario to life. Here was a special 'Dambusters' edition for the Lancaster, complete with breached dam wall! Several Corgi 1/50th scale trucks and the 1/50th scale Routemaster bus also received the 'Sights & Sounds' treatment. ◉

GET A SUBSCRIPTION TO
DIECAST COLLECTOR

Subscribe for just £8.99 per quarter on direct debit plus:

- ■ **Get every issue delivered direct to your door**
- ■ **Get your copy before it's even on sale in the shops**
- ■ **Save over 15% on the shop price**

SUBSCRIBE NOW

 Call 01778 392006 quoting the code DCC/CORGI16

 Or subscribe online at newsub.diecast-collector.co.uk

 Or return the form below to: Diecast Collector subscriptions, Warners Group Publications, FREEPOST:WARNERSGROUP   Offer ends 30th Sept 2016.

- ✂ - - -

I would like to subscribe to *Diecast Collector*, saving 15%, for just £8.99 per quarter.

YOUR DETAILS

Mr/Mrs/Miss/Ms   Initial(s)

Surname

Address

                    Postcode

We'd like to let you know about our latest offers.
If you do not wish to receive direct mail from the publisher please tick here ☐
If you do not wish to receive direct mail from selected third parties please tick here ☐

Email

I am happy to receive special offers via email from:
Warners Group Publications ☐ Selected third parties ☐
I would like to receive the *Diecast Collector* enewsletter by email ☐

Telephone

I am happy to receive special offers via telephone from:
Warners Group Publications ☐ Selected third parties ☐

DCC/CORGI16

Instructions to your Bank or Building Society to pay by Direct Debit

Name(s) of Account Holder(s)

Bank/Building Society account number   Branch Sort Code

Name of your Bank or Building Society

Reference Number (*Office use only*)

Service User Number   9 4 2 2 4 0

Banks and Building Societies may not accept Direct Debit Instructions for some types of account

DIRECT Debit

INSTRUCTION TO YOUR BANK OR BUILDING SOCIETY
Please pay *Warners Group Publications Plc* Direct Debits from the account detailed in this instruction subject to the safeguards assured by the Direct Debit Guarantee. I understand that this instruction may remain with *Warners Group Publications Plc* and, if so, details will be passed electronically to my Bank/Building Society.

Signature(s)   Date

MARCEL VAN CLEEMPUT

Gijs Noordam champions the visionary man whose incredible intelligence, imagination and drive was behind so much at Corgi Toys

When playing with my Corgi toys in the sixties, I did not realise at the time that there was a genius behind them: Marcel Van Cleemput. As a designer he was there at the birth of Corgi Toys in 1956, together with Howard Fairbairn, Mettoy's technical director. Their aim was to beat the popular Dinky Toys and Matchbox ranges and that proved very successful.

Marcel René Van Cleemput was born on 2 May 1926 in Croix, France, to fairly poor but hardworking parents, as he says in his autobiography that is included in the second edition of his *New Great Book of Corgi*. The family origins can be traced back to Belgium, hence his surname, which at the time was still a part of the Netherlands so he claims to be of Dutch descent.

In 1935 his family moved to England as his father was in charge of the installation of a textile plant for a French company in Marsden, West Yorkshire. Only speaking two words of English, he faced a hard time at school and regularly had to stand his ground as "Froggy". However, just like his parents he was a hard worker, mastering the English language very quickly and doing well in secondary school and college. Just after the start of World War Two, he enrolled at Huddersfield Technical College, following in the technical footsteps of his father whom was somewhat of an inventor. When his father changed jobs, the family moved to Loughborough so the young Van Cleemput switched to Loughborough Technical College School to further his engineering education.

His ambition being to become an architect, he attempted to study at an art college, but due to the war he was left to fill his time with

Born in France during 1926, Marcel van Cleemput moved with his family to England in 1935. After a few years back in his native homeland, he returned to England after the war to marry his sweetheart and then began an incredible career lasting nearly three decades that shaped the future of the diecast industry.

all sorts of odd jobs like assisting a vet, working as a draughtsman on tools for the aviation industry (including parts for the de Havilland Mosquito) and freelance designing from home. This experience must have been of great help when he joined Mettoy.

By the end of the war his parents decided to move back to France, just after he met his future wife Molly. Young Van Cleemput continued his work in France as a tooling designer but, upon applying for a passport to return to England to discuss his engagement plans, he found that he had to first fulfil his military service for France. After his dismissal from service, he returned immediately and went straight to England, to

marry his beloved Molly. This would bring him two daughters, Patrice and Ginette.

On 1st January 1954, he joined the Mettoy Company and he immediately felt part of a well organised team, driven hard by directors Henry Ullmann, son of the founder Philipp Ullmann, and Howard Fairbairn, the technical director. Both appeared to be early adopters of the now famous "management by walking around" style, unexpectedly popping up in any department of Mettoy and involving themselves in technical matters, design and marketing. The management went by the principle "company first", which did cause some problems for Van Cleemput during his many years of service with Mettoy but, as he says in his autobiography, the love for his job saw him through.

Van Cleemput was hand picked by Fairbairn to work closely with him on the development of a range of new toys that would compete with Dinky Toys. Fairbairn himself had a background in a casting company and, together, they chose the first six cars to start the Corgi range in 1955. Van Cleemput created the first drawings of the Ford Consul and Austin Cambridge, catalogue numbers 200 and 201.

This would be the start of a very productive period of new releases for almost 20 years after which the success regretfully started to wane, ending with Mettoy's demise in 1983. Van Cleemput attributes this to a number of reasons. In the beginning of the sixties, boys up to the age of 16 collected model cars but by the mid-seventies children of that age were more interested in electronic games and Transformers. Secondly, competition from other diecast and toy companies had grown substantially, especially in the Far East.

Although Corgi retained its number one

> His autobiography does not seem to answer the important question; where he found inspiration for the avalanche of features that he designed

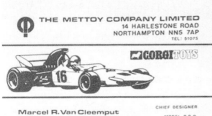

position in the field of TV and film, it was not sufficient to support the production of the more regular ranges. Mettoy desperately spent a lot of money on hiring a child psychiatrist, who advised on what toys children would like, but this could not stop the slide, let alone improve Mettoy's market and financial position.

Van Cleemput left Mettoy at the beginning of 1983, observing that his twenty eight years as Corgi's chief designer had been very exciting and rewarding, meeting many interesting people from very different walks of life and also realised that he was too young to retire. He registered his own companies, Acorn Technical Design Services and Acorn Models & Patents Company, through which he continued to work for Mettoy but now as an independent entrepreneur. Nowadays we would call that outsourcing. He also produced the wonderful *Great Book of Corgi*, published in 1989, chronicling the history of the company right up to his retirement.

During his years at Mettoy and Acorn, he miraculously found time to enjoy a great number of hobbies like photography, collecting postcards and stamps, badger watching and sports. Even during retirement he simply pushed on with a great many other interests and activities that makes me admire his energy and dedication.

His autobiography does not seem to answer the important question; where he found inspiration for the avalanche of features that he designed for the Corgi range during the years. "The one with windows", opening parts, spring suspension, steering, detachable wheels, Trans-o-lite, to name just a few. Probably he thought this self-evident: just like his father he was essentially an inventor and Mettoy gave him a free reign in this, provided he beat the competition.

On 15 March 2013 Marcel René Van Cleemput passed away at the age of 86 and was no doubt still considering new projects. He certainly deserves his place in history, not only for his many talents, but most of all as the one and only "Mr Corgi". ◉

Clockwise from top: Marcel van Cleemput with Corgi's former Marketing Manager, Martyn Weaver, at the company's Margate premises in November 2011; One of his many post-retirement projects, the fabulous Great Book of Corgi; The first two Corgi Toys designed by Marcel, the Ford Consul (No 200) and Austin Cambridge (No 201); Judging by the type of racing car, this was his business card during the early 1970s.

CORGI
The early years...

Gijs Noordam guides you through the early days of Mettoy and the launch of Corgi Toys

Wars always cause havoc, destruction and human suffering but sometimes something good comes from them. The German pre war toy industry was concentrated in, Bavaria where successful and innovative toymakers like Tippco had their workshops. Their main products were pressed tin toys, most of them with clockwork mechanisms. Tippco was founded in 1912 by Mr and Mrs Carstens, maiden name Tipp. In 1913 Philip Ullman joined the company and who was later followed by the son of a South African cousin, Arthur Katz. Ullman and Katz, like many German toymakers were Jewish and had to flee from the rise of National Socialism that in the early Thirties was particularly strong in Bavaria. In 1933 they both took refuge in England, a country with which the German toy industry had traditional long relations.

In Winteringham they set up The Mettoy Company Ltd, which continued the earlier German production of tin toys with clockwork mechanisms. The business again proved successful and many tin toys were exported to America which explains the strong position that Corgi Toys would acquire in that market in the late Fifties and Sixties.

During World War II the British toy industry was ordered to contribute to the war effort. Like other toymakers Mettoy changed to producing Jerry cans, shell fuses, landmines and magazines for Sten and Bren guns. Mettoy showed its quality and was awarded by the Ministry of Supply the management of a new factory

From top: Karrier "Bantam" Two Tonner (455); The first Corgi: Ford Consul (200); "Battle of scales"; Massey Ferguson Combine (1111)

complex in Fforestfach on the outskirts of Swansea in South Wales. By the end of the war this would provide Mettoy with a jumping board to the future. The new and extended factory was opened in 1949 by King George VI and there all administration was centralised, including tool and sample making, design and development. Mettoy's board consisted of Arthur Katz and Philipp Ullman and they were joined by the latter's son Henry.

Tin toys appeared somewhat outdated by the time Mettoy started making cast aluminium clockwork models for Marks and Spencer. These new models were possibly inspired by the success of Dinky Toys with its zinc alloy cast toys. The models were produced by the Birmingham Aluminium Casting Company under the name Castoys. In the early 1950s Howard Fairbairn, in charge of development of Birmingham Aluminium, made the switch to Mettoy in order to supervise and develop their investments in pressure die casting. For this and other new products a new company was formed, Playcraft Toys Ltd.

Due to the Korean war in the early '50s the use of zinc, the main metal used in diecasting, became restricted but when this ban was lifted Mettoy started to have a go at market leader and monopolist Meccano and its successful Dinky Toys. Through its old contacts Mettoy employed skilled

CORGI TOYS — SPRING SUSPENSION SEATS AND STEERING WHEEL — RENAULT "FLORIDE" — 222

CORGI TOYS — RENAULT "FLORID[E]"

> Like other toymakers Mettoy changed to producing Jerry cans, shell fuses, landmines and magazines for Sten and Bren guns

Bedford TK Cab with Carrimore Transporter (1101)

Above left: *Jaguar Fire Chief Car (213)* **Above right:** *Land Rover 109 W.B. (first casting, 406)*

Above: *the first 7 models selected by Howard Fairbairn and Marcel Van Cleemput:*
Ford Consul (200), Austin Cambridge (201), Morris Cowley (202), Vauxhall Velo

German toolmakers and hired the very talented designer Marcel Van Cleemput, a Frenchman whose life and career are described in more detail in the previous feature.

A Karrier Bantam carrier promoting CWS soft drinks served as a pilot for the new Corgi Toys range, named after the national Welsh dog and a tribute to the Fforestfacht factory in Wales. The fact that at that time the young Queen Elizabeth II was often spotted with Corgi pet dogs may

> ## In 1956 Corgi also launched the Corgi Model Club, a clever way of creating a bond with young collectors

have been a lucky PR coincidence.

Marcel Van Cleemput contributes the successful launch of Corgi Toys mainly to the drive and single-mindedness of Howard Fairbairn who only thought Corgi. Together they selected 7 popular British saloon cars of the era, the Ford Consul, Austin Cambridge, Morris Cowley, Vauxhall Velox, Rover 90, Hillman Husky and Riley Pathfinder, the latter having the advantage that it could easily be "made over" to the police car that was in use by various police forces of that time.

A problem however was scale. Looking at Dinky Toys they found that no standard scale was used at all and they consequently created the Corgi bible of scales that kept the scale of each new model within a certain predetermined size. And indeed, with due respect for Dinky Toys, if one compares similar models made by Dinky and Corgi, for instance the Jaguar 3.4 where you will find the Corgi model (208) to have a more robust and "real life" appearance compared to the Dinky (195).

Fairbairn and Van Cleemput also realized that in beating Dinky at its own game Corgi should offer something special and they decided that all models should have windows. "The first with windows" became the new and inspiring slogan. To add further advantage over Dinky they added a secondary line of these models with a mechanical flywheel device that by retracting the car, would propel it forward. Their inspiration come no doubt from the earlier tinplates with a clockwork

From top down: Riley Pathfinder (205) and the "make over" Riley Policecar (209); Citroën DS 19 (210); Jaguar 2.4 Litre Saloon (208 and 208S); the first Corgi: Ford Consul (200)

mechanism but regretfully the idea was short lived due to disappointing sales, especially in export markets. It did have the advantage that by installing the flywheel, Corgi had to redesign the tinplate chassis to a diecast base that gave another sales argument over Dinky.

The distribution of the new range, including the flywheel line, started in July 1956 and did well. That same year Corgi added a number of British sports cars, notably the Triumph TR2 ("frog eye", 301) and Austin Healey (301) that are still much sought after classic cars nowadays. Also a series of Bedford "Utilicon's" vans were released in different liveries, showing that Corgi at an early stage understood that by doing so it could sell more of the same without extra design and tooling cost. Also another British workhorse of the era made its entrance, the Commer lorry, one of them already showing the upcoming trend of merchandising model cars: the Commer "Wall's" Refrigerator Van promoting Wall's ice cream on the side panels (453).

In 1956 Corgi also launched the Corgi Model Club, a clever way of creating a bond with young collectors. The Corgi Club published a newsletter on a regular basis and each subscriber received a numbered certificate of membership and a cast Corgi lapel badge. A big force behind the Corgi Club was its secretary Bill Baxter who was much involved with Corgi's marketing, advertising and PR.

In 1957 the Corgi range was rapidly extended. Helped by the introduction of the first Corgi catalogue showing models to come, and new folded leaflets in all boxes showing other Corgi models, plus advertising on television and in youth magazines. Retailers also agreed to automatically take monthly new sample releases that helped production planning.

The new models that year included the Karrier "Bantam" Two Tonner (455), based on the earlier Mettoy C.W.S. soft drinks van; a Jaguar 2.4 Litre Saloon (208 and 208M) that was named Mark 1 after the introduction of the Mark 2; Land Rover 109 W.B. (406) that was to become the first of more than 10 million pieces sold in different guises; and the Bedford TK with Carrimore Car Transporter (1101), the first Corgi Major and also the basis for the first Corgi Gift Set. As a possible tribute to Van Cleemput's French roots the Citroën DS 19 (210) was released at the end of that year as the first foreign car in the range and the first to have a diecast base outside the flywheel line.

In 1958 Corgi enhanced the playability of its models by designing trailers, a service ramp and Carrimore Low Loaders with a detachable rear axle. The first "Rocket" models made their entry and in general Corgi improved quality so that new items could withstand a four foot drop test from a filing cabinet! The greatest non-event of that year (as Van

Cleemput puts it himself in his Great Book) was the simultaneous introduction of a real life new Rover and its model, the famous Road Rover (intended 212) that did not make it but certainly influenced the design of the first Range Rover. Regretfully the few castings, made by Corgi in great secrecy, were melted down when Rover ditched the project, with only 2 models and boxes surviving somewhere in the cabinets of very lucky collectors.

In 1959 Corgi did some re-vamping of existing models, like a two tone colour variation of the original saloon cars that were released in 1956 and a Jaguar re-make into a fire chief car (213). But there were also new castings like the Ford Thunderbird (214), made up from a separate main body and hardtop. The same construction was used for the sleek and famous Mercedes 300 SL Hard Top (304). Also, a wonderfully tooled Massey Ferguson Combine (1111) entered the arena of farm related toys. The innovation of the year was spring suspension, "Glidamatic" that was even registered by Corgi as a trademark and would soon be the standard on all new Corgi releases.

Top: The first with "Glidamatic" suspension: Renault Floride (222)

Above: Corgi Jaguar 3.4 (208) versus Dinky Jaguar 3.4 (195)

Below: Two tone versions: Ford Consul (200), Auston Cambridge (201), Rover 90 (204) and Standard Vanguard (207)

The first car to be fitted with this ingenious system of two wires staked to the inside of the chassis and resting on the axles was the Renault Floride (222). It was also the first to have new vacuum formed interior with a steering wheel fitted.

The end of the decade was near but the Sixties were already waiting around the corner promising to become possibly the most exiting part of Corgi's history. ◉

Sources: "A concise history of CORGI TOYS and other Mettoy products" by Rod Ward, "The Great Book of Corgi" by Marcel Van Cleemput

The Swinging Sixties

Gijs Noordam remembers the golden age of Corgi Toys

After Corgi's successful start the range really took off in the beginning of the 1960s. In this chapter we will focus on Corgi's innovations during this decade.

In March 1960 Corgi issued the Aston Martin DB4 Saloon (218), the first diecast model to have an opening bonnet which revealed a detailed engine. This car would later form the basis for the very popular James Bond DB5.

Early 1960 saw a new theme - the Chipperfields Circus range. Starting with the Circus Crane Truck (1121. A nice combination of the already existing International Tow Truck (1118) and Mettoy's tinplate toy experience.

The 1961 highlight was no doubt the Bentley Continental (224). It had self-centering steering, another first which operated by slightly pressing on the left or right side to move in that direction. It was also the first Corgi to be fitted with jewelled headlights which found their way to many later models. Also the spare wheel under the opening trunk was a nice touch and of course something to get lost easily. Mr Katz, Corgi's CEO at the time, used this model as his "business card" during his two months World Sales Drive that took him from the New York Toy Fair to Japan, Hong Kong and Australia.

The Ford Consul Classic 315 (234) had a bonnet that was automatically opened by pushing down the front of the car activating a keg on the front spring. The Ecurie Ecosse Racing Car Transporter (1126) also had enlarged self-centering steering and of course great play value as it could carry three racing cars. The Triumph Herald Coupe (231) had a fully opening bonnet just like the real car, revealing a detailed engine including a separate black air filter.

The same year Corgi introduced kits that one could build to enliven your own toy car scene. A gold plated

Main image:
Bentley Continental with self-centering steering (224)

From the top:
Chevrolette Sting Ray witch retractable jewelled headlights (310) in metallic grey and cerise; Ford Consul Classic 315 (234)

Golden Guinea Gift Set was issued that proved the stepping stone for other the gold plated Trophy Models which were sold through Marks & Spencer at the time. Today you won't come across these models at specialised shops and auctions very often. If you do, they would command high prices in mint boxed condition.

1962 was another busy year for Corgi with the release of 12 re-vamps and Gift Sets onto the market. A Jaguar E-Type with detachable plastic hard top (307), a Fordson Power Major Tractor with half Tracks (54) and a Jaguar Mark X Saloon with opening bonnet and boot, including two small suitcases. A major new feature was TRANS-O-LITE, a system by which a battery operated flash light was piped to the four corners of the Superior Ambulance on a Cadillac Chassis (437). TRANS-O-LITE was developed further for other models and even became a Corgi Trademark.

1963 saw many new developments

> ## "The Priestman "Cub" Shovel had an ingenious mechanism that enabled shovelling, lifting and discharging the grab in one fluent motion

1960

for the company. These included TRANS-O-LITE being used without the help of a battery on the Volkswagen Toblerone Van (441). The light source "bounced" via highly polished mouldings or rods from one end of the car to the other. Another Volkswagen, the Kharman Ghia (239) had the automatic bonnet system, first used on the Ford Consul Classic. Under the bonnet one finds a spare wheel and a small suitcase. Underneath the boot lid is a detailed engine, found under a transparent cover. This was also the first Corgi saloon to receive an injection moulded plastic interior. In Mister Softee's Ice Cream Van (428) the vendor rotates through a knob on the base plate, serving his customers on either side of the van through sliding windows. In the Citroën ID 19 Safari (436) the rear

seat also rotates, be it horizontally, by means of a thumb wheel in the base plate. The tailgate also opened in an upper and lower part, just like the real car. The Priestman "Cub" Shovel (1128) had an ingenious mechanism that enabled shovelling, lifting and discharging the grab in one fluent motion. The Commer Police Van (464) was fitted with the battery operated flashlight seen on the earlier Superior Ambulance. The Chevrolette Sting Ray (310) was fitted with retractable jewelled headlights and a newly designed plastic spring suspension system. With the Constructor Gift Set (GS24) various liveries could be tried out on two Commer chassis. The Hillman Imp (251) included folding rear seats and an opening rear window, with a suitcase on the rear parcel shelf. The

Clockwise from above left: Citroën ID 19 Safari with rotating rear seat (436); Aston Martin DB4 Saloon, the first Corgi with an opening bonnet (218); Volkswagen Kharman Ghia (239); Bentley Continental with self-centering steering (224); Bedford TK with Carrimore Machinery Carrier and detachable rear axle (1131)

Carrimore Machinery Carrier (1131) had a detachable rear axle to lower the platform during loading and unloading operations and the year's highlight was no doubt the Ghia L 6.4 (241) that was literally packed with gimmicks like an opening bonnet, boot, doors, tip up seats and a small Corgi dog on the rear parcel shelf.

In 1964 Corgi introduced the Classic Range with very detailed and highly finished models of icons such as the Model T Ford (9011) and the Bentley Le Mans (9001). The Austin A60 Driving School Car had a steering system mounted as a roof sign that made playing more fun compared to earlier self-centering steering. It came in a Right and Left Hand Drive edition (236 and 255). The Buick Riviera (245) again had the TRANS-O-LITE feature, now on both front and rear lights. The Simon Snorkel Fire Engine (1127) provided great play value with its operating booms and retractable stabilising legs. Another first, this time on the Mercedes Benz 600 Pullman (247) were operating windscreen wipers. They were actually rotating clear discs with painted wipers close to the windscreen which was spotted with raindrops.

1965 saw the start of the Film & TV related models which made Corgi a true "Merchandiser". These models will be dealt with in a separate chapter.

Other firsts from this time can be found in the finely detailed spoked hubs and working conveyor belts that the Forward Control Jeep (64) came with. The Lotus Elan S2 (318) had sliding side windows and seats that could fully tip up. The Chrysler Imperial (248) did not only carry the usual features like an opening bonnet, trunk and doors but also a surprise in the boot, a nicely detailed golf trolley with bag and clubs. The wheels were newly styled louvred diecast that would soon find their way to other models soon. The Ford Cab with Detachable Trailer (1137) had a cab that could be tilted forward,

> "Separate coloured pictures could be inserted at the front of the screen to create the impression of a colour TV

Another form of merchandising can be found in the Corgi models relating to Walls Ice Cream. We have already seen the swivelling vendor in the Walls Ice Cream Van and 1965 brought two smaller cars in Walls Ice Cream livery based on the Ford Thames Chassis (447 and 4784). The latter contained a box that when cranked with a handle at the back of the car chimed the five note Walls jingle.

The Ferrari Berlinetta Le Mans (314) had an ingenious opening engine cover which reveal a detailed 12 cylinder block and a spare wheel.

showing a big engine underneath including a cooling fan. The trailer was fitted with an amazing automatic coupling system that left the trailer standing on its jockey wheels when uncoupled. Upon coupling again these wheels automatically withdrew, a very clever piece of engineering. Finally the Volkswagen 1200 East African Safari Rally (256) could be steered away from a charging rhino by turning the spare wheel mounted on the roof.

Although 1966 was another busy year for Corgi there were still new releases with remarkable innovations. The Ford Consul Cortina Estate Car

(440) thanked its woody appearance to side trims that were a part of the interior moulding, extending to the sides of the car that was tooled in an upper and lower part. The Carrimore Car Transporter (1138) was pulled by the Ford Tilt Cab, with the transporter having a clever folding system for lowering and lifting the top deck. Another first were adjustable chocks to stop the cars from rolling away. The Volkswagen Break Down Truck (490) was fitted with a winch unit. This was operated by the spare wheel fitted on it and with tool boxes with opening lids, showing sets of plated tools.

1967 proved to be Corgi's most successful year, both from the view of models sold (almost 17.5 million) and company profits (more than £1.2 million). Mettoy received its second "Queen's Award to Industry" and its second "Highest Standard Award" from the National Association of Toy Retailers. Corgi's exports markets were also performing well.

The Ford "5000" Super Major Tractor (67) could be steered realistically with the steering wheel itself. The Chevrolet Kennel Service (486) carried 4 dogs in comfort, and featured a light canopy in the roof, sliding clear windows in the sides and an opening tailgate. The Ford Tilt Cab design found its way to the Holmes Wrecker Recovery Vehicle (1142), combined with a twin lift boom system that could be operated separately or together. The Lotus Elan Hard Top (319) brought a separate chassis that could be detached from the car body and clicked back again.

From the top: Ford Consul Cortina Estate Car "woodie" (440); Volkswagen Break Down Truck (490); Corgi Classics: 1915 Model T Ford - black edition (9011); Ferrari Berlinetta Le Mans (314); Simon Snorkel Fire Engine (1127); Ford Thames Wall's Ice Cream Van (478) chiming the five note Wall's jingle

Above: *Mercedes Benz 600 Pullman with operating windscreen wipers (247)*

Another Corgi first was the battery powered television set in the Lincoln Continental Executive Limousine (262). Separate coloured pictures could be inserted at the front of the screen to create the impression of a colour TV. The interior and boot were lined with carpeting just like in a real limo. The Lancia Fulvia Sport Zagato (332) was not only a very nicely styled car but it also had a side opening bonnet and separate lens mouldings that were fitted in the radiator.

The Commer Mobile Camera Van (483) carried a platform with a camera on a tripod and cameraman that could be fitted either in front, on top or at the rear of the van.

In 1968 Corgi introduced a true innovation: Take-Off Wheels. They were fitted with "Golden Jacks" on a number of existing and new models like the Rover 2000 TC (275) and the Mini-Marcos (341). These wheels added great play-value and luckily there were spare wheel packs available for wheels that would, without failure, go missing. Although not equipped with new features the Jaguar E-Type 2 + 2 Fastback (335) should be mentioned for the front end

From the top: Ferrari
Berlinetta Le Mans (314)

opening bonnet with detailed engine underneath. It also had opening doors, tilting front seats, side opening fast back door, sliding rear seats enlarging the luggage area and a separate copper coloured exhaust casting.

The American "La France" Aerial Rescue Truck (1143), an elaborate model featuring a triple extension ladder on a rotating turntable, separate clip on ladders stowed away in the trailer, stabilising arms and a lot of detailed gear like a bell, siren, footplates, faucets and a dry-chemical extinguisher. Finally, the newly tooled Mini-Cooper "Magnifique" (334) impressed with its many opening features on such a small scale, and a brightly coloured sliding sun roof and a plated trim around the wheel arches and the bottom end of the car.

On 10 March 1969 fire swept through in Corgi's Swansea factory, destroying its warehouse along with one year's stock of Corgi models. As a consequence the production numbers of some models got lost and are referred to quoting the known production number " + 1969 Sales". Luckily the design and production areas were not structurally affected.

A wonderfully styled Italian Ghia Mangusta de Tomaso (271) was issued with a detachable chassis, mounted with a very detailed V8 engine and rolling on "magnesium type" wheels. Corgi had designed new steering systems for its models many times. This time for racing cars by means of swinging the racing driver to the left or the right. The newly designed Lotus-Climax (158) and Cooper-Maserati (159) were equipped with this innovation.

From the top: Buick
Riviera in 3 colour
variations (245)

Also in the field of farming Corgi continued to introduce new features like the hydraulic side scoop for the Ford "5000" Tractor (74). The first sign of a major strategic change, prompted by the increasing number of Corgi competitors, was the first model fitted with Whizwheels, the Ferrari 260 Dino Sport (344). Corgi models could now compete on the plastic racing tracks that became so popular by the end of the 1960s. The early Whizwheels had "Red Spot" hub centres and a number of cars, like the Ferrari, that were already in production with regular wheels received this new type of wheels. The second model to receive theseearly Whizwheels was the Chevrolet Astro 1 Experimental Car (347). Its real feature is the sliding rear section of the body that also lifts the chairs in the interior, thereby allowing easy entrance and exit from the car.

Due to market changes at the end of the '60s, Mettoy started to review its diecast ranges, introducing new collections like Qualitoys and Corgi Rockets. Regrettably this also meant that some of the successful Corgi principles, established decades before, such as the continuous drive for innovation and the quality of castings in general, fell by the wayside. Nevertheless one can hardly blame Mettoy. The toy market was changing very quickly and it was hard to predict in what direction it would go. The market of young consumers became confused, just like the youngsters themselves. ◉

Source: "The Great Book of Corgi" by Marcel Van Cleemput

Corgi TV & Film

One of the successes of the Corgi Toys range during the 1960s was the introduction of diecasts modelled after actual cars appearing in popular TV series and movies

Above: The Saint's Volvo P-1800 (258) with its "civilian" predecessor (228)

It all started with The Saint's Volvo P-1800 (258) that was released in the spring of 1965. Roger Moore, the archetypal English gentleman, played the role of The Saint in the very popular TV series with the same name. Corgi used the basic Volvo P-1800 (228), painted it white, added a driving figure with a tuxedo and the logo of The Saint on the bonnet. Three variations of this logo exist: in black on a white bonnet, in white on a red bonnet and in white on a blue bonnet. The last version is scarce and in total 1,159,000 (+ 1969 sales) cars were sold. A huge success for a relatively simple car.

In October 1965 Corgi released the even more successful James Bond Aston Martin DB5 (261). Using the existing Aston Martin body (218) which was actually a DB4, Marcel Van Cleemput and his staff cramped the model with three features not shown before: ejector seat with flip-up roof, rear bullet-proof shield and flick-out overriders and hidden machine guns. The figure of James Bond nicely resembles Sean Connery who drove this car in "Goldfinger". Also "the baddie" appears to have walked in directly from the picture: an Asiatic gunslinger in a blue overall. A total of 3,974,000 (+ 1969 sales) were sold.

In January 1966 The Avengers Set was released as Gift Set 40. A great set of two cars that were already available in the Corgi range and could be converted with little modification into a new TV related Gift Set: the 1927 3 litre Bentley

(9002) and the Lotus Elan S2 Roadster (318). The figures of John Steed (Patrick Macnee) and Emma Peel (Diana Rigg) were of course included. Emma in her very '60s white trouser suit and French beret, with John in a classic Saville Road outfit and bowler hat. A wonderful diorama offers ample room for both cars, Emma Peel standing next to her car and Steed's 3 umbrella's. On the back of the diorama there is an "in depth" story telling that the cars of cinema and TV heroes and heroines were chosen with great care to fit the characters. 190,000 (+1969 sales) passed the counter.

By already having a basic model at hand that could be re-engineered to fit a special edition, the Oldsmobile "The man from U.N.C.L.E. (497), released in August 1966, showed once again Corgi's prowess. The pre-existing Oldsmobile Super 88 Sheriff Car (237) and standard saloon version (235) formed the basis for this "Trush-buster" as used in the successful TV-series that started in September 1964. Napoleon Solo at the wheel and next to him Ilya Kuryakin, both firing their guns from the side

> ...the Batmobile racing through the cave, slashing a chain with the blade up front, at the same time firing rockets from behind

windows. Of great detail are the 3 bullet holes in the front screen. According to the text on the diorama U.N.C.L.E. stands for United Network Command for Law and Enforcement, an "organisation pledged to protect the welfare and interests of people and nations anywhere in the world from the forces of evil". So you could say the armed wing of the United Nations. The Headquarters of U.N.C.L.E were situated a few blocks away from the United Nations building. A blue and a more scarce white version of this car are known. Total sales: 1,479,000 (+1969 sales).

Another TV and film related blockbuster was the Batmobile (267), released in October 1966. Around 5 million Batmobiles were sold, becoming the best selling car for Corgi. The figures of Batman (alias Bruce Wayne) and Robin The Boy Wonder are included. The first version of the Batmobile had gold hubs and red bat emblems. The diorama coming with this first type is full of action, the Batmobile racing through the cave, slashing a chain with the blade up front, at the same time firing its rockets from behind the cockpit. On the back of the diorama the Batman story is summarized in English, French and German.

February 1967 saw the release of the *The World of Wooster* Bentley (9004), identical to the Bentley in the Avengers Gift Set. There is some doubt whether Bertie Wooster and his manservant Jeeves who played the leading parts in the famous books by P.G.Wodehouse, drove a Bentley. In any case, a Bentley

was used in the BBC TV series *The World of Wooster* and Corgi happened to have one on stock. Marcel Van Cleemput considered the model somewhat of a flop as sales in 1967 only reached 34,000. Nevertheless a clever extension of the production life of this wonderful Bentley!

With some small modifications Corgi generated another nice Gift Set from existing models like Batman's Batmobile and Batboat (Gift Set 3), issued in June 1967. Take the original Batmobile (267), fit a tow hook, add the hull of the Dolphin 20 Cabin Cruiser (104) with a new superstructure, large fin and Batman logo, use the Wincheon Trailer in a shortened version, equipped with square mudguards and two springs to clip on the Batboat, paint the trailer gold, add some operating and secret instructions and a new Gift Set is born. With sales figures over 1.5 million to boot!

The James Bond Toyota 2000 GT (336, October 1967) was again a wonderful film related model. This time from the Bond film *You Only Live Twice* in which a young Sean Connery is rescued by Aki Wakabayashi of the Japanese Secret Service, from Osato's gunmen in a cream white Toyota 2000 GT Convertible. The Toyota only existed as a saloon, two convertibles were especially made for the picture and one is still surviving in the Toyota museum. The special feature is of course the rocket firing mechanism in the boot. It sold a total of 768,000 (+1969 sales).

Daktari was a big success on British television and November 1967 saw the release of the Daktari Set (Gift Set 7). Once again it appeared a lucky coincidence that Corgi had the Land Rover (438) used by Dr Marsh Tracy already in the range. It only needed some restyling with zebra striping and the addition of figures of the doctor,

From the top down:
Napolean Solo takes a shot at the bad guys; Batmobile (267); "The World of Wooster" Bentley (9004) with blundering Bertie Wooster and his clever manservant Jeeves; Aki Wakabayahi at the wheel, one of the scarce lady drivers in the Corgi range; Chitty Chitty Bang Bang (266). **Below:** James Bond Aston Martin DB 5 (261) with its "civilian" predecessor (218)

Judy the chimpanzee, a tiger on the bonnet instead of the spare wheel and the doctor's assistant Paula sitting astride Clarence, the lion. The box has an appealing top card showing Clarence, the doctor and Paula. On the back Judy shows an elephant with a dental problem the way to the Wameru Sub-district hospital.

The Green Hornet's Black Beauty (268), released in November 1967, and selling 345,000 (+ 1969 sales) was based on an American TV series. Although the Green Hornet had the lead in the series, in real life the actual hero turned out to be Kato, played by Bruce Lee. It was the first time that his Kung Fu fighting style was seen outside the movie theatres of Chinatown. The masked figures of the Green Hornet and Kato are seated in the back and behind the wheel. The Green Hornet fires his gun from the open window. Together with the rocket firing platform behind the grill at the front, the boot with a launch pad for plastic radar scanners, green windows and an enormous Green Hornet logo on the roof. This is a great, but possibly somewhat underrated, model.

The second version of the famous James Bond Aston Martin DB5 (270) was issued in February 1968. It now had the correct silver spray and with added features compared with the first issue of October 1965 (261). It had sales of 1,172,000 (+1969 sales). The added features were the three-sided revolving number plates at the front and the rear, and the fitting of tyre slashers in the rear wheels.

Another make-over of the Land Rover (438), was in the style of the Daktari Set. Now white with the same black striping, brought the Lions of Longleat as Gift Set 8 in August 1968, with 357,000 (+ 1969 sales). Included are a warden standing up from the cabin through a manhole

and a lions den in which we find Clarence from the "Daktari" Set, be it without his glasses and 2 other new lions who would re-appear some months later with the Scammel Chipperfield's Menagerie Transporter (1139).

Chitty Chitty Bang Bang (266, November 1968) was modelled after the car that starred in "The most fantasmagorical film ever made", based on a children's book by Ian Fleming. A complicated model with a lot of nice details like the serpent horn, the exhaust system, the bonnet strap and of course the flip-out wings operated by the handbrake.

Included are the four figures from the film, Caractacus Potts played by Dick van Dyke, his two children and Sally Ann Howes as Truly Scrumptious. Packed in a very nice box, the car rests on a platform that gives the impression that it is flying through the clouds. Also included was a diorama with the castle of the wicked Baron and his balloon. 776,000 (+1969 Sales) were sold.

The Monkees Monkeemobile (227, December 1968) copies the dragster type of car used by the American pop band The Monkees in the popular TV series. The band was composed of Americans Micky Dolenz, Michael Nesmith and Peter Tork and Englishman Davy Jones, hence Mike, Davy, Pete and Micky. The Monkees scored a number of international hits, including "Last train to Clarksville" and "I'm a Believer". Although it is a detailed model there are not the usual gadgets

that Corgi included in its earlier TV and film related issues. 82,000 (+ 1969 sales) Monkeemobiles were sold.

The Beatles' Yellow Submarine (803, February 1969): originally written by the Beatles as a children's song, turned out to be a big hit and inspired a United Artist animation film in 1968. Corgi was asked to reproduce the submarine on small scale, using numerous stills from the film and adding John, Paul, George and Ringo popping up from two hinged hatch covers. The first version had a yellow and white hatch cover, the second two red ones like in the film. In total a meagre 44,000 (+ 1969 sales) were sold. Apparently the market was not waiting for this type of model, notwithstanding the many Beatles' fans all over the world.

Noddy's Car (801) was released in July 1969, and although it includes some nice figures from Enid Blyton's children's books, it is completely out of line with the other Corgi range of the 1960s. Nevertheless 280,000 (1969 sales) were consumed by the market.

In the Giant Daktari Set (Gift Set 14, May 1969) we find again a clever combination of previous models, with some modifications. The Land Rover with the same "menagerie" as the earlier Daktari Gift Set (7), the Bedford Giraffe Transporter (503) now repainted in jungle colours and decals of the "Wameru sub-district" like on the Land Rover and the Dodge "Kew Fargo" Livestock Transporter (484), having changed its load of pigs for a

Inset, top down: James Bond Aston Martin DB 5 (270), 2nd version; Oldsmobile "The man from U.N.C.L.E" (497) in blue metallic and white version; The Green Hornet's Black Beauty (268)

Main image: The Saint's Volvo P-1800 (258) with its "civilian" predecessor (228);

Inset, top left: Daktari Set (Gift Set 7)

Inset, top right: James Bond Toyota 2000 GT (336) with the re-issued model in the 007 Series (65102)

mother and baby elephant and also a jungle "Wameru sub-district" livery. Included is a diorama that can serve as a background for the models. 110,000 (+ 1969 sales) of these sets were sold.

We finish this decade of TV & Film related releases with The Hardy Boys' Rolls-Royce (805, June 1970). Marcel Van Cleemput admits that this psychedelic update of the Classics Rolls-Royce Silver Ghost 1912 (9041) should never have been. It is not clear whether he said this because of disappointing sales figures or tarnishing of the original model. After the Monkees Monkeemobile (227) and the Beatles Yellow Submarine (803) this was the third rock band that received its own Corgi status. The box tells us a little more about the background of The Hardy Boys. Joe and Frank Hardy (saxophone and guitar), sons of the famous private eye Fenton Hardy, are teenager detectives, using their rock band as cover for their war against crime. Assisted by the other band members Chubby Morton (drums), Pete Jones (guitar) and Wanda Kay (vocals) they solve. One only wonders why criminals did not go immediately underground when they spotted this brightly coloured vintage car. ◉

Sources: "The Great Book of Corgi" by Marcel Van Cleemput; "TV & film diecasts" by Dean Sheperd in Diecast Collector July 2010; "Corgi – it(s) figures!" by Gijs Noordam, produced in various Diecast Collector issues during 2015

Living in the eighties

David Boxall *looks back at the models and innovations from Corgi in the 1970s and 1980s*

Two rather significant events took place in 1969 which were to influence the beginning of the 1970's for Corgi Toys. Firstly, in March 1969, there was a very serious fire at the Swansea factory. While production continued, the warehouse and all the stock was destroyed. This created a shortfall of models required by retailers. In order to maintain their levels of stock, traders had to rely on other manufacturers, such as Dinky Toys. This was not the best way to launch into another decade. Furthermore, the records of sales for the whole of 1969 were lost in the fire.

The second event to take place in 1969 was that Mr Philipp Ullmann retired as Chairman and Director of the company, after more than thirty-five years.

Many of the cars released in 1968 and 1969 were available into the 1970's. The Hillman Hunter 'London to Sydney Marathon Winner' is a good example, released as model No 302. This model was issued in blue with a white roof and black bonnet. It was produced in a 1:43 scale, and was fitted with the 'Golden Jack's' system. It carried a spare hub and tyres on the roof, plus an opening toolbox and a swivelling spotlight. This car was purchased in a window box, with a kangaroo - to highlight the dangers of the rally. This very attractive model had jewelled lights front and rear, and came with

a pack of sponsorship transfers. The slightly larger scale was more in line with foreign manufacturers.

Two new ranges of toys were introduced in 1969. The first was the Qualitoys range. These vehicles were larger and more robust, and aimed at a younger market. There were eight brightly coloured working models altogether.

Also in 1969, came the Corgi Rockets range. These vehicles had a detachable chassis, which could be removed with the use of a key. The cars were particularly fast, hence the name. These cars had their own

Above: In 1984, the release of the Thorneycroft Van was to help sustain Corgi sales during the mid-1980's.

track system with a variety of special sections to drive over or through. Seven cars were initially available, mostly in bright metallic colours. A quantity of track and specialised accessories were released in 1970 to expand the Corgi Rockets system.

The contract to supply Husky models to Woolworth stores had come to an end, and in 1970 the range was renamed Corgi Juniors. By 1971, there were more than fifty Corgi Juniors available.

With the introduction of some of these new ventures and ranges of toys, Corgi seemed better prepared for the

1970's. It was good to begin the new decade with a few developments and innovations in hand.

As fast cars was now the growing trend for most manufacturers, the 1970's began with the introduction of the Corgi Whizzwheels. These wheels were made of plastic. They replaced the spun aluminium hub and tyre, which was far more realistic but more expensive to produce. The Whizzwheel was not only lighter but it was shaped so that a minimum amount of the plastic wheel was actually in contact with the surface. By 1971, there were thirty four diecast cars, all fitted with Whizzwheels.

In February 1970, the release of Roger Clark's V6 3 Litre Ford Capri, model No 303 was typical of the new releases. In white with a black bonnet, this model came with various transfers and a set of racing numbers. It had opening doors and was fitted with the all-new Whizzwheels.

The Rolls Royce Silver Shadow with Coachwork by HJ Mulliner, Park Ward, was released as model No 273. This car was produced in a 1:43 scale and retained the 'Take-Off-Wheels' system. It appeared in grey-blue and white with an opening bonnet and boot, opening doors, folding seats, chrome bumpers and grill, and jewelled headlights, and was a very substantial model.

While the emphasis on fast cars was to remain, there were fewer models released with the sort of features that had become commonplace.

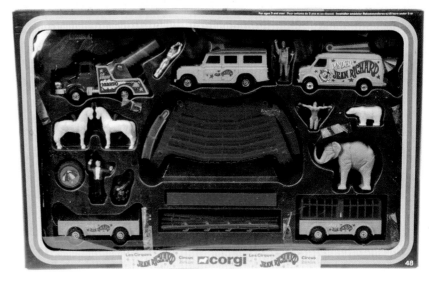

The demographic of the purchasing public was to change, with fewer older children now buying and collecting. In addition, there were many more manufacturing competitors. These two factors alone, together with the steady rise in manufacturing costs, made toy production far more difficult. With so many toy makers, Corgi's market share decreased. This led to a reduction in the number of models produced at the main factory in Northampton, and consequently, there was a reduction in the workforce. Many reasons have been cited for Corgi's reduction in size, and yet in 1971, they still managed to take the award for 'Toy of the Year' for boys, with their range of Corgi Rockets.

Furthermore, Corgi had been engaged to produce a range of toys for

From the top: The Circus was also a popular theme with the release of the Jean Richard's Circus Set, as GS 48; The 1975 Catalogue features a number of the Military models available; A quantity of track and specialised accessories were released in 1970 to expand the Corgi Rockets system; There had been a growing interest in F1 racing cars, as can be seen in the Corgi Catalogues; In 1981, Corgi released a whole new range of toys in their 'Corgitronics' and 'Corgimatics' series.

Fisher Price. They had been selected due to the very high standards of production maintained throughout the Corgi range.

The Corgi diecast range was expanded further with examples such as the Morris Marina 1.8 Coupe, No 306, and the Citroen SM, No 284. The Marina in metallic deep red or lime green, had opening doors and bonnet, which revealed a detailed engine. The Citroen in metallic yellow or mauve, had opening doors and rear hatch with a hinged parcel shelf. Both cars had Whizzwheels, although the Citroen had the addition of plated hub discs, which greatly enhanced the appearance.

An exception to the models with Whizzwheels was the Massey Ferguson '165' Tractor with Saw Attachment, released in March 1970, as model No 73. The tractor was issued in the familiar red grey and white, and had a circular saw fitted to a spring connection, which rotated with the forward motion of the tractor.

In 1972, the Police 'Vigilant' Range Rover was released as model No 461. It was issued in white and had a number of special features, including an opening rear hatch and a large storage area for emergency roadside equipment. The window box package had a policeman and a number of road signs and orange cones. It also had large swivelling roof lights in chrome, and opening side panels. This model achieved a staggering 1,055,000 sales, and was finally withdrawn in 1979.

> ## "Many reasons have been cited for Corgi's reduction in size, and yet in 1971, they still managed to take the award for "Toy of the Year', with their Corgi Rockets

1970

Corgi continued to release diverse ranges of models, such as a series of eight aircraft produced by Linn in Hong Kong. A further series of aircraft was released in 1973.

There was clearly a growing interest in racing generally, this was even reflected in the sales of Corgi dragster cars. It was the introduction of the new 1:36 scale F1 racing cars, however, which really gave sales a boost. In 1972, the Surtees TS9 was released as model No 150, and led the field for many new releases.

In 1973, the John Player Special Lotus was released as model No 154. This very popular racing car in gold and black achieved an outstanding 2,027,000 sales. This was to be followed with a larger version in 1974, produced in a 1:18 scale, as model No 190. There were more releases from the 1:36 F1 stable in 1974, and all achieved high sales figures.

Sports and Competition cars were generally in favour, The Ferrari Daytona 365 GTB/4 was released in 1973 as model No 323. This model in red, white and blue had opening doors, with a detailed interior and was produced in a 1:36 scale. A second Ferrari Daytona with Corgi & JCB logos, was released as model No 324.

There was still demand for other vehicles too. In April 1974, Corgi released the Volkswagen Driving School Car as model No 400. Issued in deep metallic blue this car had the mechanism from one of the earlier Corgi Volkswagen cars, which enabled

Clockwise from above left: The Hillman Hunter 'London to Sydney Marathon Winner' was released as model No 302; In April 1974, Corgi released the Volkswagen Driving School Car as model No 400; In 1972, the Police 'Vigilant' Range Rover was released as model No 461, and achieved a vast number of sales; Corgi continued to release gift sets such as the Mini Camping Set, released as GS 38, in February 1977; The Corgi diecast range was continually expanding with cars such as the Morris Marina 1.8 Coupe, No 306.

it to be steered. It had a gold coloured steering wheel on the roof, 'L' plates, and labels on the doors.

As Corgi approached the middle of the decade, they promoted their toys as 'the finest range of die-cast scale models in the world'. They had released a range of Military vehicles in 1974, mostly in a 1:60 scale, or similar, and had an extensive range of standard scale saloon cars, together with a growing number of 1:36 scale saloon cars.

The Mercedes-Benz 240 D, model No 285, was released in March 1975. In metallic blue or green, bronze or beige, this car had a tow bar, opening doors and boot with chrome bumpers and grill. The same car was utilised for Gift Set 24, the Mercedes-Benz 240 D and Touring Caravan.

> It was the year that the Muppets took to the road, and emergency vehicles and helicopters seemed to be in demand

Corgi continued to release gift sets such as the Mini Camping Set, released as GS 38, in February 1977. This had a Mini with opening doors, chrome bumpers and grill, detailed red interior and Whizzwheels. The camping element of the gift set was a plastic click-together tent in orange and dark blue, together with a female sunbather and a male figure standing at a barbecue.

Also in 1977, the 1902 State Landau was released as Gift Set 41, to celebrate the Queens Silver Jubilee.

The 1977 Corgi Catalogue shows that the majority of models were in a 1:36 scale, with only a few of the more traditional scale models still available. One of these is the VW 1200 Rally Car, model No 385. In blue with

Whizzwheels and chequered stripes on the roof and sides, rallying as number 5. This car had no opening features, and an all-in-one plastic moulded interior.

1978 was the 'Best Year Ever' according to Peter Katz, the Managing Director. A number of new Gift Sets were released such as the Metropolitan Police Land Rover and Horsebox, as GS 44, together with more diecast cars – all in 1:36 scale. The Circus was also a popular theme with the release of the Jean Richard's Circus Set, as GS 48.

There were also a number of individual vehicles and sets, made by Corgi and released by Marks and Spencer, under their brand name. The sets were very well designed with colourful dioramas in the background of the box.

Clockwise from the top left: In 1981, Corgi released a whole new range of toys in their 'Corgitronics' and 'Corgimatics' series; The Qualitoys range was introduced in 1969. These vehicles were larger, more robust, and aimed at a younger market. The Thorneycroft Van was released many times in a variety of colours and all with different themes and logos; The Ford Escort Van in the new dark blue window box with Corgi logo.

Finally, 1979 saw the release of more colourful cars and models, together with numerous TV and film related toys. It was the year that the Muppets took to the road, and Emergency vehicles and helicopters seem to in demand. It had generally been a good decade for Corgi Toys, with many changes undertaken to meet the demands of a fiercely competitive market. The expectation of high sales for individual models, however, had slowly diminished during the 1970's, as increasing uncertainty in the toy market had gathered pace.

The demographic of the purchasing public had continued to change, and was shrinking ever faster with much younger children now buying and playing with toys. More basic toys were clearly produced to appeal to

this younger age group, and greater diversification was undertaken. The different scales and range of toys available under the Mettoy banner, was successful according to the headline news of 1978, which cited record profits. Trading difficulties were highlighted in 1979, however, and in 1980 the company declared the first trading loss for almost a decade. Consequently, while Corgi continued to release excellent models - including many more saloon cars, there were significant job losses in Northampton.

Further saloon car releases included the Rolls Royce Corniche, in July 1979, issued in four different colours, as model No 279. It had opening doors, bonnet and boot, a detailed engine and interior plus chrome bumpers and trim.

In October 1980, the Ford Escort was released as model No 334. In three different colours, with opening doors and detailed interior, the Escort's appearance was planned to coincide with the launch of the actual car. Ford had even designed a special box for a quantity of models - these were issued as model No 333.

The Mini Metro, model No 275, was released in the same month and also had opening doors and a detailed interior, together with an opening hatch and plated headlights. A quantity of these models in different colours were bought by British Leyland and issued in a special box, which greatly enhanced the models popularity.

In 1981, Corgi released a whole new range of toys in their 'Corgitronics' and

Clockwise from the above left: In 1984, the release of the Thorneycroft Van was to help sustain Corgi sales during the mid-1980's; In 1981, Corgi released a whole new range of toys in their 'Corgitronics' and 'Corgimatics' series; The Limited Edition Model T Ford with the new Corgi logo, released in 1986; Corgi took every opportunity to promote and sell its models; The Model T was a particularly colourful range.

'Corgimatics' series. All the models had special feature and were 'Battery-operated Micro-Chip Action' vehicles. There were more than a dozen models released altogether, between 1981 and 1983. Each of the toys in the series had a different theme and all were very innovative.

In October 1981, the 'Royal Wedding Metro' was released as model No 275. In purple with an off-white interior, opening doors and hatch, this model had the Prince of Wales' crest, together with the initials C and D on the doors, in silver.

In January 1982, a series of 'Duo Packs' were produced for the French market as 'Les "Plus" de Corgi'. These consisted of a large size Corgi model and a similar small model from the

Thorneycroft Van was a major breakthrough for the company, and was to help sustain Corgi's market share for two to three years. The Thorneycroft Van was released many times in different colours and all with different themes and logos. It was joined by the AEC Lorry, the Ford Model T, and others. The Thorneycroft Bus was also a great favourite. These Vans were really models for the collector rather than toys. The different models certainly created a very colourful display and the window boxes enabled the model to be seen and protected at the same time.

Corgi Club members 'Limited Edition' models were well supported and this also ensured a certain number of sales. It is interesting how castings were used repeatedly, and that the club members bought the new issues as they appeared – all very reminiscent of the 1960's approach to increasing the potential number of sales.

A model of the Ford Escort Van was also released in abundance. All had excellent colour schemes and logos, many of which were promotional models of well known companies. All these popular models, which were continually reissued, helped to keep the cost of re-tooling down and the peripheral costs as low as possible.

Finally in 1988, a new series of vintage Sports and Saloon cars of the 1950's and 1960's was introduced. The cars were well made beautifully finished and proved to be rather popular.

It was perhaps credit due to Corgi for their hard work that made the company far more attractive - even saleable. In 1989, Corgi was purchased by Mattel Inc.,the American based makers of Hot Wheels.

Another new chapter opened and the Corgi story continued. The Corgi name and various brand symbols have brought a great deal of pleasure to numerous generations. The proof is that we are still buying obsolete Corgi toys manufactured from 1956 right up to the present day – quite an achievement. ◉

Source: Images used courtesy of Vectis Great Book of Corgi – Marcel R. Van Cleemput; The Unauthorised Encyclopedia of Corgi Toys - by Bill Manzke; TheRamsays Guide; The Corgi Years; The Barry Score Collection.

Clockwise from top left: Further saloon car releases included the Rolls Royce Corniche, in July 1979, as model No 279; While the Ford Escort Van had opening rear doors, many of the models had no opening features. (choice of 2); The 1989 Limited Edition model of the Mini, marking the thirtieth anniversary of this wonderful car; The popular Corgi Toys 'Cars of the Fifties' series appeared in 1982; In February 1970, the release of Roger Clark's V6 3 Litre Ford Capri, model No 303 was typical of the new releases; The Rolls Royce Silver Shadow with Coachwork by HJ Mulliner, Park Ward, retained the 'Take-Off-Wheels' system.

'Junior' range. Later in the year a similar idea was used as a promotion for Woolworth, under the heading of 'Little and Large, the Little one Free'.

In June 1982, the Ford Sierra 2.3 Ghia was released as model No 299. This car had opening doors and hatch together with a hinged parcel shelf. Once again, Ford bought a quantity of these models and also designed the box for their release.

The Corgi Toys 'Cars of the Fifties' series also appeared in 1982, and included the 1952 Jaguar XK 120, model No 803, and the rally version, model No 804. Also in the series was the 1956 Mercedes-Benz 300SC, model No 805, and the soft-top version, model No 806.

In 1983, after further redundancies, Mettoy decided to move all operations

to the one site in Swansea. Following a major review, however, the company finally called in the receivers in October of that year.

It was the end of Mettoy and the beginning of a new chapter for 'Corgi Toys Ltd'. Needless to say that a great deal of reorganisation took place with a quantity of left over stock to sell. The new logo comprising of a car and traffic signs was introduced, along with the deep blue window box. A silver-grey window box was also produced for the new Corgi Classics range of models, which was to be quite extensive. To accommodate the new range of toys, changes were also made to the number system, with letter prefixes to the numbers.

In 1984, the release of the

Corgi TV& Film

PART 2

*After the highs of the 1960s, **David Boxall** guides you through the various TV and film models released throughout the 1970s.*

Above: Corgi released the Magic Roundabout Musical Carousel as model No H852, in December 1972.

Film and Television models have always been very popular. After all, they receive the maximum amount of publicity and advertising. Consequently, diecast manufacturers made a real effort to create a model with that extra special feature or two. Corgi was no exception. It made some of the most popular models ever produced.

Generally, the main trends in the 1970's were towards slightly larger models in a 1:36 scale, and the use of plastic wheels which Corgi called Whizzwheels. Throughout the two decades every effort was made to produce quality toys as cheaply as possible. Film and TV models seem to be more colourful in the 1970's and non-existent in the late 1980's.

In May 1970, 'The Saint's Volvo P 180 (model No 201) was re-released with Whizzwheels. This version had a new red label on the bonnet, with the 'Saint' logo in white but was essentially the same casting as the 1960's version. Simon Templar was at the wheel, and the car was noticeably quicker – far more sprightly with the Whizzwheels. It was withdrawn in 1972.

Corgi released the Magic Roundabout Musical Carousel as model No H852, in December 1972. The model was made in Swansea but the musical movement was Swiss. The large red wheel-like button wound the carousel up – with the help of Dylan, the guitar playing rabbit. The Carousel went round to the tune of the Magic Roundabout, and the figures and model came in a colourful box.

In July 1976, the Kojak Buick was released as model No 290. It was manufactured in a 1:36 scale and appeared in deep bronze with a white interior and chrome bumpers, wheel discs and grill. This model had opening doors and a clip-on roof light in red. The Crocker figure sat in the rear seat as though firing through the rear side window, and Kojak himself stood outside the car in a firing position. A firing sound could be made by means of a wheel at the rear bumper. The Kojak package came complete with a self-adhesive New York Police Dept. Lieutenant's badge.

The James Bond Lotus Esprit was released as model No 269, in July 1977. This sleek model in white, housed the mechanics for a variety of functions. These included: firing rockets via the periscope, and the extension of the fins and rudders via the vent at the back of

Above left: In May 1970, 'The Saint's Volvo P1800, model No 201 was re-released with Whizzwheels.

In the late 1980's, the James Bond DB5 was available in a blue window box as C.271, and simply labelled 'Aston Martin'.

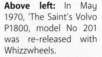

Top down: Corgi released The Saint's car as model No 320, in 1978. Simon Templar was now driving a Jaguar XJS; In 1978, Corgi released the larger 1:36 scale model of the James Bond Aston Martin DB5, as model No 271.

Left from the top down: The City of Metropolis Police Car as released as model No 260, and the Superman Van as model No 435; In October 1977, Corgi released the Starsky and Hutch Ford Torino, model No 292; Charlie's Angels, was released as model No 434, and the Incredible Hulk was issued as model No 264.

the car. This model was available in the early yellow and black window box, or the later black and white 'film edged' window box with a photo header card.

In October 1977, Corgi released the Starsky and Hutch Ford Torino, model No 292. In a 1:36 scale, this car had no features which opened but it did have chrome bumpers and grill. The car was in bright red and the distinctive white band was applied as a label. The car came in its own diorama with a roadway base and a night scene background. The figures of Starsky and Hutch together with a 'suspect' figure all formed part of the diorama. The figures were no longer hand painted for this set but were colour-moulded in plastic.

In 1978, Corgi released the larger 1:36 scale model of the James Bond Aston Martin DB5, as model No 271. This model was completely re-tooled for the new scale. The car was finished in silver and had the same features as the early 1960's model: the bullet shield, ejector seat, and extending front bumpers and guns. The wheels on this new version had a disc type wheel hub, and the radiator and bumpers were gold paint plated.

Corgi also released The Saint's car as model No 320, in 1978. Simon Templar had sold his Volvo and was now driving a Jaguar XJS. The car was issued white, naturally, with a red interior and the all-important Saint Figure on the bonnet of the car. The model had opening doors, an aerial and chrome trim, and was available until 1981.

The James Bond Lotus Esprit was released as model No 269, in July 1977.

The James Bond Citroen 2CV, from the Bond film 'For Your Eyes Only', was released as model No 272.

The Circus came to town in November 1978, when Corgi released Gift Set 48, The Jean Richard's Circus. The set contained the Human Cannon Ball vehicle, the Land Rover and Animal Trailer, and the Booking Office Van – all in 1:36 scale. The set also had a number of Circus related items, including: a 12 piece ring set, a Ringmaster, two horses, an elephant, a bear, a chimpanzee, together with a clown and the human cannon ball. The box and vehicles were in the Jean Richard's livery of red and yellow, and all had the colourful circus logos.

Another crime-prevention team released in 1978, was Charlie's Angels, issued as model No 434. The custom van was finished in pink with a colourful Charlie's Angels logo and image on the side. The blue, black and purple striped window box with a yellow interior, header card and logo, made the whole package a very attractive purchase.

The Incredible Hulk was released as model No 264. The Mazda pick-up had a caged area to the rear of the vehicle, and the Incredible Hulk was bursting through the top of the cage. The large Plastic Hulk figure looked rather animated within the Window box. This model also had a colourful header card depicting the Hulk in defiant mood.

Corgi released the City of Metropolis Police Car as model No 260, in January 1979. This very attractive model had opening doors, and was finished in bright metallic blue with an off-white

interior. It had a white roof with a double set of lights and sirens on the top. This was essentially the Buick Police Car with a 'City of Metropolis' crest on the bonnet of the car. Along with the crest, the car had Police decals on the doors, together with double stripes on the rear door and tail section. It was a much sought after car and available until 1981.

Also in January, 1979, Corgi released the Superman Van as model No 435. The van was silver, with Superman logos and images on the side. This particular van proved to be another popular Superman toy.

A year later, Corgi released The Professionals in 1980, as model No 342. The set was presented in a window box with all three main characters present. Cowley, Bodie and Doyle can be seen in various action poses around the Ford Capri. The model is a sporty version in silver, with black 'flash-by' decals along the side, black bumpers, chrome trim and a red interior. The header card had the logo and profiles of the CI5 team, and was available until 1982.

The James Bond Citroen 2CV was released as model No 272, in June 1981. This model was based on the car from the Bond film 'For Your Eyes Only'. It was issued in yellow with a red interior. As well as an opening bonnet, it had a slide back canvas-like roof in yellow plastic to match the car. The wing mirrors were finished in chrome, as were the wheel hubs. Two different box types were issued, the yellow and black with a red

From top down: Corgi released The Professionals in 1980, as model No 342. Cowley, Bodie and Doyle were all present; In 1982, Magnum PI was released as model No 298. This sports car was from the successful American TV series; 3. In July 1976, the Kojak Buick was released as model No 290.

photo header card, or the flap opening box with logo and photo on the front. This model was withdrawn in 1982.

In 1982, Corgi released Magnum PI, as model No 298. This sports car was from the successful American TV series. The car was an open top Ferrari 308 GTS, with an opening rear engine compartment. It looked rather spectacular in Ferrari red with black and cream interior and chrome trim. The red, black and yellow window box had a header card showing the title, together with a photo of the star of the series. The model was available until 1983.

As a consequence of Mettoy calling in the receivers in 1983, it seems that all existing licenses were deemed null and void, particularly for TV and Film related models.

Sadly, the camera shutters and film spools lay dormant throughout the rest of the 1980's. The re-tooling process for individual models had become far too expensive. It would be some years before TV and Film models would be produced again. The only exception, it seems, is the James Bond Aston Martin model No 271. This model was initially sold as existing stock, and then in the late 1980's, it was available in a blue window box as C.271, and simply labelled 'Aston Martin'. ◉

Images used courtesy of Vectis. Sources: Great Book of Corgi – Marcel R. Van Cleemput; Ramsays Guide; The Corgi Years; The James Bond Diecast of Corgi - by Dave Worrall.

Shaping the Diecast Hobby

Paul Lumsdon meets the man who spent 50 years designing for Corgi

To my mind one of the keys to the success of any leading brand is good product design. Here, Corgi has been uniquely lucky. From its conception, and throughout the decades, Corgi has been known for innovation in diecast design and has led the way for others to follow. It is no coincidence that for nearly 50 of those 60 years, there was one constant factor underpinning the excellence of Corgi design – and that constant was Terry Fox!

I recently caught up with Terry at his home in Northampton, where he is now happily retired and enjoying more time travelling (he has a son in Canada), walking, gardening and generally enjoying life!

Terry started working on Corgi Toys as a young apprentice in September 1963. He was employed by Corgi's parent company, Mettoy, at their design offices in Northampton. It was a five year apprenticeship which saw Terry initially working in the tool room and progressing through various other departments as he learned about all aspects of toy production. For his final six months he was moved to the drawing office and introduced to product design.

His first job was to design moulds. As Terry says; 'you really need to understand how moulds work in order to be able to design successful toys'. After successfully completing his apprenticeship Terry remained

Terry Fox and some of the US Fire Engines produced in 2000. Nearly forty years after joining the company Terry he played a key role in the design of this new bespoke range.

in the drawing office and started working on full product designs. His mentor at this time was Corgi's Chief Designer, Marcel Van Cleemput, who taught him all aspects of diecast model design, from initial research, measuring and photographing a vehicle, right through to individual component design.

The 1970s were challenging times, not only for Corgi Toys, but for all of Mettoy's

brands and in 1981, after posting record losses, the Northampton site was closed as all production moved to the company's Swansea factory. Rather than re-locate Terry and a small group of designers set up their own office in Northampton and continued to work independently, but exclusively on Corgi toy design work.

At the end of 1989 Corgi was bought by US toy giant Mattel and the offices were moved to Leicester whilst production was transferred to China. At this point Terry decided to move on and work for himself. He set up his own design studio at home and through his contacts he was lucky enough to be invited to work as a freelance designer for Mattel on Corgi's new ranges.

Further change came in 1995 when Chris Guest, head of Corgi within Mattel, led a successful management buyout and set up Corgi Classics, based in Leicester. He immediately contacted Terry and persuaded him to join the new venture as his Design Manager. Terry accepted and began the next phase of his career.

With production offices in Hong Kong and factories based in mainland China Terry's role became split. Research and design work was completed in the UK and then the design 'packs' were handed over to the far east team. To ensure everything was properly interpreted and actioned, Terry made regular trips to Hong Kong and into the factories to check the designs and product quality. This threw up some new

Classic US Fire Engines

challenges for Terry as he explains; 'In China the factories were very labour intensive so assembly times became critical. It was therefore essential to ensure designs were as simple as possible to maximise efficient production and keep the costs down'.

In 2000 Corgi established a new team in the USA and again Terry took on a key role in the design of the bespoke new US ranges. He made several trips to the Corgi Chicago offices and travelled to various parts of the USA researching primarily US fire, bus and truck ranges.

In 2008 Corgi was sold to Hornby Hobbies. Terry remained as part of a small Leicester based team working on Corgi designs for three more years until in 2011 Hornby moved the brand to its Margate offices. Terry was made redundant, just one year short of his official retirement, and having worked on the Corgi brand for 48 years in total. ◉

Classic US Fire Engines

CAREER HIGHLIGHTS

STAND OUT MODEL
'This has to be the Monkeymobile from 1968. It was the very first model that I designed in its entirety so it has a special place as a career highlight.'

STAND OUT MOMENT
'Working with Marcel Van Cleemput on the Tyrell 6-wheel Formula 1 Race Car in 1976. Not only was it a remarkable vehicle but whilst at Tyrell's works we also caught sight of Concorde flying by for the very first time.'

FAVOURITE RANGE:
'The US Fire range. I think it was the finest range I ever designed but possibly also one of the most under-rated. The US team never achieved the sales success I feel this range deserved.'

CAREER ACHIEVEMENT
'I designed every Corgi OOC (original Omnibus Collection) bus model from launch in 1995 until I left in 2011.'

SUMMARY
'I am so lucky. I consider I have had the best job in the world. I have travelled to some great places, met some really fascinating people and all to help design some fabulous toys. What job could be better? I have loads of great memories - but not many toys; I have never been a collector!'

Corgi Castings

David Boxall reviews the different ways Corgi has used the same casting for a variety of releases

It was quite apparent, right from the beginning in 1956, that Corgi would need to create a range of toys in a short period of time. Dinky Toys were their main competitor in the toy market, and they had already been producing toys for many years, sometimes using the same casting over and over again - changing the colour of the model, and replacing the logo. This enabled the production of a number of toys without the expense of constant re-tooling.

The new range of Corgi toys was to be based on the sound principles of value for money. The initial intention was to sell all the cars at the same price, and so it seemed logical to manufacture similar sized cars. A system was introduced using a line graph, which effectively 'equalised' the size of each model. It was decided that all the Corgi vehicles would have windows, and to increase the range of toys available, a

second edition of models would be mechanised.

The original Corgi toys were produced with a tinplate or diecast base to accommodate the mechanical flywheel motor. The mechanical versions were withdrawn in 1959 but the diecast bases continued for all models. The base was riveted to the main body shell, producing a very sturdy toy. The wheels were made of aluminium

Above: Corgi Toys model 412, Beford Ambulance

and placed on a 2mm axle, and the hub had a retaining groove for the tyre.

The Bedford Van is one of the best examples of an early Corgi model, as it provided the basis for lots of different toys. All these early Bedford Vans were of similar construction: a basic casting, with a tinplate or diecast base, fixed axles, smooth hubs, rubber tyres, and windows. They were all manufactured in a 1/44 scale, and the early models did not require suspension, or an interior. The Bedford Van's greatest asset by far, was its simplicity. It could be re-wrapped in a different colour and be given a new logo and launched as an entirely different model. This approach enabled Corgi to expand their range of products, whilst keeping the cost of each unit to a minimum. There are five particularly good examples of how the Bedford Van casting was re-used. The Bedford Dormobile was released

Left, from the top down: Corgi model 404, Bedford Dormobile in both cream and blue versions; Corgi model 251, Hillman Imp in bronze and below it in dark metallic blue.

as model No 404M, and had side windows and a mechanical flywheel motor. It appeared in a variety of colours including: blue, metallic maroon and turquoise. This particular Bedford was available until 1960. The non-mechanical Bedford Dormobile was released as model No 404. It was issued in cream, metallic maroon, turquoise or blue, and was a very successful model.

The Bedford 'Utilicon' AFS, model No 405, was issued in bright or dark green, and with the addition of a removable ladder clipped onto the top of the van, it had an entirely different appearance. This model proved to be another popular toy.

The Bedford 'Utilicon Fire Dept' Van was released as model No 405M. In contrast, this version appeared in red with a silver or black ladder and was available until 1959.

Finally, in November 1957, the Bedford Ambulance was released as model No 412. In this way, with a little imagination and changes to the colour and appearance, Corgi managed to expand the range of toys on offer.

> "The Bedford Van is one of the best examples of an early Corgi model, as it provided the basis for lots of different toys"

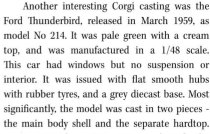

Another interesting Corgi casting was the Ford Thunderbird, released in March 1959, as model No 214. It was pale green with a cream top, and was manufactured in a 1/48 scale. This car had windows but no suspension or interior. It was issued with flat smooth hubs with rubber tyres, and a grey diecast base. Most significantly, the model was cast in two pieces - the main body shell and the separate hardtop.

In December 1959, Corgi released the Thunderbird Open Sports as model No 215. This model used the same body casting but with the addition of a cast interior, which was housed neatly into the body. It was available until 1962. It was issued with a white body, blue interior and silver seats.

The Chevrolet Impala also had a major impact on the production of Corgi toys. Due to the shape of the rear of this car, new painting techniques were developed to overcome the difficulties of spraying the overhanging underside of the fin. The painting process had to be changed from flat spraying on a conveyor belt system to rotary spraying.

Above: Corgi model 328, Monte Carlo Imp in Blue

Above: Corgi Toys 340 Sunbeam Imp Monte Carlo 1967 metallic blue car

Castings were hung or mounted individually and rotated as they travelled through a spray booth.

Corgi also increased the number of toys available by up-grading existing models. In June 1962, the all-new Thunderbird Open Sports was upgraded and released as model No 215S. The 'S' at the end of the model number refers to the new 'Glidamatic Spring Suspension' system. This car was issued in red with a

way to improve and expand the sales stock.

The designers at Corgi continued to be quite adventurous with some of the castings. The Bermuda Taxi was released in July 1962, as model No 430. This rather unusual version of the Ford Thunderbird appeared in white with a yellow interior, and had a detachable sun canopy. The plastic canopy was issued in a variety of different colours – all with contrasting coloured

up an ambulance, a milk float, a red van and a Pick-up. The different tops could be used on either of the chassis bases.

So far, the models considered have shown how Corgi made the best possible use of each available casting. Changes such as the vehicle use, and the colour scheme, could totally alter the appearance of the toy. In the same way, additional features

> These comparatively simple additions and changes had transformed the Hillman Imp, producing four different models from the same casting

yellow interior, and now had a driver at the wheel. Once again, this was the same casting of the car body, with an additional cast interior.

Also in June 1962, Corgi released the Ford Thunderbird Hardtop as model No 214S. The metallic grey body with a red top, had a lemon interior, a steering wheel, shaped hubs, and 'Glidamatic Spring Suspension', and was available until 1964. These re-released models were clearly the quickest and easiest

fringes. The model had 'Bermuda Taxi' stickers on the doors and on the boot. A taxi driver sat at the wheel of the car. Corgi certainly changed the whole context of the vehicle to great effect.

In August 1963, the release of the 'Commer' Constructor Set as Gift Set 24, was a particularly innovative issue. The set contained two chassis and four rear compartments enabling the vehicles to be put together in a number of different ways. The various elements could make

such as suspension jewelled headlights, aerials, stickers and transfers, could also result in a different, more desirable product.

The Hillman Imp was manufactured in a 1:43 scale, and had a number of excellent features. It had an opening rear window, to accommodate an item of luggage, a plastic moulded interior, and a rear seat, which folded up or down. This model had excellent suspension and a grey diecast base. The

Above: Model 405, Bedford Utilicon AFS Fire Tender

Above: Model 405m, Bedford 'Utilicon' Fire Tender

Above: Model 308, Monte Carlo Mini in Yellow

Above: Model 204, Morris Minor in blue

first Hillman Imp was released by Corgi in December 1963, as model No 251. The initial colour variations were metallic blue with a lemon interior or metallic bronze with a white side flash and an off-white interior. This first Hillman Imp was available until 1966.

The same casting was used again three years later, for the 1966 Monte Carlo Hillman Imp, which was released as model No 328. This version had a new dark metallic blue finish with a white masked flash along the side of the car. It was also given Monte Carlo plates, jewelled headlights, and rally number 107. The new colour and transfers, plus the twinkly lights, created a sporty version of the Hillman Imp. This model was only available for one year.

The following year, in March 1967, Corgi released the 1967 Monte Carlo Sunbeam Imp, as model No 340. It was issued in the same metallic dark blue with the white flash, and also wore the Monte Carlo plates but now competed as number 77. This model had an additional sump guard and six jewelled lights. These comparatively simple additions and changes had transformed the Hillman Imp, producing four different models from the same casting. The casting was used

again for a number of Police Panda Cars.

By far the most prolific model in the Corgi range, was the Mini. The first Morris Mini Minor was released as model No 226 in February 1960. It was produced in a scale of 1:42. The Mini was issued in lilac blue or pale blue, and was to have a long and successful production run until 1968, when it was finally withdrawn, having achieved 1,667,000 sales.

In May 1962, the Mini-Cooper Competition model was issued as model No 227. In blue and white, or primrose yellow and white, these cars were particularly spectacular. With their exciting new livery, competition numbers on the doors, crossed union and chequered flags on the bonnet, suspension, interior, steering wheel and jewelled headlights.

One of Corgi's most used castings was for the Monte Carlo Mini-Cooper models. All the cars appeared in red with a white roof, and were released each year, following the many successful rallies undertaken by the real cars as follows:

• In 1964, model No 317 appeared with RN 37, and had a chrome roof light.

• In 1965, model No 321 appeared with RN 52.

• In 1966, the same model No 321 appeared with RN 2, and had 'silk screened' signatures on the roof.

• In 1967, model No 333, was released as the RAC/Sun Rally Mini-Cooper 'S'.

• In 1967 Corgi model No 339 appeared with RN 177, and had a chrome roof rack containing two spare wheels.

Finally, in 1972, after Corgi had changed the wheels and tyres to all-plastic Whizzwheels, the Mini castings were used for the last time. The Corgi model No 308 appeared with RN 177. This model was issued in yellow, and had a chrome roof rack with two spare wheels.

Also in 1972, the Morris Mini-Minor was released as model No 204, with Whizzwheels. These last two models were sold in window boxes.

With the decline in the volume of sales for each individual model, across the toy industry as a whole, the days when the same casting was used for several related models was drawing to a close. ◉

Images used courtesy of Vectis.
Sources: Great Book of Corgi by Marcel R. Van Cleemput; Ramsays Guide; The Corgi Years

Above: Model 223, Chevrolet State Patrol

Above: Model 214, Ford Thunderbird in two tone mint/cream

.60th Anniversary range

60 YEARS 1956-2016

*To celebrate its very significant birthday, Corgi announced a range of limited edition models. **Rick Wilson** takes a closer look*

Featuring some of the most famous vehicles and liveries from the air and on the road, the collection is presented in specially designed commemorative 60th Anniversary packaging and all have prices significantly lower than its regular range releases.

The initial announcement comprised ten models but in early 2016 Corgi added a 60th anniversary van model, in a similar vein to the Bedford van released to commemorate its 50th in 2006, which is only available via Corgi's website.

AA27603 Hawker Hurricane Mk.I V7357/SD-F, Sgt. J.H 'Ginger' Lacey, RAF No.501 Squadron, Gravesend, Sep 1940
Scale: 1/72 Price: £24.99

The exploits of the glorious 'Few' during the Battle of Britain are the stuff of legend and standing right at the head of this illustrious group of men was James 'Ginger' Lacey, Hurricane pilot and proud son of Yorkshire. Flying throughout the Battle of Britain, Lacey was credited with eighteen aerial victories, making him the second highest scoring British fighter ace of the Battle – each of these victories was gained whilst flying the trusty Hawker Hurricane. This latest Hurricane release is an essential addition to any Battle of Britain collection.

The Hawker Hurricane is arguably the most important aircraft in the history of the Royal Air Force, specifically as it heralded the development of the modern, monoplane fighter. It combined the finest construction techniques already in place with the best biplane aircraft and was relatively easy to manufacture - the Hurricane was certainly the right aeroplane at the right time and in Britain's hour of need, proved to be absolutely crucial. During the savage dogfights of the Battle of Britain, the Hurricane accounted for more Luftwaffe aircraft destroyed than all other British aircraft combined. A magnificent gun platform, the Hurricane could also absorb significant battle damage and still bring its pilot home – this was critical in Britain's eventual success and was rather reassuring for the Hurricane pilot.

AA36012 BAE Hawk RAF Red Arrows
Scale: 1/72 Price: £29.99

Providing advanced pilot and weapons delivery training for a new or converting student pilot is perhaps one of the most important duties undertaken by any of the world's air forces. For Royal Air Force students, this means many

> It combined the finest construction techniques already in place with the best biplane aircraft and was relatively easy to manufacture

hours spent in the cockpit of the British Aerospace Hawk advanced jet trainer, which has now been in service for forty years. Replacing the diminutive Folland Gnat trainer, the Hawk proved to be a highly adaptable and extremely reliable aircraft in service, with large numbers serving with the RAF and many overseas air forces. Perhaps the Hawk is most famous for its association with the world famous Royal Air Force Aerobatic Display Team, the Red Arrows, who enjoy a reputation for excellence the world over.

AA39211 Supermarine Spitfire Mk.I R6800/LZ-N, Sqn. Ldr. Rupert 'Lucky' Leigh RAF No.66

Top, left to right: JAA27603 Hawker Hurricane, AA39211 Supermarine Spitfire and AA36012 Red Arrows BAe Hawk

Opposite page: OM46310 Classic Routemaster

Below: CC16602 Eddie Stobart Volvo FH Curtainside

Squadron, Gravesend, Sep 1940
Scale: 1/72 Price: £24.99

For young British pilots in the late 1940s, the most exciting and enigmatic aircraft that they could possibly hope to fly was the new Supermarine Spitfire. The absolute pinnacle of aviation technology at that time, the Spitfire was a thoroughbred in every sense of the word and simply a beautiful aeroplane to look at. Just a few short months after the Spitfire entered RAF service, it would be called upon to fight for the very survival of Britain and the free world, as swarms of Luftwaffe aircraft launched massed attacks against RAF airfields and strategic targets across southern England. The handsome

Spitfire would have to bare its teeth and take on the feared Messerschmitt Bf 109!

CC16602 Volvo FH, Curtainside Trailer, Eddie Stobart
Scale: 1/50 Price: £84.99

With 2,200 units, over 3,200 trailers and in excess of six million square feet of warehousing, Eddie Stobart is one of the most recognisable names in haulage and distribution. The company's entire fleet of vehicles would stretch over fifty miles in length if they were all to travel in convoy.

This new tooled Volvo FH carries the famous Eddie Stobart logo and livery, and has been designed using

Corgi's advanced CAD system to ensure every detail is accurately replicated.

DG25005 Corgi 60th Anniversary Model Van – Website Exclusive
Scale: Fit The Box
Price: £9.99

To celebrate its special birthday Corgi has produced a charming little van in a commemorative livery with special 60th Anniversary packaging. The van was produced as a gift for its retailers to mark the anniversary at the trade shows in January 2016, however a limited number have been made available exclusively on the Corgi website - so this is sure to become a collector's item! Each limited edition model is supplied with a uniquely numbered certificate of authenticity.

OM46310 Classic Routemaster, London Transport
Scale: 1/76 Price: £19.99

The Routemaster was designed and built in London by AEC and Park Royal Vehicles specifically for London Transport use. Although conventional in appearance, the design was technically sophisticated, featuring innovative construction techniques, braking systems and semi-automatic transmission. Featured on tourist souvenirs all around the Capital, the traditional red Routemaster is perhaps one of the most famous images of London with many examples of this iconic vehicle still in existence all over the world.

OM46613 New Routemaster, London United, Route 9
Scale: 1/76 Price: £19.99

The New Routemaster is a hybrid diesel-electric bus which primarily operates in central London. Designed by Thomas Heatherwick and Wrightbus, the New Routemaster features a 'hop-on hop-off' rear platform, updated to meet the requirements for modern use. Route 9, seen here en route to Hammersmith, features advertising for the world famous *The Book of Mormon* satirical musical by South Park creators Trey Parker and Matt Stone. This West End smash was named Best New Musical at

Above: DG25005 60th anniversary van alongside its Bedford CA counterpart from 10 years ago

the 2014 Laurence Olivier Awards.

VA02538 Austin Mini Cooper S Surf Blue
Scale: 1/43 Price: £14.99

When launched in 1959, designer Alec Issigonis' Mini revolutionised the automotive industry by pioneering the mass production of front-wheel-drive transverse-engine cars. Then Formula 1 World Champion team owner John Cooper, a friend of Issigonis, immediately saw its nimble handling as an opportunity to create a powerful competition car and, after building a prototype, persuaded BMC's bosses to produce it. It was launched in 1961, started winning races and rallies immediately, and became the cool must have car of the 1960s, selling in much

Below: OM46613 New Routemaster

> Designed by Thomas Heatherwick and Wrightbus, the New Routemaster features a 'hop-on hop-off' rear platform, updated to meet the requirements for modern use

larger numbers than initially envisaged. The Cooper S added more power and the example modelled here was a BMC press car tested, with enthusiasm, by Autosport magazine in August 1963.

VA05808 Morris Minor 1000, Highway Yellow
Scale: 1/43 Price: £14.99

The Morris Minor was launched at the 1948 London Motor Show, Britain's first since the cessation of hostilities, alongside another legend the Jaguar XK120. In its original form it used a 918cc sidevalve engine and its headlights were mounted low in the grille. Foreign market legislation forced the lights up into pods on the wings in 1951 and then, when Morris Motors merged with Austin in 1952 to create BMC, the Minor received the Austin-designed 803cc A-Series engine. This was updated to create the 'single screen' Minor 1000 in 1956. The Minor was Alec Issigonis' first complete car design and possessed extremely surefooted handling which was many years ahead of its competitors.

VA06519 Rover P6 3500 VIP, Brasilia
Scale: 1/43 Price: £14.99

In October 1963 Rover announced its compact 2000 model, often known colloquially by its codename P6. It was an all-new design featuring a unit-construction base skeleton covered by bolt-on body panels, independent

Above, left to right:
VA06519 Rover P6 3500, VA09519 Ford Escort MkI Mexico and VA05808 Morris Minor 1000

front suspension using horizontal coil springs, de Dion rear suspension and four-wheel disc brakes, giving it class-leading dynamics. Its radical exterior and interior styling was by David Bache and its pioneering passenger safety-cell contributed to it becoming the first ever 'European Car of The Year' in 1964. Rover's General-Motors derived all-aluminium V8 was offered as a more powerful option in April 1968, finally giving the P6 the power its chassis had always warranted. Production of the P6 ceased in 1977.

VA09519 Ford Escort Mk1 Mexico, Diamond White
Scale: 1/43 Price: £14.99

Ford were determined to win the 1970

London-Mexico World Cup Rally and, after extensive reconnaissance of the arduous 16,000 mile route, works driver Roger Clark suggested they use heavy-duty rally Escorts with simple Cortina 1600GT engines in place of the usual Lotus twin-cams; reliability being more important than performance. It worked, Hannu Mikkola and Gunnar Palm won in 'FEV 1H ' and, quick to see the value of the publicity, Ford launched the Mexico as a production replica of the winner using their rally-proven Type-49 bodyshell and crossflow engine. Built at Ford's Advanced Vehicle Operations facility in Ockendon, Essex, it was launched in 1970 at £1,150, making it the affordable performance car of its era. ◉

Below: VA02538 Austin Mini Cooper S

Corgi's new Golden Age

Paul Lumsdon and Corgi head towards the new millennium

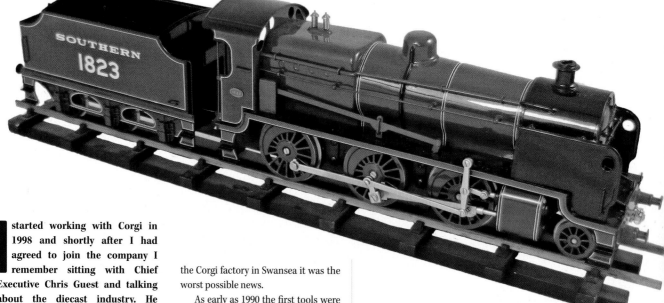

I started working with Corgi in 1998 and shortly after I had agreed to join the company I remember sitting with Chief Executive Chris Guest and talking about the diecast industry. He likened it to a roller coaster ride. 'We are all on the ride together, there will be lots of ups and downs but it will always be great fun and full of excitement'. He was absolutely right and the 1990s was to become a decade when the Corgi roller coaster was very much on the 'Up'.

It didn't start quite so positively however. Change inevitably brings a degree of uncertainty and when, at the end of 1989 Corgi Toys Limited was sold to the American toy giant Mattel, there must have been considerable uncertainty and concern at what the future might hold.

Sadly for many of the workforce at the Corgi factory in Swansea it was the worst possible news.

As early as 1990 the first tools were moved to China and the very first model, a British Racing Green MGA sports car was produced overseas and shipped to the UK, heralding the start of a new era in Corgi manufacturing.

Throughout 1990 many more tools were shipped to China and on 21st January 1991, Corgi officially moved from its long established factory at Fforestfach, Swansea, to Mattel's UK headquarters on the Meridian Business Park in Leicester.

With the injection of investment from Mattel, coupled with a far cheaper manufacturing base in the Far East, Corgi was set to grow and the future for the brand looked bright.

Main image:
*Bassett Lowke 2-6-0
Southern N Class Mogul*

THE 'GUEST' FACTOR

Mike Rosser had led the 1983 management buyout that saw the formation of Corgi Toys Ltd, following the collapse of Mettoy. In 1985 he appointed Chris Guest as Sales and Marketing Director. As a classically trained marketing professional, Chris set about changing the focus of Corgi from being a product-driven brand to one driven by the requirements of its customers. He quickly identified two distinct market sectors – toys and collector products. Corgi Classics was launched as a brand aimed at the adult

> " Chris set about changing the focus of Corgi from being a product-driven brand to one driven by the requirements of its customers

1990

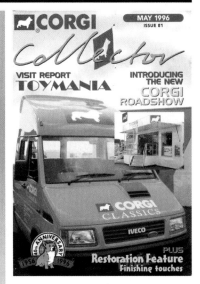

Left: Corgi MGA first made in China (photocourtesy www.little-wheels.net)

Above: Marketing material for The Corgi Roadshow

Above:
1998 Early Modern trucks in large perspex display case

collector market and proved an instant success.

Following the Mattel acquisition, Chris was invited to make the move to Leicester where he became Managing Director for the Corgi brand within Mattel. Much to the delight of the new adult collectors, Chris continued to develop the collector market, in particular with 1/43 scale classic cars and vans of the 1950s and 1960s – the nostalgia years for the early post-war baby boomers.

At the same time Corgi Toys were able to attract an international audience through Mattel's established worldwide distribution network.

These were successful years for both Corgi and Mattel, with Corgi sales growing strongly and establishing a position of pre-eminence in the collector market. Increased detail and accuracy, coupled with limited editions and attractive packaging led to unprecedented demand. This was the new 'Golden Age of Diecast'.

Over time it became clear that Mattel's focus was far more on the

On August 7th, 1995, it was officially announced that a management consortium, headed by Chris Guest and backed by venture capitalists, Cinven, had successfully bought the business from Mattel. Corgi Classics Limited was born!

The separation was complete when on 29th October 1995, the new business moved to its own premises on the Meridian Business Park, Leicester, just half a mile away from the Mattel offices.

Original Omnibus Company (OOC) and 1/50 American trucks, buses and fire appliances. With its new found independence the pace of new launches increased. A 1/50 scale Routemaster bus in 1996, Heavy Haulage in 1997, Modern Trucks and Aviation Archive in 1998, Vintage Glory Steam Wagons, plus O Gauge Bassett-Lowke locomotives and Icon collectable figurines in 1999. French and German collector ranges were also introduced as the company

Above: *1998 Early Modern trucks in large perspex display case*

> There was nothing lucky about Corgi's success during this period. It was down to a good understanding of the customer needs, hard work and strong focus from a dedicated workforce. Good marketing played a very important role as well

high volume, international toy market, whereas Chris could see the growth potential and profitability of the adult market, particularly within the UK and USA. It was becoming increasingly apparent that the Corgi business was growing apart from the core Mattel, mass market toy business. Early in 1995, the Corgi roller coaster took a sudden dip when Chris Guest departed the company.

However, the story was far from over. Throughout the spring of 1995 the rumour mill was rife with speculation around the future of the Corgi brand. It was soon to emerge that Chris had been working with a team of financiers with a view to buying the Corgi collector brand, 'Corgi Classics' from the parent company Mattel.

ON THE UP AND UP!

With the focus of the business now firmly on the adult collector market, and investment money available, Corgi Classics continued to grow strongly throughout the second half of the 1990s. In 1996 Corgi acquired the name of 'Bassett-Lowke', the prestigious, Northampton based model engineering brand, and at the end of 1999, following the collapse of Lledo plc, the 'Lledo', 'Days Gone' and 'Vanguards' brands also joined the Corgi fold.

It seemed as if everything Corgi touched turned to gold and the new management was quick to move into new sectors of the market in order to continue the growth. 1994 had seen the first 1/76th scale buses with the hugely successful launch of the

spread its distribution into Europe

Alongside the dedicated collector ranges there were also more populist releases under the heading of 'TV and Film Favourites'.

HARD GRAFT

There was nothing lucky about Corgi's success during this period. It was down to a good understanding of the customer needs, hard work and strong focus from a dedicated workforce. Good marketing played a very important role as well. The Corgi Collector Club was at its peak during the early 1990s with over 11,000 members signed up for the regular newsletters, proving an invaluable communications and dedicated advertising medium. In 1992 Corgi held it's first 'Biggest Little Motor

Show' at Telford in Shropshire. It was hugely successful and further events were held in 1993 and 1994 at the British Motor Heritage Centre, Gaydon. 1995 saw the show move to Donington Park and it was hailed as the biggest and best yet! However in 1996 the show was replaced by a new initiative – The Corgi Roadshow. This was a custom built Iveco Ford truck kitted out like a miniature showroom and allowing Corgi to travel all around the country to meet its customers and to preview new ranges to the trade. It made its debut in March 1996 at the London Classics Motor Show and the reaction was such that people were queuing 30 deep to get on board! Other marketing initiatives during the 1990s included the 'Gold Star' retailer scheme, the issuing of points with models for redemption against a special release, a collector of the year award, the foundation of a Corgi Collector 'Council of Experts' for assistance with model research, plus the sponsorship of the Plant Brothers rallying Minis. At weekends the sales team were to be found supporting store openings, often assisted by James Bond, Jaws or Del-Boy-Trotter look-a likes. Yes, it was hard work, but yes, it was great fun and exciting!

ONE MORE SURPRISE!

Remember I said this was a roller coaster ride? One thing that is for certain in life is that nothing stays the same forever, and in Corgi's case it seemed that nothing stayed the same for long. Venture capitalists invest in companies in the short term but they tend to like to cash in and move on

Above: Chris Guest leads MBO 1995

Above: Corgi team move to Leicester 1991

every four to five years. And so it was with Corgi.

In July 1999, after four years of strong growth and profitability, the roller coaster had another brief blip as it was announced that Corgi had been bought by the Hong Kong based, US Collectables specialist and NASDAQ listed company, Zindart.

However, key to this move was that Chris Guest and the management team were to be kept in place to continue running the business. Further positives were also that Zindart had its own turnkey manufacturing plant in China, thus giving Corgi a manufacturing base. Zindart was also keen to expand in the USA and just before the end of the decade a dedicated Corgi sales and marketing team was established in Chicago to develop the US market.

With the new millennium fast approaching Corgi had enjoyed a decade of constant growth and huge success. The company was without doubt the UK's No1 diecast manufacturer with a huge band of dedicated and loyal collectors. The roller coaster was still riding high and everyone at Corgi was still enjoying the ride! ◉

Corgi MGA first made in China
(photo courtesy www.little-wheels.net)

It gets complicated

Hope, optimism and new toys!

With the Corgi roller coaster riding high throughout the 1990s there was unsurprisingly plenty of hope and optimism going into the new millennium. The acquisition of the company in 1999 by Zindart had little effect on the day to day running of the business, other than the addition of a US team based in Chicago.

Corgi had launched an impressive, bold and distinctive new catalogue for the new millennium. It had a gold and black cover and for the first time moved away from the traditional A4 format. It also combined ranges like 'Modern truck' and 'Vintage Glory' under the general heading of 'Collectables' as separate catalogues were becoming expensive and time consuming.

2000 also saw some other significant firsts for Corgi. At the New York Toy Fair that year the new US operation launched its very first catalogue. Utilising to a large degree existing tooling the new models were however enhanced with a considerable amount of additional details to bring them up to standard for the discerning collector market. These were known as 'Premier' models and they covered collecting themes such as Texaco, Guinness, US Buses and Fire Appliances, as well as a small collection dedicated to Canadian

Main image:
AN01103 Raw Cast Ford Consul Saloon

Opposite page, clockwise from top left:
Raw cast Ford Consul and box; 25th Anniversary Kermit from 2002; 25th Anniversary Muppets; Miss Piggy in 25th Anniversary pack

collectors.

In the UK the team were kept extremely busy following the acquisition in late 1999 of Lledo including the Vanguards and Days Gone brands. The first priority was to launch a new Vanguards catalogue. Corgi had already been working on a proposed 1/43rd scale car offering of its own, to be called 'Motorcade'. Once the decision had been taken to continue with the 'Vanguards' brand name it was a reasonably easy and quick task to merge the two ranges together. The resultant new catalogue benefitted from new Lledo and Corgi tooling and in my opinion was one of the strongest model car ranges ever launched for the UK collector.

Over a period of years since the 1995 Management Buyout, Corgi had been slowly reintroducing a range of toy vehicles to its ranges. It was important to recruit the adult collectors of the future by introducing the Corgi name to a younger audience. This was stepped up in 2001 when Corgi secured a license with Enid Blyton to produce a range of Noddy and Friends vehicles. There was considerable new tooling investment and a raft of new vehicles as Noddy, Big Ears, PC Plod, Tessie Bear and more all took to the road in a variety of colourful cars. 2001 also saw a new range of Muppet releases. Based on the original 1979 tooling, the models were nevertheless upgraded to

2000

"

These were known as 'Premier' models and they covered collecting themes such as Texaco, Guinness, US Buses and Fire Appliances, as well as a small collection dedicated to Canadian collectors

celebrate the 25th anniversary of the Muppets UK TV debut.

These were the first shoots of a toy revival but there was much more to come on the toy front.

CHANGE IS IN THE AIR

For the first few years of the new millennium it was pretty much carry on as usual for Corgi, business and profits were good. However, 'limited edition' production quantities were still relatively high and releases were coming thick and fast. Was this sustainable or was the roller coaster about to take a big dip?

Well there was certainly an air of change on the horizon. Early in 2004, after 19 years with Corgi, Chris Guest left the business to 'pursue other

being 100% in the adult collector/ hobby area.

The results were indifferent. There were some fantastic products like 'Little Red Tractor', then a new childrens' series from the BBC. Corgi won the license and in 2004 produced a fabulous range of tractors and other farm vehicles associated with the show. Sadly it was beaten to the screens by Tractor Tom and was not the success it might otherwise have been.

Then there was 'Lil Handfuls'. This was a range of bean filled dolls with magnets in their hands so they would 'climb, hug and hold' by gripping each other around chair/cot/rocking horse legs etc. This is only a personal opinion but to my mind they were ugly, uninteresting and about as far

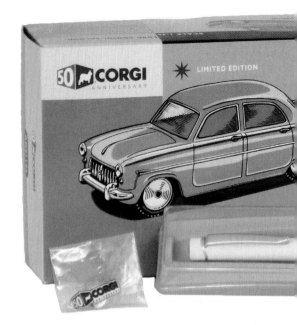

For a while the Corgi offices were awash with Light Sabers, Millennium Falcons and Harry Potter wands, to mention but a few

interests'. Zindart Ltd announced that American toy industry veteran, George Volanakis was to be the new President and CEO, based in Chicago, whilst Dave Turner, former Managing Director of Tyco Toys, would be in charge of the UK operation.

There now followed a period of intense toy development as Corgi strived to realign itself more towards the volume toy market rather than

away from everything that Corgi stood (and stands) for as you could get. That they were developed at great cost and brought to market at all is quite beyond me. But yes, in 2005 they were launched onto the market and then quickly proceeded to sink without trace. Enough said!

2006 THE GREAT 50TH BIRTHDAY PARTY

The highlight of 2006 was undoubtedly

Above: Ford Consul goody bag received as part of the 50th Anniversary celebrations

Below: a special 'raw casting' version of the Ford Consul

the Corgi 50th Anniversary celebrations. A special catalogue was launched containing unique anniversary releases and top amongst these was the Ford Consul. This had been the very first Corgi model releases back in 2006 and the new version was retooled to replicate the original in every way. Each of Corgi's popular collector categories featured special anniversary releases – trucks, buses, aircraft, cars and fire engines. Each catalogue also included, as a loose leaf insert, an announcement of a brand new Mettoy release for 2006. This was to be a beautiful tinplate, clockwork driven Routemaster bus, and was heralded as the first of a range of fabulous new tinplate toys to be released under the Mettoy name in 2007.

To complete the celebrations, on a beautiful summers day Corgi held a 50th birthday party in the grounds around the Leicester offices and every attendee received a goody bag containing a special 'raw casting' version of the Ford Consul. I remember Dave Turner telling the gathered crowd that he was merely the current custodian of the Corgi brand, and that the brand would continue when he was long gone. As it turned out, that was quite a prophetic statement!

DECEMBER 2006 – THE COMPLICATED BIT

In December 2006, after changing the Zindart company name to Corgi International, a number of major changes took place almost simultaneously. Zindart Manufacturing was sold to Chris Franklin, who was General Manager of the manufacturing division anyway. Chris had previously worked with Lledo, then Corgi before taking on the role of running the Zindart factory. At the same time Corgi International also announced that it had purchased a company, Cards Inc and merged with another company, Master replicas Inc. George Volanakis stood down and Michael Cookson, founder and Chairman of Master Replica, was appointed as the new President and CEO of Corgi International. Dave Turner departed early in 2007, to be replaced by Dennis Horton, another experienced toy man, and former MD at Radica.

WHAT DID ALL THIS MEAN?

Master Replicas Inc., based in Walnut Creek, California, was a leading manufacturer and marketer of movie and television prop replicas. Having licenses with Star Wars, Pirates of the Caribbean, Narnia, Lord of the Rings, Spider Man, X-Men, Star Trek and Men In Black, the range was a staggering

From the top: The Magisterium Sky Ferry was a huge, Zeppelin-like airship, featured in the Golden Compass film. The model was extremely accurate and beautifully finished. The central 'spine' of the craft, including the rudder and gondola, was diecast, while the rest was plastic; The Magisterium carriage is a bizarre type of taxi which it appears very briefly in the film... in fact, so briefly that if you blink you might miss it. Again, this is a terrific model. The chassis and wheels are diecast, while the coachwork is mostly plastic. Most impressive are the leadlight windows on the carriage doors, and the atomic power element inside the front wheel; Lee Scoresby's airship is a weird, Jerry-built craft that appears to be cobbled together from an old boat and a pair of patched-up hot air balloons. Visually, this model is probably the least appealing of the three, being painted in shades of grey rather that the brilliant red and gold of the previous two. Still, it's not a bad model, and comes complete with a Lee Scoresby figure and his jackrabbit daemon, plus a detachable stand.

array of high end collectable replicas.

Cards Inc. Limited, based in Watford, England, was a manufacturer and distributor of pop culture collectables, gifts and toys. They had just won a license for Harry Potter, adding to existing licenses for Star Wars, Transformers and Pirates of the Caribbean gifts and collectables.

For a while the Corgi offices were awash with Light Sabers, Millennium Falcons and Harry Potter wands, to mention but a few. The emphasis was on creating less diecast and more plastic, as the business moved into the film replica collectables market. Who remembers 'The Golden Compass'? Corgi produced a superb range of licensed products – a Magisterium Carriage, Zeppelin Sky Ferry, and Lee Scoresby's airship. Sadly the film was a box-office disaster and the weird but beautifully produced Corgi vehicles were clearly not what Corgi Collectors were looking for. I still recall a tour of the warehouse to see the racks upon racks of Golden Compass boxes, all waiting to be jobbed off to the highest bidder. Very sad!

THE NEXT CHAPTER

It has to be said that the mis-match between Master Replicas/Cards Inc and Corgi was glaringly obvious and so it was no great surprise when in April 2008, Corgi International announced the sale of the Corgi collector business to Margate based Hornby Hobbies. Hornby, famous for it's OO scale Model Railways, already owned a considerable hobby portfolio including Scalextric, Airfix and Humbrol Paints and Glues. Corgi immediately felt far more at home here as the emphasis turned immediately back towards the collector market. A small team from the old Corgi remained in place in Leicester to continue the range development, whilst Hornby were able to offer the latest technology CAD design and 3-D scanning to bring the range right up to date in terms of accuracy and detail. This latest chapter in Corgi's roller coaster story looked like having a happy ending and as the first decade of the new millennium drew towards an end, the future for Corgi looked bright once again. ◉

SUBSCRIBE TO COLLECTORS GAZETTE FOR JUST £7.99

Subscribe today at **£7.99** per quarter, saving over 15%

PLUS Get every issue delivered direct to your door each month.

SUBSCRIBE NOW

 Call 01778 392480 quoting the code GAZ/CORGI16

or subscribe online at www.ccofgb.co.uk

Corgi TV & Film

PART 3

*TV and Film related models are an essential part of Corgi's culture going back to the earliest days. **Paul Lumsdon** looks back at models from the 1990s*

The popularity of James Bond's Aston Martin DB5, The Batmobile and Chitty Chitty Bang Bang during the 1960s are the stuff of legend and have also helped to drive the collector market that we all enjoy today.

There can also be no doubt that in the modern era of specialist adult collectable diecast models, TV and Film related models have a more populist appeal and help to bring diecast to a broader, younger mass audience. This was never more so than in the 1990s when the adult collector market was growing to its peak. Let's take a look at some of Corgi's fabulous TV and Film related models from that period...

96758 *Some Mother's Do 'Ave 'Em* Morris Minor Saloon

In one episode of the classic 1970s comedy, the hapless Frank Spencer is given the use of a Morris Minor Saloon for his job on a chicken farm. He decides to take wife Betty for a picnic by the coast and true to form Frank ends up driving the car to the cliff edge where it dangles perilously, hundreds of feet above the English Channel. Michael Crawford (Frank) and Michelle Dotrice (Betty) both performed their own stunts during this daring but hilarious scene which was watched by 15 million viewers. The Morris Minor achieved its own celebrity status and was released by Corgi in 1/43 scale in 1995.

C98751/05301 Chitty Chitty Bang Bang

During the 1990s, first under Mattel ownership and later as the independent Corgi Classics, TV and Film related models were constantly featured and it is rather neat that the decade started and ended with very different releases of one of the most famous cars of all – Chitty Chitty Bang Bang.

In 1991 to celebrate the 25th anniversary of the film, Corgi produced a superb, limited edition version of the car (C98751) moulded from the original 1968 (266) tooling. It incorporated all the original features including the four figures, pop-out red and yellow wings and clip-on front and rear stabiliser wings. The model was presented in a beautiful sealed blue box, on a wooden plinth and had a numbered certificate.

The 1998 release (05301) was billed again as a 'Corgi Original' but sadly

Above: Chitty Chitty Bang Bang with Caractacus Potts behind the wheel

suffered from being an expensive model to produce. So much so that this release only featured one figure, Caractacus Potts, the pop-out wings were single colour red only, whilst the front and rear stabiliser wings were left out altogether. It was presented in a colourful window display box. This 'economy' version was all to hit a margin at a certain price point. Corgi may have been independent again but the financial backers were constantly scrutinising the profitability!

96012 *Spender* Ford Sierra

Jimmy Nail played gritty Geordie detective Freddie Spender in this Newcastle upon Tyne based cop show from the early 90s. Spender's car in the series was a Ford Sierra Sapphire Cosworth provided by the Ford Motor

Company. When the first car provided was stolen from the set and later found burnt out, a new vehicle was provided and it then had to be allocated its own security guard for the third and final series. Corgi's model was an existing toy tool with opening front doors and bonnet. It was produced in 1995 in 1/43 scale.

57401 *The Professionals* Ford Capri

Aired between 1997 and 1983, *The Professionals* was an all-action drama about a fictional British law enforcement department, CI5. Bodie and Doyle (Martin Shaw and Lewis Collins) under the control of Cowley (Gordon Jackson) became a huge hit, as did the cars they used. Foremost amongst these was the Ford Capri 3.0S MkIII. Initially Bodie drove a silver version but in later series Doyle also had a gold Capri. Corgi's 1/36 scale model produced in 1999, was in silver and was another 'Corgi original' using the 342 tooling from 1980. Bodie and Doyle figures were also included but not a Cowley figure which did feature in the original 1980 release.

57402 *Starsky and Hutch* Ford Torino

Running from 1975 to 1979, Starsky and Hutch were two street-wise southern California cops who bust criminals with the help of their their red-and-white Ford Torino and a police snitch called Huggy Bear. The Ford Torino, nicknamed 'The Striped

Tomato' became as big as the central characters of the show. Corgi's 1999 1/36 scale model was billed as a 'Corgi Original', meaning it was produced from the original 1970s tooling. It also featured two nicely sculpted Starsky and Hutch figures.

18302 *Moving Story* Bedford Pantechnicon

Moving Story was a comedy drama that aired over two series between 1994 and 1995. It followed the adventures of a team of removal workers. The Corgi 1/50 scale Bedford Pantechnicon released in 1995 was only loosely based on the vehicle used in the series, which wasn't actually a Bedford at all. Still the series quickly disappeared without trace so is anyone really that bothered? I suspect not.

Above: 05506 Italian Job Mini set

Below: 57401 Ford Capri which featured in The Professionals

01803 *Inspector Morse* Jaguar MkII

First broadcast in 1987, Inspector Morse (played by John Thaw) was a rather grumpy but highly intelligent CID officer with the Oxford Police Force. The show was almost as famous for the stunning location scenery around Oxford and for Morse's famous Mk II Jaguar, as it was for the plots. Corgi's 1/43 scale model was launched in 1998.

96757 *Lovejoy* Morris Minor Convertible

Lovejoy, a comedy drama about a roguish East Anglian antiques dealer (played by Ian MacShane), ran from 1986 to 1994. During the second series Lovejoy borrowed a car from his love interest, Lady Jane Felsham, and

01704 *Daktari* Land Rover

The popular 1960s series *Daktari* followed the adventures of vet Dr Marsh Tracey looking after sick animals in Africa. This Corgi model is based on the 1/43rd scale Series 2 Land Rover tool and is a replica of the vehicle originally issued as Gift Set 7 (GS7) in 1967. It appeared in 1998 with Judy the chimp and Clarence the boss-eyed lion figures

18901 *Soldier Soldier* Bedford Dropside

Soldier Soldier was a hugely popular Army drama that aired between 1991 and 1997. It made household names of Robson Green and Jerome Flynn, the two lead actors, who also developed a singing career as an offshoot of the show. The 1/50 scale Corgi Beford High Dropside truck released in 1997, was typical of those used in the British Army at the time and the set was completed with the addition of two hand painted uniformed figures.

04419 *Mr Bean* Mini

Rowan Atkinson's brilliant Mr Bean followed the adventures of a grown man with the mind of a child. His hilarious exploits ran as a TV series from 1990 to 1995 and there have been two subsequent films. Bean's 1976 Mini has starred throughout and was nicely reproduced in 1998 by Corgi in 1/36 scale. The standard Mini tool was even modified to feature the bolt and padlock locking system on the driver's door. ◉

'Miriam' a Morris Minor Convertible became his trusty transport thereafter. Corgi's model was produced in 1995 from the existing 1/43 scale tooling, even though the real car used in the series was actually a saloon that had been converted to a convertible.

05201 *Only Fools and Horses* Reliant Van

Probably the most famous Reliant Regal Supervan III there has ever been, Corgi rushed this 1/36 scale model out for 1999 having been beaten to market by Lledo with a 1/43 scale version. The larger Corgi model featured opening front doors and rear door, plus an opening suitcase for Del-Boy's swag! Ironically shortly after this model was released Corgi acquired Lledo and its tooling, so they inherited their version of the Reliant as well.

04302 James Bond *Tomorrow Never Dies* Aston Martin DB5

The iconic Aston Martin DB5 first appeared with agent 007 in 1964's *Goldfinger* and went on to make further appearances in *Thunderball*, *GoldenEye*, *Tomorrow Never Dies*, *Casino Royale*, *Skyfall* and *Spectre*. This Corgi Model was released in 1998 to mark the DB5's appearance in *Tomorrow Never Dies* and is based on the original 1/32 scale (271) tooling from 1978. It has the original working features of ejector seat, flip-up bullet proof shield and pop-out guns on the front bumper.

57403 *Kojak* Buick Regal

Kojak was a 1970s US cop show featuring Telly Savalas as the tough, New York cop, Theo Kojak. In the early episodes Kojak smoked but in an effort to give up he took to sucking lollipops. These became his trademark, along with the phrase 'Who Loves Ya baby?' and his trust bronze Buick Regal. Corgis 1/36 scale model from 1999 is another 'Corgi Original' using the original tooling.

05506 *The Italian Job* Mini Set

Who can forget this classic comic caper from 1969? Charlie (Michael Caine) and a bunch of hardened crooks try to steal a consignment of gold from the streets of Turin. The getaway cars are three Mini Coopers in red, white and blue. It is probably fair to say that the Minis made the film and the film made the Mini Cooper! The 3-car set from Corgi featured the 1/36 scale Mini with additional bonnet mounted spot lights and was first released in 1998.

00101 *The Avengers* Bentley

Airing from 1961 to 1969, *The Avengers* was a slightly 'off-the-wall' Spi-Fi series. It starred the suave John Steed (Patrick McNee) alongside a succession of attractive and assertive female assistants. Steed drove a number of Bentleys throughout the series. Corgis 1/43 scale model from 1998 was a remake of the original model from the 1966 Avengers Gift Set (GS40) but in green and with a standing Steed figure.

Above: 57402 Starsky and Hutch Ford Torino

From top down: 04302 James Bond's Aston Martin DB5 from the film *Tomorrow Never Dies*

The 'rock' at the Collectors Club

*Some people are 'Corgi' through and through. Susan Pownall is one such employee, **Paul Lumsdon** caught up her at home to find out more*

We used to joke at Corgi that there were certain employees that were like a stick of rock. Break them in half and you would see 'Corgi' written through the middle of them. Susan Pownall was one of those employees. She was the 'Rock' of the Corgi Collector Club for 29 years, pretty much from Day 1, until she retired in 2014. I caught up with her recently at her home in the north east of England where she chatted about her long career with Corgi.

■ Swansea Days

Susan joined Mettoy in Swansea in April 1983 as the PA to Sales and Marketing Director. However later that year the Mettoy Company went into receivership. Fortunately for the workforce, a management buyout led by Mike Rosser was successful and in March 1984, Corgi Toys Ltd was formed. Susan continued to work in the Marketing Department, where she met Art Director, Don Fuller. As the new company took off, Don found himself fielding an ever growing number of queries from diecast collectors. He became so busy that he decided to pre-empt many of the queries by issuing a bi-monthly newsletter. This started life as a simple typed sheet that was duplicated and posted out to customers. Issue 1 went out in August 1984.

It was around this time that Corgi Management identified an adult collector market for diecast products which heralded the launch of Corgi Classics. The first model, the Thornycroft, was released in 1985, and the need for detailed product information increased as a result. Don recruited Susan to help with the newsletter early in 1985 and together they grew the membership from around 200 to well over 2,000.

Susan at home, surrounded by some of the many newsletters she helped produce over the course of 29 years.

A charge of £2 per year was levied to cover postage and with the introduction of computers in to the workplace Susan began to allocate membership numbers and cards. The newsletters improved and by issue 7 there was spot colour. However, the biggest success for the club in its early days was the launch of a free members' model. The first was C832 Thorneycroft Van, sent out in 1985 to mark the first anniversary of the new company. Of course collectors were quick to appreciate that the value of the club model more than compensated for the cost of membership and more and more applied to join. The initial run

of 2000 Thornycrofts had to be supplemented by a second run of 1200 models to cope with demand. Just as an aside, the first release gave the Corgi address incorrectly as 'Fforestfach Industrial Estate'. The second run had this corrected to read 'Swansea Industrial Estate'. Both variants have become very collectable.

In October 1985 Mike Broadfield took over from Don Fuller as the Club Magazine Editor and Susan was made Assistant Editor. In 1986 Issue 11 marked the 30th anniversary of Corgi manufacturing and became the first issue produced in full colour. Shortly afterwards Mike Broadfield moved on to become Corgi's Business Development Director and Susan was promoted to Editor.

In 1990 Susan's hard work and huge success with the Club received formal recognition. She won a well-deserved *Collectors Gazette* award for services to the Toy Industry.

■ Off to Leicester

1991 saw further change as the Corgi business moved to Leicester, having been bought by US toy giant Mattel. Susan decided to remain in Swansea but continued to run the club from home on a part time basis. How she coped I have no idea as her main job was as Marketing Manager for the Wales Tourist Board. The annual free members' model was an ever popular draw, the Club Magazine became a high-quality 16-page publication packed with news and information, and membership continued to grow rapidly, peaking in the early 1990s at over 11,000!

In 1995 there was more change as Chris Guest led a new management buyout and Corgi became independent again. In 1996 Susan re-joined as a full time employee (albeit based in

Swansea). By the spring of 1998 she launched a separate Original Omnibus Company (OOC) Club (assisted by Gavin Booth) called 'Bus Route'. This ran bi-monthly until January 2004 when it was merged with the main Club magazine. Similarly, in 2001, Susan launched and managed 'Flight Recorder' for enthusiasts of the Aviation Archive range. This continued as a bi-monthly stand-alone publication until 2011, when it also merged into the main Club magazine.

■ The Hornby Era

At the beginning of 2012 a decision was taken to merge the Lledo (Vanguards) and Corgi Collector magazines into one and Susan Pownall and Jennifer Shaw became joint editors of the one magazine. Still called 'The Corgi Collector' it covered all the Corgi brands including Days Gone and Vanguards from the Lledo fold.

In 2014, exactly 30 years after Don Fuller published the first Corgi newsletter in-house, Hornby decided to bring the magazine in-house again and produce it from Margate (now Sandwich). Susan decided it was time to retire after working for the Corgi Club for 29 of those 30 years.

■ Dig This!

Mind you she's not one for the quiet life. Now living in the North East of England it's fair to say she likes a bit of gardening! So much so that she has become Chairman of the 'Newcastle Allotments Working Group' looking after 62 allotments in the city. She also chairs her own local allotment association and helps to run the allotment shop. Then just to keep her eye in with writing she is now editor of the regional allotment newsletter, 'Dig This' and writes the Moorside Allotment Association newsletter.

So clearly she has no plans to vegetate in retirement – or does she? ◉

Clockwise from top: 1 of 5500 1/43 scale Thornycroft Box Vans produced to mark the 21st Anniversary of the Corgi Collectors Club; Scania R Fridge, 30th Anniversary Corgi Club Exclusive; A selection of magazines spanning the decades; Corgi Mini Cooper 2007 Collectors Club limited edition

A positively Corgi family!

To find a father and daughter team, who between them have amassed some 47 years with the same company is not only unusual, but also shows loyalty and dedication to be much admired.
Paul Lumsdon *went to find out more*

Don and Adrienne Fuller were just that team and both had a real passion for Corgi – they were truly part of the Corgi family!

I worked at Corgi with Adrienne and met Don on several occasions after his retirement, so when I popped over to talk to 'Ade' about both their careers, there was a fair bit of catching up on old times to be done!

■ Don Fuller

Don Fuller was a man of rare talent. He was a classically trained graphic designer, who also happened to be a superb artist and illustrator.

Born in Middlesex in 1934, his early career was shaped in the cut and thrust of a London advertising agency. There followed several years working as an in-house designer with the pharmaceutical company Pfizer, before making the huge decision to move to New Zealand, where he worked as an Art Director.

In 1967 Don and his family returned to the UK and he joined the Mettoy Company. His first job was to set up the packaging design unit, for Corgi Toys and many other brands owned by Mettoy.

Corgi however became Don's passion and his superb designs and illustrations played a key part is the success of Corgi's packaging. Despite the many changes over the years, Don remained fiercely loyal to Corgi and moved

Adrienne and Don

Above: *Don presenting a James Bond cake to children at Rushton Hall, near Northampton*

with the business as it relocated from Swansea to Leicester under Mattel ownership, and then back into independent ownership in 1995.

Don retired a couple of years later giving him more time to pursue his dual love of aircraft and painting. He was particularly keen on De Havilland aircraft and was often to be found painting at the Moth Club rallies at Woburn Park, or at Leicester aerodrome. Sadly Don passed away in February 2011 at the age of 77.

■ Adrienne Fuller

Adrienne first started working for Corgi in Swansea in 1983. She had been looking for a job and so Don arranged a few weeks work for her, helping him to draw the tampo-print artwork for models. She excelled and the temporary role soon became permanent. Although most of the early work was on toys, the first Corgi collectable ranges were being introduced and 'Ade' remembers working on the artworks for the first Thorneycroft Vans and Buses.

In 1987, she decided to move on. She sold her house and used the money to fund a move to Spain, where she bought a bar. For 5½ years she enjoyed the sunshine lifestyle, until one day in 1993 she received a call from her dad. Corgi was now part of Mattel and Chris Guest was the MD. He asked Don to see if Adrienne would return to take up a 6 month contract to produce a new range called 'Corgi Cameos'. She agreed

CAREER HIGHLIGHTS

DON FULLER

STAND OUT MODEL
This has to be 'Chitty Chitty Bang Bang' for reasons that will become clear below.

STAND OUT MOMENT
Being invited to Hollywood for the film-premiere of 'Chitty Chitty Bang Bang'. Don attended the post-launch studio party where he met the stars of the film, including Dick Van Dyke and Sally Ann Howes.

CAREER ACHIEVEMENT
Don's legacy lives on in the wonderful packaging and superb artworks he produced for 'Corgi Classics'. I come across his work at every toy fair I attend.

ADRIENNE FULLER

STAND OUT RANGE
'It has to be the buses, and in particular the classics. Researching the colourful liveries and historical coats of arms and crests was just something I found really interesting and challenging in equal measure.'

MEMORABLE MOMENT
'Taking part in the Goodyear All-Ladies 4x4 Challenge. I was part of a 4 lady Corgi team in a sponsored Vauxhall Frontera 4x4. We were lucky enough to make the final in France where we encountered daily gruelling driving and intellectual challenges. We didn't win, in fact we came 5th, but we had such a good time!'

CAREER ACHIEVEMENT
'Working with Chris Guest and the rest of the team during the heyday of the Corgi Classics era was probably the highlight of my career. The camaraderie was incredible and it really did feel like we were one big, happy, family. Great times!'

SUMMARY
Adrienne's research and development work, particularly in the early days of Corgi Classics, helped create many of the diecast collectable ranges that we enjoy to this day, and of course she continues the good work with Oxford Diecast's current ranges.

> There followed several years working as an in-house designer with the pharmaceutical company Pfizer, before making the huge decision to move to New Zealand, where he worked as an Art Director

Above: DCorgi Ladies 4x4 Challenge team - Ade on left

Above: Ade in her office at home

Below: Corgi Ladies 4x4 Challenge Team (Ade on right) newspaper cutting.

TEAM IN GEAR FOR ON-ROAD CHALLENGE

Below: Corgi Ladies 4x4 Challenge team - Ade on left

and within 2 months the position was made permanent. Adrienne became the Product Development Co-ordinator for the entire Corgi range. When Chris Guest led a management buyout in 1995 Adrienne became the Product Manager for Corgi Classics Limited.

As the Corgi ranges grew so too did the development team but Adrienne remained a key part of it through until 2007, when Corgi was facing financial difficulties and Adrienne, along with many others, was made redundant.

Luckily she was immediately snapped up by Lyndon 'Taff' Davies to work for his Oxford Diecast Company. Lyndon himself was formerly employed by Mettoy at Swansea so this in many ways was a re-uniting of old colleagues and 'Ade' has been working happily as Oxford's Product Development Manager ever since. ◉

Gift Sets

Gijs Noordam looks at the highlights covering 1956 - 1970

With the innovation of Gift Sets, Corgi took the lead in the diecast toy market. But other toy makers were soon to follow. For example, before WWII, Dinky Toys introduced lines in motorcars, racing cars and planes that were specially packaged at gift sets. Corgi was not undone however, and managed to outstrip the competition releasing a series of special Gift Sets in rapid succession in 1956; cleverly combining classic models and new releases. Including the classic models, that were already designed and tooled for production, reduced their costs and allowing freedom to develop the concept and branding of the Gift Sets.

TRANSPORTERS

In October 1957 Corgi introduced its first major model, the Carrimore Car Transporter (1101). It featured an ingenious casting with simulated hydraulic rams between the two decks. The Transporter was drawn by

Above: R.A.F. Land Rover with Bloodhound Guided Missile, Trolley and Launching Ramp (Gift Set 4)

Above: Corporal Missile with Erector Vehicle, Launching Platform and International Army Truck (Gift Set 9)

Below: Land Rover evolution 1958 - 1968

the first series Bedford "TK" cab that, like in the real world, was replaced by the newer cab design in 1962 (1105). Corgi possibly tried to beat Dinky's Pullmore Car Transporter (982-G) that was already introduced in 1954) and similarly Corgi's Carrimore may have inspired Dinky to release its Car Carrier and Trailer (983-G) in 1958. All of them provided great play value.

It was Dinky who first saw the possibility of offering its transporter carrying existing saloon cars, releasing its Car Transporter Set (990-G) in 1956. Corgi followed suit with its first Gift Set in December 1957. The four cars included were the Austin Cambridge (201), Jaguar 2.4 Litre (208), Austin Healey (300) and MG A Sports car (302).

This Gift Set was reintroduced in 1963 with the new cab design (GS 28), again with 4 existing but updated saloon cars. There are many variations in the types of cars in this set, some original, some created especially.

This was followed in 1966 by the newly designed Car Transporter with the Ford Tilt cab (1137). A few months

later Gift Set 41 appeared, packed with 6 cars, in a number of variations.

In 1970 the Car Transporter was fitted with a third deck and coupled to a Scammell Handyman MK III Tractor Unit (1146). With the addition of 6 cars, among them The Saint's Volvo (258), resulted in Gift Set 48.

MILITARY

One highlight of the Military Sets collection is no doubt Gift Set 6 with the Rocket Age Models. Only 10,000 were sold and it is therefore quite rare. The set was released in 1959, and included existing military models like the Bristol Bloodhound Missile (1108), the Thunderbird Guided Missile (350), the Decca Radar Van (1106) and assorted related cars. The artwork of the box is quite eye-catching and even somewhat chilling, remember that those were the days of the Cold War.

Some of the military models were also issued as separate Gift Sets, like the Thunderbird Missile with the R.A.F. Land Rover (GS3), the Bloodhound Missile again with the R.A.F Land Rover (GS4) and the Corporal Missile with Erector Vehicle and Army Truck (GS9).

CIRCUS

Chipperfields was one of the leading circus names in Great Britain and over the years Corgi build a close relationship with its owners. The first of many Chipperfield models was the Circus Crane Truck (1121) in 1960, cleverly based on the pre-existing International Tow Truck (1118).

From top down:
Chipperfield Circus Set (Gift Set 23), first issue with Circus Booking Office (426); Ford Tractor and Conveyor (Gift Set 47); Car Transporter Set (Gift Set 28), with newly designed Bedford cab, Renault Floride (222), Studebaker Golden Hawk (211S), Mercedes-Benz 220 SE (230)

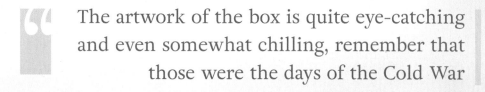

> The artwork of the box is quite eye-catching and even somewhat chilling, remember that those were the days of the Cold War

Clockwise from top right: Corporal Missile with Erector Vehicle, Launching Platform and International Army Truck (Gift Set 9); R.A.F. Land Rover (351) and Thunderbird Guided Missile on Trolley (350), together forming Gift Set 3; Car Transporter with Ford Tilt Cab (1137), reconstructed as Gift Set 41; Four generations of Car Transporters: 1957, 1963, 1966 and 1970, resp. Gift Sets 1, 28, 41 and 48

After some smaller gift sets like the Circus Crane Truck and Cage Wagon (GS 12) and an Elephant Cage (GS 19), Corgi issued the wonderful Chipperfield Circus Set (GS23) in 1962. It consisted of 6 models and a number of circus animals. The first issue contained the Circus Booking Office which was replaced by a Bedford Giraffe Transporter in the second.

UTILITY

Corgi shaped its mini world with a close eye to the real world and included utility models like fire engines, police cars, towing trucks, milk vans and ambulances. These could of course also serve as a Gift Set. First issued in 1961, early examples are the Jeep Hydraulic Tower Wagon

and Lamp Standard (GS14) including a technician fitting a new lamp, and the ERF Milk Truck and Trailer (GS21) carrying a load of milk churns.

Highlights in this category are the Constructor Set (GS24) that contained 2 Commer Cab, Chassis units and 4 different backs that could be combined to form different vans. The Shell or BP Garage Layout (GS25) comprising a number of kits to be built, accompanying cars and coloured layout on which the whole set could be positioned and played with.

AGRICULTURE

Another fertile field for Corgi was the farm and agriculture range. Here the Land Rover proved to be an excellent groundbreaker, starting in 1958 with

Clockwise from top right: The three racing cars forming Gift Set 5: Stirling Moss Vanwall (150), Le Mans Lotus XI (151) and BRM (152); Ecurie Ecosse Racing Transporter (1126 - Gift Set 16); Farming Models (Gift Set 22); Monte Carlo Rally Set (Gift Set 38) with Mini-Cooper S (321), Rover 2000 (322) and Citroën DS 19 (323); Lotus Racing Team Set (Gift Set 37)

the charming set of a Rice's Pony Trailer (GS 2) with two ponies. This set was updated in 1962 with a spring suspension version and replaced in 1968 by Gift Set 15. The Land Rover is now towing a Rice's Beaufort Horse Box with additional front ramp.

Apart from a number of Gift Sets based on Massey-Ferguson and Fordson Tractors with trailers, ploughing equipment and elevator (Gift Sets 1, 7, 9, 13/18, 32, 33 and 47) the centre pieces of this range were the Farming Models (GS22) and the Agricultural Set (GS5). The Farming Models were grouped around the Massey Ferguson Combine Harvester (1111). Issued in 1962 and followed in 1967 by the Agricultural Set it included the Dodge "Kew Fargo" Livestock Transporter (484) as well as the Land Rover, Massey Ferguson Tractor, Farm Tipper and Tandem Disc Harrow. This truck of American origin must have stood out in the English countryside!

MOTOR SPORTS

Corgi's design team closely followed the many British successes in motor racing. When the Mini Coopers made mash potato of their competitors in successive Monte Carlo Rally's Corgi very quickly issued models of the different winning Mini's. This resulted in the now much sought after Monte Carlo Rally Set (GS 38).

The Gift Sets in this range date back to 1959 when Corgi put a winning Stirling Moss Vanwall with a Le Mans Lotus XI and a BRM (GS 5). The release of the Ecurie Ecosse Race Transporter was immediately followed by a Gift Set based on this one off which included three Corgi racing cars that may vary (GS16). The indestructible Land Rover made its reappearance, now towing the Ferrari "Shark nose" Formula 1 on a trailer (GS 17).

In 1966 the Land Rover was replaced by the Volkswagen Breakdown Van in the Lotus Racing Team Set (GS37). It was accompanied by the sleek Lotus Elan with detachable chassis that had been issued the year before, be it in different colours. The Volkswagen returned in the Racing Set (GS6), now towing a trailer with a Cooper-

Maserati Formula One.

That same year Corgi started the "All Winners Set" (GS46 and 45) that came with varying sports and racing coupes that were released earlier.

The top set is no doubt the Silverstone Racing Layout (GS15) that a box full of kits, models, figures, and a layout sheet to place it all and have your own racing day. Anyone lucky enough to receive this set as a Christmas or birthday present will no doubt have built the kits so not many of the 8,000 sold will be around in the original mint and boxed condition. The current price range for this set in that condition is around £2,000-2,500 and seems staggering but if you add up the single items at their present market value it is in fact a bargain. At the same time be prepared for a dilemma: if you start putting the kits together the value will no doubt drop with each box that you open...

HOLIDAY AND LEISURE

Also in this field Corgi and Dinky as the two brand leaders were tough rivals. Dinky came up first with sets focussing on the holiday and recreation theme and Corgi quickly followed. At the end of 1965 the Riviera Gift Set (GS 31) was issued, a nice combination of the existing Buick Riviera with the Dolphin Cabin Cruiser on a trailer. Figures of a captain and a waterskier completed the set that came in a box with a diorama and suggestive artwork of life on the Riviera.

In Gift Set 36 the marine theme continued with the Oldsmobile Toronado towing a newly designed Glastron speedboat on a trailer. This set possibly started with the Rambler Marlin, another American car that appeared shortly thereafter in its own set (GS10). It towed the earlier Pennyburn trailer without the tools but including 2 kayaks and a paddling figure. The box artwork is impressive and makes you want to pack for the holidays! Also with an eye to the holidays and possibly meant to needle the French Dinky design team, Corgi released in 1968 the Tour de France Set (GS13) featuring a new casting of the

From the top down: Rambler Marlin with Kayak and Trailer (Gift Set 10); Oldsmobile Toronado and Speedboat (Gift Set 36); variations in the water skying figures!; Tour de France Set (Gift Set 13); Camera man on platform appeared earlier with the Commer Mobile Camera Van (483)

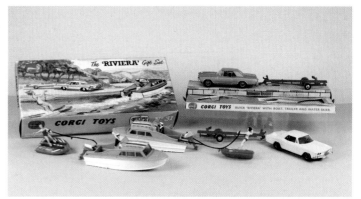

Top: Land Rover with Ferrari on Trailer (Gift Set 17) and Volkswagen Breakdown Van with Cooper-Maserati on Trailer (Gift Set 6)

Above: Riviera Set (Gift Set 31) with Buick Riviera (245) and Dolphin Cabin Cruiser on Trailer (104)

Right: Tour de France Set (Gift Set 13) with converted Renault 16 on basis of the basic Renault 16 (260)

GIFT SET 13

Renault 16. It came with a rear camera platform that was used earlier with the Commer Mobile Camera Van (479) and a toiling Tour de France cyclist.

AMERICAN MARKET

By the late 1950s Corgi's overseas sales accounted for nearly a third of the company's turnover. The USA had become an important market since the introduction of a number of American cars like the Studebaker Golden Hawk, Ford Thunderbird and Chevrolet Impala. Distribution in the USA was run by Reeves International in New York. Two important outlets were the toyshops of FAO Schwarz in New York and Marshall Field's in Chicago. For these retailers Reeves put together some special Gift Sets,

tailored to the American market. Within the limits of this chapter only two sets can be mentioned, the Tow Truck Set containing the Holmes Wrecker Recovery Vehicle (1142) and a Buick Riviera (245) and the Hiway Patrol Set, including the two cars from the Tow Truck Set. Added was a typical American police car, the Chevrolet Police Patrol Car (481). In total there are 6 of these special sets known but possibly other sets will come to light, even after all these years. They are, in any case, extremely rare and therefore expensive. ◉

Sources: the Great Book of Corgi and the series of articles on Corgi Gift Sets by Andrew Ralston in Diecast Collector 2010/2011.

Accessorize to survive

*Corgi didn't just make vehicles, as **Gijs Noordam** reviews the numerous characters and accessories*

From the start Corgi and Dinky were not only competing for better diecast but also for enhancing the "play value" of its models. Corgi did so by adding figures of drivers and animals like those seen in its Chipperfield's circus range. During the late 1950s and the '60s Corgi also added a variety of other accessories like planks and other loads for trucks and trailers, suitcases and golf trolley's, lamp standards, trailers with boats and racing cars, self-adhesive packs with number plates and racing numbers, spare wheels and tires, bollards and hay bales and a number of do-it-yourself plastic kits.

Corgi was not the first to start with figures and accessories. The history of figures goes further back than model cars of course, for example toy soldiers. Figures with car models originated from Dinky as accessories to Hornby 0 gauge trains. Only later on did Dinky launch model cars under the name Dinky Toys.

As Corgi produced a great number of figures with its models we will only be able to deal with some of the highlights.

The Corgi figures can be divided in a number of categories:

■ CAR AND RACING DRIVERS

The first driver figure was a very small one, matching the scale of the Proteus Campbell Bluebird Record

Car (153). The figure is wearing white racing overalls and helmet. Larger racing figures, although some of them without legs, appeared in the B.R.M. F1, Vanwall F1 and Lotus Mark XI (152S, 150S and 151). The Lotus driver was the prelude to Corgi's own Stig, the figure of Jim Clark in the Lotus Climax Formula 1 car (155). This figure did not only have a white racing overall and helmet but also silver goggles and re-appeared in a number of later sports and racing cars. The ultimate racing driver figures were first sold as a separate set, together with spectators,

Main image: The Hardy Boys with their Rolls Royce (805)

race track, press officials and garage attendants (1501 – 1505). They all found their way to the wonderful and rare Silverstone and Shell/BP Service Station Sets (GS 15 and 25).

More sophisticated was the driver with the red bow tie in the Thunderbird Open Sports (215S) who changed car to a Mercedes-Benz 300 SL Roadster (303S). Classical outfits can be found in the Corgi Classic Series of Veteran and Vintage class vehicles like the 1915 Model "T" Ford (9011 and 9012) and the 1910 Daimler 38 HP (9021). Looking really posh are the couple in

Clockwise from top left: Poodles and charming dog trainer with Chipperfield Chevrolet Circus Truck (511); London Passenger Set (Gift Set 35) with cab driver, bus driver, "clippy" conductor and Bobby; Lion Clarence with spectacles and Paula on his back; Aki Wakabayahi at the wheel, one of the scarce lady drivers in the Corgi range; The Monkees Monkeemobile (227) with Micky Dolenz, Michael Nesmith, Peter Tork and Davy Jones; Farming figure with brown leather jacket and yellow scarf used in Gift Set 22 and later farming models

evening dress in the Chevrolet Astro 1 Experimental car (347).

■ FARM

Corgi's farm and agricultural range has been strong from the beginning. Its roots go back to the introduction in 1957 of the first of many Land Rover's models to come. In combination with the Rice's Pony Trailer (Gift Set 2) the first Corgi figures were born by way of two ponies. Soon after Corgi put the Agricultural Set (Gift Set 22) on the market, a combination of farm equipment including a combine and two tractors appeared. Driven by two different farm figures that would re-appear again in the seats of later tractor editions. Both sturdy men, one in a green overall and the other in a brown leather jacket and both with a yellow scarf. Of course a farm cannot do without animals, see the four calves in the Beast Carrier coupled to the Fordson Power Major Tractor (Gift Set 33), a farm hand working the sacks onto the Conveyor Belt with Jeep FC 150 (64), the five pigs in the back of the Dodge "Kew Fargo" Livestock Transporter (484) and again horses but now a mare and foal with the updated Land Rover and Rice's Beaufort Double Horse Box (Gift Set 15).

■ CIRCUS

The Chipperfield range is impressive, both in models and in figures, be it that they are mostly animals. Lions and polar bears with the Circus Animal Cage (1123), a friendly elephant with the Circus Land Rover and Elephant Cage on Trailer (Gift Set 19). Majestic circus horses with their stable on wheels are found in the Circus Horse Transporter (1130), while elegant giraffes feature in the Circus Giraffe Transporter (503). A yellow skirted chimpanzee attracts attention to the circus on the Circus Land Rover Parade Vehicle (487), tigers and partly newly moulded lions and bears in transparent cages on the Scammel Circus Menagerie Transporter (1139) and finally the charming performing poodles on a green plastic disc with the Chevrolet Circus Truck (511). Also charming, as it is only here that we find a human figure in this range - the pretty female poodle trainer. She is possibly modelled after one of the members of the big Chipperfield family who started and owned this circus empire.

■ TV AND FILM

Corgi really became famous in the 1960 due to its TV and Film related models. Of course these models could not do without their corresponding figures. Starting with the Saint in

Right: Jim Clark or Corgi's own Stig? Lotus- Climax Formula 1 Racing Car (155)

his white Volvo P-1800 (258) who is, unfortunately, not really recognizable behind the wheel. This was followed up with the most successful of them all, James Bond in his Aston Martin D.B.5 (261) from the Bond film "Goldfinger". This time Corgi depicted a good look-a-like figure behind the wheel and included a "baddie" in blue overalls. After this Corgi really took off with this range. The detailed figures of *The Avengers* John Steed and Emma Peel with their Bentley and Lotus Elan (Gift Set 40), Napoleon Solo and Ilya Kuryakin as The Man from U.N.C.L.E. in their Oldsmobile "Trushbuster" (497), Batman and Robin in the Batmobile (267 and later also in the Batboat, 107), Bertie Wooster and his manservant Jeeves with "The World of Wooster Bentley" (9004), again James Bond but now with Aki Wakabayashi from the Bond film *You only live twice* in the Toyota 2000 GT (336), and Dr Marsh Tracy as "Daktari" in the Daktari Set (Gift Sets 7 and 14). Also lesser known characters were staged like *The Green Hornet* in The Green Hornet's Black Beauty (268) and *The Hardy Boys* with their Rolls Royce (805). Tailored for the US market, which was important to Corgi in those years, may explain the extravagant Chitty Chitty Bang Bang (266) from the American film with the same title. Dick van Dyke, Sally Ann Howes and their two children wonderfully reduced to 1/43! Also from the other side of the Transatlantic came the pop band The Monkees with Micky Dolenz, Michael Nesmith, Peter Tork and Davy Jones in their Monkeemobile (227) and from England the most famous rock band ever, The Beatles, in their Yellow Submarine (803).

MARINE

Trailering a boat did of course also enhance playability of diecast so Corgi produced the Dolphin Cabin Cruiser on a trailer as part of the Rivièra Set (Gift Set 31). Towed by a Buick "Riviera", with a neatly dressed captain at the helm and a young female on water skis. The Glastron Sportsman Speedboat V171 with the Oldsmobile Toronado was a worthy successor (Gift Set 36) with a happy crew of three enjoying

Sunbeam Imp Police "Panda" (506)

Dutch and German policemen in their Volkswagen 1200 Police Car (492)

Firefighters with the American "LaFrance" Aerial Rescue Truck (1143)

Firefighters with the Chevrolet Fire Chief Car (439)

Rotating ice vendor in Mister Softee's Ice Ceam Van (428)

Driving teachers and pupils in RHD and LHD Austin A60 De Luxe Saloon Driving School Car (263 and 255)

the sun and no doubt they will have come across the surfing Adonis who parked his Austin Mini Countryman with surfboards near the beach (485). For those who prefer paddling, Corgi issued the Rambler Marlin Fastback with Kayaks (Gift Set 10) with a figure in a kayak holding a paddle.

UTILITY

Corgi however did not forget about life on the street which added to a realistic toy scene.

A technician repairing a lamp with the Hydraulic Tower Wagon (Gift Set 14), taxi drivers spanning the globe from Bermuda with a Ford Thunderbird Taxi (430), to New York with a Chevrolet Impala Yellow Cab (480) and finally

Above: *Skier with Citroën Safari Corgi Ski Club (475, second issue)*

to London with the Austin taxi in the London Passenger Set (Gift Set 35). That set also came with a bus driver in the immortal Routemaster double deck bus and a London 'Bobby' directing the traffic from a platform. Corgi gave him a number of colleagues like the police dog handler with the Austin Mini Police Van (448), the austere cops in the Chevrolet Impala Police Car (481), a local keeper of the peace with the Sunbeam Imp Police "Panda" (506) and Dutch and German policemen in their Volkswagen 1200 Police Car (492).

Fire fighters are also well represented in this range. The Chevrolet Fire Chief Car (439), the popular Simon Snorkel Fire Engine (1127) and the impressive American

Team manager and driver in Citroën Tour de France Team Manager's Car (510)

Decca Airfield Control Radar 424 Scanner (353)

Politicians with the Land Rover Public Address Vehicle (472)

Ford Consul Cortina Estate Car "woodie" (440) with golfer and caddie and golf bag on trolley

Chrysler Imperial with two golfers and a surpise in the boot (248)

The Beatles in their Yellow Submarine (803): Paul McCartney, John Lennon, George Harrison and Ringo Starr

"LaFrance" Aerial Rescue Truck (1143) could be purchased.

We meet a milkman in the Commer Constructor Set (Gift Set 24), ice vendors in the Karrier Bantam Mister Softee Ice Cream Van (428) and also the Ford Thames Wall's Ice Cream Van (447), and snackbar vendors in the Karrier Bantam Joe's Diner Mobile Canteen (471). There are also driving teachers, both right and left hand drive, with the Austin A60 De Luxe Saloon Driving School Car (263 and 250) and even politicians with the Land Rover public address vehicle (472).

SPORTS
Sporting figures played a large part in the Corgi scene. Golfers with the

Chrysler Imperial (246) and Ford Cortina Estate Car (440), skiers and their rescuers with the various Citroën Safari Olympic editions (475, 499 and 513) and cyclist with Tour de France Set Renault 16 (Gift Set 13), driver, cameraman and Citroën Tour de France Team Manager's Car (510).

Finally, we should not forget the most famous Corgi figure of them all: the Corgi dog lying on the parcel shelves of the Ghia L 6.4 Chrysler (241) and Ford Mustang Fastback 2 +2 (320).

VARIOUS ACCESSORIES
Although figures formed the major part of Corgi's playing field there are some interesting further accessories. For example, a service ramp that could

be raised or lowered by cranking a lever at the front (1401). To accompany the military range there was a Radar Scanner mounted on a box structure (353). Still found on Corgi models in specialised shops and at auctions: self adhesive number plates, Running In labels, Road Fund licences, sports discs and white wall tyre trims. They all made the Corgi model car world more realistic (1460 -1464). The same goes for planks, bricks, milk churns and cement sacks loads that could be fitted on Corgi trucks and trailers (1485 – 1488). There were suitcases big and small for Corgi models with opening boots, bonnets or rear windows like the Jaguar Mark X Saloon (238), the Volkswagen 1500 Karmann Ghia (239) and the MGB GT (327).

At this point Corgi kits should also be mentioned. In a time when plastic do-it-yourself kits of airplanes, warships and cars were very popular Corgi added its own kits to the range that could be used to built your own Corgi city. There were simple lamp standards (606), AA and RAC Telephone Boxes (602) and Bartley Garages (601). More complicated and therefore more fun to build were the Motel Chalet (611) and the wonderful stands that formed part of the Silverstone Racing Track: the Racing Pits (603), the Press Box (604) and the Clubhouse/Timekeeper's Box (605). The ultimate kit was the Shell/BP Service Station (608). A last special mention for a rather unique and rare accessory: the Corgi Carry Case containing a Shell service station with roof parking and underground storage (X400).

Corgi created a world of it's own for young children who belonged to the Babyboom generation. The Corgi world was filled with a great variety of diecast models that actually populated the roads and neighbourhoods of the real world and accessories like those mentioned above made this world even more realistic. ◉

Sources: "The Great Book of Corgi" by Marcel Van Cleemput, "TV & film diecasts" by Dean Sheperd in Diecast Collector July 2010 issue and "Corgi – it(s) figures!", a series of articles by Gijs Noordam in various Diecast Collector 2015 issues

Above: Rescuer and St Bernard rescue dog with Citroën Safari Alpine Rescue Car (513)

Simon Snorkel Fire engine

Released: *August 1963* **Withdrawn:** *1968*
Sales: *1,163,000 (plus 1969 figures, lost in fire)*

The Simon Snorkel Fire Engine, released in September 1964, was a superb replication of one of the very latest types of fire engines in use at the time. It is a perfect example of Corgi's ability to engineer in miniature to the highest standard and at the same time incorporate top notch playability, all the while having enough appeal to sell well. Initially packaged in a Styrofoam moulded base with a very attractive box lid featuring excellent artwork of the unit in action, the model would be sold in the less appealing but more sales point friendly window box during the later years of its life.

The boom rises and lowers by way of a beautifully engineered pantograph mechanism that keeps the yellow cage at the business end level at all times, just like the real thing. Two thumb wheels each operate a very clever rack and pinion system to move the whole arrangement up and down to the desired height, which is mounted on a simple turntable giving more manoeuvrability and flexibility. To keep the whole combination on an even keel are four extending steadying legs.

An operating fire engine wouldn't be complete without firemen of course and Corgi wouldn't leave us disappointed with six suitably attired figures – two in the front of the cab (one is a driver of course), three in the back of the cab, facing backwards, and that all important brave soul in the cage, ready to aim the hose.

Fabulously finished in red of course, the toy was much loved and well played with. But with well over one million sold during its twelve years in the shops, it is fairly easy to find one in this good boxed condition today and the example photographed here cost just £25 from an online auction website in February 2016. ◉

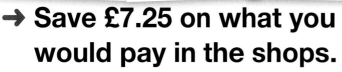

Commer Constructor set-GS24

*Released: August 1963 **Withdrawn:** 1968 **Sales:** 345,000*

Corgi Toys first released the Commer ¾ ton chassis in the form of the No 464 County Police van in June 1963, followed by No 465 Commer Pick-up one month later featuring the innovative Trans-o-lite system that used natural light to illuminate the headlights using a clear plastic moulding between the cab roof and the front of the cab.

If this wasn't exciting enough, there was a fantastic surprise in store for the following month, August 1963, which saw the release of the Pick-up as part of the superb Gift Set 24 Commer Constructor Set.

The set comprised two basic Commer cab and chassis units, one red and one white, plus four different interchangeable backs, a milk bottle load, a bench seat and a milkman figure. From these, a variety of combinations could be built up, offering plenty of playability. The

parts were packaged in a Styrofoam moulded base with an attractive box lid depicting the eight combinations possible and this initially went on sale for just 15 Shillings.

The red Trans-o-lite chassis was joined by a white version without the feature and the four backs made either of these into a van, an ambulance, a milk float (hence the milkman figure) and a pick up. The latter was yellow, so when matched with the red chassis, this combination was the same as the No 465 release the previous month. The combination of the white chassis with the ambulance back was released separately in February 1964 as No 463, and with the milk float back as No 466 in April 1964. The van, although never released in the colours from the set, was the basis for several releases in ensuing years. Corgi certainly made good use of the basic casting!

Available until 1968, the Commer Constructor Set achieved sales of 345,000 and, as a result, this means that there are still many available today although, given the superb playability of the set, most of these are in varying states of playworn condition. ◉

"Nevva Wazzas"

Paul Lumsdon *tells the stories behind some of the Corgi 'What Might Have Been' models that nearly made it to production but were in fact cancelled at the last minute*

Product development isn't a precise science and despite all the checks and measures that are put in place by companies to ensure that the process is as foolproof as possible, there will always be products that are planned but which, for a variety of reasons, fail to make it to production and are cancelled at the last minute. From my experience this certainly happened at Corgi from time to time and here are the stories behind just a few examples along with photographs of what are now very unique, 'what might have been' items.

MOLEART VWS – THE 'BUGS' THAT NEVER WERE

Going right back to my earliest days at Corgi, there was always a nagging doubt about the longevity of the diecast collector market and a fear that it would gradually decline as collectors aged, and (to be blunt) eventually died! Recruiting new and younger collectors was always a key goal and the Corgi development team were constantly coming up with ideas that might appeal to a broader, younger, mass audience. Some, like the 'Icon' gift figurine range, made it to full production, but most fell by the wayside much earlier, and never even progressed beyond a sketch pad.

'Moleart VWs' was one idea put forward at Corgi around 1999, that made it well beyond the drawing board but just fell short of going into production. It was based around the then large market for customised VW Beetles (or Bugs) amongst 20 and 30-plus year olds. The idea was to create a range of caricature-type 'Bug' vehicles – cartoons in 3-D if you like, with the idea that these would appeal as whimsical, but still collectable, gifts.

The first stage with many new model ideas that appear to have potential beyond two dimensional sketches, is to get an idea of what the product would look like in three dimensions. The cheapest way to do this back then was to roughly carve the product from blue foam. That's exactly what Corgi did with the 'Bugs' and the end result looked rather promising. So much so that a range of finished resin prototype models were then commissioned, albeit slightly smaller than the foam renditions. These were to be finished to a high standard to be used as trade preview prototypes and possibly even for catalogue photography.

Two styles were progressed, one slightly more cartoon-like than the other and the

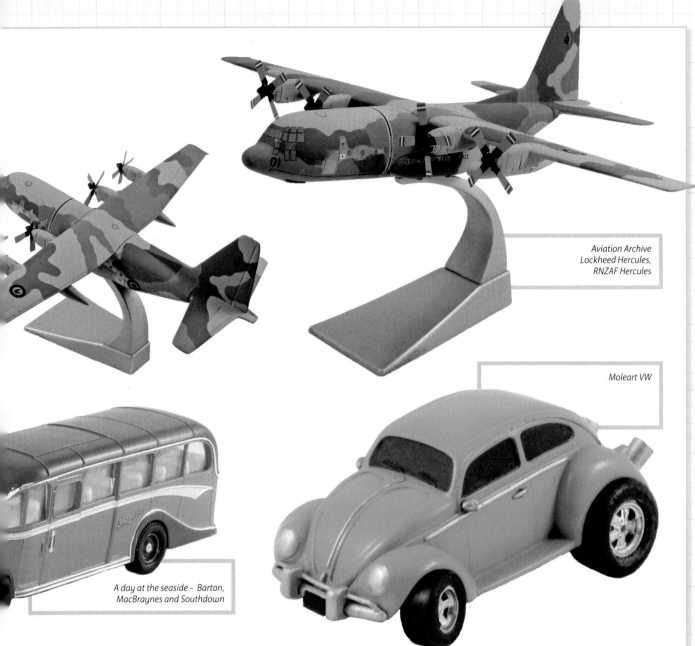

Aviation Archive
Lockheed Hercules,
RNZAF Hercules

Moleart VW

A day at the seaside - Barton,
MacBraynes and Southdown

finished prototypes looked very good. Both captured the essential recognisable features of the 'Bug', and both featured that classic Californian 'slammed' look with lowered suspension, huge oversize rear wheels and massive exhaust tailpipes. Why this range was suddenly dropped without even making it into a catalogue I really cannot say. My guess would be that the target market was so far removed from the existing Corgi distribution (more Clinton Cards than Modelzone) that the cost of entering this completely new area would have been considerable and was perhaps considered a risk too far. At this time Corgi was financially supported by venture capitalists looking for a fast return on their investment. My guess is that a few new diecast trucks and buses would have

delivered their short term objective quicker and without major risk.

So the 'Moleart VW' range was dropped and disappeared without ever being publicly aired. Fortunately, as a bit of VW enthusiast myself, I was able to rescue some of the foam-carved models and resin prototypes from the skip, and after many years sitting in a box under my desk, I eventually brought them home and they have been in safe storage ever since.

CLASSIC BUS - A DAY AT THE SEASIDE

Designed to evoke memories of carefree family day trips by coach to the seaside, this series was an opportunity to reintroduce to the range some of the classic 1/50 scale coach tools that had not be used for 10 years or more. To enhance the series a sign-written advertising 'A' board was

to be included with each model as well as a specially commissioned seaside 'saucy' postcard.

Hand decorated samples of three models were produced with authentic liveries and seaside destinations. The range was photographed and product numbers were allocated as follows:
• **CC25101** Bedford OB, Southdown
• **CC25301** AEC Regal, MacBraynes
• **CC25401** Burlingham Seagull, Barton

If the editor is brave enough to show the 'saucy' postcards (created by Corgi model makers, Code 3 Models) it may be of interest to know that the MacBranes one featured a caricature of my good self.

This was a very attractive and colourful range and offered something different for the 2008 first half year catalogue. So why did it not go ahead? Quite simply the price. The range development went ahead to hit catalogue deadlines but when product quotes were received, the costs for the relatively limited volumes proposed were high giving a retail price of close to £50. Even with the extra features included this was considerably more than the secondary market prices for the original 1/50 scale coach models. As a result pre-order sales were poor and the decision was taken in November 2007 to cancel this entire series.

The models depicted here are the hand-decorated models produced for catalogue photography. No factory produced pre-production models were ever made so these are the only examples of this proposed range that exist.

AVIATION ARCHIVE LOCKHEED HERCULES – ROYAL NEW ZEALAND AIR FORCE

Around 2000, Diane Brown, the newly promoted Export Manager at Corgi Classics set about developing sales to overseas markets. In particular, Corgi's collectable ranges had enjoyed great popularity in the southern hemisphere markets of Australia and New Zealand, Diane was therefore keen to offer Corgi distributors in these territories bespoke products that would have appeal to local collectors. Working closely with the New Zealand distributor at the time she researched the Royal New Zealand Air Force's Hercules aircraft. Corgi had added a 1/144 scale Hercules to the Aviation Archive range in 1999 so the tooling was available and hand decorated samples were commissioned. Two models were produced with one being sent to New Zealand for approval, whilst the other was retained in the UK for reference. The product number AA31302 was allocated to the Hercules. At the same time the Hong Kong office was briefed so that factory quotes could be obtained.

However, it wasn't the cost that caused this model to be dropped but more the minimum production run required by the factory. I can't remember the exact number but I know the New Zealand distributor felt it was too many units for his market alone, whilst the UK sales team felt they could not help spread the risk by committing to a significant quantity for the UK collectors. There was no option but to cancel the model. No factory pre-production samples were ever made so the two hand-made samples were the only examples of this model that were ever made.

CORGI SHOWCASE – MILITARY COLLECTION

Corgi Showcase was launched in 2003 as an attempt to bring collectable diecast models to a larger and younger audience. It was the brainchild of Corgi Classics CEO, Chris Guest who was aware of the ageing profile of many collectors and the declining production numbers associated with the increased costs of high end collectables.

Resin versions of the Moleart VWS

This model later became the generic 66401 Crawler Loader

Chris wanted something collectable but cheaper!

At the same time Corgi had opened a USA office and they were keen to launch a range with international flavour that would appeal to the American consumer.

Corgi Showcase covered popular themed areas including aviation, space flight, military and emergency services. The models were sized to fit a standard box rather than a recognised scale and were cleverly designed to offer maximum detail with a minimum of parts so that the cost could be kept low. The plan was to further enhance the models with attractive colour schemes and markings.

All went well initially and the team in the USA were particularly enthusiastic to get the product trialled across several large Walmart stores. For a full roll-out across the USA a huge development plan was going to be necessary so that the range could be constantly refreshed to keep the interest of customers/collectors. The Corgi development team was working flat out and further new models were produced specifically for the US market. Despite this,

the Walmart trials were not as successful as had been hoped and the big roll-out never happened. Much of the Showcase development was shelved. More military vehicles had been proposed but sadly they never saw the light of day. Two of these are pictured here – The German King Tiger (or Tiger II) Heavy Tank and the Sdkfz 250 Half Track were both planned for the WW2 ranges but were cancelled at the model making stage. The models shown are the resin prototype samples, hand produced from rubber moulds. They were painted in a white undercoat prior to being decorated for catalogue photography. Sadly they never progressed to this stage and were never allocated product numbers. To the best of my knowledge these are the only prototype models that ever existed.

CORGI TOY – JCB/KS PLANT CRAWLER LOADER

To the casual observer this yellow and black Crawler Loader may look exactly

JCB 110B Crawler Loader

Resin prototype versions
of the Showcase Sdkf2 250
Half Track and German King
Tiger Heavy Tank

Only Fools and
Horses Gold Plated
Reliant Regal Van,
still in its original
packaging

like the model that was widely available in the Corgi Toy range from around 2001 as product number 66401. Now look again and you may spot why this model is in fact a 'Nevva Wazza'. Here's the story:

It began life in 1976 as Corgi Majors model number 1110 – a JCB 110B Crawler Loader. It was produced in authentic period JCB red, yellow and white livery and was very popular, remaining in the range until 1980, when a reissue appeared in the scheme of 'Block Construction'. This was less popular and was withdrawn the following year with the tooling then going into retirement.

When in the late 1990s Corgi Classics were looking for a low-cost range of new toys, the Crawler Loader, with its fabulously engineered working features was an obvious contender. The tooling was available so the development team set about updating the model with the latest JCB yellow and black scheme. The model shown is one of just a handful of pre-production samples produced by the factory to full

production standard including printed livery.

The problem was that the model had the JCB logo printed on the cab door. When the original 1976 Corgi Majors model had been produced the world was a very different place. In the ensuing decades licensing became big business and a source of revenue for many well-known brands including JCB. Sadly Corgi Classics did not have a JCB license and they would not grant permission for Corgi to produce the model, claiming (quite rightly) that the yellow and black livery was completely wrong for 110B's period.

To get around the problem Corgi set about making changes. The most obvious was the removal of the JCB logo from the cab, but also on the underside the engraving was changed to remove all reference to JCB 110B. At the same time the Corgi Majors engraving was replaced with the latest Corgi logo and a cheaper rubberised caterpillar track was introduced. This then became the generic Crawler Loader that went into production as model number 66401. The model as depicted here was never produced and is one of only two factory-prepared pre-production models that I am aware of.

ONLY FOOLS AND HORSES – GOLD PLATED RELIANT REGAL VAN

I have to confess that this 'Nevva Wazza' has me rather stumped. I really can't recall what this Gold Plated Trotter Van was designed for, or why it never went into production. The sample depicted is a fully production finished model, sealed on a blister card. This same style of packaging was used for a standard 1/43 scale 'yellow' Trotter van based on the Vanguards range tooling. It was included with a 2002 BBC video release of the Christmas 2001 feature length episode of Only Fools and Horses 'If They Could See Us Now'.

The gold version is mounted on the very same blister card but differs from the video release version by virtue of the fact that it has no bar code printed on the reverse. I can only assume that this was proposed for a special limited video release that did not go ahead, or that it was rejected by the BBC, or that it was too expensive to produce.

The only thing I can say for sure is that there are two examples in existence (which was normal for a pre-production model) but apart from these, I have never seen or heard of another. ◉

Cataloguing the past

Since the very earliest days of Corgi, product catalogues have presented the product range and inspired generations. With some of these catalogues now becoming almost as collectable as the toys and models within the pages.
Rick Wilson *delves into his archives*

C atalogue designs over the past six decades have not just served as promotional tools, they have also reflected the changing face of diecast toys and, latterly, the rise of collecting, so are very useful for tracking the history of Corgi. From the coloured drawings in the first catalogues, actual photography has been the mainstay for most of the catalogues since. With modern production processes and commercial reasons meaning that finished models are sometimes not ready until after the latest brochure has gone to print, things have almost gone full circle with CAD renderings featuring more and more these days, harking back to the pre-photographed brochures.

MEMORIES OF CATALOGUES PAST

Ever since I can remember, the prospect of a new Corgi catalogue has given rise to excitement levels of pre-Christmas proportions. So with six decades of such publications to pore over, this article has been a delight to put together, using many of my own collection for reference, but a big nod of appreciation is due to my fellow contributor Paul Lumsdon for his help in plugging many of the gaps.

Catalogues over the years have appealed to both children and adult collectors alike and, despite a wide variance and many changes in their design, Corgi's catalogues have always managed to thrill. Mine were always at the top of the pile on the

Above:
Three from the 1970s compared to the 2016 January/ June edition.

Far left:
The first proper catalogue 1958 cover.

Left:
1961's catalogue was worth it for the front cover alone.

coffee table, serving as a day dreaming device for me and a useful present list for my parents/relatives for birthdays and Christmas each year. Pocket money would be piled up alongside to help with my saving inspiration too. As a result though, it meant that they were well thumbed and dog-eared by the end of the year, not to mention the strategic marking with a biro or folded over page corners, so simply got discarded when replaced by the latest edition. But there are still many of the earlier catalogues to be found in immaculate condition amazingly, and at a reasonable price too.

The early seventies examples photographed here have cost me just

Above: *The wraparound cover of the 1970 catalogue, featuring the No 385 Porsche 917 in pursuit of the No 388 Mercedes-Benz C111.*

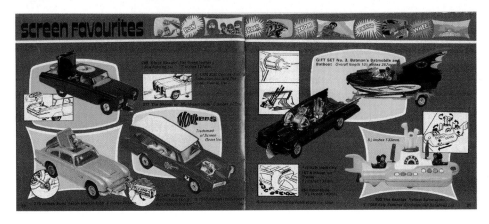

a couple of pounds each thanks to a little careful searching coupled with a large degree of patience and will power to avoid paying over the odds and not just snapping up the first one I've seen. Go back a few years into the sixties though and it's a different story and as for the fifties it is very hard indeed to find a pristine copy without delving into deep pockets.

Middle : *The catalogue had quite a range to cover including the very popular Corgi Rockets range complete with track system, seen alongside a call to action to join the Corgi Model Club.*
Bottom: *1970 also featured plenty of favourites from TV and film.*

SIX DECADES OF DIECAST PRODUCTION

Without wanting to repeat large sections covered elsewhere, it would have been easy to fill these lines with the history of the company's production but as the catalogues were very visual tools, I will leave largely that to the images selected, so evocative of each era that they

Top: *1997 July-December Classics cover.*

Middle: *January to June 1993 Classics cover.*

Bottom: *Classic Corgi cover, January - June 1992.*

Above, left to right: *One of my all time favourite covers, with the dramatic JPS Lotus 72 at speed announcing the arrival of the big 1/18 scale No 190. Equally as eye-catching was the 1978 cover featuring James Bond's underwater Lotus Esprit escaping from the Stromberg Helicopter. The cover images got more lifelike but no less dramatic, this is the second half odf the year cover for the Aviation Archive range in 2002.*

Above, left to right: *This selection clearly shows the 60th anniversary 2016 catalogue cover (right) harking back to former glory days of the 1960s with 007's Aston Martin DB5 (1966 cover) and the fabulous Chitty Chitty Bang Bang flying high for the 1969 cover with the "Take Off Wheels" Chevrolet Camaro on the ground.*

represent.

From the early issues hand drawn to the modern day hi-res photography and pre-production renderings, each style is a real sign of the times. I can spend hours looking at the pages within my collection of catalogues. Some bring memories of Corgis I owned, or dreamt of owning. Then there were the years when I was away doing 'other things', including raising a family, which then brought me right back into the toy and model emporiums and the land of temptation. Bizarrely, it was one of Corgi's least successful ranges, announced in its 2007 catalogue, that proved to be the tinder box that caused my diecast collecting fire to reignite; the Golden Compass film range. So the power of the catalogue still worked on someone who was well into their fifth decade at the time!

PERSONAL FAVOURITES

We are all going to have very different favourites when it comes to catalogues, just like we do when it

comes to the models actually on the pages within. Please bear with me while I don my rose-tinted spectacles for a few lines... Born in the first half of the 1960s, it is no surprise that I was introduced to Corgi by way of a car transporter on my third birthday. My fondest catalogue memories are of those in the latter half of the sixties and then pretty much the whole of the

seventies.

From Chitty Chitty Bang Bang to the Formula 1 racers, with a nod to the Beatles Yellow Submarine, I love flicking through the pages and reliving the memories. So many of the releases during those years passed

through my hands, into the mud roads fashioned in the back garden on sunny days and then off to the local hospital when they'd seen better days. Today the modern equivalent would be the local charity shop or auction websites for those of us more financially motivated. It was through the acquisition of catalogues from that same era that my latter years'

collecting gathered momentum. Together with more recent catalogue releases, proving that the force is still strong in the modern equivalent, in particular the 2016 60th anniversary version with its fabulous retrospective look. How many of the anniversary

> " So many of the releases during those years passed through my hands, into the mud roads fashioned in the back garden on sunny days

Above, left to right: *As the years progressed, Corgi covers evolved to reflect the shift in market sector, catering more in later years for adult collectors so the covers became more serious, demonstrated here by the July - December 2005, October 2010 to March 2011 and April/June 2012 catalogues. The latter is notable as being the first release of the current style of catalogue.*

range did I have on pre-order within days? Some would say too many.

Back in the days when Corgi actually produced several catalogues, the Aviation Archive versions always seem to be able to grab my attention, even now. The 'action' poses, complete with spinning propellers, always serve to raise my level of interest. But one in particular stands out and that is the special 60th anniversary D-Day catalogue, released in 2004. As it said on the cover: "A unique collection of 1:50 scale die-cast models meticulously recreated to commemorate the 60th anniversary of 'Operation Overlord'."

They all make for fabulous reading, so now I'm extending my catalogue collecting to those wilderness years, when I was otherwise distracted with seemingly more serious matters, and even the years before I was a twinkle in my dear Dad's eyes.

FROM TOYS TO COLLECTABLES

One of the most obvious changes that has gone hand in hand with the style transitions over the last 60 years is the transformation from toys to collectables for Corgi products. Corgi of course do still produce a range of toys for the younger collector but its core market for new products these days is very different to what it was six decades ago. Of course those fabulous original toys are just as much sought after today as they were all those years ago by many of the same people and for different reasons now.

With such powerful brands as Hauliers of Renown, Aviation Archive,

Right:
Special D-Day 60th Anniversary Collection catalogue from 2004.

Left:
Another from 2004, this is the "Second Half" version for the main ranges.

Right:
Sometimes less is more, as shown by the 1985 cover, cleverly adapting road signs for the numbers.

Original Omnibus Company and Vanguards, each cater for a specific market. I dabble across them all, but many people will specialise. Our collecting tastes are different and the catalogues have to work hard to cater for all of our tastes. Corgi's most certainly hit the spot and even now, well into my sixth decade, I still feel the thrill of anticipation when I know a new Corgi catalogue is imminent.

MODERN DAY MARKETING

The first of the modern style A5 landscape catalogues, harking back to earlier size and format, appeared in April 2012. It announced Corgi's new look logo, still in use today, and had a rather striking rendition of a Tornado jet diving across a selection of new releases. With this new style, I felt that diecast temptation had officially been immortalised in print – and any ambitions to top up my savings account at any time soon were promptly discarded. Darn those marketing people.

With internet sales on the increase, it was only a matter of time before Corgi began to tap into this market. Separate digital Corgi Direct brochures, in the same format as the paper version, rather temptingly dropped into my inbox from time to time. See above comment re. those marketing types!

I wonder what the future holds for Corgi? One thing is for sure and that is for the best way to chart the history of this much-loved enterprise, don't throw those catalogues away, they will provide cherished memories for years. ◉

Boxing Clever

The packaging used over the last sixty years has gone through many evolutions but one thing that hasn't changed is the effectiveness of the appearance — you always know when you're looking at something by Corgi. **Rick Wilson** *thinks (about the) outside of the box*

Main image:
The first two types of box with the wonderful James Bond DB5 box from 1965 behind.

Below: *Fabulous artwork featured on many of the Corgi Majors releases.*

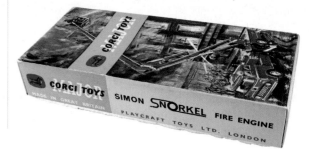

If you talk to a casual observer, the notion that an original box on its own might be worth more than the actual model it was designed for is a difficult concept to grasp sometimes. However that is exactly the case with many of the early Corgi Toys, especially when the box in question is in mint condition.

In my formative years, I was just as guilty as many of us when it came to getting home from the toy shop, or having just opened a Christmas or birthday present and the first thing discarded after the insignificant shop bag or wrapping paper was the box. The eagerness to play with our latest acquisition was paramount and

little thought was given to the fact that if we had kept the box, it might actually keep our treasure in better condition for longer, let alone the idea of the box's value in later life. I blame whoever came up with the toy box! It meant that our toys took up far less space but also went a long way to accelerating the playworn state of our beloved models.

When Corgi Toys burst onto the scene in the original style blue boxes, its products became instantly recognisable. Fast-forward just under three years to June 1959 and the famous yellow and blue box appeared, first being issued with the early two-tone models. The box design

gradually evolved and the artwork was particularly notable on the No 261 James Bond Goldfinger DB5 and No 267 Batmobile releases.

In December 1966, the Corgi window box began to transform shop displays as it meant that you could see exactly what you were going to get. It meant that any box art was

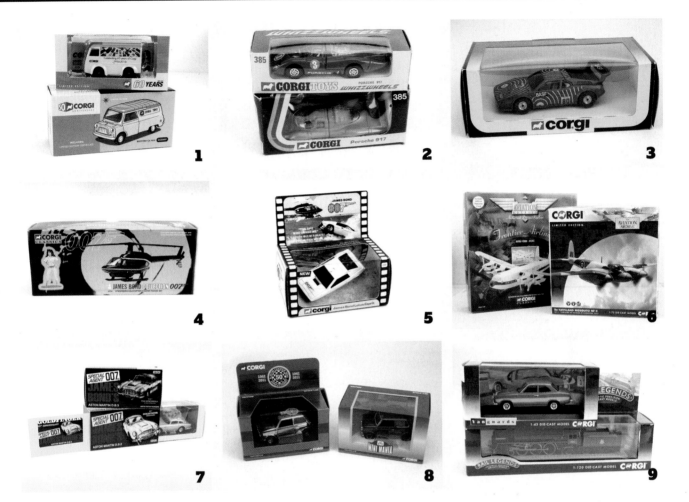

Clockwise from above left: 1 Contrasting retro styles for the 50th and 60th anniversary special models *2* Both types of Porsche 917 No 385 window box *3* The spacious window box was introduced in June 1981 *4* A typical Corgi Classics box *5* A great box design was made specifically for 007's underwater Esprit *6* Early and current Aviation Archive style boxes *7* Corgi pulled out all the stops for the 2015 release of the Goldfinger 50th anniversary DB5 *8* Two very colourful themes for the marvellous Mini *9* Current box styles for the Vanguards and Rail Legends ranges.

then restricted to the rear but, at the time, the excitement of seeing the real thing without first having to open the box more than compensated for this. The wonderful window boxes first appeared with the Gift Set 1 Ford 5000 Super Major Tractor and Beast Carrier Set.

The next evolution of the window box brought the red and yellow Whizzwheel style, which then evolved into the angled window box in May 1973, first seen with No 396 Datsun 240Z. June 1981 saw the introduction of the spacious black frame box, first seen with No 345 Honda Prelude.

Many further evolutions have taken place since, right up to the vibrant modern versions, as can be seen in the accompanying photos.

But if the above has left you feeling the same way as I do about any rashness during our formative years, don't despair as there are plenty of reproduction box manufacturers out there ready to provide you with replacement boxes of the earlier examples that are difficult to distinguish from the originals, even down to the type of card used! My two usual sources are DRRB Boxes (regulars on the toy fair scene) and 20th Century Box (www.20thcenturybox.co.uk). These companies both regularly help to relieve any regrets I may still be harbouring!

...don't despair as there are plenty of reproduction box manufacturers out there ready to provide you with replacement boxes of the earlier examples that are difficult to distinguish from the originals

The Great Book of Corgi

Marcel Van Cleemput's Corgi Masterpiece

For those who have never seen a copy of *The Great Book of Corgi* how would I describe it? To be honest it is difficult to conjure up sufficient superlatives to do it justice. Meticulously researched, beautifully produced, a treasure trove of childhood memories and essential reading for any toy enthusiast, are but a few. Quite simply it is the definitive reference guide to Corgi, charting the lifetime's work and passion of its author from 1954 to 1983 – it is a masterpiece!

About The Author

Marcel René van Cleemput was born near Lille in France on 2nd May 1926. In 1935 his family moved to Marsden in West Yorkshire where his father was charged with installing a new textile plant. The nine year old Marcel started school at Marsden National School initially knowing just two words of English, 'yes' and 'Christmas'. In September 1940 he enrolled at the Huddersfield Technical College but later moved to study engineering at Loughborough Technical College. After completing his studies his first job was in support of the war effort as a draughtsman for Westbourne Engineering. Here he began designing parts for aircraft including the famous de Havilland Mosquito.

THE **NEW** GREAT BOOK OF
CORGI
1956–2010

MARCEL R VAN CLEEMPUT

Above: Cover artwork taken from The New Great Book of Corgi

Opposite page: A thank you note signed by Marcel van Cleemput

After the war, in 1947, Marcel met his wife to be Molly and just three weeks later they became engaged. Sadly he was soon to be separated from his new fiancé as the Van Cleemput family returned to France. Marcel was conscripted into the French Army where he started an officer training course. However, just eight months later he returned to England and to his fiancé and they settled in Northampton where he found a job working for Express Lifts. In 1950 he married Molly and they went on to have two daughters, Patrice and Ginette.

On 1st January 1954 Marcel joined the Mettoy Company. At that time he knew plenty about lift designs but very little about toy moulds. He was a very quick learner and within months he was promoted to Chief Designer. Two years later Corgi Toys was launched by Playcraft, a sister company of Mettoy and Marcel had been working on the drawings for the very first Corgi Car, a Ford Consul. He has the great and unique distinction of having then designed or overseen the design of every Corgi model produced from 1956 until the company's demise in 1983. Marcel's reputation for design innovation was apparent from the offset with Corgi models being fitted with clear plastic windows. This was a first at the time and gave rise to the famous slogan; 'The ones with windows'. First year sales for the new Corgi brand achieved some 2.75 million models, immediately making it a serious contender for its biggest rival Dinky. Working features soon followed and these found fame in some of the most popular diecast toys of all time. Acknowledged classics like the James Bond Aston Martin DB5, the Batmobile from the TV series and Chitty Chitty Bang Bang to name but a few, were to propel Marcel to become a legend of the toy industry in his own lifetime.

By the late 1970s the popularity of diecast toys began to decline and Corgi suffered as a result. In 1983 the company went into liquidation and Marcel set up his own company, Acorn Technical Design Services. He continued working on diecast designs for the re-formed Corgi Toys Ltd, but also took on projects in other areas and worked with the likes of Boots and Thorn EMI. In 1986 he set up a new enterprise, Acorn Memories producing and selling 3-D artworks.

In 1989 he produced 'The Great Book of Corgi', a 543 page 'bible' for Corgi Collectors and in 2010 he followed it up with an updated version 'The New Great Book of Corgi'.

For the final 23 years of his life Marcel and Molly lived in a small cottage in the Northamptonshire village of Great Brington. Marcel immersed himself in village life and was an active member of the village committee, helping to plan and organise a great many village events.

Marcel van Cleemput, affectionately known as 'Mr Corgi', died on 15th March 2013, aged 86.

Writing 'The Great Book of Corgi'

In the Great Book of Corgi Marcel Van Cleemput mentions that he 'had an arrangement' whereby he received one of every model produced. What a clever move!

By 1978 he had amassed so many models that he in fact stopped collecting them. He and Molly were looking to move to a small country cottage and he would not have been able to store them. Friends Jack and Jean Smith came to the rescue and agreed that the collection could be stored in their loft.

In the late 1980s Marcel was working for a local Northamptonshire businessman, Nigel Turner of Turner's Magical Musical Merry-Go-Round. He learnt of the unique Van Cleemput collection of Corgi models and felt strongly that it should be on permanent display, preferably in Northampton. After a little persuasion Marcel agreed to sell the entire collection to Nigel for £7250.00, on the understanding that he would build a museum to display it. True to his word Nigel built a museum as an added attraction to his existing business. He also set about replacing some of the models that had gone missing from the collection over the years and was able to add most of the models produced from 1978 to 1983 after Marcel had stopped collecting.

With the collection pretty much complete Nigel approached Allen Levy of New Cavendish Books about

> Fortunately, with all the models together in the museum photographing them was relatively simple, although it did take a full three weeks to complete

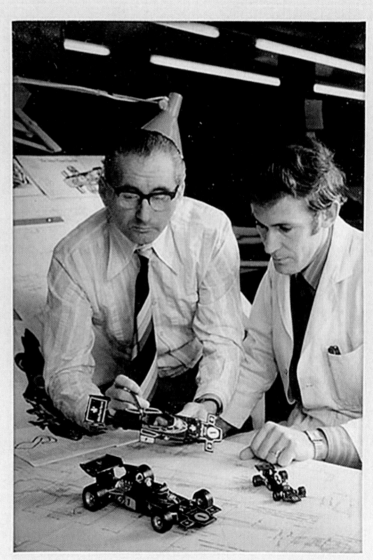

Above: A signed photograph from Marcel van Cleemput

the possibility of producing a definitive reference book based on the collection. Allen was, and still is a great toy historian and he was very keen on this idea. He then left Nigel to persuade Marcel to write the book. After a short period of constant pressure Marcel agreed and was set a six month deadline. Fortunately, with all the models together in the museum photographing them was relatively simple, although it did take a full three weeks to complete, during which the museum had to be closed.

The rest, as they say, is history. *The Great Book of Corgi* was published in 1989 and has become the definitive reference work for all who have an interest in the Corgi brand, both its history and products. Not only is it beautifully illustrated with product photographs, but Marcel also amassed a huge number of original design drawings as well as catalogues and other marketing material, many of which are also included to add another fascinating dimension to the book. It was said at the time that nothing better had ever been written about Corgi, and nor was it likely to be in the future – but hold on ....

The New Great Book of Corgi

In 2010 Marcel launched a second Great Book of Corgi, *The New Great Book of Corgi*. Once again published by New Cavendish Books this volume was billed as bringing the story up to date by chronicling the entire Corgi production from 1956 to 2010. It is another beautifully produced volume and once again follows the production of Corgi models in chronological order, year by year. In fact the new book is effectively a slightly condensed reprint of the original, but brought up to date with invaluable access to Hornby's Corgi archive.

There can be no doubt that for collectors who missed out on the original book this is a 'must have, must read' edition. With the original edition out of print for some years, the cost of the new book will also be considerably cheaper than trying to find a good original.

However, if I am honest, this book does not cover the later years from 1984 to 2010 in anything like the detail of the earlier years and as such, it is slightly disappointing in this area. Many of the post-1983 years are illustrated with reproductions of relevant catalogue pages rather than the superb individual product photographs of the original. In many respects this is no great surprise given that Marcel had little if anything to do with the Corgi business over this latter period, but I think it does leave the door ajar for a really detailed history of these years still to be produced. In other words, the original has still not been bettered – in my opinion.

When Corgi celebrated 50 years in 2006, there were rumours that someone closely associated with Corgi from the 1980s period was planning to cover the later years in similar depth to Marcel's original, but to date this has not come to fruition.

I hope one day it does because this famous old brand deserves it! ◉

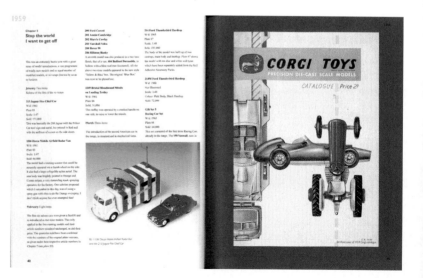

Above: Inside pages and artwork featured in The New Great Book of Corgi

James Bond Moon Buggy

Released: *June 1972* **Withdrawn:** *1973* **Sales:** *189,000*

For a model with relatively low sales compared to some of Corgi's big hitters at the time and one that was only on sale for a single year, No 811 is a very well-remembered release. It is also one that commands a high price in top condition today. Due to the superb playability, few have survived in truly mint condition as the model was well 'loved' in its day. Even the playworn examples, thanks to the readily available supply of reproduction parts, can be brought back to resemble the day they left the shop and provide many more years of joy, although it is more likely to be as display pieces this time around.

A pretty good representation of the actual moon buggy used in the James Bond film *Diamonds Are Forever*, the model had been carefully planned alongside the film (released in December 1971). The vehicle has two articulating jointed arms, one on each side, with sprung claw grips at the end that actually worked. The radar scanner dish at the back rotates as the model moves. The domed canopy flips up to reveal our hero, played by Sean Connery in the movie. Moon rover style wheels moulded in yellow plastic finish off the look.

Re-released in 1997 under Corgi

Below main image: *Original and classic versions of the model*

Inset: *Just one of the many advertising posters produced*

Classics branding as "Special Edition" No 65201, complete with 54mm high hand-painted white metal Sean Connery 007 (and later as CC04401 without the figurine), this time the model took on a much more accurate look in terms of colours, closely resembling those of the actual film version. All the same playability was there but, despite the more accurate appearance of the model and identical features, this version is very easy to find in mint boxed condition at around £15-£20. ◉

Still at the Vanguard of diecast

*20 years on **Paul Lumsdon** gives a unique and personal insight into the story behind Corgi's 'Vanguards' range of popular classics*

2016 isn't only the 60th Anniversary of Corgi. It is also the 20th Anniversary of the company's popular 1/43 scale classic car and commercials brand 'Vanguards', which were launched at the beginning of 1996, not by Corgi but by Lledo. It wasn't until 1999, when Lledo went into receivership, that Corgi bought the Days Gone and Vanguards brands and tooling. Since then the Vanguards range has continued to thrive and develop – despite some early gloomy predictions from Jack O'Dell, the founder and Chairman of Lledo.

THE EARLY DAYS

The Vanguards story really begins at Lledo PLC in Enfield, Middlesex sometime during 1994. Bert Russell, Managing Director of Lledo and his fellow directors had enjoyed huge success for over ten years with the 'Days Gone' range and its premiums offshoot, 'Lledo Promotionals'. However by late 1994 they were concerned that sales were beginning to level out and that the existing product range had little scope for further expansion. Bert decided to engage the services of a Marketing Consultant and Paul Warner was introduced to the business early in 1995 on a temporary basis, to evaluate the market and to suggest ways forward that would enable Lledo to compete with competitors such as Corgi. My life and career changed almost overnight as a result!

It soon became evident why Paul Warner had been selected. He was clearly a very astute operator and very capable of getting quickly under the skin of the business to both analyse the current position and make positive recommendations for the future.

Above:
A selection of popular classics

Below:
Hand made resin prototypes

He also very quickly determined the massive workload this would entail and so he enlisted two lieutenants. They were Len Mills (previously of Corgi) on the engineering development side and Paul Lumsdon (that's me!) on the product marketing side!

I was promoted from Product Manager to Marketing Manager, and then basically told I would be working pretty much every waking hour under the sun until the job was done!

That job was to write a 3-Year Marketing plan for the launch of a brand new range of highly detailed

scale models, present it to the board and have it approved by them. Then I would have to implement the full launch plan to both the trade and consumers – all in time for the key Toy Fairs in January and February 1996. It was one of the busiest years of my working life, but also one of the most fulfilling and I can now look back on it with a feeling of immense pride.

The first 3 months were taken up working on the Marketing Plan. To convince the board, including former Lesney boss and Lledo founder Jack O'Dell that they should invest literally hundreds of thousands of pounds into the new project was going to take some doing and the argument had to be robust and comprehensive. Paul Warner and I set about researching the market to determine where the opportunities might lie. Where Paul was particularly clever was in quickly appreciating that Corgi's strengths appeared to lie within Classic Commercials - Trucks, Buses and Emergency Vehicles. Classic British saloon cars and vans of the 1950s and 1960s appeared to be the gap that Corgi had not successfully filled. To cut a long story short the result of months of hard work was a range to be called 'Vanguards'. Len

refer to the new models as 'The suicide range'. Jack's whole philosophy of model making was based on creating a good boxful of product. Scale was irrelevant as long as it filled the box and looked good value! It has to be said this philosophy had always borne fruit at Lesney with the Matchbox range and during the early days at Lledo with the Days Gone range.

The trouble was that the market was rapidly changing. Corgi Classics had

Top: VW Golf Mk1 and Beetle Cabriolet

Above: Sunbeam Alpine, Triumph Spitfire, MGA and Triumph Stag

From top down: Lledo and Corgi packs; Ford police collection with packs; 2004 pack style

modelled before since the heyday of Corgi and Dinky in the 1960s and like their predecessors Vanguards were 100% designed and built in England. Models like the Ford 105E Anglia, Triumph Herald and Morris Traveller were seen as a breath of fresh air by the trade and consumer alike. Follow up models like the Rover P4, Ford 100E Popular, Hillman Imp and Austin Mini, plus van variants where appropriate, soon followed as the range gained both momentum and credibility. Sadly it was ultimately too little, too late for Lledo the company, but the brands were soon to find a new home.

ENTER THE MOTORCADE

In 1998 I made a career move from Lledo to Corgi and one of the first questions CEO Chris Guest asked me was: 'What do we need to do to produce a successful model car range?' Clearly the launch of Vanguards by Lledo had made an impact and Chris always wanted Corgi to lead the market.

It became a major project and by 1999 a plan was coming together. The Lledo Vanguards range was good but I felt it was held back somewhat by the cost of UK production and tooling and certain compromises that had to be made to make production economic and as automated as possible. With Chinese manufacturing most of these

> ## He was clearly a very astute operator and capable of getting under the skin of the business

Mills, assisted by Dick Finch in the toolroom was tasked with designing the brand new range of 1/43 scale cars and 1/64 scale trucks to a level of detail that was hitherto unknown at Lledo.

THE 'SUICIDE RANGE' GETS APPROVAL

Prototypes were created to support the plan and the entire package was presented to the board. It was enthusiastically received by all but Jack O'Dell himself. By this time Jack was Chairman so his dissenting voice carried less weight but he did famously

emerged as a successful competitor and had identified a fast growing area of adult collectable models that were authentic scale models. Lledo's quaint and attractive 'Yesteryear' style collectable toys were quickly losing ground to their competitor.

Vanguards launched early in 1996 and the reception was fantastic. Lledo finally had a credible scale model range. What's more its philosophy of replicating the everyday family cars that dad or a favourite uncle drove in the 50s and 60s struck the right chord too. Many of these had never been

constraints were lifted and I felt that Corgi could produce a far more detailed and authentic product for less money. In particular the Chinese were extremely good at mask spraying and hand applied small parts and details.

The new Corgi Car range was presented and approved by the board – The Motorcade range was set to go into production. Tooling was started on an Austin A60 Cambridge, Austin Allegro, Morris 1300 Estate and Ford Zephyr 6 Mk111, all in 1/43rd scale. In addition it was planned to upgrade a number of existing Corgi car models to augment the range. To differentiate the models from the competition all 'Motorcade' models were designed with an 8-point specification plan as follows:

• Faithful shapes, accurately scaled
• Precisely matched authentic colours and high quality paint finish
• Accurate interiors including dashboard, gearstick, steering wheel and rear view mirror
• Detailed wheels, hubs and tyres (all separate parts)
• Detailed chassis with all assembly fixings hidden
• Working suspension
• Photo-etched chrome detail parts
• Jewelled headlights

Interestingly all the specification points were designed to increase authenticity and realism with the exception of the jewelled headlights which were added as a touch of nostalgia, having been used on many Corgi models back in the heyday of the 1960s and 70s. As the range developed over next few years the jewels were gradually phased out in favour of more realistic clear plastic light lenses, as collectors became ever more discerning!

TWO BECOME ONE!

In October 1999, with the Motorcade range development well advanced, the news came through that Lledo had ceased trading. There was a furious week or so of activity at Corgi as we speedily evaluated the potential for acquiring the Lledo brands and very quickly a deal was done with the receivers. Corgi bought the Lledo name, along with the 'Days Gone' and 'Vanguards' brand names and all the tooling. Suddenly we owned the very well received Vanguards brand and a decision was quickly taken to abandon the Motorcade name and instead merge the new Corgi car tooling with the existing Vanguards models, including two planned new tools that Lledo had announced but not produced, a Vauxhall Victor F and Singer Chamois.

Behind the scenes there was a huge amount of work to be done, not least to ship all the tooling to China and make sure it could be used on the Chinese diecasting machines. Fortunately Len Mills and Terry Fox were probably the best and most experienced diecast toy design engineers in the UK so Corgi had the best men for the job. Not only did the tools have to run successfully but the existing Vanguards had to be gradually upgraded to meet the proposed higher Corgi level of detail. A number of old Corgi Classics models were also identified as being suitable for the new range and these too had to be upgraded to suit. Compiling the new range was Product Manager Robert Hinchcliffe ably assisted by former Lledo graphic designer and self-confessed car nut, Mark Pinnigar, who has worked on the artworks for Vanguards from 1996 to the present day.

The new enhanced Vanguards

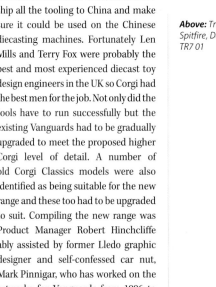

Above: Triumph Herald, Spitfire, Dolomite and TR7 01

Below: Vauxhall Victor test shots

range was launched at the 2000 London Toyfair with a beautiful new retro-styled catalogue. It remained faithful to the traditional values of Vanguards but now produced to the even higher 8-point level of specification and for the first time introducing cars of the 1970s with the new (love it or loath it) Austin Allegro, complete with authentic square steering wheel.

STRONG CATEGORY THEMING

Whilst the new Vanguards continued to concentrate on the familiar family saloons of the period, Corgi very quickly introduced some strong sub-categories to move the range into different areas and broaden the collector appeal. Each category was clearly identified by different contrast colour flashes on the packaging and included Police vehicles, Motorsport, Sports Cars and, for the 2nd half of 2000, Classic Commercials. The commercials category concentrated on saloon based vans in 1/43rd scale rather than the 1/64th scale light trucks that had been a significant part of the original (Lledo) Vanguards. This was the one area of the old Vanguards that did not live up to expectation, being a largely US based scale unknown in the UK, so these were

Above: *Triumph Spitfire, TR4 and Stag*

quickly dropped. In addition Corgi already had a very successful 1/50th scale classic commercials range, plus a relatively new modern truck range so the larger commercials were already well covered.

Segmenting the range into different themes allowed collectors to focus on specific areas of interest and has remained an important factor in the range development to this day.

A NEW APPROACH

In 2004 the Vanguards brand underwent its first significant facelift since its launch, in an effort to widen the appeal of the range beyond just diecast collectors. Firstly, to attract full-size car enthusiasts, the old theming was ditched in favour of a more marque driven approach. All-new packaging was unveiled that now segmented the range based on the manufacturer of the real vehicle. The bold new packaging was much more modern and featured individual designs for BMC, Ford, Rootes Group, Vauxhall, MG Rover and later Land Rover. For greater on-shelf impact the models were also presented on a black display plinth with a clear perspex lid which formed the pack window. There was also a pack for general 'Classics'

to cover all other marques and police vehicles had a new bespoke pack design. Finally to introduce a younger audience, in 2005 the range came right up to date with the introduction of the Rover 75, MG ZT, Vauxhall Astra, Land Rover Defender and 3rd generation Range Rover. Vanguards now covered over half a century of motoring from the 1950s to the 2000s.

In 2007 there was a brief attempt to further broaden the appeal of Vanguards to a younger audience with another rebranding exercise. This saw the range name changed to 'Drive Time' and the sub-ranges within were known as 'Emergency Motors', 'Road Traders', 'Motorsport' and 'Vanguards Classics'. The packaging was, in my opinion rather toy-like and the logo design could almost have been mistaken for Disney's 'Cars' movie logo. You may well gather that I was not overly keen on this period in the Vanguards history and so I was very pleased to be able to lobby for a further change when Hornby took over the Corgi brands in 2008.

THE MODERN CLASSICS

Under Hornby ownership I was part of a small Corgi team retained in Leicester to help integrate the Corgi brands into

Top: *Ford Collection*

From top down:
2008 Hornby pack style; 1999 Motorcade pack proposal; 2007 Drive Time pack style; Vauxhall Cresta VA064 my personal favourite

the Hornby fold. I am pleased to say that as a result the 'Drive Time' name was soon dropped and we reverted to the well-established 'Vanguards' brand in a new but more traditional style of pack, designed by Mark Pinnigar. This had echoes of the original designs, returning to the card lid and base style. It has subsequently been upgraded by a plinth and clear lid style pack but still retaining the traditional yellow/black Vanguards logo.

By 2008 the range was firmly established in the 1970s era and future plans were soon in place for 70s classics like the MGB Mk3, VW Golf Mk1, Ford Fiesta Mk1, Escort Mk2 and 3, Cortina Mk4 and Granada Mk2. The late 1960s have also been included with the Mini Clubman and Ford Capri Mk1, both of which overlapped into the 1970s.

But Vanguards had yet to break into what we might term the 'Modern Classics' of the 1980s. This was to be the major change during the early years of Hornby ownership. What this also meant was that the traditional UK manufacturers would be less represented to reflect the changes in the real automotive industry as overseas marques became more dominant.

So it has come to be that the past few years has seen some wonderful new models but with a far more international flavour. 1980s cars like The Peugeot 205 and 309, Subaru Legacy, Ford Sierra XR4i and RS Cosworth, Audi Quattro, Vauxhall Astra Mk2, Carlton Mk2 and Cavalier Mk3, BMW 3 Series and VW Golf Mk2 have given the range a more modern makeover.

WHAT OF THE FUTURE?

No one can say for sure but perhaps some clues have already been given. The Vanguards motorsport ranges have in recent years introduced more modern vehicles. Cars like the Ford Focus, Subaru Impreza, Skoda Fabia Turbo and Citroen Xara Turbo have started to introduce rally vehicles from the 1990s and early 2000s. Certainly over the next decade there must be scope to model the next generation of road going classics from these eras to keep the Vanguards range relevant to a younger model collecting audience. We shall see! ◉

From Little Acorns

The Aviation Archive Range was launched in 1998, but it was a very different range to the one we know today. **Paul Lumsdon** *charts the history and key developments of Corgi's hugely popular diecast aircraft range*

When Corgi launched the Aviation Archive range in 1998 it marked a first for aviation enthusiasts. Here was a range of accurate scale models, finished to 'museum' standard that were 'ready to display'. Today, some 18 years later, the range has developed to become a major category within the Corgi collector portfolio, covering a century of aviation history in various scales. Here I have set out a timeline of some of the key developments and innovations that have shaped the range and helped it to grow and maintain its position as a market leader.

1998 – A CHANCE DISCOVERY

Interestingly, the original thinking from Corgi was to fill in the gaps that the major plastic kit manufacturers had previously not covered. As a result Aviation Archive launched with a range of mainly civilian propliners of the WW2 and early post war period,

in the rather unusual 1/144 scale. The scale was chosen to keep these large aircraft at a manageable and affordable size in model form. The launch models were a Douglas DC-3 (Dakota), Lockheed Constellation, Avro York, Avro Lancastrian and most importantly, the Avro Lancaster. By today's standards they were a little basic with printed window detail and formed tinplate propellers, but they were accurately scaled and beautifully finished.

With any new diecast range there is a high investment involved and a risk of failure. So the Corgi accountants were pleased to see that the tooling for the trio of Avro models made

Top: *1/32 Mustang*

Above:
Avro Lancaster

Below:
1/72 Sunderland Ian Crawford; 1/144 Constellation and Viscount

maximum use of common parts for the wings, engines and tailplanes. The Lancaster was included for just this reason, even though it didn't fit the 'propliner' theme.

However it was a chance discovery that was critical, and it helped to shape the range from that point on. You see the Aviation Archive was generally very well received by aviation enthusiasts and diecast collectors alike, but the order book for the Lancaster was around 3 times more in volume, than the next most popular item. What that told Corgi's management was that just because an aircraft had been widely produced as a plastic kit, didn't mean to say that it would not sell as

a fully finished model. Dispelling this fear suddenly opened the door to a whole new world of opportunities and was the catalyst for Aviation Archive becoming one of the biggest and most important categories within the Corgi portfolio.

1999 - MILITARY DOMINATION BEGINS

With tooling lead times being around one year, it would prove difficult to make wholesale changes quickly, but for the 2nd half 1998 catalogue the range was already amended to show a clear Military category, separate from the Civilian aircraft. 1/144th scale still dominated but by 1999 the range was further segmented to include Civilian, WW2 Military and Post War Military. New tooling included the Vickers Viscount, Boeing Stratocruiser and De Havilland Comet on the civilian side and the B-17, Short Sunderland, Lockheed Hercules and Avro Vulcan for the Military category, which was also augmented by military versions of the Comet, DC-3 and Constellation. The Stratocruiser tooling would also later become the basis of the B-29 Superfortress. Conversely a modified variation of the Short Sunderland

Above: 1/48 Fokker DR1 Triplane

Above: 1/72 Sopworth Camel

...but the order book for the Lancaster was around 3 times more in volume...

tooling was also used in the Civilian range to produce a BOAC Hythe Class seaplane. However, even at this early point in the life of Aviation Archive, the military subjects were proving popular and beginning to dominate, but not overwhelm, the range.

2000 - MAJOR CHANGES FOR THE NEW MILLENNIUM

The January to June 2000 range heralded a major change in the strategy of Aviation Archive. To commemorate the 60th Anniversary of The Battle of Britain, Corgi announced a range of WW2 fighter aircraft, all to be produced in 1/72nd scale. Corgi now had the

confidence in its aircraft range to take the plastic kit manufacturers head on in both scale and subject matter, and the opening line-up was impressive. A Spitfire Mk1, Hurricane Mk1 and Messerschmitt 109E were all launched in Battle of Britain schemes, whilst a P-51D Mustang was also included to maintain a US interest (Corgi was just about to open a new US office in Chicago). All featured interchangeable (deployed or retracted) undercarriage, rubbers tyres, removable engine covers, spinning propellers, clear cockpit covers with pilot figure and a display stand, as well as highly detailed, authentic colour schemes

Below: 1/72 Lancaster

and markings.

The move into 1/72nd scale was further strengthened in the 2nd half of 2000 with the introduction of post-war jet fighters as Corgi announced the English Electric Lightning and Hawker Hunter.

2001 - BIG NEWS IN MORE WAYS THAN ONE

Success is always a magnet for competitors and so the challenge at Corgi was to stay one step ahead as others began to enter the diecast aviation market. And so they did! In 2001 they announced what was to become another milestone in the story of the Aviation Archive and created a category where, to this day they remain the market leaders and innovators – the 1/72nd scale 'Heavy Bomber'. The first was an absolute classic – The Avro Lancaster. This introduced the concept of large scale super-detailed models

and the 'Lanc' featured rotating turrets with moving guns, a full set of crew figures, opening bomb bay doors, as well as four rotating propellers, up/down undercarriage options and a posable cradle-style stand. But for me what set this model apart was its sheer size and weight. This was a large, high quality piece and it is fair to say that it set new standards in diecast collecting and, many would argue, set new requirements for display space as well!

2002 – CHOPPERS

Helicopters is another category where Corgi has excelled over the years and created a successful niche collector market. The first model produced was the 1/72nd Sikorsky/Westland Sea King which made its debut in 2002. The model featured a detailed interior with crew figures, a sliding door, interchangeable undercarriage and uniquely two sets of rotor options – flying and static. This has become a feature of Corgi helicopter releases and is typical of the innovative thinking of the design team. The Chinook followed in 2003 with a clever contra-rotating rotor mechanism and operating rear loading door and ramp. Subsequent releases have included the Blackhawk, Wessex, Whirlwind, Lynx and Puma in 1/72nd scale, whilst mainly for the US market there have been 1/48th scale models of the Bell Huey Iroquois, Cobra and Sioux.

2002 – SETTING THE BAR EVEN HIGHER

2002 saw the launch of a brand new scale which underlined Corgi's ambition to remain at the forefront

of innovation. A 1/32nd scale Spitfire Mk1 was launched and with it a whole new dimension to detailed, diecast modelling. With a wingspan of 350mm the features were almost endless. There were operating control surfaces including flaps, removable engine covers revealing a detailed Merlin engine and sliding cockpit canopy revealing a detailed interior and pilot figure. The undercarriage was hinged to retract and deploy authentically, the hatch behind the cockpit could be opened to reveal the radio, and the gun covers on the wings could be removed to reveal the Browning 0.303 machine guns. Later versions brought 'Sights and Sounds' with authentic Merlin engine sounds, driven propeller, undercarriage legs that would deploy and retract automatically, plus working wingtip navigation lights. These features were all powered from batteries located in the cradle-style display stand.

Above: 1/72 Lightning

Below: 1/72 Vulcan C Scott

The Spitfire was the first in a line of 1/32nd releases that would eventually include the P-51D Mustang, Hawker Hurricane, Messerschmitt 109G and for me, probably still the definitive diecast aviation model ever produced, the Mosquito.

2004 – THE BIG WOODEN WONDER

Overshadowing everything else in the 2004 range was the magnificent 1/32nd scale Mosquito, de Havilland's 'Wooden Wonder' and arguably one of the finest aircraft of WW2. With a huge wingspan of 518mm this was a true triumph of diecast engineering, offering exceptional levels of detail. In addition to all the features of the previous 1/32nd scale releases the 'Mossie' also incorporated opening bomb bay doors and included a detailed ground crew, bomb trolley and 'Cookie' bomb.

The Mosquito certainly presented problems in terms of display space, and not surprisingly perhaps, releases have been limited to just six, three of these as bomber and photo-reconnaissance variants in 2004, followed by an eight year gap before a much modified fighter/bomber variant was released in 2012. Personally, I think every serious WW2 aircraft enthusiast should have at least one of these as a centrepiece to their collection!

2007 – WIND IN THE WIRES

The decision to extend the Aviation

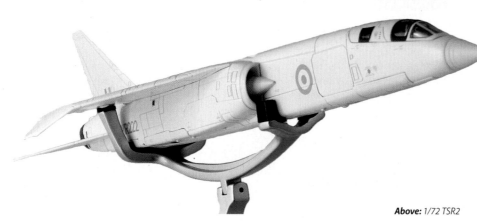

Above: 1/72 TSR2

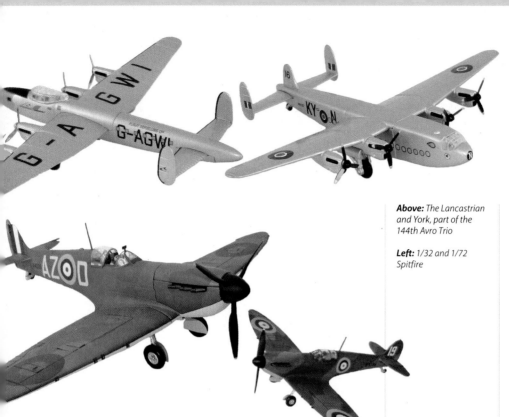

Above: The Lancastrian and York, part of the 144th Avro Trio

Left: 1/32 and 1/72 Spitfire

Below: 230 Puma A Osbourne; Queens Flight Wessex; Blackhawk Down; Sea King; Lebanon Chinook

Archive range to cover WW1 aircraft threw up a couple of major challenges for Corgi. A key element of these (mainly) biplane aircraft was the rigging that was used to strengthen the canvas covered structures of the aircraft. Corgi felt it was important to replicate these fine wires but this then brought the size into question. As these aircraft were quite small, models at 1/72 scale would also be small and too intricate to successfully and realistically rig with wires. The decision was therefore taken to increase the scale to 1/48th. This was already a well-known model scale in the USA but was not so popular in the UK. 2007 saw the first models launched; the SE5a, Spad XIII and Albatross DV. These were followed up the following year by the Sopwith Camel and Fokker DR1 Triplane and finally by a Fokker DVII in 2009. There is no denying that the models at this scale were beautifully detailed and the rigging wires certainly added to the realism.

Sadly, however the sales numbers were something of a disappointment.

Whether this was down to the scale or just the subject matter being beyond living memory I am not sure. No further new tooling has been added since 2009 and whilst occasional re-colours have appeared, the range has rather stagnated. Ironically, perhaps due to the lower numbers produced and the fact that they are very attractive models, many have become extremely collectable and now achieve premium prices on the secondary market.

2009 – BOLD MOVE

Corgi has never shirked from making bold decisions with the aviation range and the 2009 launch of a TSR2 was a huge financial gamble. The ill-fated TSR2 project of the 1960s saw only one aircraft fly and all but two of the prototypes were destroyed when the programme was scrapped. Corgi's model options were therefore extremely limited but it went ahead in 1/72nd scale. It is a hugely impressive model of a true icon of the British aviation industry. Only 3 releases have ever been produced covering the flying prototype, XR219 and the only

survivors, XR220 and XR222.

Whether Corgi has ever made a return on its investment is open to debate, but I suspect that, like the real aircraft, the Corgi TSR2 project has probably also been prematurely scrapped!

2011 TO DATE – KEEPING AHEAD OF THE GAME

Recent years have seen the Aviation Archive range continue to develop into new areas. In particular in 2011 there was a move into the inter-war years with 1/72nd scale models of the Hawker Hart, Demon and Audax, followed by the elegant Hawker Fury fighter. The range has also consolidated on its strengths and the much anticipated Short Stirling has become another classic model in the 'Heavy Bomber' category. This has recently been followed by another magnificent 1/72nd scale release, the Short Sunderland which has an awesome presence at this size.

However all the talk in recent years has centred on a heavy bomber of a different era, the 'cold war' era. That bomber is of course the Avro Vulcan and the excitement generated by Corgi's announcement that it was to produce a monstrous 1/72nd scale model in diecast can only have been matched by the frustration caused by the production delays as the technicalities of producing such a large model were overcome. In the autumn of 2014, and boasting a wingspan of 472mm, it finally arrived. Whilst there were the inevitable gripes from some quarters about the cost, the colours, the plastic versus diecast content, the quantity produced etc., there can be no doubt that Corgi has once again produced a quite superb model and one that clearly keeps them ahead of the game. The latest Vulcan release from 2015 represents a 617 Squadron aircraft in anti-flash white and, in my opinion, it is one of the finest diecast models ever produced and one to challenge the fabulous 1/32nd scale Mosquito as my all-time favourite.

In fact it leaves me with the question – how can Corgi ever top this? Only time will tell! ◉

The backbone of Corgi's success

*Post-war Britain was rebuilt around its industry and the lifeblood of that industry was the goods that were transported across the length and breadth of the country by road transport. **Paul Lumsdon** takes a look at the models which resulted*

Top: *Scania 111 with tandem axle box trailer in the livery of Montgomery Transport from Northern Ireland*

Above:
An impressive pair of MAN TGA tractor units. The Curtainsider is in the livery of Ken Thomas of Guyhirn, whilst the Powder Tanker is in the colours of John Mitchell

In 1948 under Clement Atlee's labour government, road transport was nationalised and the Road Transport Executive created BRS (British Road Services) as the national carrier. The road haulage industry had always been vehemently opposed to nationalisation and lobbied hard to get the conservative party to reverse the decision. When they came to power in 1951 that's exactly what they did. BRS remained but was joined by a mass of transport operators all keen to profit from the massive growth in the transportation of goods by road in the UK. This was a golden era for road haulage in the UK and the huge variety of truck types, styles and operators created a diverse and colourful industry that would have a historical interest and nostalgia all of its own to future generations.

To my mind there can be no doubting that the backbone of Corgi's new found success during the 1990s and beyond, was centred around the development of its haulage ranges from the classic era of the 1950s and 1960s right the way up to the most current modern cab units. It would take a book to cover these in any detail, so for the purposes of a short article such as this, I will give a brief overview of some of the key developments across these ranges.

CLASSIC TRUCKS

By the early 1990s Corgi's 1/50 scale Classic Commercial range had developed from the vintage Thorneycroft, AEC Cabover and Renault Vans that were introduced during the 1980s as the early 'Corgi Classics'. New models like the Bedford Pantechnican and Bedford Box Van had moved the range into the post war period and Corgi took every opportunity to reproduce these vehicles in a wide range of liveries. In 1993 the Foden FG 8-wheeler and Scammell Scarab were both significant new releases that led the way for an explosion of new classics over the next few years. 8 wheelers in particular became a trademark part of Corgi's classic truck ranges with a wide range of cab styles being produced. Corgi's design team were clever. Particularly following the 1995 management buy out, the investment in new model lorries grew at a pace. Each new cab was designed with a degree of modularity. This was to enable a maximum number of configurations to be produced from each tool. So there would be 4-wheelers, 6-wheelers, 8-wheelers, flatbeds, dropsides, boxbacks, canvas backs, plus articulated versions – the list was almost endless. Themes would include everything from famous haulage companies, famous breweries, utilities like Royal Mail, Post Office Telephones etc., to classic collector themes like circus and showman's collections. The market seemed to swallow up everything Corgi had to offer. And just to give an indication of market size the limited edition certificates in 1995 included some huge numbers. A Carters Circus Scammell with trailer and caravan – 13,300 pieces. A Leyland 8-wheeler with flatbed and load in J&A Smith of Maddiston – 12,300 pieces. I think most would agree that 'limited editions' in these quantities were a challenge to the definition of 'limited'. These levels of production could not be sustained and it is interesting to review similar releases from just two years later in 1997 – 5,500 pieces became the norm. This is still good by today's standards where 1,000 to 1,200 pieces is normal and I really question whether Corgi or their customers (or both) were being carried away by the euphoria of those early post Mattel days.

HEAVY HAULAGE

The introduction of the Heavy Haulage range in 1997 took Corgi's transport ranges to a whole new levels in terms of detail, authenticity and sheer size! Even in 1/50 scale model form these 'monsters' of the haulage industry

have a presence to make them the centrepiece of any collection. I can only imagine what it must have been like to witness them for real on the roads in the 1950s and 1960s. By utilising the existing Diamond T military truck tooling in civilian liveries, along with brand new items like the Scammell Constructor, Corgi was able to present a very impressive new range for a modest investment and risk in new tooling.

Below: The Volvo F12 was one of the workhorses of the Pickfords Heavy Haulage fleet during the 1980s. This model is coupled to a 5-axle King trailer and is carrying a cold-cast resin load.

> So there would be 4-wheelers, 6-wheelers, 8-wheelers, flatbeds, dropsides, boxbacks, canvas backs, plus articulated versions – the list was almost endless

Clever use of cold cast resin loads added colour and variety to further enhance the models. Limited Edition runs of over 10,000 pieces were the norm at launch back in 1997!

Cold cast resin was used for these loads because it is produced from low cost rubber moulds rather than expensive hard tooling. As such relatively low quantities could be produced fairly economically. The big disadvantage of this material is that it is not 100% stable. It shrinks as the resin hardens and predicting the exact amount of shrinkage is not an exact science. Corgi found this out with the Annis and Co Diamond T Ballast with Girder Trailer and Locomotive load (31007) released as part of the 1997 ➡

range. The models were all shipped and delivered to customers but due to the complexity of the locomotive drive mechanism and valve gear, combined with the variable rates of resin shrinkage, the quality of the locomotive was rather unreliable to say the least. Eventually a decision was made to recall the locomotive and to issue an alternative, somewhat simpler generator load. As far as I recall the trade thought Corgi were up to something and the uptake was really low. The feeling was that by returning the locomotive loads, whatever the quality, they would become quite rare and sought after and so very few trade customers took up the offer. If I am honest I don't recall having ever seen a set offered for sale since with the alternative load. So perhaps my example shown here is in fact the rarer version?

Despite this minor hiccup the Heavy Haulage range was well received and developed over the years into a comprehensive series reflecting the broad range of vehicles used to transport abnormal loads during the post war period right through to modern times. Specialist tractor units like the 1960s/70s period Scammell Contractor reflect Corgi's strength in this sector. With the introduction of the Modern Trucks category in 1998, so the opportunity for Modern Heavy Haulage was developed with vehicles like the Volvo FH Ballast Tractor, DAF XF Four Axle Unit and the Scania T Cab. Nicholas Bogies, King and Nooteboom trailers have expanded greatly the options for the loads. Possibly amongst the most impressive of them all were the massive Wynn's and Pickfords

Industrial sets, both utilising 2 x Scammell Contractors with Nicholas Bogies carrying a massive girder trailer and resin stator load and generator load respectively. Both when fully assembled were close to 90cm (almost 3ft) long. That's a lot of diecast metal!

MODERN TRUCKS TO MODERN CLASSICS

The first Corgi 'Modern Trucks' range was launched in 1998 with 1/50th scale DAF 85 and ERF EC articulated cabs plus curtainsider, box and tanker trailers. The launch heralded the new range as a 'New Era of Road Transport' and the presentation of each model in a large perspex case was certainly very impressive. Initial sales however were slightly disappointing. What Corgi had failed to appreciate was that the collector of modern trucks was not so much interested in the distribution of Boddingtons Beer or Royal Mail, but more in the independent haulage companies like James Irlam and Eddie

Above: Early models in the Corgi Heavy Haulage range featured the Scammell Constructor shown here in Pickfords blue and the Diamond T shown here in Annis & Co. red and black. The cold cast resin generator load is the replacement offered when Corgi recalled the original locomotive load. It seems most customers chose to keep the loco despite quality issues so this load is quite rare.

Below: Two trucks from a similar period – the BRS Bedford S Type is very authentic whilst the Eddie Stobart Leyland Beaver platform Lorry is completely made up, yet looks very believable in period scheme.

Stobart. This set the trend in modern truck collecting and is still as relevant today. In fact as the market for modern trucks has developed so Corgi has come to appreciate that often the smaller the haulage company the more desirable the model. Location is also important and Scottish and Irish hauliers in particular have proven to be very popular as well.

To reflect the market, the brand name 'Modern Trucks' and the 'fish tank' perspex case were very quickly dropped in favour of 'Hauliers of Renown' and a more modest window style presentation box. In this format the range has developed to become one of the biggest collector categories in the modern Corgi range. Keeping up to date with the latest real truck releases has been important and Corgi has worked closely with the major truck manufacturers to bring the latest models, Sadly for several years now, particularly through the last recession, most new truck designs have been merely facelifted upgrades.

However, the requirements of the latest Euro 6 emission controls have forced the truck companies into new cab designs. Corgi has so far produced the Mercedes Actros MP4 and I have heard rumour that a new Volvo FH4 may be in tooling so watch this space. With all-new cab designs from DAF, Iveco and Renault also already on the market, there is plenty of scope for Corgis future models too!

The lack of brand new modern truck designs did have one major knock-on effect for Corgi's truck range. To keep the offering fresh in recent years, Corgi have set a trend back in time to what might be termed 'Modern Classics'. Great cabs like the Scania 110/111/140/141, Seddon Atkinson Strato, Volvo F10/F12/F16 and Volvo F89 have allowed Corgi to move into one of the most interesting eras of trucking (in my opinion). To me the stories of long haul road trips to the Middle East by the so-called 'Cola Cowboys' are what real trucking is all about. The Scania 110 with period TIR sealed Tilt Trailer in Chapman and Ball orange livery (CC15304), complete with under-chassis storage panniers is a great example of this type of truck and has been beautifully reproduced.

THEMES AND LICENSES

No article on Corgi's road haulage ranges would be complete without at least a brief mention of some of the themes and licenses that have become so popular with collectors over many years. Amongst the first to feature in the range were the vehicles of British Road Services and Pickfords.

The sheer size of both fleets during the classic years of the 1950s, 60s and even 70s made the liveries familiar sights on the roads and generated a strong collector following. Pickfords in particular ran a diverse range of vehicles across its haulage, bulk liquid transport and household removals businesses and Corgi has covered everything from a Land Rover to huge heavy haulage rigs featuring multiple Scammell or Diamond T tractor units coupled to girder trailers with massive resin loads. In recent years the range has featured a Volvo F12 with five axle King trailer and load in the mid-1980s livery of Pickford Haulage Division.

Whilst Pickfords managed to retain its brand name following the 1948 nationalisation of the road transport industry, most of its competitors were swallowed up by, and became part of, BRS (British Road Services). Once again the diversity of vehicle types made life easy for Corgi to produce a wide range. This coupled to the fact that the powers that be at the time decided to differentiate between different arms of the business with distinctive livery schemes, gave great scope for a colourful and interesting spread of models. Road Services vehicles were red, Parcels green, Meat Haulage blue and cream whilst tippers were in grey. Everything from a Morris Minor Van in BRS Parcels green to a

Top left: Brand new tooling Volvo FH with curtainside trailer is a special release to mark the 60th anniversary of Corgi

Top right: This Scania R Highline with tanker trailer is part of Eddie Stobart's specialist fuel transportation fleet.

Above left: The Mercedes Actros MP4 is one of the latest breed of modern trucks to have been modelled by Corgi. This one is in the livery of Middlebrook Transport

Above right: MAN TGX with flatbed trailer and load in the smart livery of Collett & Sons Specialist Transport

Below: In it for the long haul! The drivers of these Chapman and Ball Scania 110s to the Far East were known as 'Cola Cowboys'. They drank Cola on the long and often dangerous journeys across the desert because it was cheaper than water!

Scania 110 with Tilt Trailer in BRS Road Services Red have been covered, plus a multitude of models in between, which would be enough for a full article in its own right.

We however don't have space for such depth, particularly as we have still to cover the one themed license that has dominated Corgi's haulage ranges for twenty years or more. I am speaking of course of the phenomenon that is Eddie Stobart.

Corgi has seen fit to pretty well 'Stobartise' everything and anything in its range. At its best some of the recent modern truck releases in the latest liveries are quite superb, whilst Reliant three-wheelers, real though they may be, are pushing it a bit for me. However, such has been the strength of feeling for the Cumbrian based haulage company that it would seem it is all very collectable! So we now have everything from steam wagons in make-believe pre-war Stobart designs, to the beautifully accurate and detailed contemporary designs of today, all available from Corgi. The Eddie spotters have never had it so good! ◉

Trackside

Emerging from the shadow of Days Gone and Corgi

Corgi's Trackside range is, as the name suggests, designed with the model railway enthusiast in mind. Produced to 1/76th scale the models are ideal accessories for OO scale model railway layouts but have also proven popular with model vehicle collectors, where the smaller scale allows for a larger collection if display space is at a premium.

However, despite its popularity I can't help but feel that the Trackside range has struggled to find an identity of its own - until recent years that is. Let me explain further...

EVOLUTION NOT REVOLUTION

The Trackside range was officially launched in 2000 shortly after Corgi had taken over the Days Gone brand name in late 1999. However its origins go back much further to the heyday of Days Gone, and the launch of the DG44 Scammell six wheeler in 1990. Collectors very quickly latched onto the fact that despite being scaled to fit the standard Days Gone box, this model was in fact an accurate 1/76th scale model. As such it gained popularity beyond the regular Days Gone collectors with a new audience of OO railway enthusiasts. A Scammell Ballast Tractor (DG80) followed in

1996 based on the DG44 tooling and so unwittingly the seeds had been sown for what was to become the Trackside range.

One of Corgi's first dilemmas following the acquisition of Lledo was the question of how to move the Days Gone brand forward. The solution was to create a sub-brand and begin to create a range of scale models. Utilising the 1/76th scale tooling already available 'Days Gone Trackside' was created. Utilising the Scammell six wheeler, Scammell Ballast Tractor and a new Sentinel Ballast Tractor the new range evolved as a slightly underwhelming scale version of Days Gone.

The next range in 2001 progressed to a brand new AEC Mammoth cab utilising the ballast tractor chassis, plus an articulated low loader back for use

with a new Scammell tractor and the existing ballast tractors. Cold cast resin loads added colour and variety without the expense of hard tooling. 2001 also saw the launch of a nicely detailed new Burrell Showman's Wagon and Road Roller, both in 1/76th scale.

MIRRORING THE CLASSICS

The next major move for Trackside borrowed much from the 1/50th Corgi Classic Truck models as the range started to mirror its Corgi 'big brother', albeit in reduced scale. 2002 saw the launch of a classic Foden F21 'Mickey Mouse' cab with flatbed trailer and a Guy Pantechnican. The flatbed trailer was also paired with an AEC Mammoth tractor. A Scammell Scarab with its own dedicated articulated flatbed trailer was also launched. Further new models followed at a pace

including a Scammell Mechanical Horse, Scammell Handyman, ERF LV and BMC Noddy Van, plus Leyland Octopus and Guy Big J Tipper 8-wheelers.

In 2005 Trackside lost its Days Gone identity and became a sub-brand of Corgi. As if to reinforce this message the highlight of the new tooling that year was the Scammell Contractor, huge even at 1/76th scale, and a further move into Corgi territory, this time mirroring 1/50th scale 'Heavy Haulage' range.

SMALLER IS BETTER!

In 2006 Trackside took yet another cue from its Corgi 'big brother'. This time it was from the Vanguards range as the new tooling turned to smaller commercials with a Morris LD, Bedford CA, Austin J2 and Ford Transit Mk1. Although quite small in 1/76th scale, these vans nevertheless gave the range greater breadth and popular themes such as Royal Mail, PO Telephones, and newspaper delivery vans were covered. A Scammell Townsman was also added to complete the trio of mechanical horse vehicles.

In 2007 the range went even smaller as saloon cars and car-derived vans were introduced. 3-car sets included a Vauxhall Viva HA, Morris 1000 and Ford 105E Anglia in different colour variations, whilst the commercial variants of each were released as individual models. To contrast with these smaller models in late 2007 a beautiful Harrington Horsebox appeared. These were used by the pre-nationalisation railway operators as reflected by the first two releases in LNER and Southern Railways liveries. 2008 saw a return to smaller vehicles with the diminutive Mini and Minivan, Ford Escort and Escort van, alongside a larger Thorneycroft Nippy with articulated trailer.

TRACKSIDE FINDS ITSELF!

2009 is when I believe the Trackside range really began to emerge from its Days Gone and Corgi shadow. This began with the release of a Fire Engine. This time it was not reflecting the old Corgi 1/50th scale 999 range. This time it was tackling a subject that Corgi had

> ## Cold cast resin loads added colour and variety without the expense of hard tooling

previously not dared to take on.

The Green Goddess Fire Engine had been much requested by collectors for years but the high cost of tooling coupled with a lack of liveries had always relegated it to the 'not commercially viable' file. However, at Trackside scale and with some clever design to minimalize components, the tooling was approved. Trackside had made its mark!

It was quickly followed by the Dennis F12 to create a small sub-range of fire appliances.

The 2010 range featured another ground breaking launch for Trackside with Vintage Construction vehicles. The Ruston Bucyrus 19 was a workhorse of mining, quarrying and railway construction, with a long operational lifespan from around 1930. As such it was an ideal choice for pre- and post- nationalisation railway layouts and the wide range of variants such as face shovel, drag shovel, skimmer and crane meant the tooling use could be maximised. The models were also impressively rigged for additional realism.

2011 saw the addition of a Coles

Argus 6-ton Crane, another workhorse of many a railway yard, and still in use today on some preserved railways.

UNCERTAIN FUTURE

Sadly just as the range started to find its own identity, development of new Trackside models appears to have ceased. There has been no further tooling investment since the Ruston Bucyrus and Coles Crane. What the future holds in not certain at this moment but we can only hope there will be new announcements from Corgi in the not too distant future – especially as Trackside has now found itself! ◉

John Player Special
Lotus 72
Formula 1

Released: April 1974 **Withdrawn:** *1977* **Sales:** *347,000*

The story of this model actually begins with the introduction of model No 154, the 'John Player Special' Lotus, in March 1973. Modelled in 1/36 scale along with several other top Formula 1 cars of the time, Corgi produced an accurate toy replica in correct JPS cigarette livery, something that would be unheard of today. The range was a masterstroke as it appealed to all ages given the popularity of the cars on the Grand Prix racing circuits around the world. Sales of this model in particular were staggering (more than 2 million over a six year run) and sufficiently so to begin with that Corgi took the brave step of literally thinking big and doubling the size of the model to 1/18 scale, adding the feature of removable wheels using an included wheel brace, as No 190.

But this could have been a very different story as a licensing disagreement threatened to throw a spanner in the works before the release of the smaller model. This was settled after Marcel van Cleemput personally travelled to Jarama, just outside Madrid, to meet Lotus boss Colin Chapman, leading to a meeting soon afterwards that smoothed things out, allowing production to go ahead.

The larger model that we are focusing on here really was a new venture for Corgi, but the company was confident enough to feature just this model on the cover of the 1974 catalogue. The larger size allowed for slightly finer detail and made for impressive desktop presence for any Formula 1 fan of the era. There are still a good number to be found in excellent condition, although finding one with the wheelbrace and spare

Right: *Time for a quick pitstop. A detailed picture of the model in pieces*

wheel nuts is a harder task. Even so, expect to pay around £50-£85 for a good boxed example like this, definitely towards the upper end with the accessories. ◉

THE CORGI PRICE GUIDE

CORGI TOYS CARS 1956–1983
See also 'Emergency', 'Novelty, Film and TV-related' sections.

150 **Vanwall Racing Car**, 1957-61, green body, yellow seat, large or small 'Vanwall', flat hubs, RNs '1', '3' or '7', clear or blue screen. 'Made in Gt Britain' or 'British Made' and large 'CORGI TOYS VANWALL' cast along base. Blue box with leaflet **£80-100**
Vanwall Racing Car, 1957-61, green body, silver seat, clear screen. 'Made in Great Britain' cast along base. 'CORGI TOYS VANWALL' small across base. Flat hubs. RN '3'.....................**£80-100**
Vanwall Racing Car, 1957-61, vermillion red body, silver or yellowseat, small or large 'Vanwall', blue or clear screen. RN '1', '3' or '7'. 'CORGI TOYS VANWALL' cast small across or large along base. Flat or spoked hubs. Blue/yellow box..........**£125-175**
Vanwall Racing Car, 1957-61, gold plated finish red seats, criss-cross cast wheels with original profile publications leaflet.............
....**£80-100**

150S **Vanwall Racing Car**, 1961-65, (with 'suspension')
Vanwall Racing Car, 1961-65, vermillion red body, blue/white bonnet design plus black RN '25', white driver, silver seat, small 'Vanwall', 'Made in Gt. Britain' cast along the base. '150S CORGI TOYs VANWALL' across base.............................**£80-100**
Vanwall Racing Car, 1961-65, same with 150S sticker on 150 box ....**NGPP**
Vanwall Racing Car, 1961-65, same but with Crimson body........
....**£150-175**
Vanwall Racing Car, 1961-65, promotional: 'Vandervell Products' finish...**NGPP**

150 **Surtees TS9 Formula 1**, 1972-74, metallic purple or metallic blue body, 'BROOKE BOND OXO' logo, 8-spoke Whizz-Wheels......**£40-50**
Surtees TS9 Formula 1, 1972-74, metallic turquoise body, cast 8-stud WhizzWheels..**£30-40**
Surtees TS9 Formula 1, 1972-74, 1975-76 blue/yellow body DUCKHAMS', (GS 29 only)...**GSP**

151 **Lotus XI Le Mans Racing Car**, 1958-61, blue body, red or maroon seats, clear or blue-tinted windscreen, RN '1', '3' or 7
....**£150-200**
Lotus XI Le Mans Racing Car, 1958-61, silver body, red seats, RN '3'. or 7 blue tinted screen....................................**£120-150**
Lotus XI Le Mans Racing Car, 1958-61, red body, beige seats, RN '1', blue tinted screen..**£200-250**

151A **Lotus XI Le Mans Racing Car**, 1961-65, blue body, red seats, red/white bonnet stripe, white driver, black RN '7' **£100-125**
Lotus XI Le Mans Racing Car, 1961-65, blue body, no bonnet stripe, red seats, white driver, black racing number '7'
....**£100-125**
Lotus XI Le Mans Racing Car, 1961-65, lemon body, RN '3', driver...**£130-160**

151 **Yardley Mclaren M19A**, 1974-76, white body, 'YARDLEY', RN '55', 8-spoke or stud WhizzWheels...........................**£40-50**
Yardley Mclaren M19A, 1974-76, with blue stripe on white helmet, WhizzWheels, (GS30 only)...**GSP**

152 **B.R.M. Racing Car**, 1958-61, light or dark green body, yellow seat, no driver, RNs '1', '3' or '7' blue box with leaflet........**£90-110**
B.R.M. Racing Car, 1958-61, turquoise body, Union Jack on bonnet, RN's '1', '3' or '7'. Blue/yellow box, no leaflet **£90-110**

152S **B.R.M. Racing Car**, 1961-65, (with 'suspension')
B.R.M. Racing Car, 1961-65, turquoise body, Union Jack on bonnet, white driver, RNs '1', '3' or '7', blue/yellow box, no leaflet
....**£140-160**
B.R.M. Racing Car, 1961-65, same with 152S sticker on 152 box.
....**NGPP**

152 **Ferrari 312 B2**, 1974-75, red body, 'Ferrari/Shell' logo, RN '5', white driver, orange/blue helmet, 8-spoke or 8-stud cast hubs
....**£30-35**

153 **Bluebird Record Car**, 1960-61, blue body, UK and US flags on nose, metal hubs..**£175-200**

153A **Bluebird Record Car**, 1961-65, blue body, UK and US flags on nose, plastic hubs **£130-150**
Bluebird Record Car, 1961-65, blue body with two Union Jacks on nose, plastic hubs **£100-130**

153 **Team Surtees TS 9B**, 1972-74, red body, blue or blue/white driver (Rob Walker), RN '26', 8-spoke hubs **£50-60**
Team Surtees TS 9B, 1972-74, red body, 'NORRIS', (GS 30 only) ...
....**GSP**

154 **Ferrari Formula 1**, 1963-72, red body, Ferrari bonnet badge, white driver, RN'36'. Plain blue/yellow card box **£60-80**
Shaped or cast wheels.
Late issue in blue and yellow window box.

154 **'JOHN PLAYER SPECIAL' Lotus**, 1974-79
(drivers Emerson Fittipaldi or Ronnie Petersen)
'JOHN PLAYER SPECIAL' Lotus, 1974-79, black body, gold trim, RN '1' or '4', 'JPS' logo, black/red helmet, 8-stud hubs, 'Fittipaldi' on box **£40-50**
'JOHN PLAYER SPECIAL' Lotus, 1974-79, 'JPS' logo, black or blue helmet, 'Petersen' on box **£40-50**
'JOHN PLAYER SPECIAL' Lotus, 1974-79, 'JPS TEXACO' logo, red helmet **£40-50**
'JOHN PLAYER SPECIAL' Lotus, 1974-79, 'JPS TEXACO', black helmet, 12-spoke hubs
(GS32 only) ....**GSP**

'JOHN PLAYER SPECIAL' Lotus, 1974-79, 'JPS SHELL' logo, black/red helmet, (GS30 only)..**GSP**
'JOHN PLAYER SPECIAL' Lotus, 1974-79, Marks & Spencers issue: No 'Corgi' on base, 'TEXACO' logo, orange (?) helmet
....**GSP**

155 **Lotus Climax Racing Car**, 1964-69, British Racing green body, yellow stripe on bonnet, white driver, blue helmet, RN '1'............
....**£40-50**

155 **'SHADOW' Formula 1**, 1974-76, black, 'UOP', driver (Jackie Collins) white/maroon helmet, RN '17' **£40-50**

156 **Cooper-Maserati**, 1967-68, dark blue body, RN '7', silver or bronze hubs, white driver, blue helmet..............................**£40-50**
Cooper-Maserati, 1967-68, yellow, white upper body, cast hubs, race No '6' pre-production colour trial............................**£150-200**

156 **Graham Hill's Shadow**, 1974-76, white/red, RN'12', 'EMBASSY RACING'..**£30-40**
Graham Hill's Shadow, 1974-76, special issue model: Presentation box has outer sleeve with 'Graham Hill OBE, Honoured Guest of the National Sporting Club Café Royal - Monday 24th, November 1975', plus the menu for the day...**£300-450**

158 **Lotus Climax Racing Car**, 1969-73, orange and white body, blue driver, white helmet, black RN '8' & bonnet stripe.............**£40-50**

158 **Elf Tyrrell Ford F1**, 1975-78, blue body, RN '1', 'ELF', Jackie Stewart driving..**£40-50**

159 **Cooper-Maserati**, 1969-72, yellow and white body, black bonnet stripe, blue driver, white helmet, cast wheels, yellow number '3'..
....**£40-50**

159 **Indianapolis Racing Car**, 1974-76, red, RN '20' Patrick Eagle driving **£30-35**

160 **'HESKETH' 308 F1, 1975-78**, white body, black helmet, 4-spoke or 8-stud hubs..**£30-35**
'HESKETH' 308 F1, 1975-78, yellow body, 'CORGI TEAM' logo, orange driver (James Hunt), black helmet, blue belts, (GS26 only)
....**GSP**
'HESKETH' 308 F1, 1975-78, Marks & Spencers issue:
'HESKETH' 308 F1, 1975-78, white body and driver, 'CORGI' on some, orange helmet...**GSP**

161 **Santa Pod 'COMMUTER'**, 1971-73, red 'Dragster' body, chrome engine, RN '2', WhizzWheels..**GSP**

161 **'ELF-TYRRELL' P34**, 1977-78, blue and yellow body, 'ELF' logo, red or blue helmet, 8-stud hubs, yellow RN '4' **£25-30**

162 **'ELF-TYRRELL' P34**, 1978-79, blue/white, 'FIRST NATIONAL BANK' logo, red or orange helmet **£25-30**

162 **'QUARTERMASTER' Dragster**, 1971-72, green/white, driver, plastic hubs..**£50-60**

163 **Santa Pod Dragster 'GLOWORM'**, 1971-73, white, blue trim, red chassis, driver...**£30-35**

164 **Ison Bros Dragster 'WILD HONEY'**, 1972-73, yellow/black, green glass, WW...**£25-35**
Ison Bros Dragster 'WILD HONEY', 1972-73, yellow wooden mock-up model painted with "Wild Honey" decal to one door and 'Ison Bros Racing' decal to other, Jaguar decal to bonnet, plastic WhizzWheels..**£300-350**

165 **Adams Brothers 'DRAG-STAR'**, 1972-74, red/yellow, 4 x V-8 engines, WW..**£25-35**

166 **Ford Mustang 'ORGAN GRINDER'**, 1971-74, yellow/green body, RN '39', driver..**£30-35**

167 **USA Racing Buggy**, 1973-74, white/red, RN '7', driver, US flag....
....**£30-40**

169 **'STARFIGHTER' Dragster**, 1974-77, blue/silver/red body, 'FIRESTONE'..**£30-35**

170 **John Woolfe's Dragster**, 1974-77, 'RADIO LUXEMBOURG', '208'.
....**£35-45**

190 **'JOHN PLAYER' Lotus**, 1974-77, 1:18 scale, black/gold, RN '1', driver, removable wheels, tools included in box.................**£40-50**

191 **'TEXACO MARLBORO'**, 1975-80, F1 Mclaren. 1:18 scale

'TEXACO MARLBORO', 1975-80, white/red, RN '5', removable wheels, tools included in box......***£40-50***

200 **Ford Consul**, 1956-61, (this was the first 'Corgi Toys' model). Flat spun hubs, no suspension, leaflet with early issues.
Ford Consul, 1956-61, cream body......***£75-100***
Ford Consul, 1956-61, dark or pale green body......***£125-150***
Ford Consul, 1956-61, tan or dark tan body......***£125-200***
Ford Consul, 1956-61, blue body......***£125-150***
Ford Consul, 1956-61, light greyish-brown body......***£110-140***
Ford Consul, 1956-61, bright green body......***£175-250***
Ford Consul, 1956-61, pale grey and green body......***£150-200***

200 **BLMC Mini 1000**, 1976-78, metallic blue body, silver roof, red or white interior......***£20-25***

200A **BLMC Mini 1000**, 1978-83, met. blue or silver body, white or red interior, Union Jack stripe on roof, WhizzWheels......***£25-35***

200M **Ford Consul** (with flywheel motor), 1956-59, flat spun hubs, no suspension, leaflet with early issues.
Ford Consul (with flywheel motor), 1956-59, blue......***£100-150***
Ford Consul (with flywheel motor), 1956-59, dark green......***£150-175***
Ford Consul (with flywheel motor), 1956-59, bright green......***£130-160***
Ford Consul (with flywheel motor), 1956-59, two-tone green......***£130-160***
Ford Consul (with flywheel motor), 1956-59, green/cream......***£130-160***
Ford Consul (with flywheel motor), 1956-59, silver/cream......***£130-160***
Ford Consul (with flywheel motor), 1956-59, pale grey over green......***£130-160***

201 **Austin Cambridge**, 1956-61, flat spun hubs, no suspension, leaflet with early issues.
Austin Cambridge, 1956-61, pale blue body......***£100-120***
Austin Cambridge, 1956-61, turquoise body......***£125-150***
Austin Cambridge, 1956-61, light grey body......***£150-200***
Austin Cambridge, 1956-61, mid-grey body......***£125-150***
Austin Cambridge, 1956-61, green/cream......***£125-150***
Austin Cambridge, 1956-61, two-tone green......***£125-150***
Austin Cambridge, 1956-61, silver/metallic green......***£175-200***
Austin Cambridge, 1956-61, empty dealers trade box......***£25-50***

201M **Austin Cambridge**, 1956-59, (with flywheel motor). Flat spun hubs, leaflet with early issues.
Austin Cambridge, 1956-59, cream body......***£130-160***
Austin Cambridge, 1956-59, red body......***£130-160***
Austin Cambridge, 1956-59, slate grey body......***£130-160***
Austin Cambridge, 1956-59, medium grey body......***£130-160***
Austin Cambridge, 1956-59, silver or metallic blue......***£130-160***
Austin Cambridge, 1956-59, burnt orange body......***£250-300***

201 **BLMC Mini 1000**, 1979-82, silver, 'TEAM CORGI'/'8' on some......***£25-40***
BLMC Mini 1000, 1979-82, same model but with orange body......***£25-40***
BLMC Mini 1000, 1979-82, dk. blue, without 'TEAM CORGI'......***£25-40***
BLMC Mini 1000, 1979-82, dark blue, 'ESSO' and 'MICHELIN' labels......***£25-40***

202 **Morris Cowley**, 1956-61, flat spun hubs, no suspension, leaflet with early issues.
Morris Cowley, 1956-61, bright green body......***£150-175***
Morris Cowley, 1956-61, grey body......***£125-150***
Morris Cowley, 1956-61, blue body......***£75-100***
Morris Cowley, 1956-61, grey/blue body......***£125-150***
Morris Cowley, 1956-61, blue/cream body......***£125-150***
Morris Cowley, 1956-61, pale green/blue body......***£150-240***
Morris Cowley,1956-61, white/blue body......***£125-150***

202M **Morris Cowley**, 1956-59, with flywheel motor. Flat spun hubs, leaflet with early issues.
Morris Cowley, 1956-59, pale green body......***£150-175***
Morris Cowley, 1956-59, mid-green body......***£130-160***
Morris Cowley, 1956-59, dark green body......***£130-160***
Morris Cowley, 1956-59, off-white body......***£120-150***

202 **Renault 16TS**, 1970-72, blue/silver, yellow interior, WW..***£35-40***

203 **De Tomaso Mangusta**, 1970-72, met. dark green, gold stripes, RN '1'......***£25-35***

203 **Vauxhall Velox**, 1956-61, flat spun hubs, leaflet with early issues.
Vauxhall Velox, 1956-61, red body......***£125-150***
Vauxhall Velox, 1956-61, cream body......***£100-150***
Vauxhall Velox, 1956-61, yellow body......***£100-150***
Vauxhall Velox, 1956-61, yellow/red body......***£150-175***
Vauxhall Velox, 1956-61, blue body......***£500-750***

203M **Vauxhall Velox**, 1956-59, (with flywheel motor). Flat spun hubs, leaflet with early issues.
Vauxhall Velox, 1956-59, red body......***£175-200***
Vauxhall Velox, 1956-59, orange body......***£250-300***

203 **De Tomaso Mangusta**, 1971-72, green/gold, white interior, WW......***£50-75***
De Tomaso Mangusta, 1971-72, green body, white interior, silver base, WhizzWheels......***£50-75***

204 **Rover 90**, 1956-61, flat spun hubs, leaflet with early issues.
Rover 90, 1956-61, cream or off-white body......***£130-150***
Rover 90, 1956-61, light or dark grey body, flat hubs......***£150-175***
Rover 90, 1956-61, mid or dark green body, flat hubs......***£150-175***

Rover 90, 1956-61, metallic green body, flat hubs......***£140-160***
Rover 90, 1956-61, met. red lower body, cream upper..***£140-160***
Rover 90, 1956-61, metallic cerise over grey body......***£140-160***

204M **Rover 90** (with flywheel motor), 1956-61, flat spun hubs, leaflet with early issues.
Rover 90 (with flywheel motor), 1956-61, bright mid-green or dark green......***£100-150***
Rover 90 (with flywheel motor), 1956-61, grey body......***£150-175***
Rover 90 (with flywheel motor), 1956-61, metallic green body......***£175-225***

204 **Morris Mini-Minor**, 1972-73, all have WhizzWheels.
Morris Mini-Minor, 1972-73, dark blue body, lemon interior......***£100-130***
Morris Mini-Minor, 1972-73, met. blue body, lemon interior......***£100-125***
Morris Mini-Minor, 1972-73, all-orange body, lemon interior......***£125-150***
Morris Mini-Minor, 1972-73, orange body, black roof......***£275-350***

205 **Riley Pathfinder**, 1956-62, flat spun hubs, leaflet with early issues.
Riley Pathfinder, 1956-62, red body......***£130-160***
Riley Pathfinder, 1956-62, blue body......***£130-160***

205M **Riley Pathfinder**, 1956-59, (with flywheel motor) Flat spun hubs, leaflet with early issues.
Riley Pathfinder, 1956-59, red body......***£200-250***
Riley Pathfinder, 1956-59, mid blue body......***£200-250***
Riley Pathfinder, 1956-59, navy blue body......***£150-175***

206 **Hillman Husky Estate**, 1956-59, flat spun hubs, leaflet with early issues.
Hillman Husky Estate, 1956-59, tan or greyish light-brown body......***£125-150***
Hillman Husky Estate, 1956-59, metallic blue and silver body......***£150-175***

206M **Hillman Husky Estate**, 1956-59, (with flywheel motor).
Hillman Husky Estate, 1956-59, flat spun hubs, leaflet with early issues.
Hillman Husky Estate, 1956-59, cream body......***£150-175***
Hillman Husky Estate, 1956-59, mid-blue body......***£150-200***
Hillman Husky Estate, 1956-59, dark blue body......***£150-200***
Hillman Husky Estate, 1956-59, grey body......***£100-150***
Hillman Husky Estate, 1956-59, turquoise body......***£250-300***

207 **Standard Vanguard III**, 1957-62, flat spun hubs, leaflet with early issues.
Standard Vanguard III, 1957-62, off-white body (red roof top)......***£100-120***
Standard Vanguard III, 1957-62, grey body (red roof)..***£120-140***
Standard Vanguard III, 1957-62, red over green body..***£120-140***

207M **Standard Vanguard III**, 1957-59, (with flywheel motor). Flat spun hubs, leaflet with early issues.
Standard Vanguard III, 1957-59, primrose yellow body......***£190-230***
Standard Vanguard III, 1957-59, pale green body, red roof pillars......***£145-175***

208 **Jaguar 2.4 litre**, 1957-60, flat spun hubs, leaflet with early issues.
Jaguar 2.4 litre, 1957-60, white body......***£100-120***

208M **Jaguar 2.4 litre** (with flywheel motor), 1957-60, flat spun hubs, leaflet with early issues.
Jaguar 2.4 litre (with flywheel motor), 1957-60, metallic dark blue body......***£200-250***

208S **Jaguar 2.4 litre**, 1960-63, (with spring suspension).
Jaguar 2.4 litre, 1960-63, flat spun hubs, lemon body..***£150-175***
Jaguar 2.4 litre, 1960-63, flat spun hubs, pale lemon body......***£150-175***

210 **Citroën DS19**, 1957-60, flat spun hubs, leaflet with early issues.
Citroën DS19, 1957-60, yellow body, red roof, grey or silver baseplate......***£120-160***
Citroën DS19, 1957-60, met. dark green body, black roof......***£140-180***
Citroën DS19, 1957-60, as previous but with bulge in base to take flywheel motor. Note that a '210M' was not produced....***£120-160***

210S **Citroën DS19** (with suspension), 1960-65, red body, lemon interior, grey base......***£130-160***

211 **Studebaker Golden Hawk**, 1958-60, flat spun hubs, leaflet with early issues.
Studebaker Golden Hawk, 1958-60, blue body, gold rear wing flashes......***£120-150***
Studebaker Golden Hawk, 1958-60, white body, gold rear wing flashes......***£120-150***

211M **Studebaker Golden Hawk**, 1958-59, (with flywheel motor).

Flat spun hubs, leaflet with early issues.
Studebaker Golden Hawk, 1958-59, white/gold body ***£170-200***
211S **Studebaker Golden Hawk**, 1960-65, (with spring suspension).
Studebaker Golden Hawk, 1960-65, gold ('plated') body, red interior, white flash, shaped hubs ***£100-125***
Studebaker Golden Hawk, 1960-65, gold (painted) body, shaped hubs ***£125-150***
212 **Road Racer**, 958 not released, one example known to exist ***NPP***
214 **Ford Thunderbird Hardtop**, 1959-65, flat spun hubs, leaflet with early issues.
Ford Thunderbird Hardtop, 1959-65, pale green (cream hardtop), '1959' rear no. plate ***£100-120***
Ford Thunderbird Hardtop, 1959-65, same but blank rear plate ***£100-120***
Ford Thunderbird Hardtop, 1959-65, grey body (red top), '1959' No. plate ***£100-120***
214M **Ford Thunderbird Hardtop**, 1959-60, (with flywheel motor). Flat spun hubs, leaflet with early issues.
Ford Thunderbird Hardtop, 1959-60, pink (black top), '1959' rear No. plate ***£150-200***
Ford Thunderbird Hardtop, 1959-60, pale green body, cream hardtop ***£170-200***
214S **Ford Thunderbird Hardtop**, 1962-64, (with spring suspension).
Ford Thunderbird Hardtop, 1962-64, shaped spun hubs, metallic grey/red body, lemon interior ***£100-120***
Ford Thunderbird Hardtop, 1962-64, black/red body, lemon interior ***£100-120***
215 **Thunderbird Open Sports**, 1959-62, white body, flat spun hubs, blue interior ***£100-120***
Thunderbird Open Sports, 1959-62, blue body, silver interior ***£100-120***
215S **Thunderbird Open Sports**, 1962-64, (with spring suspension
Thunderbird Open Sports, 1962-64, red body, yellow interior/ driver ***£125-150***
216 **Austin A40**, 1959-62, flat spun hubs, leaflet with early issues.
Austin A40, 1959-62, two-tone blue body ***£100-120***
Austin A40, 1959-62, red body, black roof ***£100-120***
216M **Austin A40** (with flywheel motor), 1959-60, flat spun hubs, leaflet with early issues.
Austin A40 (with flywheel motor), 1959-60, red body, black roof ***£200-225***
Austin A40 (with flywheel motor), 1959-60, all-red body ***£130-160***
217 **Fiat 1800 Saloon**, 1960-63, light blue (lemon interior), smooth or shaped hubs ***£60-70***
Fiat 1800 Saloon, 1960-63, two-tone blue (lemon interior), smooth or shaped hubs ***£80-90***
Fiat 1800 Saloon, 1960-63, light tan body, lemon interior***£60-70***
Fiat 1800 Saloon, 1960-63, mustard yellow body, bright yellow interior ***£100-120***
218 **Aston Martin DB4**, 1960-62, red body (bonnet vent on some), flat or shaped hubs ***£100-120***
Aston Martin DB4, 1960-62, 1961-62 red body, red interior, cast 'spoked' hubs ***£80-100***
Aston Martin DB4, 1960-62, primrose yellow body with bonnet vent, red interior, flat spun hubs ***£80-100***
Aston Martin DB4, 1960-62, same model, but with cast 'criss-cross' wheels ***£140-170***
219 **Plymouth Suburban Sports**, 1959-63, cream with fawn roof, red interior, smooth flat hubs ***£50-75***
Plymouth Suburban Sports, 1959-63, light blue body with red roof spun hubs ***£90-100***
220 **Chevrolet Impala**, 1960-65, all have spun hubs.
Chevrolet Impala, 1960-65, metallic red body, red or lemon interior, leaflet ***£70-80***
Chevrolet Impala, 1960-65, same, powder blue body ***£70-80***
Chevrolet Impala, 1960-65, pink body, lemon int. ***£130-160***
Chevrolet Impala, 1960-65, sky blue body, red interior ***£80-90***
221 **Chevrolet Impala Cab**, 1960-63, yellow body, 'NEW YORK TAXI', red interior, smooth/shaped spun hubs, roof box ***£150-175***
221 **Chevrolet Impala State Patrol**, 1960-63, see 'Emergency Vehicles' section.
222 **Renault Floride**, 1959-65, dark red/ maroon body; red, white or yellow interior, flat or shaped hubs ***£60-70***
Renault Floride, 1959-65, light olive, red interior, flat hubs ***£70-80***
Renault Floride, 1959-65, metallic blue body, red interior, flat or shaped hubs ***£100-125***
Renault Floride, 1959-65, harder to find version: metallic blue with lemon interior, shaped hubs ***NGPP***
224 **Bentley Continental**, 1961-65, opening boot with removable spare, special lights.
Bentley Continental, 1961-65, cream over metallic apple green, red interior ***£120-140***
Bentley Continental, 1961-65, black over silver body, red int. ***£100-120***
Bentley Continental, 1961-65, two-tone green or gold body ***£120-140***
Bentley Continental, 1961-65, white over metallic green body ***£140-160***
Bentley Continental, 1961-65, cherry red body, lemon interior ***£120-140***
Bentley Continental, 1961-65, gold plated body, red interior ***£200-250***
225 **Austin 7 (Mini) Saloon**, 1961-65, red body, yellow interior, spun hubs ***£130-160***
Austin 7 (Mini) Saloon, 1961-65, primrose-yellow body, red interior, flat hubs ***£400-500***
Austin 7 (Mini) Saloon, 1961-65, mid-blue body, red interior, shaped hubs ***£400-500***
Austin 7 (Mini) Saloon, 1961-65, Danish promotional: 'JENSEN'S'
Austin 7 (Mini) Saloon, 1961-65, red body, lemon interior, flat spun hubs ***£1,000-1,200***
Austin 7 (Mini) Saloon, 1961-65, pale/light yellow body, red interior, smooth cast hubs ***£1,000-1,200***
226 **Morris Mini Minor**, 1960-68, pale blue body, red or yellow interior, flat or shaped hubs ***£100-120***
Morris Mini Minor, 1960-68, red body, flat or shaped hubs ***£100-120***
Morris Mini Minor, 1960-68, metallic maroon, lemon interior, detailed cast hubs ***£120-140***
Morris Mini Minor, 1960-68, metallic maroon, lemon interior, detailed cast hubs with Ralley Monte Carlo Rallye on bonnet Race No.6 on door ***£200-250***
Morris Mini Minor, 1960-68, promotional: Link House Magazine.
Morris Mini Minor, 1960-68, metallic red, yellow interior silver cast hubs no hole in base ***NGPP***
Morris Mini Minor, 1960-68, promotional: Coleman's Mustard.
Morris Mini Minor, 1960-68, yellow, yellow interior silver cast hubs no hole in base 'Mustard Mania' lable on roof, 'Colman's Mustard' label on doors ***£1,500-2,000***
Morris Mini Minor, 1960-68, Danish promotional:
Morris Mini Minor, 1960-68, 'JENSEN'S', pale blue body, red interior, flat spun hubs ***£1,200-1,400***
Morris Mini Minor, 1960-68, deep blue body (only in Gift Set 11) ***GSP***
Morris Mini Minor, 1960-68, NB the light blue version of 226 was also used for a short time by a US games manufacturer in a table-top racing game. This model has a large drive-pin hole in the base and 'EAST AFRICAN RALLY' stickers on the bonnet, RN '3'. Not separately boxed ***£200-300***
227 **Mini Cooper Rally**, 1962-65, bright blue body, white roof and bonnet, yellow interior, spun hubs, Union Jack and chequered bonnet flags, racing numbers '1', 3' or '7' ***£300-400***
Mini Cooper Rally, 1962-65, same but bright blue body and bonnet, white roof ***£200-300***
Mini Cooper Rally, 1962-65, primrose yellow body, red interior, white roof and bonnet with flags and RNs '1', '3' or '7' ***£300-400***
Mini Cooper Rally, 1962-65, primrose yellow body and bonnet, flags, RN '1' ***£200-300***
228 **Volvo P-1800**, 1962-65, beige body, red interior, spun hubs ***£100-130***
Volvo P-1800, 1962-65, red body, lemon interior, spun hubs ***£80-100***
Volvo P-1800, 1962-65, pink body, lemon int. ***£55-65***
229 **Chevrolet Corvair**, 1961-66, mid-blue body, bright yellow interior, spun hubs ***£60-70***
Chevrolet Corvair, 1961-66, pale blue body, lemon or red interior, shaped hubs ***£60-70***
Chevrolet Corvair, 1961-66, gold body, (in 'Golden Guinea' set) ***GSP***
230 **Mercedes-Benz 220 SE**, 1962-64, shaped spun hubs, spare wheel in boot. Cream (red interior) ***£130-150***
Mercedes-Benz 220 SE, 1962-64, maroon body, lemon interior ***£100-130***
Mercedes-Benz 220 SE, 1962-64, black body, lemon interior ***£150-190***
Mercedes-Benz 220 SE, 1962-64, dark blue body, lemon interior ***£70-80***
231 **Triumph Herald**, 1961-65, gold top/bottom, white in centre, red interior, smooth flat hubs ***£100-130***
Triumph Herald, 1961-65, mid-blue top/bottom, white centre, red interior, shaped hubs ***£75-100***
232 **Fiat 2100**, 1961-63, pale pink with mauve roof, lemon interior, spun hubs ***£60-70***
233 **Heinkel Trojan**, 1962-72, spun hubs or detailed cast hubs.
Heinkel Trojan, 1962-72, red body, lemon interior ***£75-80***
Heinkel Trojan, 1962-72, dark blue body, lemon int ***£100-125***

Heinkel Trojan, 1962-72, lilac body, lemon interior........***£75-100***
Heinkel Trojan, 1962-72, orange body, lemon interior...***£75-100***.
Heinkel Trojan, 1962-72, pink body, lemon interior........***£75-100***.
Heinkel Trojan, 1962-72, metallic blue body, spun hubs..***£75-100***.
Heinkel Trojan, 1962-72, fawn body, spun hubs...............***£75-100***
Heinkel Trojan, 1962-72, turquoise body, spun hubs......***£75-100***
Heinkel Trojan, 1962-72, empty Box for 233........................***£20-25***
Heinkel Trojan, 1962-72, pre-production:
Heinkel Trojan, 1962-72, light blue body, red interior flat spun hubs colour trial..***£100-175***
Heinkel Trojan, 1962-72, NB this was the first Corgi model to have 'By Special Request' flash on the box.

234 **Ford Consul Classic**, 1961-65, beige body, pink roof, lemon interior ***£80-120***
Ford Consul Classic, 1961-65, beige/pink body including base, pink roof, lemon interior..***£80-160***
Ford Consul Classic, 1961-65, gold body..............................***£70-80***

235 **Oldsmobile Super 88**, 1962-66, all with spun hubs.
Oldsmobile Super 88, 1962-66, black body, white side flash...***£90-100***
Oldsmobile Super 88, 1962-66, metallic steel blue, white side flash, red interior...***£90-100***
Oldsmobile Super 88, 1962-66, light blue body, red interior, white side flash ***£130-150***

236 **'CORGI' Motor School**, 1964-68, (Austin A60).
'CORGI' Motor School, 1964-68, light blue body, two figures, 'Highway Code' leaflet, r/h drive..***£110-120***

237 **Oldsmobile Sheriff Car**, 1962-66, two-tone black top on white, red interior, red roof light, round Sheriff transfer on door, spun hubs...***£130-150***

238 **Jaguar Mk10**, 1962-67, all issues have spun hubs, luggage in boot. Blue/yellow box with leaflet.
Jaguar Mk10, 1962-67, pale blue body, red interior ***£100-120***
Jaguar Mk10, 1962-67, mid-green body, red interior....***£100-120***
Jaguar Mk10, 1962-67, pale green body, red interior....***£250-300***
Jaguar Mk10, 1962-67, deep blue body, red interior ***£150-175***
Jaguar Mk10, 1962-67, kingfisher blue body, lemon int.***£100-120***
Jaguar Mk10, 1962-67, sea-green body, red interior ***£200-300***
Jaguar Mk10, 1962-67, metallic blue-grey body, red int. ***£125-150***
Jaguar Mk10, 1962-67, metallic deep blue body, red or lemon interior ***£150-200***
Jaguar Mk10, 1962-67, metallic sea-green body, red int***£175-200***
Jaguar Mk10, 1962-67, metallic cerise body, lemon int.. ***£120-140***
Jaguar Mk10, 1962-67, metallic silver body, red int......***£175-200***
Jaguar Mk10, 1962-67, metallic green body, red int......***£150-200***

239 **VW 1500 Karmann Ghia**, 1963-68, spare wheel/suitcase in boot, spun hubs.
VW 1500 Karmann Ghia, 1963-68, cream body (red interior)...***£80-90***
VW 1500 Karmann Ghia, 1963-68, gold body, red or yellow interior ***£90-100***
VW 1500 Karmann Ghia, 1963-68, red body, white or yellow interior ***£80-90***
VW 1500 Karmann Ghia, 1963-68, plum body, red interior...***£90-100***
VW 1500 Karmann Ghia, 1963-68, orange body, yellow interior...***£130-160***

240 **Fiat 600 Jolly**, 1963-64, spun hubs, two figures.
Fiat 600 Jolly, 1963-64, metallic light blue, silver/red top, red interior ***£150-200***
Fiat 600 Jolly, 1963-64, met. dark blue body, red interior . ***£150-200***
Fiat 600 Jolly, 1963-64, blue body, red interior ***£120-140***
Fiat 600 Jolly, 1963-64, yellow body, red interior ***£140-170***

241 **Chrysler Ghia L64**, 1963-69, all have shaped spun hubs or detailed cast hubs and a Corgi dog on the rear shelf.
Chrysler Ghia L64, 1963-69, met. blue/white body, cream int...***£70-80***
Chrysler Ghia L64, 1963-69, metallic green body, cream interior...***£70-80***
Chrysler Ghia L64, 1963-69, metallic gold body..............***£90-110***
Chrysler Ghia L64, 1963-69, metallic silver blue body, red int...***£120-150***
Chrysler Ghia L64, 1963-69, metallic copper......................***£70-80***
Chrysler Ghia L64, 1963-69, lime green, yellow interior .. ***£100-125***

242 **Ghia Fiat 600**, 1965-66, orange-yellow body, red interior, two figures in swim gear, windscreen but no canopy............***£250-350***

245 **Buick Riviera**, 1964-68, model has 'Trans-O-Lites', towbar.
Buick Riviera, 1964-68, metallic gold body, red interior, spoked hubs...***£100-120***
Buick Riviera, 1964-68, same, but with cast hubs.........***£110-130***
Buick Riviera, 1964-68, metallic steel blue (red interior) ***£70-80***
Buick Riviera, 1964-68, metallic greenish blue body ***£70-80***
Buick Riviera, 1964-68, pale blue body, spun or cast hubs ***£70-80***

246 **Chrysler Imperial Convertible**, 1965-68, shaped spun or detailed cast hubs. All issues should include driver and passenger, golf trolley in boot, blue/yellow box with inner packing. Red car, green car on box.
Chrysler Imperial Convertible, 1965-68, red/deep red body, pale blue or green interior ***£80-140***
Chrysler Imperial Convertible, 1965-68, metallic turquoise body, green interior...***£80-100***

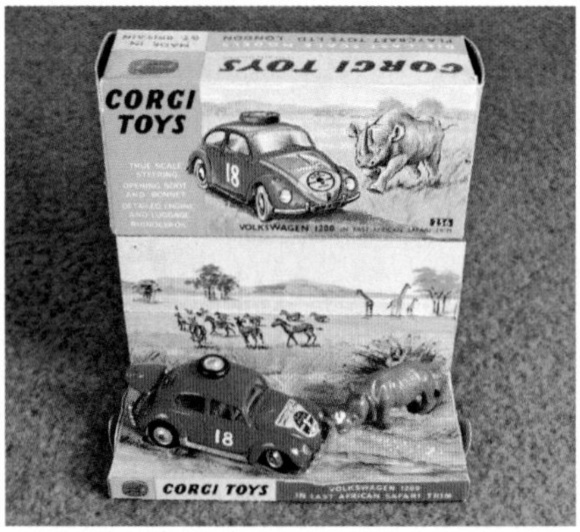

Chrysler Imperial Convertible, 1965-68, metallic blue body, pale blue interior ***£110-130***
Chrysler Imperial Convertible, 1965-68, met. kingfisher blue, green int ***£300-480***

247 **Mercedes-Benz 600 Pullman**, 1964-69, metallic maroon body, cream interior, wind-screen wipers, instruction sheet. ***£100-110***
Mercedes-Benz 600 Pullman, 1964-69, metallic red body, cream interior, spun hubs ***£90-100***

248 **Chevrolet Impala**, 1965-67, light brown body, cream roof/interior, shaped spun hubs...***£90-140***

249 **Morris Mini-Cooper DeLuxe**, 1965-69, black body, red roof, lemon interior, 'Wicker' panels, spun or cast hubs........ ***£125-150***

251 **Hillman Imp**, 1963-66, model has spun hubs and luggage.
Hillman Imp, 1963-66, metallic blue body, yellow int.......***£50-75***
Hillman Imp, 1963-66, metallic bronze body, white side stripe and interior ***£100-150***
Hillman Imp, 1963-66, Danish promotional: 'JENSEN'S', light blue body, yellow interior, logo.................................... ***£1,000-1,200***

252 **Rover 2000**, 1963-66, spun hubs; leaflet in box.
Rover 2000, 1963-66, metallic light blue or steel blue body, red interior ***£90-110***
Rover 2000, 1963-66, metallic maroon body, red or yellow interior ***£250-300***

253 **Mercedes-Benz 220 SE**, 1964-68, maroon body, luggage, spare wheel..***£80-100***
Mercedes-Benz 220 SE, 1964-68, metallic blue, luggage, spare wheel..***£100-110***

255 **Motor School A60**, 1964-68, dark blue body, l/h drive, 5 language leaflet, (Export issue of 236) ***£125-150***

256 **Volkswagen 1200 Rally**, 1965-68, orange body, RN '18', 'EAST AFRICAN RALLY', steering wheel on roof, red/yellow cardboard roof fitting, rhinoceros figure..***£250-300***
Volkswagen 1200 Rally, 1965-68, pre-production: metallic red, cream interior, spun hubs including roof turning disc, with 'Nairobi' rear window decal, factory colour trial............ ***£500-600***

259 **Citroën 'Le Dandy'**, 1966-69, metallic dark red, yellow interior, wire wheels..***£125-150***
Citroën 'Le Dandy', 1966-69, metallic blue body, white roof/boot ***£125-150***

260 **Renault 16 TS**, 1969-69, metallic maroon, yellow interior cast hubs..***£80-100***

262 **Lincoln Continental Executive Limousine**, 1967-69, box should also contain a picture strip for use with the on-board 'TV set'.
Lincoln Continental Executive Limousine, 1967-69, metallic gold, black roof...***£90-100***
Lincoln Continental Executive Limousine, 1967-69, light blue, light tan roof..***£100-125***

263 **Rambler Marlin Sports**, 1966-69, red body, black roof white interior, spun or cast hubs ***£50-75***
Rambler Marlin Sports, 1966-69, white body, blue roof, (GS10 only)...***GSP***

264 **Oldsmobile Toronado**, 1966-69, met. medium or dark blue body, smooth or cast spoked hubs, cream interior ***£50-60***

271 **Ghia Mangusta De Tomaso**, 1969-69, blue/white body, gold stripes ***£40-60***
Ghia Mangusta De Tomaso, 1969-69, orange-red body ***£80-100***

273 **Rolls-Royce silver Shadow**, 1970-71, with 'golden Jacks', 'Take-Off wheels', and a spare wheel.
Rolls-Royce silver Shadow, 1970-71, metallic silver/blue....***£75-95***
Rolls-Royce silver Shadow, 1970-71, pearlescent white over grey, blue int...***£80-100***

273 **Honda Ballade**, 1982-83, 'BSM' Driving School Car.
Honda Ballade, 1982-83, yellow body, red side stripes.... **£25-35**

274 **Bentley 'T' Series**, 1970-72, bright pink body, cream interior, special lights, WhizzWheels..***£40-50***

275 **Rover 2000 TC**, 1968-70, with 'Golden Jacks', 'Take-Off wheels', and a spare wheel.
Rover 2000 TC, 1968-70, metallic olive green body, brown or red interior, amber roof panel...***£70-90***
Rover 2000 TC, 1968-70, same but with white int........... **£90-120**
Rover 2000 TC, 1968-70, white body, maroon interior, amber roof panel...**£150-200**
Rover 2000 TC, 1968-70, metallic maroon body............. **£90-120**
Rover 2000 TC, 1968-70, gold plated version..................**£150-250**

275 **Mini Metro**, 1981-84, blue, purple or red body, yellow int.**£10-15**
Mini Metro, 1981-84, gold body.. **£45-50**
Mini Metro, 1981-84, 'Royal Wedding' metro mauve body, silver 'Charles & Diana' crest, special mauve box ***£20-25***

276 **Oldsmobile Toronado**, 1968-72, with 'Golden Jacks', 'Take-Off wheels'.
Oldsmobile Toronado, 1968-72, met. blue or red body...***£45-65***
Oldsmobile Toronado, 1968-72, metallic gold body, cream interior ***£45-65***
Oldsmobile Toronadoo, 1968-72, metallic green body, cream interior ***£45-65***
Oldsmobile Toronado, 1968-72, metallic brown body, cream interior ***£50-75***

276 **Triumph Acclaim**, 1982-83, metallic blue, or cream body, steering control...***£15-25***

277 **Triumph Acclaim**, 1982-83, 'BSM' Driving School Car.
Triumph Acclaim, 1982-83, yellow body, black 'wheel' steering control on roof...***£15-25***

278 **Triumph Acclaim**, 1982-, 'CORGI MOTOR SCHOOL' Car.
Triumph Acclaim, 1982-, yellow body, with steering control..***£25-35***

279 **Rolls-Royce Corniche**, 1980-, metallic dark red body, opening doors/bonnet/boot...***£20-35***

280 **Rolls-Royce silver Shadow**, 1970-78, metallic silver upper body, blue lower body, brown interior, WhizzWheels...................***£25-35***
Rolls-Royce silver Shadow, 1970-78, met. blue body, brown interior, WW ***£35-40***

281 **Rover 2000 TC**, 1971-7 2, metallic red body, yellow interior, amber or clear roof, WhizzWheels...***£60-75***
Rover 2000 TC, 1971-7 2, purple body, amber roof....... ***£120-140***

281 **'DATAPOST' Metro**, 1982-, blue/white body, RN '77', adverts...***£9-12***

282 **Mini Cooper Rally**, 1971-74, white/black/yellow, number '177', special lights, WhizzWheels ***£55-65***

283 **DAF 'City' Car**, 1971-74, red/black body, white interior, WW...***£20-30***

284 **Citroën SM**, 1970-76, metallic green body, pale blue interior, spoked wheels...***£30-40***
Citroën SM, 1970-76, metallic cerise, pale blue interior, spoked wheels...***£30-40***

285 **Mercedes-Benz 240 D**, 1975-81, silver, blue, bronze or beige (all Metallic), WhizzWheels...***£25-35***

286 **Jaguar XJC V-12**, 1975-79, blue/black, red/black, red, pearl, blue or Orange (all metallic), WW...***£25-35***

287 **Citroën Dyane**, 1975-78, metallic green, duck decal, WW*£25-35*
Citroën Dyane, 1975-78, same metallic yellow/black.......*£25-35*
Citroën Dyane, 1975-78, metallic bronze, duck decal, WW..*£25-35*
288 **Minissima**, 1975-79, beige/black/yellow body *£25-35*
289 **VW Polo 'DBP'** (German issue), 1976-80, yellow/white body, l/h drive, WW...*£55-75*
Volkswagen Polo, 1977-81, lime green or orange body....*£25-35*
VW Polo 'ADAC' (German issue), 1977-81, as previous model but yellow body *£55-75*
291 **AMC Pacer**, 1977-80, met. red, opening doors/hatch........*£20-25*
Mercedes Benz 240 Rally, 1982-, muddy cream body, RN '5', 'EAST AFRICAN.
293 **Renault 5 TS**, 1977-80, orange, silver or silver/blue, WW *£20-25*
Renault 5 TS, 1977-80, RALLY' or 'E.A.R.' logos...................*£20-25*
293 **Renault 5 TS**, 1977-80, orange, silver or silver/blue, WW *£20-25*
294 **Renault 5 TS Alpine**, 1980-84, black body with white stripe.........
....*£25-30*
298 **Magnum P.I. Ferrari 308GTS**, 1982-83, see 'Novelty, Film and TV-related' section.
299 **Ford Sierra 2.3 Ghia**, 1982-, metallic light brown/black stripe, dark brown or grey interior, brown or dark grey base. In special two-tone blue 'Ford' box..*£40-50*
Ford Sierra 2.3 Ghia, 1982-, metallic light brown, metallic blue, red or yellow. Packed in white/red 'Ford' box or normal black/ yellow/red box...*£40-50*
300 **Austin Healey 100-4**, 1956-65, flat spun hubs, leaflet with early issues.
Austin Healey 100-4, 1956-65, red with cream interior. *£175-200*
Austin Healey 100-4, 1956-65, cream with red interior. *£175-200*
Austin Healey 100-4, 1956-65, blue body with cream interior ....
....*£175-200*
Austin Healey 100-4, 1956-65, pale blue with red interior ....
....*£750-900*
300 **Chevrolet Corvette Stingray**, 1970-70, with 'Golden Jacks'/ 'Take-Off Wheels', and luggage. 'Plated' bright green, dark red or green body...*£85-95*
Chevrolet Corvette Stingray, 1970-70, metallic red body, black bonnet *£60-75*
Chevrolet Corvette Stingray, 1970-70, metallic green body, black bonnet *£60-75*
Chevrolet Corvette Stingray, 1970-70, NB models without box header cards contained instructions.
300 **Ferrari 'DAYTONA'**, 1979-82, green, multicoloured flash, RN '5'..
....*£20-25*
301 **Triumph TR2,** 1956-61, cream body, red seats, flat spun hubs......
....*£150-200*
Triumph TR2, 1956-61, red body, cream seats, flat spun hubs.......
....*£150-200*
Triumph TR2, 1956-61, deep green body with cream seats, flat spun hubs *£175-200*
Triumph TR2, 1956-61, cream, red seats, smooth cast hubs..........
....*£150-200*
301 **Iso Grifo 7 litre**, 1970-73, metallic blue body, black bonnet, white interior, silver or black roll-bar, WW............................*£50-75*
301 **Lotus Elite Racing Car**, 1979-82, yellow/red, RN '7', 'FERODO'....
....*£20-25*
302 **MG 'MGA'**, 1957-65, red (shades exist), cream seats, smooth or chrome spun hubs...*£175-200*
MG 'MGA', 1957-65, cream with red seats........................*£200-240*
MG 'MGA', 1957-65, mid or dark metallic green body, cream or yellow seats, smooth or shaped spun hubs......................*£200-225*
302 **Hillman Hunter Rally**, 1969-72, blue body, white roof, matt-black bonnet, RN '75', equipment, kangaroo, 'golden Jacks', transfers, toolbox, leaflet, instructions *£110-140*
302 **VW Polo**, 1979-82, metallic brown/red, RN '4', adverts.....*£20-25*
303 **Mercedes-Benz 300 SL**, 1958-60, (Open Roadster)
Mercedes-Benz 300 SL, 1958-60, off-white body, blue seats, smooth hubs, blue box..*£125-150*
Mercedes-Benz 300 SL, 1958-60, blue body, white seats, smooth hubs, blue box...*£100-125*
Mercedes-Benz 300 SL, 1958-60, cream body, blue seats, smooth hubs, blue box..*£100-125*
Mercedes-Benz 300 SL, 1958-60, NB if in rare plain overprinted box, add...*£20-30*
303S **Mercedes-Benz 300 SL**, 1961-63, (open sports with suspension).
Mercedes-Benz 300 SL, 1961-63, off-white body, yellow interior, red bonnet stripe, flat spun hubs, RNs '1' to '12' *£100-125*
Mercedes-Benz 300 SL, 1961-63, off-white body, light blue interior red bonnet stripe, flat spun hubs *£175-200*
Mercedes-Benz 300 SL, 1961-63, mid-blue body, yellow interior, red bonnet stripe, RNs '1' to '12' *£150-175*
Mercedes-Benz 300 SL, 1961-63, plated finish pale yellow brown interior with driver figure race No.3 detailed cast hubs......
....*£130-160*
Mercedes-Benz 300 SL, 1961-63, first version; blue with white interior or white with blue interior, smooth hubs.
Mercedes-Benz 300 SL, 1961-63, second version; has shaped hubs. No decals.
Mercedes-Benz 300 SL, 1961-63, NB 'Open Sports' models were housed in 303S 'Open Roadster' boxes.
303S2 **Mercedes-Benz 300 SL**, 1963-64, (open sports with driver with suspension).
Mercedes-Benz 300 SL, 1963-64, with driver dressed in grey suit, white shirt and red bow-tie. white body, yellow interior, red bonnet stripe, RNs '1' to '12', shaped spun hubs *£100-130*
Mercedes-Benz 300 SL, 1963-64, blue body, yellow int., red bonnet stripe, RNs '1' to '12', shaped spun hubs *£100-130*
Mercedes-Benz 300 SL, 1963-64, chrome plated body, lemon/ brown interior, Red bonnet stripe, spoked or cast hubs, RNs '1' to '12'..*£175-200*
303 **Roger Clark's Ford Capri**, 1970-72, white body, black bonnet, RN '73', decal sheet, WhizzWheels *£100-140*
Roger Clark's Ford Capri, 1970-72, as previous model but with red spot hubs. yellow/red box with: '9 transfers for you to apply!'
....*£110-170*
304 **Mercedes-Benz 300 SL Hardtop**, 1959-61, yellow body, red hardtop, spun hubs, no suspension..*£100-125*
Mercedes-Benz 300 SL Hardtop, 1959-61, yellow body/top, flat spun hubs *£300-400*
304S **Mercedes-Benz 300 SL Hardtop**, 1961-63, (with Suspension).
Mercedes-Benz 300 SL Hardtop, 1961-63, chrome body, red hardtop, stripe, smooth or shaped hubs, '3' or '7' *£100-130*
Mercedes-Benz 300 SL Hardtop, 1961-63, white body, red hardtop, RN '7', shaped hubs...*£300-400*
304 **Chevrolet Camaro SS350**, 1971-72, dark blue body, white bonnet band, detachable roof, special lights........................*£40-50*
305 **Triumph TR3,** 1960-63, metallic olive green or cream body, red seats, smooth or shaped hubs *£150-175*
305S **Triumph TR3**, 1962-63, (with spring suspension).

Triumph TR3, 1962-63, light green, shaped spun hubs.. *£175-225*
Triumph TR3, 1962-63, cream body, shaped spun hubs
....*£175-225*
305 **Mini Marcos GT 850**, 1972-73, white body, blue/white stripes, red interior, RN '7', WhizzWheels...*£75-100*
306 **Morris Marina 1.8 Coupé**, 1972-73, met. red body, cream interior, WW *£45-55*
Morris Marina 1.8 Coupé, 1972-73, met. lime green, cream int., WW...*£40-45*
306 **Fiat X1/9S**, 1980-81, metallic blue body with red/yellow bands, racing number '3' or '6'..*£15-20*
307 **Jaguar 'E' type**, 1962-64, metallic grey body with red removable hard-top, brown interior, spun hubs, box has inner packing..........
....*£100-125*
Jaguar 'E' type, 1962-64, plum to red body and top, inner packing...*£125-150*
307 **Renault Turbo**, 1981-82, yellow/red body, 'CIBIE', RN '8', adverts
....*£10-15*
308 **Mini Cooper 'S'**, 1972-76, 'MONTE CARLO'.
Mini Cooper 'S', 1972-76, yellow body, '177', two spare wheels on roof-rack, WW (339 update)...*£75-100*
Mini Cooper 'S', 1972-76, gold-plated body (only 144 thought to exist)...*£1,000-1,500*
308 **BMW M1**, 1982-82, yellow/black, '25', 'TEAM BMW' *£10-15*
309 **Aston-Martin DB4 Competition**, 1962-65, turquoise/white body, lemon interior, UK flags on bonnet, spun hubs, RN '1', '3' or '7 ....*£125-150*
Aston-Martin DB4 Competition, 1962-65, variation with spoked hubs *£125-150*
309 **VW 'TURBO**, 1982-, white/orange, RN '14', red decals *£25-30*
310 **Chevrolet Corvette Stingray**, 1963-67, met. cerise, lemon int., shaped hubs *£70-80*
Chevrolet Corvette Stingray, 1963-67, metallic silver body, lemon interior, 'wire' wheels *£70-80*
Chevrolet Corvette Stingray, 1963-67, metallic bronze body, lemon interior, 'wire' wheels *£100-125*
310 **'PORSCHE' 924 Turb**, 1982-, black/gold, 'GOODYEAR'....*£25-35*
311 **Ford Capri V6 3-litre**, 1970-72, orange body, gold wheels with red WW hubs, black interior *£80-100*
Ford Capri V6 3-litre, 1970-72, fluorescent orange, WhizzWheels..*£50-60*
Ford Capri V6 3-litre, 1970-72, fluorescent orange, red WW hubs...*£70-90*
Ford Capri V6 3-litre, 1970-72, red body/WW hubs, black bonnet *£70-90*
312 **'E' type Jaguar**, 1964-68, silver (vacuum plated) body, RN '2', driver, spoked hubs...*£90-120*
Marcos Mantis, 1971-74, met. red, white int., spoked hubs ..*£25-30*
Ford Capri 'S', 1983-, white, '6', hinged parcel shelf, ads..*£20-35*
313 **Ford Cortina GXL**, 1970-73, metallic blue body, black roof, black & white interior, Graham Hill figure, WW..........................*£80-100*
Ford Cortina GXL, 1970-73, metallic bronze body, black roof, white int *£80-100*
Ford Cortina GXL, 1970-73, yellow body, black roof.... *£175-220*
Ford Cortina GXL, 1970-73, metallic pale green body, black roof, white interior...*£80-90*
Ford Cortina GXL, 1970-73, promotional: tan body, black roof, red interior, left-hand drive, 'CORTINA' number plate . *£250-350*
314 **Ferrari Berlinetta 250 LM**, 1965-72, red body, RN '4', wire wheels...*£75-100*
314 **Fiat X1-9**, 1976-79, metallic lime green/black body...........*£25-35*
Fiat X1-9, 1976-79, silver/black body *£25-35*
314 **Supercat Jaguar XJS-HE**, 1982-, black body, red or tan interior...
....*£20-35*
315 **Simca 1000 Sports**, 1964-66, plated silver, red interior, RN '8', red/white/blue racing stripes *£75-100*
Simca 1000 Sports, 1964-66, metallic blue body, RN '8', red/ white/blue stripes *£120-140*
315 **Lotus Elite**, 1964-66, red or yellow with white seats..........*£20-25*
316 **NSU Sport Prinz**, 1963-66, metallic red body, yellow seats, spun hubs...*£50-60*
316 **Ford GT 70**, 1971-73, metallic lime green body, black engine cover, white interior, RN '32', (unapplied) decal sheet........*£30-40*
317 **Mini Cooper 'S'**, 1964-65, 'MONTE CARLO 1964'.
Mini Cooper 'S', 1964-65, red body, white roof, yellow interior, RN '37', roof spotlight. (Paddy Hopkirk)...............................*£200-250*
Mini Cooper 'S', 1964-65, red body, pink roof variation. *£250-300*
318 **Mini Cooper 'S'**, 1965-66, 'MONTE CARLO 1965'.
Mini Cooper 'S', 1965-66, red body, white roof, 'AJB 44B', racing number '52', no roof spotlight...*£175-200*
318 **Lotus Elan S2 Open Top**, 1965-67, metallic Steel blue, RN '6' or '8', driver, 'I'VE GOT A TIGER IN MY TANK', 'tiger' decal, logo on boot lid, blue/yellow box, unapplied decals.....................*£220-280*
Lotus Elan S2 Open Top, 1965-67, white body, black interior, same 'tiger' decal, spun hubs, unapplied decal sheet (RN '7'), figure...*£500-600*
318 **Lotus Elan S2 Open Top**, 1965-68, dark green body, yellow stripe with black or red interior (Gift Set 37)............................*GSP*
Lotus Elan S2 Open Top, 1965-68, white body, black interior (GS40), 'tiger' label, unapplied decals................................*£250-300*
Lotus Elan S2 Open Top, 1965-68, met. copper body, decals sheet..*£200-250*

Lotus Elan S2 Open Top, 1965-68, yellow body, green stripe, black interior, spun hubs.............................**£150-200**

318 **Jaguar XJS**, 1981-, blue/cream body with red line.............**£15-20**

Jaguar XJS, 1981-, 1983-? black/red/white body, RN '4', 'MOTUL', 'JAGUAR'.............................**£15-20**

319 **Lotus Elan S2 Hardtop**, 1967-69, (with racing numbers).

Lotus Elan S2 Hardtop, 1967-69, yellow body (green top), shaped hubs.............................**£100-150**

Lotus Elan S2 Hardtop, 1967-69, blue body (white top), shaped hubs.............................**£100-125**

Lotus Elan S2 Hardtop, 1967-69, red body, white top, cast hubs. **£75-100**

Lotus Elan S2 Hardtop, 1967-69, red body, red top, cast hubs. **£75-85**

Lotus Elan S2 Hardtop, 1967-69, blue body, white top, cast hubs **£40-60**

Lotus Elan S2 Hardtop, 1967-69, green and yellow lift-off body **£75-85**

Lotus Elan S2 Hardtop, 1967-69, red body with white top, WW.. ....**£75-85**

Lotus Elan S2 Hardtop, 1967-69, NB 1967-69 boxed issues should include a sheet of self-adhesive racing numbers '1' to '12'.

319 **Lamborghini P400GT**, 1973-74, metallic silver body, purple/ yellow stripes, RN '7', WW.............................**£25-30**

319 **Jaguar XJS**, 1978-81, met. red body, black roof.............................**£20-35**

320 **Ford Mustang Fastback 2+2**, 1965-67, metallic silver opening doors, suspension, Corgi dog, sliding windows, red interior, detailed cast hubs.............................**£90-110**

Ford Mustang Fastback 2+2, 1965-67, metallic deep blue cream interior detailed cast hubs, spoked hubs.............................**£90-110**

Ford Mustang Fastback 2+2, 1965-67, light green body cream interior, spoked hubs.............................**£100-110**

Ford Mustang Fastback 2+2, 1965-67, metallic lilac body, cream interior spoked hubs.............................**£175-200**

Ford Mustang Fastback 2+2, 1965-67, metallic deep yellow body, black bonnet and interior, cast hubs.............................**£500-750**

321 **Mini Cooper 'S'**, 1965-66, 'MONTE CARLO 1965'.

Mini Cooper 'S', 1965-66, (Timo Makinen). Red body, white roof without spotlight, 'AJB 44B' on bonnet, RN '52'.............**£200-250**

Mini Cooper 'S', 1965-66, same, but in 317 picture box with 'No. 321' and 'MONTE CARLO WINNER' flash **£350-450**

Mini Cooper 'S', 1965-66, red body, white roof with spotlight, RN '52', in 321 regular box.............................**£200-250**

321 **Mini Cooper 'S'**, 1966-67, 'MONTE CARLO 1966'.

Mini Cooper 'S', 1966-67, red body, white roof with RN '2' and 'TIMO MAKINEN' and 'PAUL EASTER' signatures, no spotlight. white sticker on box reads: '1966 MONTE CARLO RALLY AUTOGRAPHED MINI-COOPER 'S' in red lettering.......**£250-350**

Mini Cooper 'S', 1966-67, same but in 321 pictorial box with 'RALLY' text printed in red panel.............................**£350-450**

321 **Porsche 924 Saloon**, 1978-81, metallic green body with hook...... ....**£40-45**

Porsche 924 Saloon, 1978-81, red body.............................**£20-25**

Porsche 924 Saloon, 1978-81, met. light brown body, red interior.............................**£60-70**

322 **Rover 2000**, 1967-67, 'Monte Carlo'.

Rover 2000, 1967-67, met. maroon body, white roof, red int., '136', rally plaques, leaflet.............................**£250-300**

Rover 2000, 1967-67, same model but with green interior *NGPP*

Rover 2000, 1967-67, model boxed in rare 252 box with '322' labels over the box ends.............................**£200-250**

Rover 2000, 1967-67, 'INTERNATIONAL RALLY FINISH' and box flash. Paint shade differences are known.............................**£300-350**

Rover 2000, 1967-67, white body, black bonnet, red interior, white/ orange label on doors with black RN '21', cast hubs. 322 box with red 'ROVER 2000 INTERNATIONAL RALLY FINISH' and box flash. Paint shade differences are known.............................**£300-350**

323 **Citroën DS19**, 1965-66, 'MONTE CARLO 1965'.

Citroën DS19, 1965-66, pale blue with white roof, lemon interior, rally plaques and no. '75', suspension.............................**£200-250**

323 **Ferrari Daytona 365 GTB/4**, 1974-78, white/red/blue body, RN '81'.............................**£20-25**

324 **Marcos Volvo 1800 GT**, 1966-69, white, green bonnet stripes, red interior **£80-100**

Marcos Volvo 1800 GT, 1966-69, blue body, white bonnet stripes, blue interior **£100-125**

Marcos Volvo 1800 GT, 1966-69, white, blue bonnet stripes, red interior **£100-150**

Marcos Volvo 1800 GT, 1966-69, NB boxed models should include an unused decal sheet with RNs '4' and '8'.

324 **Ferrari Daytona Le Mans**, 1973-75, yellow, RN '33', 'A. BAMFORD' **£25-35**

325 **Ford Mustang Competition**, 1965-69, white body, double red stripe on bonnet, roof and boot. Blue interior, spun hubs or 'wire' wheels or cast 'alloy' wheels.............................**£80-120**

Ford Mustang Competition, 1965-69, white body, double red stripe on bonnet, roof and boot plus red side stripe, cast 'alloy' wheels.............................**£200-300**

Ford Mustang Competition, 1965-69, NB an unused sheet of four racing numbers should be enclosed with this model.

325 **Chevrolet Capric**, met. light green or dark green.............**£20-25**

Chevrolet Capric, 1981-, metallic silver over dark blue (US export).............................**£70-80**

327 **MGB GT**, 1967-69, dark red body, blue or light blue interior, spoked wheels, black suitcase, leaflet.............................**£125-150**

327 **Chevrolet Caprice Taxi**, 1980-81, yellow, 'THINK TWA'..**£20-25**

328 **Hillman Imp**, 1966-67, 'MONTE CARLO 1966'.

Hillman Imp, 1966-67, metallic dark blue/white, 'FRW 306 C', rally plaques & No. '107', spun hubs.............................**£175-200**

Hillman Imp, 1966-67, NB if 'HILLMAN IMP 328' yellow/red advertising card is with model, expect price to be 20% higher.

329 **Ford Mustang Rally Car**, 1973-76, (391 special).

Ford Mustang Rally Car, 1973-76, metallic green, white roof, RN '69'.............................**£25-30**

329 **Opel Senator**, 1980-82, dark blue or bronze, opening doors......... ....**£15-20**

Opel Senator, 1980-82, silver body.............................**£25-30**

330 **Porsche Carrera 6**, 1967-69, white body, red bonnet and doors, RN '60', cast hubs, blue engine cover.............................**£60-80**

Porsche Carrera 6, 1967-69, some with RN '1'.............**£80-100**

Porsche Carrera 6, 1967-69, white body, dark blue bonnet and doors, RN '60', cast hubs, orange engine cover.............**£130-150**

331 **Ford Capri GT Rally**, 1974-76, white body, black bonnet and interior, red roof stripe, red/black 'TEXACO' logo, RN '5'..**£40-60**

332 **Lancia Fulvia Zagato**, 1967-69, metallic green, metallic blue, or orange body, cast hubs.............................**£60-70**

Lancia Fulvia Zagato, 1967-69, yellow body, black bonnet **£125-150**

333 **Austin Mini Cooper 'S'**, 1966, 'SUN - RAC Rally'. Leaflet in blue/yellow box.

Austin Mini Cooper 'S', 1966, red body, white roof (without spotlight), RN '21' and 'SUN RAC INTERNATIONAL RALLY' decals, 225 box with white label: '1966 RAC INTERNATIONAL RALLY' in blue. (Tony Fall/Mike Wood).............................**£275-325**

Austin Mini Cooper 'S', 1966, same model but with Morris grille **£500-800**

334 **Mini Cooper 'Magnifique'**, 1968-70, metallic dark blue or green, jewelled lights, sunshine roof, cream int **£50-75**

334 **Ford Escort 1.3 GL**, 1981-, blue, green or yellow body......**£12-15**

Ford Escort 1.3 GL, 1981-, red body with 'AVIS' logo on roof......... ....**£25-35**

335 **Jaguar 4.2 litre 'E' type**, 1968-70, met. dark red body, black int., spoked wheels, wing flap bubble pack.............................**£75-100**

Jaguar 4.2 litre 'E' type, 1968-70, metallic blue, black interior, wing flap bubble pack.............................**£75-100**

Jaguar 4.2 litre 'E' type, 1968-70, orange body, black roof, wing flap bubble pack.............................*NGPP*

336 **James Bond Toyota 2000GI**, 1967-69, see 'Novelty, Film and TV-related' section.

337 **Chevrolet Stock Car**, 1967-69, 'STINGRAY'.

Chevrolet Stock Car, 1967-69, yellow body, red interior, RN '13'.. ....**£75-100**

338 **Chevrolet SS 350 Camaro**, 1968-71, metallic lime green/black red interior gold/black or bronze/black, 'golden Jacks'...**£75-100**

338 **Rover 3500**, 1980-83, metallic blue, red/black or bronze/brown.. ....**£20-35**

339 **Mini Cooper 'S'**, 1967-71, 'MONTE CARLO 1967'.

Mini Cooper 'S', 1967-71, (i) red body, white roof, RN '177', 2 spare wheels on roof-rack, Austin grille, cast hubs, in 227 box with white flash label with: '1967 MONTE-CARLO WINNER B.M.C. MINI-COOPER 'S' in red lettering, red '339' flash on box end.............................**£250-350**

Mini Cooper 'S', 1967-71, (ii) as (i) but shaped spun hubs, slight silver detail.............................**£250-350**

Mini Cooper 'S', 1967-71, (iii) as (i) but with Morris grille.............. ....**£250-350**

Mini Cooper 'S', 1967-71, (iv) as (i) but in 339 picture box with 'Winners' text in red lettering on box front. Special leaflet........... ....**£125-150**

Mini Cooper 'S', 1967-71, (v) as (i) but in 339 box with the 'Winners' text in red panel.............................**£150-175**

Mini Cooper 'S', 1967-71, (vi) as (i) but in blue and yellow window box.

340 **Sunbeam Imp**, 1967-69, 'MONTE CARLO 1967'.

Sunbeam Imp, 1967-69, (i) metallic blue, RN '77', spun or cast hubs, flashed 328 box with '1967 MONTE CARLO SUNBEAM IMP WINNER PRODUCTION CARS UP TO 1000cc' text in blue capitals plus model no. '340'.............................**£150-200**

Sunbeam Imp, 1967-69, (ii) as (i) but in 340 pictorial box with 'Winner' text printed in red on box front plus cast detailed hubs.

Sunbeam Imp, 1967-69, (iii) as (i) but met dark blue body, cast detailed hubs, 'winner' text in red panel on box front..... £250-350

Sunbeam Imp, 1967-69, (iv) as (i) but in plain box with no 'winner' flash £60-80

340 **Rover 'TRIPLEX'**, 1981-84, white/red/blue, RN '1'............ £25-35

341 **Mini Marcos GT 850**, 1968-70, metallic maroon body cream seats, 'Golden Jacks' and 'Take-off' wheels £60-70

341 **Chevrolet Caprice**, 1981-82, red/white/blue body, RN '43', 'STP', white tyres £10-15

342 **Lamborghini P400 Miura**, 1970-72, red body, white interior, black plastic fighting bull figure, WW. 1st type box: blue/yellow with 'Revised specification' label for 'Take-off' wheels £85-95

     Lamborghini P400 Miura, 1970-72, 2nd type box: red/yellow box with 'Revised specification' label £75-100

     Lamborghini P400 Miura, 1970-72, lime green, red interior, bull figure... £75-100

     Lamborghini P400 Miura, 1970-72, pre-production: **Lamborghini P400 Miura**, 1970-72, white body, red interior and spot wheels with pale blue and turquoise plastics also with Lamborghini pin badge mounted on blank original Corgi label.... £700-800

342 **'The Professionals' Ford Capri**, 1970-72, see 'Novelty, Film and TV-related' section.

343 **Pontiac Firebird**, 1969-73, met. silver/black, red seats, gold/red 'Take-Off Jacks', 'Golden Jacks' £35-45

     Pontiac Firebird, 1969-73, with red-hub WhizzWheels £50-60

343 **Ford Capri 3 litre**, 1980-81, yellow or silver body, black designs .. £30-35

344 **Ferrari Dino Sports**, 1969-73, yellow with black doors ('23'), WW.. £40-50

     Ferrari Dino Sports, 1969-73, red with white doors ('30'), WW .. £40-50

     Ferrari Dino Sports, 1969-73, with red-hub WhizzWheels £50-60

345 **MGC GT 'Competition'**, 1969-69, yellow body, black bonnet/ tailgate/interior, spoked wheels, black suitcase. 'MGB GT' on box overprinted 'NEW MGC'. Self-adhesive numbers enclosed. £90-130

     MGC GT 'Competition', 1969-69, orange body, black interior, spoked wheels. In early Car Transporter Gift Sets 41 and 48 only . GSP

345 **Honda Prelude**, 1981-82, metallic blue body, sunshine roof.......... £10-15

     Honda Prelude, 1981-82, cream/green body, sunshine roof.......... £10-15

     Honda Prelude, 1981-82, metallic yellow body, sunshine roof.......... £10-15

346 **Citroën 2cv**, 1982-84, yellow/black body £15-25

     Citroën 2cv, 1982-84, burgundy/black body £15-25

     Citroën 2cv, 1982-84, red/white body £15-25

     Citroën 2cv, 1982-84, grey/red body £15-25

     Citroën 2cv, 1982-84, german promotional: **Citroën 2cv**, 1982-84, yellow, black roof, 'REISGOLD' .. £100-120

347 **Chevrolet Astro Experimental**, 1969-74, met. dark blue body, red-hub WW £75-100

     Chevrolet Astro Experimental, 1969-74, metallic green body, red-hub WW £40-50

     Chevrolet Astro Experimental, 1969-74, as previous but with plain WW £30-40

348 **Ford Mustang 'Pop Art'**, 1968-69, blue body and interior, red/ orange 'Flower-Power' labels, RN '20'. Not shown in catalogues .. £150-175

     Ford Mustang 'Pop Art', 1968-69, light blue body without labels ... £60-70

349 **Morris Mini**, 1967-67, 'POP ART' red body, lemon interior, 4 psychedelic labels, 'MOSTEST' logo, few only made . £2,000-2,750

     Morris Mini, 1967-67, pre-production model.

     Morris Mini, 1967-67, blue body, red int., cast hubs. £1,800-2,000

370 **Ford Cobra Mustang**, 1982-, white/black/red/blue, 'MUSTANG', with or without tailgate stripe... £10-15

     Ford Cobra Mustang, 1982-, white, red interior, blue/red design... £10-15

371 **Porsche Carrera 6**, 1970-73, white/red, RN '60', plated blue engine cover, WWs, (330 update)... £30-40

372 **Lancia Fulvia Zagato**, 1970-72, orange body, black bonnet, black interior, WhizzWheels... £35-45

373 **Peugeot 505**, 1981-, red body, silver or black lining.......... £10-15

374 **Jaguar 'E' type 4.2 litre**, 1970-76, red or yellow, WW, (335 update).. £55-65

374 **Jaguar 'E' type 5.3 litre**, 1973-, yellow or metallic yellow body, 'New' on box label... £55-65

375 **Toyota 2000 GT**, 1970-72, metallic translucent 'candy' blue body, white interior, WW, (modified 336), leaflet...................... £50-60

     Toyota 2000 GT, 1970-72, met. purple body, white int., WW £50-75

     Toyota 2000 GT, 1970-72, met. blue cream int., red spot wheels ... £250-300

376 **Chevrolet Corvette Stock Car**, 1970-72, silver body, racing number '13', 'GO-GO-GO', WW, (337 update)................ £40-50

     Chevrolet Corvette Stock Car, 1970-72, met. blue body, red int., '13', red Spot WW £300-350

377 **Marcos 3 litre**, 1970-72, yellow body, black bonnet stripe and interior, WW, (324 conversion)...................................... £40-50

     Marcos 3 litre, 1970-72, white body, grey sunroof, WW £50-60

     Marcos 3 litre, 1970-72, Metallic blue-green body, black interior, bonnet decal, WhizzWheels.. £35-50

378 **MGC GT**, 1970-72, deep orange body, black bonnet, interior and suitcase, WhizzWheels, (345 update) £80-90

     MGC GT, 1970-72, red, (in GS 20).................................... GSP

378 **Ferrari 308 GTS**, 1982-, red or black, pop-up headlights . £35-50

380 **Alfa Romeo P33**, 1970-74, white, gold rollbar, red seats, WW........ £25-30

     Alfa Romeo P33, 1970-74, white, gold rollbar, orange seats, red Spot wheels £350-400

380 **'BASF' BMW M1**, 1983-, red/white, RN '80', aerofoil........... £15-20

381 **VW Beach Buggy**, 1970-76, met. red/white, blue/white, orange/ white or red/white, 2 maroon surfboards, WW................... £15-30

381 **'ELF' Renault Turbo**, 1983-, red/white/blue, RN '5', 'FACOM' £25-35

     'ELF' Renault Turbo, 1983-, blue/white, number '13', 'ELF' £20-35

382 **Porsche Targa 911S**, 1970-75, metallic silver-blue body, black roof with gold stripe, black interior, WW............................ £30-40

     Porsche Targa 911S, 1970-75, same but with red int............. £35-45

     Porsche Targa 911S, 1970-75, metallic olive-green body, black roof with or without gold stripe, WW.................................... £30-40

382 **Lotus Elite 22**, 1983-, metallic blue body, 'Elite 22'......... £15-20

383 **VW 1200 'Flower Power'**, 1970-76, red with psychedelic Grenadine and green daisy labels on bonnet/doors.......... £40-50

     VW 1200 'Flower Power', 1970-76, red body, green base, white interior, no flower decals.. £25-35

383 **Volkswagen 1200 'ADAC'**, 1970-73, see 'Emergency Vehicles' section.

     Volkswagen 1200 'ADAC', 1970-73, volkswagen 1200 'PTT' yellow/black body, red interior, Swiss................................ £70-90

383 **Volkswagen 1200 Rally**, 1977-78, blue, '5', chequered roof and sides £20-35

383 **Volkswagen 1200**, ??, orange, cream interior WW £30-40

383 **Volkswagen 1200**, ??, yellow, light brown interior WW £50-75

384 **Volkswagen 1200 Rall**, 1978-, blue body, RN '5', chequered stripes £35-45

     Volkswagen 1200 Rall, 1978-, same model but with 'CALEDONIAN AUTOMINOLOGISTS' logo £100-125

     Volkswagen 1200 Rall, 1978-, blue body, cream interior, WW, '40th Anniversary 1938 - 1978' £100-120

384 **Adams Brothers Probe**, 1970-73, red body, silver base, WhizzWheels.. £30-40

     Adams Brothers Probe, 1970-73, metallic gold body, WhizzWheels.. £30-40

     Adams Brothers Probe, 1970-73, green body, white interior........ £30-40

384 **Renault 11 GTL**, 1983-84, dark cream body, (export issue) £25-30

     Renault 11 GTL, 1983-84, maroon or metallic mauve body £25-30

385 **Porsche 917**, 1970-76, metallic blue or red body, RN '3', cast or WhizzWheels, with leaflet... £25-30

386 **Bertone Barchetta**, 1971-74, yellow/black 'RUNABOUT', WW ... £20-25

387 **Corvette Stingray Coupé**, 1970-73, metallic blue body, black bonnet, roof emblem, WhizzWheels................................ £45-55

     Corvette Stingray Coupé, 1970-73, metallic pink body, black bonnet, black interior £35-45

388 **Mercedes-Benz C111**, 1970-74, orange/black body, WhizzWheels.. £20-25

389 **Reliant Bond 'BUG' 700 ES**, 1971-74, orange body, 'BUG' labels, cream interior, WW £35-45

     Reliant Bond 'BUG' 700 ES, 1971-74, lime green body, WhizzWheels.. £65-75

391 **James Bond Ford Mustang**, 1972-72, see 'Novelty, Film and TV-related' section.

392 **Bertone Shake Buggy**, 1973-76, pink and green body, detailed engine, flag, WhizzWheels... £20-30

     Bertone Shake Buggy, 1973-76, yellow body, black or green interior £20-30

393 **Mercedes-Benz 350 SL**, 1972-79, white body, pale blue interior, chrome spoked wheels £25-30

     Mercedes-Benz 350 SL, 1972-79, metallic blue or dark blue body, chrome disc wheels £20-30

Mercedes-Benz 350 SL, 1972-79, metallic green body, brown interior *£65-75*
Mercedes-Benz 350 SL, 1972-79, pre-production:
Mercedes-Benz 350 SL, 1972-79, metallic copper, light blue interior, alloy style Whizzwheels, red and yellow window box *£400-500*

394 **Mercedes-Benz 350 SL**, 1972-77, 'East African Safari Rally' finish. Red body, RN '11', 'CASTROL' and 'JAPAN' logos *£30-35*

395 **Fire Bug**, 1972-73, orange body, WhizzWheels, red/black or pink/black stripe, yellow ladder (381 Beach Buggy) *£20-30*

396 **Datsun 240 Z 'US Rally'**, 1973-76, 'US Rally' finish: red/white body, RN '46','JOHN MORTON' and 'DATSUN' logos *£40-50*

397 **Porsche-Audi 917-10**, 1974-76, white/red body, 'L&M', RN '6', 'CORGI', driver *£25-30*

400 **Volkswagen 1300**, 1974-75, 'CORGI MOTOR SCHOOL'.
Volkswagen 1300, 1974-75, metallic red, roof steering wheel, cones *£80-100*
Volkswagen 1300, 1974-75, metallic blue body *£40-50*
Volkswagen 1300, 1974-75, metallic blue body, 'CORGI FAHR SCHULE', (German) *£75-100*

401 **Volkswagen 1300**, 1975-77, as C400 but with 24 'bollards' and diorama for driving practice *£45-55*

406 **Land Rover '109 WB'**, 1957-63, yellow body, black roof, smooth hubs, thin tyres *£160-200*
Land Rover '109 WB', 1957-63, met. dark blue body, cream roof, smooth or shaped hubs, thin or thick tyres *£80-120*
Land Rover '109 WB', 1957-63, green body with Tan tinplate cover, smooth hubs, thin or thick tyres *£60-70*
Land Rover '109 WB', 1957-63, 'ETENDARD' variant.
Land Rover '109 WB', 1957-63, as previous issue but with 'ETENDARD' decals, plus red/white/green roundels on front wings *£350-450*

406s **Land Rover '109 WB'**, 1963, yellow body, red seats, shaped hubs, suspension *£250-300*

411 **Mercedes Benz 240 D**, 1976-79, orange/black or cream, 'TAXI' on roof *£15-25*
Mercedes Benz 240 D, 1976-79, German issue: black body, red 'TAXI' roof sign, 'TAXI' on doors *£35-45*

415 **Mazda Camper**, 1976-78, red body with drop-down tailboard, white caravan *£25-30*

418 **Austin FX4 'TAXI'**, 1960-65, black, flat or shaped hubs, no driver *£50-60*
Austin FX4 'TAXI', 1960-65, black, flat or shaped hubs, 'younger' driver figure *£40-50*
Austin FX4 'TAXI', 1960-65, black body, flat or shaped hubs, 'older' driver figure *£35-45*
Austin FX4 'TAXI', 1960-65, maroon body, lemon interior, grey base, orange/yellow window box *£80-110*

419 **AMC Jeep CJ-5**, 1978-79, metallic green body with white plastic top, or metallic dark green body *£25-35*

420 **Ford Thames 'Airborne' Caravan**, 1978-79, two-tone green, brown interior *£100-140*
Ford Thames 'Airborne' Caravan, 1978-79, blue/cream, red interior *£175-200*
Ford Thames 'Airborne' Caravan, 1978-79, blue/green, brown interior *£100-140*
Ford Thames 'Airborne' Caravan, 1978-79, two-tone Lilac, beige interior *£100-140*

421 **Land Rover Safari**, 1977-80, orange body, black roof rack with ladder, spare wheel *£20-25*
Land Rover Safari, 1977-80, red body, white roof rack with ladder, 'FOREST FIRE WARDEN' logo *£20-25*
Land Rover Safari, 1977-80, Land Rover Workman's Bus yellow/red body, no rack or ladder .... *NGPP*

424 **Ford Zephyr Estate**, 1961-65, pale blue body, dark blue bonnet and side flash, lemon interior, luggage, flat or shaped spun hubs *£50-75*

425 **London Taxi (FX4)**, 1978-, black body, 'TAXI', WW *£10-15*
London Taxi (FX4), 1978-, maroon body, red int., WW *£80-100*

430 **Ford Bermuda 'TAXI'**, 1978-, (Ford Thunderbird).
Ford Bermuda 'TAXI', 1978-, white body, yellow/red canopy *£100-130*
Ford Bermuda 'TAXI', 1978-, white body, Lime green/red canopy *£100-130*
Ford Bermuda 'TAXI', 1978-, white body, blue and red canopy *£100-130*
Ford Bermuda 'TAXI', 1978-, metallic blue body, red canopy *£200-300*

436 **Citroën ID19 'SAFARI'**, 1963-65, yellow body, driver and passenger, detailed interior, roof luggage *£100-120*

436 **Citroën ID19 Safari Hearse**, ??, pre production trial colour black, a driver and a coffin *£2,500-3,000*

438 **Land Rover 109 WB**, 1963-77, model has plastic canopy. Earlier issues have metal towhooks (plastic later), suspension.
Land Rover 109 WB, 1963-77, dark green body grey or tan/cream canopy, lemon or red interior, shaped hubs *£100-125*
Land Rover 109 WB, 1963-77, dark green body cream canopy, lemon interior, spun hubs *£175-200*
Land Rover 109 WB, 1963-77, dark brown body, Lt. brown canopy, red interior, shaped hubs *£100-125*
Land Rover 109 WB, 1963-77, metallic green body, olive-green canopy, yellow interior, shaped hubs *£100-150*
Land Rover 109 WB, 1963-77, metallic green body, olive-green canopy, Chrome hubs *£60-80*
Land Rover 109 WB, 1963-77, metallic green body, olive-green canopy, WhizzWheels *£60-70*
Land Rover 109 WB, 1963-77, red body, brown tilt, red interior, shaped hubs *£60-70*
Land Rover 109 WB, 1963-77, tan body, cream plastic canopy, red interior, spun hubs *£100-125*
Land Rover 109 WB, 1963-77, light blue body, cream plastic tilt spun hubs (Gift Set issue). No box. *£130-150*
Land Rover 109 WB, 1963-77, red body, cream plastic tilt, lemon interior, spun hubs (Gift Set issue) *£50-75*
Land Rover 109 WB, 1963-77, tan body, cream plastic tilt, red interior, spun hubs (Gift Set issue) *£50-75*
Land Rover 109 WB, 1963-77, 'LEPRA' variant:
Land Rover 109 WB, 1963-77, metallic green body, cream or olive green canopy with 'LEPRA' logo, yellow interior, shaped hubs, silver steering wheel *£300-400*
Land Rover 109 WB, 1963-77, red body, blue canopy, (in Gift Set 19) .... *GSP*
Land Rover 109 WB, 1963-77, promotional issue:
Land Rover 109 WB, 1963-77, white body, red interior, grey base, knobbly black plastic wheels, white body, red interior, grey base, knobbly black plastic wheels, "10 millionth Corgi Land Rover" paper sticker decals to doors *£50-75*
Land Rover 109 WB, 1963-77, promotional issue:
Land Rover 109 WB, 1963-77, dark green body, grey plastic canopy, lemon interior, spun hubs, tow hook ,green and yellow 'BP' decals to side doors. With white lift off lid box with "BP" label to front also with "BP" British Racing Circuits booklet and "BP Motor Sport 1964" booklet, plus chrome ashtray *£200-250*

440 **Ford Consul Cortina Super Estate**, 1966-69, metallic dark blue with brown side panels, cream interior, plastic golfer, caddie and trolley *£125-175*

441 **'GOLDEN EAGLE' Jeep**, 1979-83, brown/tan or gold/white, spare wheel on some *£15-20*

443 **Plymouth US Mail Car**, 1963-66, white, mid blue bonnet and side flash, red interior, spun hubs 'Address Your Mail Carefully' on doors *£100-120*

445 **Plymouth Suburban**, 1963-66, Sports Station Wagon.
Plymouth Suburban, 1963-66, pale blue or eggshell blue body, red roof, lemon interior, silver stripe, spun hubs *£90-130*
Plymouth Suburban, 1963-66, beige body, tan roof *£55-65*

447 **'RENEGADE' 4x4 Jeep**, 1983-, yellow, RN '5' (As 448 but without hood). Gift Set 36 model .... *GSP*

448 **'RENEGADE' 4x4 Jeep**, 1983-, yellow body, red hood, RN '5' *£10-15*

450 **Peugeot Taxi** (French issue), 1983-, beige with blue label, '739:33:33' *£30-35*

451 **Ford Sierra Taxi**, ??, ??, cream body *£20-30*

457 **Talbot Matra Rancho**, 1981-83, red/black or green/black, tilt seats *£10-15*
Talbot Matra Rancho, 1984-, orange/black or white/blue body, brown seats *£20-25*

475 **Citroën Safari 'Olympic Winter Sport'**, 1964-65, white/yellow Citroën Safari, '1964', roof-rack, skier, skis. Diorama 'By Special Request' box *£90-110*

475 **Citroën Safari 'CORGI SKI CLUB'**, 1965-68, Citroën Safari with Off-white body, red roof-rack, 4 yellow skis and 2 poles, bonnet transfer, brown dashboard/rear seats, green front seats ... *£90-110*
Citroën Safari 'CORGI SKI CLUB', 1965-68, white body, yellow Roof-rack, 4 red skis and 2 poles, green dashboard/rear seats, brown front seats *£110-130*

480 **Chevrolet Impala Taxi**, 1965-66, yellow body, red roof, spun hubs *£75-100*
Chevrolet Impala Taxi, 1965-66, same but detailed cast wheels *£75-100*

485 **Mini Countryman with Surfer**, 1965-69, sea-green body, lemon interior, 2 surfboards on roof-rack, male figure, special leaflet *£90-120*
Mini Countryman with Surfer, 1965-69, same but with unpainted grille shaped or cast wheel hubs *£100-150*

491 **Ford Consul Cortina Estate**, 1966-69, all have brown/cream side/rear panels.

Ford Consul Cortina Estate, 1966-69, metallic red, metallic blue...£90-110
Ford Consul Cortina Estate, 1966-69, met dark grey.......£90-110
Ford Consul Cortina Estate, 1966-69, NB no golf equipment issued with this model (see 440).

499 Citroen '1968 Winter Olympics', 1967-69, white/blue, 'Grenoble Olympiade', red or yellow roof rack, yellow or red skis/poles, male tobogganist, female skier. Blue/yellow 'window' box, instruction sheet.....................................£150-200

507 Chrysler Bermuda Taxi, 1969, pre-production model finished in Kingfisher blue, cast hubs, chrome trim decals to bonnet and side, complete with luggage, this model was never issued, can be seen in the 1969 catalogue (without canopies) includes three extra figures and luggage case.....................£800-1,200

510 Team Manager's Car, 1970-73, red Citroën, 'Tour De France', figures, spare wheels, 'Paramount'.....................£100-120

513 Citroën Safari 'Alpine Rescue', 1970-72, white/red car, yellow roof-rack, St Bernard, sled, skis, male figure. blue/yellow 'window' box.....................................£150-200

2894 VW Polo 'Deutsche Bundespost', ??, no details.............£40-50

2895 VW Polo 'PTT', ??, no details.............................£40-50

CORGI LARGE SCALE MODELS 1/35

Presented in yellow/red endflap boxes each displaying an excellent picture of the model contained within.

Handcart, 19??, With 'MILK' logo and Milkman.........................£150-175

718 Paxton Observation Coach, 1956-58, metallic blue and gold body with silver raised roof section and base, red door with brown plastic male passenger. Destination board shows 'PRIVATE' and registration 'MTY 718'...............£250-350
1956-58, metallic brown and pink body with silver raised roof section and radiator, with green female passenger.....£200-300

810 Jowett Javelin, 1948-51, cream, red or green body, red interior, 'MTY 810', clockwork............................£100-200

820 Streamline Bus, 1948-51, cream, green or red body, clockwork mechanism, red pressed tin seating, solid rubber wheels, unpainted chassis. Registration No 'MTY 820'.........£200-250
1948-51, as previous model but with opening door, registration No. 'MTY 720'..£200-250

830 Racing Car, 1948-51, light green, 6" long approx, 'METTOY' cast in base, tinplate hollow printed wheels with motor and brake......£100-200

840 Articulated Lorry, 1948-58, metallic blue cab with grey rear body, silver radiator and hubs........................£350-400

850 Fire Engine, 1948-51, red body, silver ladder, crank.....£100-200
1948-51, red body, silver extending ladder, no crank.....£100-200

860 Tractor, 1948-51, no models seen but shown in 1951 catalogue with yellow/red body.......................................NPP

863 Ferguson TE20 Tractor and Trailer, 1950, red/blue tractor, yellow trailer, red hubs, painted plastic driver..............£200-300

870 Delivery Van, 1948-51, plain, without advertising, dark blue, cream, green or red.......................................£200-300
Delivery Vans, 1952-55, with advertising or logo 'EXPRESS DELIVERY' yellow or blue body with red logo and design on sides, clockwork.......................................£300-350
'POST OFFICE TELEPHONES', 1955-58, green body, white logo, Royal crest in gold, silver two part extending ladder.....£300-500
'ROYAL MAIL', 1955-58, red body, silver trim, yellow logo and Royal crest, 'MTY 870'................................£300-500
'AMBULANCE', 1955-58, cream, blue logo on sides.....£200-300
'BOAC', 1956-58, blue body, silver trim, white 'Fly By BOAC' on roof...£400-600

920 Luxury Motor Coach, red with silver wheel flash, clear plastic see-through top showing red seats, with movable figures and luggage. Illustrated box............................£75-100

Special 1/18 scale issue for Marks and Spencer
'VANWALL' Racing Car, 1958, diecast body, perspex screen, driver, VANWALL' transfers, 'push and go' motor in some. 'The famous British Racing Car Grand Prix Winner' cast in base. green body, racing number '7' or '18', no Mettoy logo on base...£200-250
1958, French blue body, racing number '20', no Mettoy logo on base..£450-500
1958, red body, racing number '7' or '5' no Mettoy logo on base.....£350-450
1958, cream body, race No. unknown......................NGPP

Small scale models 1/45
Karrier Bantam Soft Drinks Van, 1955-57, dark red body, number plate 'CWS 300', spun huns, logo on rear: 'CWS SOFT DRINKS - THIRST COME - THIRST- SERVED'.......................................£300-400

'Miniature Numbers' series
502 Standard Vanguard Saloon, 1951, shown with green body in catalogue, (2 7/8" inches long).......................£60-90
505 Rolls-Royce Saloon, 1951, red or blue body, 3"...........£60-90
510 Standard Vanguard Police Car, 1951, black with white 'POLICE' logo on doors; roof siren and bell.............£60-90
511 Standard Vanguard Taxi, 1951, shown in 1951 catalogue with yellow body and red roof rack........................£60-90
512 Standard Vanguard Fire Chief, 1951, red, white 'FIRE CHIEF' on doors; single silver ladder on roof.................£60-90

Larger versions:
602 Standard Vanguard Saloon, 1951, blue body shown in catalogue (larger version of 502, 4¼")....................£60-90

603 Standard Vanguard Saloon, 1951, as 602 but with automatic 'to and fro' bump feature.....................................£60-90
605 Rolls-Royce Saloon, 1951, yellow body shown in catalogue (larger version of 505, 4½")...............................£60-90
606 Rolls-Royce Saloon, 1951, as 605 but with automatic 'to and fro' bump feature...£60-90

Corgi Toys 'Cars of the 1950s' Series
801 1957 Ford Thunderbird, 1982, white/tan, cream/orange or cream/black...£10-20
802 Mercedes 300 SL 1982, 1982, burgundy or silver, suspension...£10-20
Mercedes 300 SL 1982, 1982, red body, no suspension.......£10-20
803 1952 Jaguar XK120 Sports, 1983, red body/black hood...£10-20
803/1 Mercedes 300 SL 1982, 1983, cream body, RN '56'............£10-20
Mercedes 300 SL 1982, 1983, white body, rally number '56'..£10-20
804 Jaguar 'Coupé des Alpes', 1983, cream/Grey, RN '56' or '414', some have rear wheel 'spats'.............................£10-20
805 Mercedes 300 SL 1982, 1983-87, black body, Tan hood....£10-20
Mercedes 300 SL 1982, 1983-87, maroon body.............£10-20
Mercedes 300 SL 1982, 1983-87, beige body and hood.....£10-20
Mercedes 300 SL 1982, 1983-87, grey, black hood, (export)..£10-20
806 1956 Mercedes 300SL, 1983-86, black body, grey/black hood.......£10-20
1956 Mercedes 300SL, 1983-86, black/green body, beige seats.....£10-20
1956 Mercedes 300SL, 1983-86, red, cream int., export...£10-20
1956 Mercedes 300SL, 1983-86, blue body.................£10-20
810 1957 Ford Thunderbird, 1983-87, white, pink, red.........£10-20
1957 Ford Thunderbird, 1983-87, cream body, orange roof.....£10-20
1957 Ford Thunderbird, 1983-87, black/white, red/white int......£10-20
811 954 Mercedes SL, 1984-87, silver, red....................£10-20
954 Mercedes SL, 1984-87, grey/black body, export model......£15-25
812 1953 MG TF, 1985, green/tan sides.......................£10-20
813 1953 MG TF, 1985-87, red/black..........................£10-20
1953 MG TF, 1985-87, cream/red, export model............£10-20
814 1952 Rolls-Royce Silver Dawn, 1985-86, red/black........£10-20
1952 Rolls-Royce Silver Dawn, 1985-86, white/beige.....£10-20
1952 Rolls-Royce Silver Dawn, 1985-86, silver/black, export model........£15-25
815 1954 Bentley 'R' type, 1985-86, black or cream body........£10-20
1954 Bentley 'R' type, 1985-86, dark blue and light blue body....£10-20
1954 Bentley 'R' type, 1985-86, cream/brown, export model.........£15-25
White body, black roof..................................£10-20
816 1956 Jaguar XK120, 1985, red body, black tonneau, '56'...£10-20
1956 Jaguar XK120, 1985, red body, cream hardtop.........£10-20
819 949 Jaguar XK120, 1985, white body, black hood, '7'......£10-20
825 1957 Chevrolet Bel Air, 1985-87, red body, white roof and flash..£10-20
1957 Chevrolet Bel Air, 1985-87, black/white, export model.......£10-20
869 MG TF Racing Car, 1987, royal blue body, beige seats, RN '113' £10-20
870 Jaguar XK120, 1986, green body, yellow seats, RN '6', export model....£15-25

'CORGI CLASSICS' CARS (ORIGINAL MID-1960S ISSUES)
ORIGINAL ISSUES. A factory fire ended production in 1969 of this original series of 'Classics' cars. Boxes are of two types: one with separate lid with coloured line-drawings printed on it and containing a separate picture of the model; and type two which has the model attached to a sliding-drawer style base in an outer box with half-flaps (similar printing to 1st type). Early issues have reference numbers '901' onwards which were changed to '9001' etc just before release.

9001 **1927 3-litre Bentley**, 1964-69, British Racing green, RN '3', detachable hood, drive £30-50

1927 3-litre Bentley, 1964-69, four examples as above still sealed in original factory shrink wrap £140-160

9002 **1927 3-litre Bentley**, 1964-68, red body, civilian driver, no RN, detachable hood £30-50

9004 **'WORLD OF WOOSTER' Bentley**, 1967-69, as previous model but in green or red and with Jeeves and Wooster figures.£90-100

9011 **1915 Model 'T' Ford**, 1964-68, black body, driver, passenger, brass radiator £30-50

Pre-production: chrome plated body, black seats, with two figures, red wheels with white & yellow original box without labels £100-125

9012 **Model 'T' Ford**, 1965-68, yellow/black body, black or yellow wheels £30-50

9013 **1915 Model 'T' Ford**, 1964-69, blue/black body, detachable hood, spare wheel, driver cranks £30-50

9014 **1915 'LYONS TEA' Van**, 1967, appeared in 1967/68 catalogue but was not issued ....NPP

9021 **1910 38 hp Daimler**, 1964-69, red body, driver and three passengers, folded hood £30-50

9022 **1910 38 hp Daimler**, 1966, appeared in the 1966 catalogue but not issued ....NPP

9031 **1910 Renault 12/16**, 1965-68, lavender/black body with carriage lamps £30-50

9032 **1910 Renault 12/16**, 1965-69, same model but primrose yellow and black body £30-50

9041 **1912 Rolls-Royce Silver Ghost**, 1966-70, silver and black body, carriage lamps, spoked wheels £30-50

Maroon body, silver roof and bonnet........................£75-85

RE-INTRODUCED ISSUES.
Four of the 'Classics' were re-introduced in 1985 when original tools were discovered. They have new numbers, 'SPECIAL EDITION' on their baseplates and are packed in Grey/red boxes which do not contain a picture of the model. 13,500 of each colour were made.

C860 (9041) 1912 Rolls-Royce Silver Ghost, silver, black or ruby red body...£20-25

C861 (9002) 1927 3-litre Bentley open top, British Racing green, black or Ruby Red body £20-25

C862 (9031) 1910 Renault 12/16, yellow, pale blue, cream or brown body £20-25

C863 (9012) 1915 Model 'T' Ford, black, red or blue body £20-25

CORGI TOYS DUO PACKS
These packs combine standard models with (mainly) similar 'Junior' models. Launched early in 1982 in France with the name 'Les Plus de Corgi', the packs later became available in the UK in Woolworths as 'Little and Large; the Little One Free'. See also 'Novelty, Film and TV-related' section for additional details.

53	Triple Pack (1982), 'Stunt Bikes':	
171	**Street Bike**	*NGPP*
172	**Police Bike**	*NGPP*
173	**Café Racer**	*NGPP*
173	**'Les Plus de Corgi' Duo Pack range:**	
1352	**Renault 5 (307) Metro (C275)**	*£25-30*
1353	**Austin Metro**	*£20-30*
1354	**Texaco Lotus (C154) Junior 53**	*£30-60*
1355	**Talbot Matra Rancho (457)**	*£30-60*
1356	**Fiat XI/9 (306)**	*£30-60*
1357	**Golden Eagle Jeep (C441)**	*£30-60*
1358	**Citroën 2CV**	*£20-30*
1359	**Ford Escort (334), Junior 105**	*£30-60*

F.W. Woolworth's 'Little & Large' Promotional Duo Pack selection:

1352	**Renault 5 (307) Metro (C275)**	*£50-75*
1353	**Austin Metro**	*£30-60*
1355	**Talbot Matra Rancho (457)**	*£30-60*
1356	**Fiat XI/9 (306)**	*£30-60*
1359	**Ford Escort (334), Junior 105**	*£30-60*
1363	**Buck Rogers (607)**	*£50-60*
1364	**Space Shuttle 'NASA' (648)**	*£50-60*
1365	**469 Routemaster Bus, E71 taxi**	*£20-30*
1371	**Volkswagen Turbo (309)**	*£30-60*

Other Duo Packs (most available in UK)

1364	**Space Shuttle 'NASA' (648)**	*£50-60*
1365	**469 Routemaster Bus, E71 Taxi**	*£30-60*
1372	**Jaguar XJS (319)**	*£30-60*
1373	**Ford Capri (312) Junior 61**	*£30-60*
1376	**Starsky & Hutch**	*£75-100*
1378	**Porsche 924,** yellow	*£30-60*
1380	**Mercedes 240D,** metallic grey.	*£30-60*
1381	**Ferrari 308GTS,** red	*£30-60*
1382	**Ford Mustang (320)**	*£30-60*
1383	**Mack Fire Pumper**	*£30-60*
1384	**Ford Thunderbird,** cream/orange	*£30-60*
	Ford Thunderbird, cream/black	*£30-60*
1385	**Austin Metro 'DATAPOST'**	*£30-60*
1389	**Ford Sierra (299) Junior 129**	*£30-60*
1390	**Porsche 924,** black	*£30-60*
1393	**447 Jeep and E182 Jeep**	*£30-60*
1394	**448 Jeep and E183 Jeep**	*£30-60*
1395	**495 Mazda, E184 Range Rover**	*£30-60*
1396	**Space Shuttle**	*£30-60*
1397	**BMW M1 'BASF' (380)**	*£30-60*
1400	**Lotus Elite and E10 TR7**	*£30-60*
1402	**1133 Tipper plus E85 Skip Truck**	*£30-60*
1403	**Mercedes Tanker, E185 Van**	*£30-60*
1405	**Jaguar**	*£30-60*

Corgi Toys Commercial Vehicles, 1959–1983 See also 'Novelty, Film and TV-related' section.

100 **Dropside Trailer,** 1957-65, cream/red or yellow body, wire drawbar or fixed towing 'eye', blue box £50-60
Dropside Trailer, 1957-65, yellow and blue box............£50-60

101 **Dropside Trailer,** 1958-63, grey/yellow or silver/blue or silver/lemon body...£60-70

109 **'PENNYBURN' Trailer,** 1968-69, blue body, yellow chassis, tools include: shovel, pick-axe & brush, plastic towing 'eye', leaflet yellow & blue box £40-50

403 **Bedford 12 cwt Van,** 1956-60, 'DAILY EXPRESS' dark blue, box with leaflet...£100-150
Bedford 12 cwt Van, 1956-60, same model but deep blue body ...
....£150-175

403M **Bedford 12 cwt Van,** 1956-60, 'KLG PLUGS', with flywheel motor
....£150-175
Bedford 12 cwt Van, 1956-60, bright red body, leaflet in box ....
....£200-250

403 **Thwaites Skip Dumper,** 1974-79, yellow/green tipping body, driver, WhizzWheels...£20-30

404 **Bedford Dormobile,** 1956-62, smooth or ribbed roof, smooth or shaped hubs. Early issues have divided windscreen. Blue box with leaflet...£20-30
Bedford Dormobile, 1956-62, cream, a blue roof on some ....
....£120-140
Bedford Dormobile, 1956-62, turquoise £120-140
Bedford Dormobile, 1956-62, blue £100-120
Bedford Dormobile, 1956-62, red or metallic red £120-140
Bedford Dormobile, 1956-62, yellow body, pale blue roof ....
....£200-250
Bedford Dormobile, 1956-62, yellow lower half, blue upper half
....£200-250
Bedford Dormobile, 1956-62, all-yellow body, with suspension ..
....£100-150
Bedford Dormobile, 1956-62, cerise, split windscreen
....£100-130

404M **Bedford Dormobile,** 1956-60, (with flywheel motor)..£100-130
Bedford Dormobile, 1956-60, blue box also contains leaflet........
....£100-130
Bedford Dormobile, 1956-60, red or metallic red £160-200
Bedford Dormobile, 1956-60, turquoise body.................£160-200
Bedford Dormobile, 1956-60, blue body..........................£160-230

405 **Ford Transit Milk Float,** 1981, 'DAIRY CREST'.................£20-30
Ford Transit Milk Float, 1981, 'MILK MARKETING BOARD' on each side and 'MILK' on rear...£20-30
Ford Transit Milk Float, 1982, blue/white, 'LOTTA BOTTLE' ......
....£10-15

406 **Mercedes-Benz Unimog,** 1971-75, yellow/green body, blue interior £25-35
Mercedes-Benz Unimog, 1971-75, yellow/red body with blue interior £25-35
Mercedes-Benz Unimog, 1971-75, blue/red body with blue interior £25-35
Mercedes-Benz Unimog, 1971-75, pre-production £25-35
Mercedes-Benz Unimog, 1971-75, white chassis, maroon body, brown plastic tilt, maroon hubs are painted silver to outside including axle ends, chassis/body secured with slotted round head bolts £75-90
Mercedes-Benz Unimog, 1971-75, pre-production: £75-90
Mercedes-Benz Unimog, 1971-75, yellow, white cab, yellow rear body, 'Recycling' to sides, black chassis, grey drive train, hubs are painted sliver including axle ends £75-90
Land Rover (109 WB), 1957-63, yellow, black roof, smooth cast hubs, silver detail...£90-120
Land Rover (109 WB), 1957-63, metallic blue, white roof, smooth cast hubs..£100-130

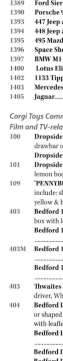

407 Smiths Karrier Bantam, 1957-62, 'HOME SERVICES HYGIENIC MOBILE SHOP'...........£100-130
Smiths Karrier Bantam, 1957-62, pale blue body, red logo, smooth hubs £100-125
Smiths Karrier Bantam, 1957-62, off white body, smooth hubs....£120-150

409 Forward Control Jeep, 1959-65, light blue body, red grille, smooth or shaped hubs £70-90
Unimog Dumper, 1976-77, white/red or blue/yellow body, suspension, hook £20-30
Unimog Dumper, 1976-77, pre-production £20-30
Unimog Dumper, 1976-77, blue/white, black plastic wheels with painted silver hubs and axle ends, plastic chassis to tractor unit has two slotted bolts to secure...........£75-100
'ALLIS CHALMERS' Forklift, 1981-?, yellow body, pallets/load/driver...........£15-20
'ALLIS CHALMERS' Forklift, 1981-?, promotional for Allis Chalmers...........£15-20
'Unimog Dumper, 1981-?, black/white body pallets/load/driver red/white closed box...........NGPP

411 Karrier Bantam Van, 1958-62, 'LUCOZADE'...........NGPP
Karrier Bantam Van, 1958-62, yellow body, grey shutter, smooth hubs, blue box...........£130-150
Karrier Bantam Van, 1958-62, shaped hubs, blue/yellow box...........£120-140

413 Smiths Karrier Bantam, 1960-64, mobile butchers...£120-140
Smiths Karrier Bantam, 1960-64, white/blue van, spun hubs, 'FAMILY BUTCHERS', meaty decals, blue box w/leaflet £150-175
Smiths Karrier Bantam, 1960-64, same model but with suspension £125-150
Mazda Motorway Maintenance, 1976-78, yellow/black body, figure, road signs, bollards, decal sheet enclosed, (modified 478/493)...........£20-35

417 Land Rover, 1960-62, 'BREAKDOWN SERVICE'...........£20-35
Land Rover, 1960-62, red body, yellow tinplate canopy, spun hubs...........£75-100

417s Land Rover, 1963-65, 'BREAKDOWN SERVICE' (with suspension)...........£75-100
Land Rover, 1963-65, red body, yellow tinplate canopy, lemon interior, shaped hubs...........£160-190

420 Ford Thames Airborne Caravan, 1962-66, pale green top, metallic olive green bottom, brown interior, spun hubs .£80-100
Ford Thames Airborne Caravan, 1962-66, lilac top, mauve bottom, dark cream interior spun hubs...........£100-120
Ford Thames Airborne Caravan, 1962-66, off white top, blue bottom, cream interior, red table...........£100-120

421 Bedford 12 cwt Van, 1960-63, 'EVENING STANDARD' £100-120
Bedford 12 cwt Van, 1960-63, black body, silver ridged roof, smooth hubs, undivided windscreen...........£150-175
Bedford 12 cwt Van, 1960-63, black lower body, silver upper and roof...........£110-130
Bedford 12 cwt Van, 1960-63, medium blue body, 'AVRO BODE' logo...........£250-300

422 Bedford 12 cwt Van, 1960-62, 'CORGI TOYS'...........£250-300
Bedford 12 cwt Van, 1960-62, yellow body, blue roof, smooth or shaped hubs...........£300-350
Bedford 12 cwt Van, 1960-62, reversed colours: blue body, yellow roof, smooth hubs...........£400-500
Bedford 12 cwt Van, 1960-62, variation: blue lower half with yellow upper body and roof...........£400-500

424 Security Van, 1977-79, black/yellow/white, 'SECURITY'.£15-25

426 Chevrolet Booking Office, 1978-81, van 'PINDER'...£15-25
Chevrolet Booking Office, 1978-81, yellow/red body, 'PINDER JEAN RICHARD', WW, two loudspeakers £35-45
Chevrolet Booking Office, 1978-81, NB the 'clown's face' poster may be at the front or the rear on the n/s of the model. ...£35-45

428 Karrier Ice-cream Van, 1963-66, 'MR SOFTEE'...........£35-45
Karrier Ice-cream Van, 1963-66, blue/white body, detailed chassis, salesman swivels...........£200-300

431 Volkswagen Pick-Up, 1964-66, yellow body, red or olive-green canopy, red 'VW' emblem...........£100-150
Volkswagen Pick-Up, 1964-66, met. gold body, red 'VW' emblem, red canopy and interior, spun hubs...........£400-600

431, 432, 433 Chevrolet Vans, 1964-66, ('VANATIC', 'VANTASTIC' and 'VANISHING POINT'). See 'Novelty' section...........£400-600

433 Volkswagen Delivery Van, 1962-64, red/white body, red or yellow interior...........£100-150
Volkswagen Delivery Van, 1962-64, promotional issue: Dutch 'VROOM & DREESMANN', grey body, spun hubs...........£350-450

434 Volkswagen Kombi, 1962, metallic pale grey over green body, red interior, spun hubs...........£90-120
Volkswagen Kombi, 1962, two-tone green, red or yellow interior...........£65-80

435 Karrier Bantam Van, 1962-63, blue/white/yellow, 'DRIVE SAFELY ON MILK'...........£100-120

437 Chevrolet Van 'COCA-COLA', 1979-80, red body, white logo, tinted roof windows, crates...........£15-20

440 Mazda Custom Pick-Up, 1979-80, orange/yellow/red, US flag...........£20-30
Mazda Custom Pick-Up, 1979-80, metallic blue and silver..£20-30

441 Volkswagen Van, 1963-67, 'CHOCOLATE TOBLERONE' Blue body, lemon interior, 'Trans-o-lite' headlamps ...£130-150

447 'WALLS ICE CREAM' Van, 1965-66, blue/cream Ford Thames van, salesman, boy, spare transfers. Blue/yellow card box, inner base, correct folded leaflet, unapplied decal sheet...........£350-500

450 Austin Mini Van, 1964-67, green body with unpainted grille, red interior...........£130-160
Austin Mini Van, 1964-67, green body, painted grille, red interior...........£130-160
Austin Mini Van, 1964-67, promotional: Dutch...........£130-160
Austin Mini Van, 1964-67, metallic green body, grey base, red interior, white 'FDR1.2009/17' logo. In original 450 box with club slip...........£300-400

452 Commer Dropside Lorry, 1956-63, red and cream body (raised ridge on some cab roofs), smooth or shaped hubs.........£100-120
Commer Dropside Lorry, 1956-63, blue body, cream back...........£80-100

453 Commer Refrigerated Van, 1956-60, 'WALLS ICE CREAM'...........
Commer Refrigerated Van, 1956-60, dark blue cab, cream back, smooth roof, flat spun hubs...........£350-400
Commer Refrigerated Van, 1956-60, light blue cab, cream back, cast roof, flat spun hubs...........£125-150

454 Commer Platform Lorry, 1957-63, metallic blue cab and chassis, silver-grey platform, flat hubs, leaflet...........£120-170
Commer Platform Lorry, 1957-63, yellow cab/chassis, silver platform...........£120-170

455 Karrier Bantam 2-ton, 1957-60, blue, red or grey body, red platform, smooth hubs...........£80-100

456 ERF 44G Dropside Lorry, 1960-63, yellow cab and chassis, metallic blue back, smooth/shaped hubs...........£70-100
ERF 44G Dropside Lorry, 1960-63, two-tone blue or yellow/blue body, smooth hubs...........£100-150

457 ERF Flatbed Lorry, 1958-65, light blue cab/chassis, dark blue back with load, silver trim, flat spun hubs, tow hook......£75-100

458 E.R.F. Earth Dumper, 1958-66, red/yellow, 'ERF' cast-in, smooth or shaped hubs...........£80-100

459 ERF 44G Van, 1958-60, 'MOORHOUSES LEMON CHEESE' 'MOORHOUSES JAMS' yellow/red...........£150-200
Raygu Rascal Roller, 1973-78, yellow/green body, 'Road Roller'..........£20-30

460 ERF Neville Cement Tipper, 1959-61, 'TUNNEL CEMENT'

Lemon cab/chassis, silver base, metal filler caps...........£40-50
ERF Neville Cement Tipper, 1959-61, as previous version, but with red plastic filler caps...........£70-80

462 Commer Van 'CO-OP', 1970-?, white/blue body, blue/yellow box...........£80-100
Commer Van 'HAMMONDS', 1971-?, promotional...........£80-100
Commer Van 'HAMMONDS', 1971-?, green/blue/white, cast hubs. In un-numbered Corgi box with '462' handwritten...........£125-175
Commer Van 'HAMMONDS', 1971-?, promotional: Combex Industries. Grey...........£200-300

465 Commer Pick-Up Truck, 1963-66, red/yellow, yellow/red or green/grey, 'Trans-O-Lites'...........£90-120

466 Commer Milk Float, 1964-66, white cab/chassis and load; blue rear roof and sides...........£80-100
Commer Milk Float, 1964-66, promotional...........£80-100
Commer Milk Float, 1964-66, as previous model but with 'CO-OP' labels. Plain card box...........£100-110

470 Forward Control Jeep, 1965-72, blue/grey, mustard yellow, pale green or light blue body, detachable canopy...........£50-75

471 Karrier Bantam Snack Bar, 1965-66, blue/white, 'JOE'S DINER', figure, opening hatch...........£150-200
Karrier Bantam Snack Bar, 1965-66, Belgian issue: blue/white, 'PATATES FRITES'...........£200-250

472 Land Rover Public Address, 1964-1966, vehicle green, yellow rear body with two figures, "Vote for Corgi" to sides, red interior, spun hubs...........£200-300

474 Musical 'WALLS ICE CREAM' Van, 1965-68, Ford Thames van in blue/cream, musical movement (must function for top price), diorama but no figures, blue/yellow card box with correct folded leaflet, fresh decal sheet...........£250-300

477 Land Rover Breakdown, 1966-67, red body, yellow canopy with spotlight and 'BREAKDOWN SERVICE' logo, rubber (or later plastic) 'tyre' crank, shaped or cast hubs...........£50-75
Land Rover Breakdown, 1966-67, same, but with large or small silver crank, WW...........£50-75

478 Jeep Tower Wagon (Forward Control), 1965-68, green, yellow and silver, red interior, figure...........£40-50
Jeep Tower Wagon (Forward Control), 1965-68, green, yellow and silver, cream interior, figure...........£50-75

479 Commer Mobile Camera Van, 1968-71, 'SAMUELSON FILM

COMPANY LTD', blue/white body, shaped/spun hubs, camera and operator, equipment case ***£150-200***

483 **Dodge Tipper Truck**, 1968-72, 'KEW FARGO' white cab, blue tipper, cast hubs ***£60-70***

484 **Dodge Livestock Transporter**, 1968-72, see 'Agricultural Models' section ***£60-70***

486 **'KENNEL CLUB' Truck**, 1967-69, white/orange Chevrolet Impala with 'Vari-View' dachshund picture, four dogs, cast hubs ***£80-100***

490 **Volkswagen Breakdown Truck**, 1966-72, light olive green, red interior and flatbed load, 'Breakdown' sticker to one door, detailed cast hubs ***£75-100***

Volkswagen Breakdown Truck, 1966-72, white, yellow interior, red rear body, spun hubs, 'Racing Club' door labels ***£80-100***

493 **Mazda B 1600 Pick-Up**, 1975-78, blue/white or silver/blue body ***£20-25***

494 **Bedford Tipper**, 1967-72, red cab/chassis, yellow tipper ***£60-70***

Bedford Tipper, 1967-72, red cab/chassis, silver tipper ***£100-125***

Bedford Tipper, 1967-72, red cab/chassis, grey tipper ***£150-175***

Bedford Tipper, 1967-72, yellow cab/chassis, blue tipper ***£110-130***

Bedford Tipper, 1967-72, blue cab/chassis, yellow tipper ***£130-150***

Bedford Tipper, 1967-72, late issue. Red cab and chassis. Yellow tipper in blue and yellow window box ***£130-150***

508 **Commer Minibus 'Holiday Camp Special'**, 1967-72, white/orange, green luggage, spun hubs, leaflet ***£100-150***

70 **Inter-City Mini-Bus**, 1974-80, orange body, yellow labels, WW ***£10-15***

Inter-City Mini-Bus, 1974-80, MAJOR PACKS ***£10-15***

1100 **Bedford 'S' Carrimore**, 1958-63, (Low-loader) ***£10-15***

Bedford 'S' Carrimore, 1958-63, yellow cab, metallic blue low-loader trailer, smooth or shaped hubs ***£140-240***

Bedford 'S' Carrimore, 1958-63, red cab, metallic blue low-loader trailer, winch ***£140-170***

Mack Truck, 1971-73, 'TRANS-CONTINENTAL' ***£140-170***

Mack Truck, 1971-73, orange cab, black/orange/silver trailer ***£40-50***

Mack Truck, 1971-73, orange/metallic lime green ***£70-80***

1101 **Bedford 'S' Carrimore**, 1957-62, Car Transporter ***£70-80***

Bedford 'S' Carrimore, 1957-62, blue cab, yellow transporter body, 'CORGI CAR TRANSPORTER' ***£200-275***

Bedford 'S' Carrimore, 1957-62, red cab, blue transporter body, smooth hubs ***£140-170***

Bedford 'S' Carrimore, 1957-62, cerise cab, blue transporter body, smooth hubs ***£300-350***

Bedford 'S' Carrimore, 1957-62, yellow cab and transporter body, silver ramps ***£200-250***

Mobile Crane, 1976-81, yellow/blue, 'Warner & Swasey' ***£25-30***

1102 **'EUCLID' TC-12 Bulldozer**, 1958-62, yellow body, pale grey tracks. Box has inner lining ***£120-140***

'EUCLID' TC-12 Bulldozer, 1958-62, same model but with black tracks ***£120-140***

'EUCLID' TC-12 Bulldozer, 1958-62, pale lime-green body ***£120-140***

Crane Freuhauf, 1974-76, (Berliet Dumper) ***£120-140***

Crane Freuhauf, 1974-76, yellow cab, orange dumper body, 'Road Maker Construction' logo ***£30-35***

1103 **'EUCLID' Crawler Tractor**, 1960-65, yellow or pale lime-green body, pale grey tracks ***£125-150***

'EUCLID' Crawler Tractor, 1960-65, same model but with black tracks ***£125-150***

1104 **Bedford 'S' Carrimore**, 1958-63, Machinery Carrier ***£125-150***

Bedford 'S' Carrimore, 1958-63, red or blue cab, silver trailer, smooth hubs, operable winch ***£140-170***

Bedford 'S' Carrimore, 1958-63, yellow cab silver trailer, smooth cast hubs ***£100-120***

Bedford 'S' Carrimore, 1958-63, yellow cab, metallic blue high sided trailer, smooth cast hubs ***£80-100***

Bedford 'TK' type, 1974-77, horse transporter ***£80-100***

Bedford 'TK' type, 1974-77, green or metallic green, orange top 'NEWMARKET RACING STABLES', 4 horses and boy ***£50-60***

1105 **Bedford 'TK' type**, 1962-66, 'Corgi Car Transporter' ***£50-60***

Bedford 'TK' type, 1962-66, red cab, blue/white trailer, collapsible decks ***£100-120***

Berliet Racehorse Transporter, 1976-80, brown/white, 'NATIONAL RACING STABLES' four horses ***£40-50***

1106 **Mack Container Truck 'ACL'**, 1972-77, yellow/black/white body, two red containers ***£35-40***

Mack Container Truck 'ACL', 1972-77, promotional: for the '3M' company ***£120-140***

1107 **'EUCLID' with Dozer & Driver**, 1963-66, yellow body, black or grey tracks ***£150-200***

'EUCLID' with Dozer & Driver, 1963-66, red body ***£150-200***

'EUCLID' with Dozer & Driver, 1963-66, lime-green body ***£80-100***

Berliet Container Lorry, 1978-79, 'UNITED STATES LINES' ***£80-100***

Berliet Container Lorry, 1978-79, blue cab, white chassis, two Grey containers ***£20-30***

1108 **Ford Truck 'MICHELIN'**, 1982, blue/white artic. body, 2 containers ***£40-50***

1109 **Ford Truck 'MICHELIN'**, 1979, blue/yellow body, 2 containers ***£20-30***

Ford Container Lorry, Dutch promotional issue white cab, orange trailer, two red container with DSM logo ***£125-175***

Mercedes Benz Tractor And Trailer, blue cab, white chassis, blue back with white 'Sealink' containers, cast hubs, with Sealink free travel sticker to box ***£25-35***

1110 **Bedford 'S' Tanker**, 1959-64, 'MOBILGAS' red/white articulated body, detachable cab, lemon interior cast hubs ***£150-200***

Bedford 'S' Tanker, 1959-64, same but with shaped spun hubs ***£150-200***

Bedford 'S' Tanker, 1965-67, 'SHELL BENZEEN' ***£150-200***

Bedford 'S' Tanker, 1965-67, blue/white articulated tanker, Dutch model ***£2,500-3,500***

'JCB' Crawler Loader, 1976-80, yellow/white body, red bucket, black tracks, driver ***£30-35***

'JCB' Crawler, 1976-80, yellow and white body, driver ***£30-40***

'JCB' Crawler, 1976-80, light blue/orange with light blue chassis ***£30-40***

'JCB' Crawler, 1976-80, yellow body, light blue cab, red bucket ***£30-40***

'JCB' Crawler, 1976-80, red body, light blue cab and bucket ***£30-40***

'JCB' Crawler, 1976-80, orange body, 'BLOCK CONSTRUCTION' ***£30-40***

1113 **'HYSTER' Handler**, 1981-86, yellow or black/white main body, 'US Lines', hoist ***£100-125***

'HYSTER' Handler, 1981-86, yellow or black/white main body,

'SEALINK', container, export model ***£100-125***

'HYSTER' Handler, 1981-86, white/dark blue/yellow, MICHELIN', container ***£100-125***

1116 **Refuse Lorry**, 1979-?, (Shelvoke and Drewry Revopak) ***£100-125***

Refuse Lorry, 1979-?, orange/silver or red/silver body ***£20-30***

Refuse Lorry, 1979-?, 1988 blue cab, white tipper, 'BOROUGH COUNCIL' ***£15-20***

1117 **'FAUN' Street-sweeper**, 1980-85, orange and yellow or all-yellow, with operator ***£50-75***

1119 **Mercedes Load Lugger**, 1983, yellow/red body, 'CORGI' ***£15-20***

1120 **Express Coach**, 1961, Midland red Motorway Coach, red with black 'Birmingham-London Motorway Express', early version in Major box later model in standard box ***£60-100***

1121 **Ford Tipper (Corgimatic)**, 1983, orange/beige body, 'CORGI' ***£15-20***

1126 **Racing Car Transporter**, 1961-65, 'ECURIE ECOSSE' ***£15-20***

Racing Car Transporter, 1961-65, metallic dark blue body, logo in yellow lettering ***£200-250***

Racing Car Transporter, 1961-65, later version: logo in orange lettering ***£130-160***

Racing Car Transporter, 1961-65, with logo in white lettering ***£130-160***

Racing Car Transporter, 1961-65, with logo and raised ridges in Light blue ***£130-160***

Racing Car Transporter, 1961-65, metallic light blue body with logo in red lettering ***£200-250***

Racing Car Transporter, 1961-65, metallic light blue body with logo in black lettering ***£200-250***

1128 **'PRIESTMAN' Cub Shovel**, 1963-76, red/yellow body, driver ***£100-125***

1129 **Bedford 'S' Tanker 'MILK'**, 1962-65, blue/white articulated body, detachable cab ***£200-260***

1130 **Euclid TC12 Twin Crawler Tractor**, 19??, lime green body, black tracks ***£100-125***

Chipperfields Circus Horse, 1962-71, transporter ***£100-125***

Chipperfields Circus Horse, 1962-71, red Bedford TK Cab blue & red trailer, circus lables on front with horses head on rear six white horses ***£50-75***

1131 **Bedford 'TK' Carrimore**, 1963-66, machinery low loader ***£50-75***

Bedford 'TK' Carrimore, 1963-66, blue cab, silver trailer, yellow detachable rear axle unit, spun hubs ***£120-140***

Bedford 'TK' Carrimore, 1963-66, same, but black detachable rear axle unit ***£80-100***

1132 **Bedford 'TK' Carrimore**, 1963-65, yellow cab and ramp, red low loader trailer, spare wheels, no winch ***£200-250***

1137 **Ford Articulated Truck**, 1965-71, 'EXPRESS SERVICES' ***£200-250***

Ford Articulated Truck, 1965-71, blue/silver/red body, lemon interior mechanic figure. 'H' series tilt-cab ***£100-120***

1138 **Ford Articulated Transporter**, 1966-69, 'CORGI CARS' ***£100-120***

Ford Articulated Transporter, 1966-69, red/silver tilt cab, two-tone blue trailer ***£150-200***

1140 **Bedford 'TK' Petrol Tanker**, 1965-67, 'MOBILGAS' ***£150-200***

Bedford 'TK' Petrol Tanker, 1965-67, red/silver/white artic. body, tilting cab, box includes inner packing, leaflet ***£150-240***

1141 **Bedford 'TK' Milk Tanker**, 1965-67, 'MILK' ***£150-240***

Bedford 'TK' Milk Tanker, 1965-67, blue/white articulated body, tilting cab ***£225-275***

1142 **'HOLMES WRECKER' Truck**, 1967-74, red white & black body, Grey or gold twin booms, ladder on tilt-cab, 2 spare wheels two mechanics, blue window box ***£100-125***

'HOLMES WRECKER' Truck, 1967-74, blue & yellow window box ***£100-125***

'HOLMES WRECKER' Truck, 1967-74, striped window style box ***£175-200***

1144 **Berliet Wrecker Truck**, 19??, red/white/blue, gold booms/hooks, striped window box ***£50-70***

1145 **Unimog Goose Dumper**, 1969-76, yellow/red body, '406' ***£50-60***

1146 **Scammell Carrimore Mk.V**, 1970-73, orange/white/blue Tri-deck Transporter articulated transporter with three collapsible decks ***£125-150***

1147 **Scammell Truck**, 1969-72, yellow/white, 'FERRYMASTERS INTERNATIONAL HAULIERS' ***£100-125***

1148 **Scammell Carrimore Mk.IV**, 1969-72, red/white car transporter body with yellow chucks ***£90-110***

1150 **Mercedes (Unimog 406)**, 1971-77, snowplough ***£90-110***

Mercedes (Unimog 406), 1971-77, green/black, 2 red flags, orange/silver plough ***£40-60***

Mercedes (Unimog 406), 1971-77, yellow cab and back, red chassis, silver plough ***£40-60***

1151 **Mack Tanker 'EXXON'**, 19??, red/white body, striped window box ***£50-70***

Mack Tanker 'ESSO', 1971-76, white/red/blue, Gloster Saro Tanker ***£50-75***

Mack Tanker 'ESSO', 1971-76, same model but 'EXXON' logo ***£70-80***

1152 **'BARRATT' Tipper**, 1983-, green/white body, tipper section tips ***£5-10***

1153 **'PRIESTMAN' Crane**, 1973-74, red/orange body, 'Higrab' ***£45-55***

1153 **'WIMPEY' Tipper (Scania)**, 1983-84), green/silver body (later yellow) ***£5-10***

1154 **Priestman Crane Truck**, 1974-76, yellow/red body, silver boom, hook 'Hi Lift' ***£75-100***

Giant Tower Crane, 1979, 'BLOCK CONSTRUCTION' £75-100
Giant Tower Crane, 1979, orange/yellow crane, white body........
.........£55-65
1155 'Skyscraper' Tower Crane, 1975-79, yellow/red body, black
tracks £35-40
1156 Volvo Concrete Mixer, 1977-79, yellow/red/orange body,
'RAPIER' £30-35
Volvo Concrete Mixer, 1980, orange/white body, 'BLOCK
CONSTRUCTION' £30-35
1157 Ford Tanker 'ESSO', 1976-81, white/red articulated body£25-35
1158 Ford Tanker 'EXXON', 1976, white/black artic. body, US issue ....
.........£30-50
1159 Ford Car Transporter, 1976-79, metallic blue/white articulated.
body £30-50
Ford Car Transporter, 1976-79, metallic green articulated body
.........£30-50
1160 Ford Tanker 'GULF', 1976-78, white/orange articulated body......
.........£30-40
1161 Ford Tanker 'ARAL', 1976-78, blue/white/black, German export
.........£30-50
1169 Ford Tanker 'GUINNESS', 1982, red/cream/black articulated
body £30-50
1170 Ford Car Transporter, 1982, red/white/yellow articulated body
.........£30-50

AGRICULTURAL MODELS
Agricultural models also appear in the Gift Sets section

50 'Massey-Ferguson 65' Tractor, 1959-66, bright red bonnet, seat
and metal hubs, pale grey chassis, black plastic steering wheel ....
.........£160-200
'Massey-Ferguson 65' Tractor, 1959-66, bright red bonnet, bare
metal seat, red metal hubs, grey plastic steering wheel£100-125
'Massey-Ferguson 65' Tractor, 1959-66, dark red bonnet, silver
metal steering wheel and seat, fawn engine, red plastic hubs........
.........£140-160
'Massey-Ferguson 65' Tractor, 1959-66, NB a variation with
Copper metal seat is known to exist ....NGPP
50 'Massey-Ferguson 50B' Tractor, 1974-77, yellow/black/red
body, windows £60-80
'Massey-Ferguson 50B' Tractor, 1974-77, pre-production: ....
.........£60-80
'Massey-Ferguson 50B' Tractor, 1974-77, white, cream plastic
hubs, black interior and trim £40-60
51 'Massey-Ferguson' Tipper Trailer, 1959-64, red chassis, yellow
or grey body, red metal or plastic wheels.........£40-45
53 'Massey-Ferguson 65', 1960-66, tractor with shovel.........£40-45
'Massey-Ferguson 65', 1960-66, bright red bonnet without decals,
grey plastic steering wheel, silver metal seat/shovel, cream engine,
fawn rams with black decals, red metal hubs.........£120-150
'Massey-Ferguson 65', 1960-66, as previous model, but bright red
bonnet has thin black outline decals, red plastic hubs ... £100-125
'Massey-Ferguson 65', 1960-66, same but bright red bonnet has
thin black outline decals, bare metal rams/shovel, red plastic
hubs.........£100-125
'Massey-Ferguson 65', 1960-66, red bonnet with white/black
decals, silver metal steering wheel, cream engine and rams,
cream bucket with silver interior, red plastic hubs.........£100-125
54 'Massey-Ferguson 50B', 1974-??, Tractor with Shovel.
'Massey-Ferguson 50B', 1974-??, yellow and red body and
shovel.........£60-80
54 'Fordson Power Major' Tractor, 1962-64, (Roadless Half-
Tracks).
'Fordson Power Major' Tractor, 1962-64, blue body, orange
rollers and wheels, black rubber tracks, lights in radiator grille.
Plain early box £175-225
'Fordson Power Major' Tractor, 1962-64, same but with grey
rubber tracks, lights at sides of grille, in picture box £175-225
'Fordson Power Major' Tractor, 1962-64, first type casting has
lights at side of grille. orange or pale orange plastic hubs with
grey tracks.........£175-225
55 'Fordson Power Major' Tractor, 1961-63, blue/grey/red body,
orange metal hubs, silver seat/steering wheel £100-175
'Fordson Power Major' Tractor, 1961-63, blue/grey/red body,
dull orange plastic hubs, silver seat/steering wheel......£150-200
55 'David brown 1412' Tractor, 1977-??, black/red/white body.........
.........£50-75
56 Four-Furrow Plough, 1961-63, red/brown/yellow body .£30-35
Farm Tipper Trailer, 1977-??, red/yellow or red/white body with
drop-down tailboard.........£10-15
57 'Massey Ferguson 65', 1963-66, tractor with fork.
'Massey Ferguson 65', 1963-66, red/silver/cream body, red hubs,
driver, steering wheel £150-175
'Massey Ferguson 65', 1963-66, same model but with orange
hubs.........£125-150
58 Beast Carrier, 1965-72, red/cream/blue body, four calves ....
.........£45-55
60 'Fordson Power Major' Tractor, 1964-71, blue body/steering
wheel, bare metal seat, driver, red plastic hubs £100-150
61 Four-Furrow Plough, 1964-71, blue/silver body £30-35
62 Ford Tipper Trailer, 1965-72, red/yellow body, two raves.£20-25
64 Forward Control Jeep, 1965-69, red body, yellow/white working
conveyor, farmhand figure.........£80-100

66 'Massey-Ferguson 165' Tractor, 1966-72, red/blue/white,
engine sound.........£100-120
67 'Ford Super Major' Tractor, 1967-72, blue/white/silver body,
'FORD 5000', instructions.........£100-150
'Ford Super Major' Tractor, 1967-72, blue with grey plastic
hubs, pale blue mud-guards, driver.........£100-150
69 'Massey Ferguson 165', 1967-72, tractor and shovel.
'Massey Ferguson 165', 1967-72, red/grey body, silver shovel,
driver.........£100-150
71 Fordson Disc Harrow, 1967-72, yellow/red/silver body.£30-35
72 'Ford 5000' Tractor and Towbar, 1971-73, as Corgi 67 but with
frame, bucket and pipes.........£100-150
73 'Massey-Ferguson' Tractor and Saw, 1970-73, as Corgi 66 +
yellow rotating saw.........£100-150
74 'Ford 5000' Tractor and Scoop, 1969-72, as Corgi 67 + yellow/
silver scoop.........£150-200
101 Platform Trailer, 1958-63, grey/yellow or silver/blue or silver/
lemon body.........£30-50
102 Rice's Pony Trailer, 1958-59, red body, brown chassis, wire
drawbar, smooth hubs, plastic pony.........£35-50
Rice's Pony Trailer, 1958-59, red body, silver chassis, wire
drawbar, smooth hubs, plastic pony.........£40-60
Rice's Pony Trailer, 1958-59, red body, black chassis, wire or
cast drawbar, smooth or shaped hubs.........£40-60
Rice's Pony Trailer, 1958-59, red body, silver chassis, wire or
cast drawbar, smooth or shaped hubs.........£40-60
Rice's Pony Trailer, 1958-59, cream body, red chassis, wire or
cast drawbar, smooth or shaped hubs.........£40-60

Rice's Pony Trailer, 1958-59, tan/cream body, silver chassis, cast
drawbar, shaped hubs.........£40-60
112 Rice Beaufort Horse-Box, 1969-72, blue/white horse-box with
mare and foal.........£25-50
484 Dodge Livestock Transporter, 1967-69, beige/green/graphite
grey body, spun hubs, 'KEW FARGO', 5 pigs. blue/yellow card box
.........£50-100
Dodge Livestock Transporter, 1967-69, later issue with cast
hubs blue/yellow window box.........£70-100
Dodge Livestock Transporter, 1967-69.

Major Packs (and large farming models)
1111 'Massey-Ferguson', 1959-60, combine harvester.
'Massey-Ferguson', 1959-60, red/yellow, yellow metal wheels,
metal tines, card box has internal packing.........£100-150
1111 'Massey-Ferguson 780', 1960-61, combine harvester..£100-150
'Massey-Ferguson 780', 1960-61, red/yellow, yellow metal
wheels, plastic tines, card box has internal packing £100-150
'Massey-Ferguson 780', 1960-61, red/yellow, red plastic wheels,
yellow plastic tines, card box has internal packing.......£175-225
1112 'David Brown' Tractor, 1977-78, and combine harvester.
'David Brown' Tractor, 1977-78, Corgi 55 Tractor with red/
white/black combine harvester.........£150-175

CORGI EMERGENCY VEHICLES
*Police, Fire, Ambulance and Rescue Vehicles, etc. See also 'Corgi
Commercial Vehicles' (for other breakdown recovery vehicles,
etc), and the 'Corgi Gift Sets' section.*

209 Riley Pathfinder 'Police' Car, 1958-61, black and silver body,
bell.........£125-150
213 Jaguar Fire Chief's Car, 1959-61, red body, bell, grey aerial, roof
sign, smooth spun hubs.........£150-200
213s Jaguar Fire Chief's Car, 1961-62, (with suspension).
Jaguar Fire Chief's Car, 1961-62, as 213 model but shaped hubs
.........£150-200
Jaguar Fire Chief's Car, 1961-62, deep cherry red, lemon
interior, spun hubs.........£150-200
223 Chevrolet Impala 'State Patrol', 1959-61, black body, silver
stripe, lemon interior, grey aerial.........£175-200
237 Oldsmobile Sheriff's Car, 1962-66, black body, white roof,
'COUNTY SHERIFF', clear or blue light.........£80-90
260 Buick 'POLICE' Car, 1979-81, metallic blue/white, 'CITY OF
METROPOLIS', two light bars.........£30-40
284 Mercedes-Benz 240 D, 1982-83, red body, 'NOTRUF 112',
flashing lights, German export model.........£20-25
293 Renault 5 TS, 1980-81, French issue: two-tone blue, roof light,
'S.O.S. MEDICINS'.........£80-100
295 Renault 5 TS Fire Chief, 1982-83, red/white 'SAPEURS
POMPIERS', French export.........£15-20
297 Ford Escort 'Panda' Car, 1982-86, light or dark blue, white
doors, blue warning lights, 'POLICE'.........£15-20
326 Chevrolet Caprice 'Police' Car, 1980-81, black/white body,
suspension.........£20-30
332 Opel Doctors Car, 1980-81, German issue: white/red,
'NOTARTZ'.........£30-40
339 Rover 3500 'POLICE' Car, 1980, white and red body.......£20-25
373 VW 1200 Police Car, 1970-76, green and white body, red
interior, 'POLIZEI', blue roof light, WW.........£70-80
VW 1200 Police Car, 1970-76, white body, red interior, silver
base, blue roof light, 'POLIZEI'.........£75-100
VW 1200 Police Car, 1970-76, black/white/blue, 'POLITIE' ....
.........£90-120
VW 1200 Police Car, 1970-76, white body, red interior, blue roof
light, black 'POLICE' on white decal.........£40-50
VW 1200 Police Car, 1970-76, same, but white 'POLICE'
lettering on blue decal.........£40-50
VW 1200 Police Car, 1970-76, white body, black hatch/bonnet
stripes, red interior, 2 figures, 'POLICE'.........£40-50
383 VW 1200 'ADAC', 1970-73, yellow body, black roof with '1341',
'ADAC STRASSENWACHT' logos.........£75-85
386 Mercedes 'POLIZEI', 198, green/white body, two blue warning
lights, German export model.........£30-40
395 Fire Bug, 1972-73, orange body, Whizzwheels, red/black or
pink/black stripe, yellow ladder (381 Beach Buggy)..........£20-30
402 Ford Cortina GXL Police Car, 1972-77, white/red body,
'POLICE' labels, (updated (313).........£55-65
Ford Cortina GXL Police Car, 1972-77, German issue: white/
red body, 'POLIZEI'.........£75-85
405 Bedford Fire Tender 'A.F.S.', 1956-60, bright or
dark green 'Utilicon' body, divided windscreen, silver or
black ladder, smooth or shaped hubs. Blue box with leaflet ....
.........£150-200
405M Bedford (Utilicon) Fire Tender, 1956-59, red body, divided
windscreen, silver or black ladder, 'FIRE DEPT', smooth or
shaped hubs, friction motor. Blue box with leaflet £150-250
405 Chevrolet Ambulance, 1978-80, white/orange, patient on
stretcher and two attendants £20-25
406 Mercedes Bonna 'Ambulance', white body, red/black design,
opening doors, stretcher, ambulancemen.........£15-20
Mercedes Bonna 'Ambulance', German issue: cream body,
'KRANKENWAGEN'.........£30-40

Mercedes Bonna 'Ambulance', Danish issue: red/white, 'FALCK'.
....£30-40

Mercedes Bonna 'Ambulance', Swedish issue: white/red/black body, 'SDL 951'..£30-40

407 **Mercedes Bonna 'Ambulance'**, 1981, white body, red/black design, opening doors...£15-20

408 **Bedford 'AA' Service Van**, 1957-59, yellow/black, divided windscreen, smooth hubs, blue box, leaflet..................£100-125

Bedford 'AA' Service Van, 1958-59 yellow/black, undivided windscreen, smooth or shaped hubs, blue box, leaflet ....
....£100-125

Bedford 'AA' Service Van, 1959-63 yellow/black, undivided windscreen, shaped hubs, blue/yellow box, no leaflet..£120-140

Bedford 'AA' Service Van, late issue: yellow/black, single windscreen, ridged roof, flat hubs..........................£100-140

412 **Bedford 'AMBULANCE'**, 1957-60, cream 'Utilicon' body, divided screen, smooth hubs, blue box with leaflet............£110-150

Bedford 'AMBULANCE', 1957-60, as previous model but with one-piece wind-screen......................................£150-175

Bedford 'AMBULANCE', 1957-60, Factory error: a few examples of 412 were issued with 'HOME SERVICES' front labels ......NGPP

412 **Mercedes Police Car**, 1976-79, white/black body, 'POLICE' logo, blue roof lamp..£30-35

Mercedes Police Car, 1976-79, green/white body, 'POLIZEI' logo, blue roof lamp, German issue..........................£35-45

414 **Jaguar XJ12-C**, 1975-77, white/blue body, 'COASTGUARD' ....
....£10-15

416 **R.A.C. Land Rover**, 1959-61, blue body, 'RADIO RESCUE' on cab roof sign, metal canopy, smooth hubs, blue/yellow box.£150-175

R.A.C. Land Rover, 1959-61, blue body, no cab roof sign, 'RADIO RESCUE' on canopy, shaped hubs......................£200-320

R.A.C. Land Rover, 1959-61, Belgian issue: yellow body and metal canopy, 'TS' decals on sides, 'RADIO' on roof £500-650

416s **RAC Land Rover**, 1962-64, (with suspension).

RAC Land Rover, 1962-64, blue body, Lemon interior, suspension, 'RADIO RESCUE', plastic canopy.................£100-125

RAC Land Rover, 1962-64, Belgian issue: yellow body, red interior, grey plastic canopy, 'TS' decals on doors, 'RADIO' on bonnet £800-900

416 **Buick Police Car**, 1977-79, blue body or metallic blue body, 'POLICE', two policemen window style box.........................£25-30

419 **Ford Zephyr Motorway Car**, 1960-65, white or cream, smooth or shaped hubs, 'POLICE', large or small roof light, blue and yellow box..£80-100

Ford Zephyr Motorway Car, 1960-65, Dutch export: with 'POLITIE' or 'RIJKS POLITIE' logo £200-250

421 **Land Rover Station Wagon**, 1977-79, red body, white roof-rack, 'FOREST WARDEN'..£20-25

422 **'Riot Police' Wagon**, 1977-80, red/white body, water cannon, white number '6'..£15-20

423 **Bedford 12cwt. Tender**, 1960-62, red body, black ladder, undivided windscreen, smooth or shaped hubs, 'FIRE DEPT'.........
....£110-150

Bedford 12cwt. Tender, 1960-62, red body, unpainted ladder, undivided screen, shaped hubs.............................£125-150

424 **'SECURITY' Van**, 1976-79, black/yellow/white body, mesh windows, WW..£10-15

428 **Renault 'Police' Car**, 1978-80, black/white body, (export isssue) ......
....£55-65

429 **'Police' Jaguar XJ12-C**, 1978-80, white/red/blue body, aerial, lights..£25-35

430 **Porsche 924 'Police'**, 1978-80, black/white body, warning light ..
....£15-25

Porsche 924 'Police', 1978-80, German issue: white/green 'POLIZEI'...£40-50

Porsche 924 'Police', 1978-80, French issue: white/black, 'POLICE'..£40-50

437 **Cadillac Superior Ambulance**, 1962-65, cream over red body, 'AMBULANCE' on side windows, amber roof light........£80-90

Cadillac Superior Ambulance, 1962-65, light blue over white body, 'AMBULANCE' on sides, red cross on bonnet, red roof light £100-125

Cadillac Superior Ambulance, 1962-65, met. red over Met. silver body...£100-125

439 **Chevrolet Impala**, 1963-65, red body, 'FIRE CHIEF', white stripe, lemon interior, aerial, yellow roof light, firemen, with white painted door labels with 'FIRE DEPT'.................£140-170

Chevrolet Impala, 1963-65, white rectangular label on front doors 'FIRE DEPT'...£140-170

Chevrolet Impala, 1963-65, with round red label on front doors 'FIRE DEPT'...£150-200

448 **Austin 'Police' Mini Van**, 1964-69, dark blue body, red interior, shaped or cast hubs, policeman and dog, white Police logo, pictorial stand and internal support packaging.......£125-200

461 **'Police' Vigilant Range Rover**, 1972-79, white/blue, lights, policemen, 8 'POLICE' emergency signs plus bollards..........£25-35

'Police' Vigilant Range Rover, 1972-79, white/red, 'LANGZAAM', policemen, emergency signs, Dutch model £30-50

463 **Commer 'AMBULANCE'**, 1964-66, cream or white body, red interior, blue tinted windows and roof light..............£120-140

464 **Commer 'POLICE' Van**, 1967-68, dark blue body, 'COUNTY POLICE', window bars, clear roof light, leaflet........£100-125

Commer 'POLICE' Van, 1967-68, same, but metallic light blue, with blue roof light...................................£100-125

Commer 'POLICE' Van, 1967-68, dark blue, window bars, red roof light, 'CITY POLICE', leaflet.....................£175-200

Commer 'POLICE' Van, 1967-68, dark blue, 'open' windows, blue roof light, white 'POLICE' cast into sides, with instructions..
....£90-110

Commer 'POLICE' Van, 1967-68, deep green body, 'POLICE', export model, opaque rear/side windows.............£350-450

Commer 'POLICE' Van, 1967-68, German issue.

Commer 'POLICE' Van, 1967-68, metallic green body, 'POLIZEI' ..
....£150-175

Commer 'POLICE' Van, 1967-68, French issue:

Commer 'POLICE' Van, 1967-68, metallic blue body, 'SECOURS' ....
....£150-175

Commer 'POLICE' Van, 1967-68, Dutch issue:

Commer 'POLICE' Van, 1967-68, metallic blue body, window bars, 'RIJKSPOLITIE'...£350-400

481 **Chevrolet Police Car**, 1965-69, white/black body, 'POLICE PATROL', red roof lights, two policemen.....................£100-125

482 **Chevrolet Impala**, 1966-69, red over white body, chrome stripe, bonnet logo, blue light, grey aerial, rectangular 'FIRE CHIEF' label on front doors, detailed cast or shaped spun hubs...£75-95

Chevrolet Impala, 1966-69, with round label on front doors 'FIRE CHIEF'..£75-95

482 **Vigilant Range Rover**, 1974-77, red and white body with 'AMBULANCE' logo...£25-30

Vigilant Range Rover, 1974-77, white body with blue side stripe.

Vigilant Range Rover, 1974-77, 'AMBULANCE' logo, stretcher and two ambulancemen..£25-30

483 **Belgian Police Range Rover**, 1979, white body, red stripes, warning lights, policemen, emergency signs................£75-85

484 **AMC Pacer 'RESCUE'**, 1978-80, white/orange/black body, '35'....
....£10-15

AMC Pacer 'RESCUE', 1978-80, same but with 'SECOURS' logo ...
....£40-50

489 **Volkswagen Polo**, 1980, German issue: white/green, 'POLIZEI'...
....£50-55

Volkswagen Polo, 1980, German issue: 'ADAC'...............£50-55

490 **Volkswagen Breakdown**, 1967-69, unpainted fittings, chrome tools, red 'VW' emblem, red/yellow stripe label, two spare wheels. Avocado body, shaped hubs, 'BREAK-DOWN SERVICE' labels, spun or cast hubs...................................£90-130

Volkswagen Breakdown, 1967-69, same, but in white, spun hubs in early gift sets (GS37) 'RACING CLUB' labels also in white with cast hubs..GSP

492 **VW 1200 Police Car**, 1966-70, green body, white roof, white 'POLIZEI' on bonnet, No '18' logo.....................£80-95

VW 1200 Police Car, 1966-70, white body with black 'POLIZEI' on doors and bonnet, (Germany)......................£200-250

492 **VW European Police Car**, 1966-69, dark green body, white roof and wings, red 'POLIZEI', blue lamp. Box should contain 'True Scale Steering' red/yellow cardboard roof fitting........£90-110

VW European Police Car, 1966-69, Dutch model: all-white body, light brown interior, driver, crest on doors, 'POLITIE', blue lamp...£175-225
VW European Police Car, 1966-69, Swiss model: all-white body, light brown interior, driver, crest on doors, 'POLITZIE', blue lamp...£175-225

506   Sunbeam Imp 'Panda' Car, 1968-69, white body, black bonnet and roof, blue roof light...£80-90
Sunbeam Imp 'Panda' Car, 1968-69, white body, black roof, 'luminous' door panels, blue roof light.......................£80-90
Sunbeam Imp 'Panda' Car, 1968-69, light blue body, white roof, 'luminous' door panels, blue roof light.......................£80-90

509   Porsche 911s Targa 'Police' Car, 1970-75, white/red body, black roof...£55-65
Porsche 911s Targa 'Police' Car, 1970-75, white/red body, 'POLIZEI', siren, warning lights...................................£40-60
Porsche 911s Targa 'Police' Car, 1970-75, 'RIJKSPOLITIE' export issue...£100-120

700   Motorway Ambulance, 1974-79, white/red, 'ACCIDENT'...£10-15

702   'ACCIDENT' Breakdown Truck, 1975-79, red/black, single bumper, hook...£10-15

703   Hi-Speed Fire Engine, 1976-78, red body, yellow ladder .£10-15

911   Air-Sea Rescue Helicopter, 1976-80, blue/yellow body, black 'flick-spin' rotor, 'N 428'...................................£15-20

921   Hughes OH-6A Helicopter, 1975-81, white/red, 'POLICE', 'RESCUE', warning lights......................................£15-20

921/1   'POLIZEI' Helicopter, 1975-80, white/blue, 'POLIZEI', black 'flick-spin' rotor, German issue..........................£25-30

921/2   'POLITIE' Helicopter, 1975-80, white/blue, 'POLITIE', black 'flick-spin' rotor, Dutch issue...........................£25-30

921/4   'ADAC' Helicopter, 1975-80, yellow body, 'D-HFFM', black 'flick-spin' rotor.......................................£25-30

921/6   Swiss red Cross Helicopter, 1975-80, red helicopter body, black blades, 'flick-spin' rotor..............................£25-30

922   Casualty Helicopter, 1975-78, Sikorsky Skycrane in red and white..£25-30

924   Air-Sea Rescue Helicopter, 1977-81, orange/yellow/black, 'RESCUE'...£25-30

927   Surf Rescue Helicopter, 1978-79, blue/white body, 'SURF RESCUE'...£25-30

931   Jet Ranger Helicopter, 1979-80, white/red, 'POLICE RESCUE', 'flick-spin' rotor.......................................£25-30

1001   HCB Angus Firestreak, 1980-82, red body, yellow ladder, 2 firemen plus equipment...£20-30

1103   Chubb Pathfinder, 1976-81, red/silver, 'AIRPORT CRASH TRUCK', operable pump and siren, orange logo..................£40-50
Chubb Pathfinder, 1976-81, same model but non-working siren, brick-red logo...£30-40
Chubb Pathfinder, 1976-81, red/silver, 'NEW YORK AIRPORT' logo...£80-90

1118   Chubb Pathfinder, 1981-83, red body, 'AIRPORT FIRE SERVICE', operable water pump...£60-70

1126   Dennis Fire Engine, 1977-81, 'SIMON SNORKEL' red/white/

yellow, turntable, ladder, 6 firemen...............................£30-50

1127   Bedford Fire Engine, 1964-74, 'SIMON SNORKEL' red/yellow/ Silver, turntable, ladder, 6 fireman............................£50-75

1140   Ford Transit Wrecker, 1982, white/red, '24 Hour Service', operable winch, hook..£15-20
Ford Transit Wrecker, 1982, as previous model but logo changed to 'RELAY'...£15-20
Ford Transit Wrecker, 1982 export model: red/yellow, 'ABSCHLEPPDEENST'.......................................£15-20

1143   'AMERICAN LA FRANCE', 1968-80, articulated Fire Engine in red/white/yellow, shaped spun or detailed cast wheels, 4-part extending ladder, 5 firemen, plain early box.................£50-75
AMERICAN LA FRANCE', 1968-80, as previous model but in later striped window box...£60-80

1144   Berliet Wrecker Recovery, 1975-78, red/white/gold body, with gold or grey hoists...£60-70

2029   Mack Fire Engine, 1980-83, red body, warning light, ladder, 'HAMMOND FIRE DEPT'..£15-20

MILITARY AND RAF MODELS

Unless described otherwise, all models in this listing are finished in Military-green or olive-Drab camouflage

350   Thunderbird Missile, 1958-62, blue, green or silver missile with red tip, Air Force blue loading trolley..........................£65-75

351   RAF Land Rover, 1958-62, blue body, RAF roundel, spare wheel, windows, flat spun hubs.......................................£90-110
RAF Land Rover, 1958-62, same model but with suspension, flat spun hubs...£90-110

352   RAF Vanguard Staff Car, 1958-62, blue body, Standard Vanguard with RAF roundel, blue box.......................£80-100
RAF Vanguard Staff Car, 1958-62, blue & yellow box....£80-100

353   Decca Radar Scanner, 1959-61, blue/orange, scanner rotates ....
....£35-45

354   Commer Military Ambulance, 1964-66, military green body, red interior, Red Cross, driver, blue glazing..............£125-150

355   Commer Van, 1964-65, 'US MILITARY POLICE' red interior, driver, blue roof light, leaflet in box...........................£125-150

356   VW Personnel Carrier, 1964-66, military green, red interior, driver, blue roof light, 'US Personnel'........................£115-200

357   Land Rover, 1964-66, military green, lemon interior, driver, white star, 'Weapons Carrier'.....................................£240-280

358   Oldsmobile Staff Car, 1964-68, red interior, white star, 'HQ STAF F', driver, 3 passengers, aerial.........................£150-175

359   Commer Army 'FIELD KITCHEN', 1964-66, blue interior, US star on roof, driver/attendant, 'US ARMY'..................£150-175

414   Bedford Dormobile, 1961-63, military ambulance.
Bedford Dormobile, 1961-63, olive drab body, red crosses, smooth hubs...£100-125
Bedford Dormobile, 1961-63, same model but with shaped hubs and suspension..£100-125

500   US Army Land Rover, 1963-64, rare version of model 357.............
....£200-250

900   German Tiger MkI Tank, 1974-78, brown/green, rubber tracks, fires shells (12 supplied) aerial, '144'..........................£30-40

901   Centurion Mk.I Tank, 1974-78, rubber tracks, fires shells (12 supplied), aerial, Union Jacks...................................£30-40

902   American M60 A1 Tank, 1974-80, rubber tracks, fires shells (12 supplied)...£30-40

903   British Chieftain Tank, 1974-80, fires shells (12 supplied), rubber tracks...£30-40

904   German King-Tiger Tank, 1974-78, 'B 34', rubber tracks, fires shells, (12 supplied) black crosses...................£30-40

905   Russian SU100 Tank Destroyer, 1975-76, grey, red star, fires shells, rubber tracks.....................................£30-40

906   Saladin Armoured Car, 1975-76, rubber tracks, fires shells (12 supplied), elevating gun..£30-40

907   German Rocket Launcher, 1976-80, steel blue/red, half-track, detachable limber, fires rockets (12)........................£30-40

908   French AMX Recovery Tank, 1977-80, crane, lifting dozer blade, equipment, 3 figures..£30-40

909   Tractor Gun and Trailer, 1977-80, sand-coloured British gun and trailer, fires shells (12 supplied)........................£40-50

920   Bell Army Helicopter, 1975-78, military-green with Army markings, black or green rotor.................................£15-20

923   Sikorsky Sky Crane, 1975-78, military-green, red cross, 'ARMY'...
....£15-20

MAJOR PACKS (MILITARY MODELS)

1106   Karrier Decca Radar Van, 1959-61, cream body, 4 orange bands, rotating scanner, aerials, box has interior packing.........£100-175
Karrier Decca Radar Van, 1959-61, same, but with 5 orange bands..£100-175

1108   Bristol Bloodhound Guided, 1958-60, missile and launching Ramp.
Bristol Bloodhound Guided, 1958-60, green ramp, yellow/red/ white guided missile, RAF markings.........................£125-150
Bristol Bloodhound Guided, 1958-60, first type casting has four yellow metal side rocket boosters. Launching ramp has diecast locking piece at top of ramp to hold missile.

1109   Bristol Bloodhound Guided Missile and Loading Trolley, 1959-61, green ramp, yellow/red/white guided missile, RAF markings...£130-160

1112 **Corporal Guided Missile on Launching Ramp**, 1959-62, military-green mechanical base, white missile, red rubber nose cone, instruction sheet in box... ***£175-200***
Corporal Guided Missile on Launching Ramp, 1959-62, same but with separately boxed.
Corporal Guided Missile on Launching Ramp, 1959-62, 1408 percussion head and instructions ... ***£200-250***

1113 **Corporal Guided Missile Erector Vehicle**, 1959-62, with lifting mechanism and missile, spare wheel, leaflet ... ***£300-350***

1115 **Bristol Ferranti Bloodhound**, 1958-61, yellow/red/white guided missile with RAF markings... ***£75-100***

1116 **Bloodhound Launching Ramp**, 1959-61, launching ramp for 1115. Rotates, has lifting mechanism ... ***£65-120***
Bloodhound Launching Ramp, 1959-61, first type missile with yellow metal side rocket boosters.

1117 **Bloodhound Launching Ramp**, 1959-61, for use with 1115. Military-green, spare wheel, drawbar pivots... ***£65-70***

1118 **International Tow Truck**, 1959-64, military-green with British markings (US markings on box picture) ... ***£100-150***
International Tow Truck, 1959-64, Dutch issue: silver grille and sidelights... ***£125-150***
International Tow Truck, 1959-64, US Army issues.... ***£125-150***

1124 **Launching Ramp for Corporal Guided Missile**, 1960-61, military-green, operable mechanisms, in plain 'Temporary Pack' box... ***£100-125***

1133 **Troop Transporter**, 1965-66, international six wheeled truck, 'US 7811332', hook ... ***£150-200***

1134 **'US ARMY' Fuel Tanker**, 1965-66, olive Bedford 'S' Type Artic., US Army star, 'NO SMOKING'... ***£225-275***

1135 **Heavy Equipment Transporter**, 1965-??, Bedford Carrimore, military green, US Army star, driver, red interior ... ***£450-500***
Heavy Equipment Transporter, 1965-??, military green, lemon interior ... ***£450-560***

AIRCRAFT

BOX TYPES: All these aircraft models were presented in rigid perspex cases. Helicopters and Space Vehicles are also listed in the Emergency Vehicles, Novelty and Military Sections

650 **'BOAC' Concorde**, 1973-80, white/blue with gold tail design, all-card box with 'BRITISH AIRWAYS', box has inner packing... ***£75-100***
'BOAC' Concorde, 1973-80, white/blue with red/white/blue tail, display stand, 'G-BBDG'... ***£50-60***
'BOAC' Concorde, 1973-80, version with white stripes on tail... ***£15-25***
'BOAC' Concorde, 1973-80, version with crown design on tail... ***£15-25***

651 **'AIR FRANCE' Concorde**, 1973-81, white/blue with gold tail design, all-card box... ***£40-60***
'AIR FRANCE' Concorde, 1973-81, white body, red/white/blue tail, display stand ... ***£40-60***

652 **'JAPAN AIRLINES' Concorde**, 1973-81, white/red/blue/black, all-card box, inner packing... ***£60-76***

653 **'AIR CANADA' Concorde**, 1973-81, white/red/blue/black, all-card box, inner packing... ***£60-70***

1119 **HDL Hovercraft 'SR-N1'**, 1960-62, blue/grey/white body, yellow rudders and wheels (Major Pack)... ***£75-90***

1301 **Piper Cherokee Arrow**, 1973-77, yellow/black with white wings, or white/blue, 'N 286 4 A'... ***£20-35***

1302 **Piper Navajo**, 1973-77, red/white,'N 9219 Y' ... ***£20-35***
Piper Navajo, yellow/white, 'N 9219 Y' ... ***£20-35***

1303 **Lockheed F104A Starfighter**, 1973-77, silver body... ***£60-70***
Lockheed F104A Starfighter, 1973-77, camouflage with black crosses... ***£70-90***

1304 **Mig-21 PF**, 1973-77, blue or silver, number '57', red stars, retractable undercarriage... ***£35-40***

1305 **Grumman F-11a Tiger**, 1973-??, blue 'NAVY', or silver with US stars... ***£60-70***
Grumman F-11a Tiger, 1973-??, dark metalic blue, yellow engine vents... ***£70-90***

1306 **North American P51-D**, 1973-77, Mustang.
North American P51-D, 1973-77, silver or camouflage, black props, US stars, moveable controls... ***£35-40***

1307 **Saab 35 X Draken**, 1973-77, silver or camouflage, retractable under-carriage, Swedish markings... ***£20-35***

1308 **BAC (or SEPCAT) Jaguar**, 1973-77, silver or camouflage, retractable wheels, moveable control surfaces... ***£30-45***

1309 **'BOAC' Concorde**, 1973-77, dark blue/white, retractable wheels ... ***£45-55***

1310 **'AIR FRANCE' 'BOEING 707B'**, 1973-77, white/blue body, silver wings, retractable wheels ... ***£55-65***

1311 **Messerschmitt ME410**, 1973-77, all silver body, black Iron Crosses on wings and fuselage... ***£20-35***

1312 **Boeing 727 'TWA'**, 1973-77, white body, silver wings, retractable wheels... ***£20-35***

1313 **Japanese Zero-Sen A6M5**, 1973-77, green or silver with red circles, retractable wheels... ***£20-35***

1315 **'PAN-AM' Boeing 747**, 1973-77, white body, silver wings, hinged nose, retractable wheels, 'AIR CANADA'... ***£20-35***

1315/1 **'BRITISH AIRWAYS'**, 1973-77, Jumbo Boeing 747.
'BRITISH AIRWAYS', white/silver, blue logo, hinged nose, retractable wheels... ***£55-65***

1316 **McDonnell Douglas F-4c5**, 1973-77, Phantom II in silver or camouflage with retractable undercarriage ... ***£35-45***

1320 **'BRITISH AIRWAYS' VC-10**, 1978-80, white/silver with red tail, blue logo, retractable wheels ... ***£35-45***

1325 **'SWISSAIR' DC-10**, 1978-80, white/silver with red stripe and tail, retractable wheels ... ***£35-45***

NOVELTY, FILM AND TV-RELATED MODELS

Market Price Range: Please note that the prices shown refer to pristine models and boxes. Items failing to match this standard will sell for considerably less. Note also that boxes must contain all their original additional contents. See also Corgi model identification page.

104 **Dolphin Boat on Trailer**, 1965, blue/white boat, red trailer, Helmsman, blue/yellow box... ***£50-75***

107 **Batboat on Trailer**, 1967-70, black boat (tinplate fin cover) with Batman and Robin figures, gold trailer (suspension, cast wheels). Blue/yellow pictorial box also contains black accessory towing hook for attachment to Batmobile... ***£125-160***
Batboat on Trailer, black boat (plastic fin), Batman and Robin figures, gold trailer (no suspension, WW), striped window box ... ***£100-125***

171 **Street Bike**, 1982, red, silver and black body, multicoloured swirl ... ***£5-10***

172 **'POLICE' Bike**, white/black/silver body ... ***£5-10***

173 **Cafe Racer**, 1982, silver and black RN '26', '750 cc Class'... ***£5-10***

201 **The Saint's Volvo**, 1970-72, white body, white 'Saint' logo on red label, WhizzWheels, driver, red/yellow 'window' box... ***£150-200***
The Saint's Volvo, white body, yellow interior, clear bonnet decal with black 'Saint' outline figure, WhizzWheels, driver, red/yellow 'window' box... ***£400-460***

258 **The Saint's Volvo P1800**, 1965-68, white body, black 'Saint' logo (transfer), red interior, driver, spun hubs, blue/yellow card box... ***£200-250***
The Saint's Volvo P1800, white body, white 'Saint' logo on red label, red interior, driver, cast hubs, blue/yellow card box ... ***£300-420***
The Saint's Volvo P1800, as previous version but white 'Saint' logo on blue label ... £700-900
White body, white logo on red label, yellow interior, WW ... ***£135-155***

259 **Penguinmobile**, 1979-80, white car with 'Penguin' and red/yellow parasol, black/yellow 'window' box... ***£50-75***

260 **Superman Police Car**, 1979-81, blue/white body, 'CITY of METROPOLIS', black/yellow pictorial window box ... ***£60-70***

261 **James Bond's Aston Martin**, 1965-69, (From the film 'Goldfinger') bright gold body (metal roof), red interior, wire wheels. With James Bond at the wheel, passenger seat ejector (with bandit figure). Accessories: envelope with 'secret instructions', spare bandit figure, self-dhesive '007' badge, (plus 'Model Car Makers to James Bond' Corgi Catalogue in earlier boxes). Blue/yellow picture box has inner pictorial stand... ***£350-400***
James Bond's Aston Martin, Pre-production: same model but with grey base with brass factory screws roof omponent of clear resin prototype roof... ***£1,000-1,500***

261 **Spiderbuggy**, 1979-81, red/blue jeep body with crane, Spiderman and green Goblin figures. Black/yellow pictorial window box... ***£75-100***

262 **Captain Marvel's Porsche**, 1979-80, white with flames and stars, driver, black/yellow 'window' box... ***£50-70***

263 **Captain America's Jetmobile**, 1979-81, white/red/blue body, red wheels, black/yellow 'window' box... ***£50-70***

264 **Incredible Hulk Truck**, 1979-82, bronze Hulk in red cage on Mazda pick-up, black/yellow 'window' box... ***£60-70***
Incredible Hulk Truck, same but Hulk in Grey cage... ***£70-80***
Incredible Hulk Truck, NB dark Bronze Hulk is rare – add £10 to price.

265 **Supermobile**, 1979-82, blue/red/silver body, Superman at the controls, moving 'fists'. Black/yellow pictorial 'window' box has 10 spare rockets and an instruction leaflet... ***£40-50***

266 **Chitty Chitty Bang Bang**, 1968-72, chrome, brown and red body, red/yellow retractable 'wings', figures of Caractacus Potts, Truly Scrumptious, a boy and a girl. Pictorial blue/yellow 'window' box comes in two sizes... ***£250-300***
Chitty Chitty Bang Bang, 1992 25th Anniversary replica: model on 'mahogany' display stand. Direct mail offer from Corgi... ***£60-70***

266 **Spider Bike**, 1979-83, red/blue motorcycle, Spiderman rider, black wheels, black or red handlebars forks, black or blue seat and fairing, amber or clear windshield, rocket launchers. Box also contains 10 spare rockets on sprue. Box 1: black/yellow pictorial 'window' box with header card £60-100 Box 2: black/yellow 'window' box without header card £60-100 Box 3: black/red/yellow striped 'window' box without header card... ***£60-100***
Spider Bike, same model but white wheels... ***£100-125***

267 **Batmobile**, 1966-67, (i): gloss black body, red 'Bat' logoon doors and gold cast hubs, Batman and Robin figures, 'pulsating exhaust flame', sealed secret instructions concealed in box base. 12 spare rockets (red or yellow) attached to sprue, self-adhesive 'Batman' badge. Pictorial card box with diorama, earliest versions had 'features' leaflet within... ***£400-500***
Batmobile, (ii): as previous model but with matt black body... ***£500-600***
Batmobile, As (i) but with towing hook cast into base. Blue/yellow 'window' box (some in earlier card boxes)... ***£225-275***
Batmobile, (iv): As (i) but cast silver wheels. Black/blue/yellow 'window' box... ***£225-275***
Batmobile, 1973 (v): as (iv) but with red WhizzWheels (with Chrome hubs) and without pulsating 'flame' effect. Blue/yellow 'window' box with missiles and instructions ... ***£200-300***
Batmobile, 1974-77 (vi): as (v) but with black Whizz-Wheels and without pulsating 'flame' effect. Copyright information cast in base, dark blue/yellow'window' box (header card on some), spare rockets, no instruction sheet... ***£150-175***
Batmobile, (vii): as (vi) casting but wider WhizzWheels, no Robin figure.black/red/yellow 'window' box... ***£150-175***
Batmobile, (viii): gloss black, gold slasher blade & tow hook, aerial, Batman and Robin figures, wide WW, striped 'window' box... ***£150-175***

268 **Batman's Batbike**, 1978-80, black/red rocket-firing motorcycle with red or grey Batman figure. Black & yellow 'window' box (header card on some), spare rockets... ***£100-150***
Batman's Batbike, as previous versions but in black/red/yellow striped 'window' box ... ***£100-150***

268 **The Green Hornet's 'Black Beauty'**, 1967-72, black body, green interior, driver and green Hornet figures, transfer on roof, spun hubs. Fires missiles from front, radar spinners from rear. Four of each, plus 'secret instructions' are in blue/yellow pictorial card box which should also include a greaseproof paper roof decal protector and inner pictorial card... ***£225-275***

The Green Hornet's 'Black Beauty', as above but fitted with gold coloured front grill..***£200-250***
269 **James Bond Lotus Esprit**, 1977-83, (from film 'The Spy Who Loved Me').
James Bond Lotus Esprit, white body, black windows, operable fins and rocket mechanism. Early black/yellow pictorial 'window' box with plain base must contain instruction sheet and 10 spare rockets attached to sprue............................***£100-125***
James Bond Lotus Esprit, as above with outer carded sleeve, finished in red, black and white, with "The New James Bond Corgi" to header...***£500-750***
James Bond Lotus Esprit, later pictorial 'window' box has instructions printed on base, 10 spare rockets..................***£80-100***
James Bond Lotus Esprit, 1977 10 gold-plated versions of 269 were presented to VIPs at the film's launch. These models had special mountings and boxes.......................................***£3,000-3,500***
James Bond Lotus Esprit, pre-production model: Demonstration model in a case. Red/yellow/blue/green.......................***£1,000-1,400***
270 **James Bond's Aston-Martin DB5**, 1968-76, silver body (slightly larger than 261). Features as 261, plus revolving number plates and extending tyre slashers. Box must contain inner pictorial stand, James Bond leaflet, sealed 'Secret Instructions' packet, unused '007' lapel badge (different from 261), set of unapplied no. plates and bandit figure. Variations include gold or silver coloured bumpers, metal or plastic spoked rear wheels.
James Bond's Aston-Martin DB5, Box 1: Pictorial wing-flap box. Model sits on card platform under vac-formed bubble (fragile, few made)...***£400-500***
James Bond's Aston-Martin DB5, Box 2: blue/yellow 'window' box (some with card 'upstand' till 1973, few made).......***£400-600***
James Bond's Aston-Martin DB5, Box 3: black/blue/yellow striped 'window' box (1973-76)...***£300-400***
James Bond's Aston-Martin DB5, as previous version but with fixed number plates, 'solid' chrome WW, no tyre-slashers, striped window box (no 'Secret Instructions'), ejectable passenger lodged in box inner..***£100-130***
James Bond's Aston-Martin DB5, silver, no revoling number plate fitted with red spot WW wheels..............................***£350-450***
271 **James Bond Aston-Martin**, 1978-81, silver body (1:36 scale), red interior, gold radiator/bumpers, WhizzWheels 'spoked' detail or 'alloy racing'). Early black/yellow boxes had '1:36' printed on window tag, plus header card..***£70-80***
James Bond Aston-Martin, later black/yellow boxes did not have the window tag...***£50-60***
James Bond Aston-Martin, final issues had black/red/yellow striped window boxes or purple boxes..................................***£50-60***
James Bond Aston-Martin, 1990, 'MODELAUTO' promotional: Silver, red interior, 2 figures, blue logo 'National Motor Museum Holland'...***£180-220***
James Bond Aston-Martin, reissue of C271 in clear plastic display box with plastic '007' badge...***£20-30***
271/1 **1992, Silver body (1:36 scale)**, small 4-spoked wheels....***£70-90***
271/2 **1993**, re-run of 271/1...***£70-90***
272 **James Bond Citroën 2cv**, 1981-83, (from film 'For Your Eyes Only') yellow body, opening bonnet, WW.
James Bond Citroën 2cv, box (1): black/red/yellow 'window' box with pictorial header card...***£30-40***
James Bond Citroën 2cv, Box (2): black/red/yellow 'compact' box with pictorial top flap...***£30-40***
James Bond Citroën 2cv, 1981, gold plated version: (12 only produced). 'Strada Jewellry' certificate should be present.............. ....***£2,250-2,700***
277 **'MONKEES' Monkeemobile**, 1968-72, red body, white roof, yellow logo, cast detailed wheels. Figures of Mike, Mickey, Davy and Pete plus red plastic 'Monkees' guitar. Blue/yellow 'window' box...***£175-200***
'MONKEES' Monkeemobile, same, but no 'Monkees' guitar........ ....***£200-250***
'MONKEES' Monkeemobile, in blue/yellow 'window' box with clip-in cardboard header as used for shop display purposes.......... ....***£800-900***
'MONKEES' Monkeemobile, NB pre-production model with plastic engine exists.
278 **Dan Dare's Car**, 1981, red/yellow space vehicle. Planned but not produced..***NPP***
290 **Kojak's Buick**, 1976-77, bronze body (various shades), 4-spoke or disc type wheel hubs, 'gunfire' sound, self-adhesive 'Lieutenant' badge, figures of Kojak (no hat) and Crocker (blue jacket). Black/yellow pictorial 'window' box...................***£120-150***
Kojak's Buick, same but disc type wheel hubs..............***£100-125***
Kojak's Buick, same but Kojak figure has a hat and Crocker has a black jacket. 'New' tag on some boxes.................................***£60-75***
292 **Starsky & Hutch Ford Torino**, 1977-82, red/white body, figures of Starsky, Hutch, and a suspect. black/yellow pictorial 'window' box...***£100-150***
Starsky & Hutch Ford Torino, 1986, reissued as export model (20,000 units)..***£10-15***
298 **Magnum P.I. Ferrari 308GTS**, 1982-83, red Ferrari with 4-spoke or disc wheels, black/red/yellow pictorial 'window' box..***£20-30***
320 **The Saint's Jaguar XJS**, 1978-81, white body, standard or 'dished' Whizz-Wheels. Black/yellow 'window' box (yellow or black inner)...***£40-50***
336 **James Bond's Toyota 2000 GI**, 1967-69, (from film 'You Only Live Twice').
James Bond's Toyota 2000 GI, white body, red aerial, 2 figures, rocket launchers in boot. Diorama box must have card reinforcements to protect aerial, 8 spare rockets on sprue, sealed envelope marked 'Secret Instructions' which also contains self-adhesive '007' badge...***£250-300***
342 **'The Professionals' Ford Capri**, 1980-82, metallic silver body, dished or disc hubs, figures of Cowley, Bodie and Doyle. Pictorial 'window' box..***£60-100***
'The Professionals' Ford Capri, same but with chrome wheel hubs...***£75-100***
Matt silver body, dark red interior......................................***£100-125***
348 **'Vegas' Thunderbird**, 1980-81, red body with Dan Tanner figure black/yellow pictorial 'window' box.......................................***£60-80***
391 **James Bond Mustang Mach I**, 1972-72, (from film 'Diamonds Are Forever').
James Bond Mustang Mach I, red body, black bonnet, white interior and base, WW..***£130-160***
James Bond Mustang Mach I, as above with dish wheels............ ....***£100-175***
James Bond Mustang Mach I, red/yellow 'window' box has '007' red sticker...***£150-200***
James Bond Mustang Mach I, same model but with 'CORGTOYS' shop display stand...***£300-400***

CHEVROLET VANS

423 **'ROUGH RIDER'**, 1978-78, yellow van, motorcycle labels............... ....***£100-150***
426 **'Pinder Jean Richard Circus' Booking Office Van**, 1978 ??, orange, red and blue loud speakers...***£12-15***
431 **'VANATIC'**, 1978-79, white van, polychromatic side labels ***£15-20***
432 **'VANTASTIC'**, 1978-79, black van, yellow/red design........***£15-20***
433 **'VANISHING POINT'**, 1978, Chevrolet van shown in 1978 catalogue but not issued...***NPP***
434 **'CHARLIE'S ANGELS' Van**, 1978-80, pink Chevrolet Custom van, yellow or brown interior, 4-spoke wheels. Black/yellow pictorial 'window' box..***£60-75***
'CHARLIE'S ANGELS' Van, 2nd issue with solid disc wheels........ ....***£50-60***
'CHARLIE'S ANGELS' Van, metallic silver Chevrolet 'SuperVan', black/yellow pictorial 'window' box (printing variations seen)..... ....***£35-45***
436 **'SPIDERVAN'**, 1979-80, blue Chevrolet van, 'Spiderman' design, 4-spoke wheels. black/yellow pictorial 'window' box.........***£80-90***
'SPIDERVAN', 2nd issue with solid disc wheels.................***£50-60***
437 **'COCA COLA'**, 1979-80, red Chevrolet van, white design, tinted roof windows, crates..***£30-35***
NB Various other labels were designed for the Chevrolet 'Van' series. Some prototype labels were printed but not officially used. Some of these may have found their way on to repainted van castings - they are NOT official Corgi issues. Logos include: 'Apache Patrol', 'Light Vantastic', 'Vanilla Treat', 'Cosmos', 'Columbia', 'Aquarius', 'Centaur', 'Colorama', 'Rocket Van', 'Centaur', plus four other unlettered 'psychedelic' designs.
426 **'CHIPPERFIELDS CIRCUS'**, 1962-64, Mobile Booking Office.
'CHIPPERFIELDS CIRCUS', Karrier Bantam in red and blue, with clown and circus posters, spun hubs, blue/yellow card box.. ....***£250-300***
'CHIPPERFIELDS CIRCUS', same model but with shaped hubs ***£250-300***
450 **Lunar Bug**, 1968-71, red, white, blue. Blue/yellow window box includes inner packing..***£60-70***
472 **'VOTE FOR CORGI'**, 1964-66, Corgi 438 Land Rover in green/ yellow, red interior, two figures, blue/yellow card box..***£100-120***
487 **'CHIPPERFIELDS' Parade Vehicle**, 1965-69, 472 Land Rover in red/blue, 'CIRCUS IS HERE' label, chimpanzee, clown, blue/ yellow card box...***£175-200***
497 **'The Man From UNCLE's 'Thrush Buster'**, 1966-66, Oldsmobile (235) with white body, cast wheels, cast spotlights, 'UNCLE' logo, gun sound, figures of Napoleon Solo and Ilya Kuriakin. Blue/ yellow pictorial card box (which must include internal packaging, roof packing, and 3-D 'Waverley' ring)...............................***£600-750***
'The Man From UNCLE's 'Thrush Buster', same but metallic purplish-blue body, cast or plastic spotlights....................***£250-300***
'The Man From UNCLE's 'Thrush Buster', cream with cream interior & metal lights to wings boxed with display insert. Export example..***£300-400***
503 **'CHIPPERFIELDS' Giraffe Transporter**, 1964-70, red/blue Bedford 'TK', cast or spun wheels, 2 giraffes, blue/yellow card box...***£85-125***
'CHIPPERFIELDS' Giraffe Transporter, 1970-71, as previous model but larger 'stepped' front wheels............................***£130-170***
'CHIPPERFIELDS' Giraffe Transporter, window box variation..... ....***£200-300***
511 **'CHIPPERFIELDS' Poodle Truck**, 1970-71, blue/red Chevrolet Impala Pick-Up, 'PERFORMING POODLES' labels, cast wheels, trainer (Mary Chipperfield), 4 white and 2 black poodles, blue and yellow 'window' box (should include a plastic dome over dogs)...***£250-300***
607 **'CHIPPERFIELDS' Elephant Cage**, 1963-68, a Corgi Kit with brown plastic cage and elephant mouldings, instruction leaflet. blue/yellow card box...***£50-75***
647 **Buck Rogers Starfighter**, 1980-83, white/blue, yellow retractable wings, Wilma Deering and Twiki figures, black/ yellow pictorial 'window' box, 10 spare rockets.................***£75-100***
648 **NASA Space Shuttle**, 1981-82, white/black body, 'USA Satellite', opening hatch..***£20-25***
649 **James Bond Space Shuttle**, 1979-82, from the film 'Moonraker'. **White body** (C468 casting), separate satellite (early versions retained by nylon strap). Larger pictorial black/yellow box***£50-75***
681 **Stunt Bike**, 1972, gold body, blue and yellow rider, red trolley, 'window' box, (19,000)...***£125-170***
801 **Noddy's Car**, 1969-69, yellow/red car with dickey-seat, cast hubs, chrome bumpers. Figures of Noddy, Big-Ears, and black-faced Golly. Pictorial blue/yellow 'window' box...........***£750-1000***
Noddy's Car, as previous model but Golly has light tan face........ ....***£500-600***
Noddy's Car, as previous but Golly has grey face..........***£150-200***
Noddy's Car, 1969-73, as previous but with Master Tubby (light or dark brown) instead of Golly..***£125-150***
802 **Popeye's Paddle-Wagon**, 1969-72, yellow/white body, red wings, blue paddle covers, white or yellow rear wheels, anchors, moving figures of Popeye, Olive Oyl, Swee'Pea, Bluto and Wimpey, blue/yellow pictorial 'window' box....................***£260-310***
803 **The Beatles Submarine**, 1969-72, yellow/white, psychedelic design, hatches (yellow rear, white front) open to show John, Paul, George and Ringo, pictorial window box with blue-green inner lining..***£250-300***

The Beatles Submarine, 1970-71, with two red hatch covers **£200-250**
The Beatles Submarine, with one red hatch & one white hatch. **£400-500**
The Beatles Submarine, pre-production issue: gold plated, periscope attached to sprue. Only eight issued **£600-750**

804 **Noddy's Car**, 1975-78, red/yellow car, no dickey-seat, no rear bumper. Figure of Noddy only. Dark blue/yellow pictorial 'window' box........ **£100-125**

805 **Hardy Boys Rolls-Royce**, 1970-71, 9041 silver Ghost casting in red, blue and yellow, plated wheels. Bubble-pack of five Hardy Boys figures also within the blue/yellow 'window' box .. **£150-175**

806 **Lunar Bug**, 1970-72, red/white/blue, 'Lunar Bug', windows, drop-down ramps........ **£65-75**

807 **Dougal's Magic Roundabout Car**, 1971-73, (based on 510 Citroën).
Dougal's Magic Roundabout Car, yellow/red, with Brian, Dougal and Dylan. Yellow/blue 'window' box with decal sheet........ **£100-150**
Dougal's Magic Roundabout Car, 1973-74, same but in black/yellow 'window' box, with decal sheet........ **£75-100**

808 **Basil Brush's Car**, 1971-73, red/yellow car with hand-painted Basil figure, 'Laugh tapes' and soundbox are in separate printed box within pictorial blue/yellow'window' box........ **£175-200**

809 **Dick Dastardly's Car**, 1973-73, blue/red/yellow racing car with Dick and Muttley figures. dark blue/yellow 'window' box........ **£75-120**

811 **James Bond Moon Buggy**, 1972-74, blue/white body, yellow WhizzWheels, red scanner. Roof opening mechanism should be working. Blue/yellow pictorial window box........ **£200-250**

H851 **Magic Roundabout Train**, 1972-74, red/blue, Mr Rusty and Basil in the loco-motive (engine sound), Rosalie and Paul in the carriage and Dougal in the van. Blue/yellow pictorial 'window' box with blue nylon tow-rope........ **£200-300**

H852 **Magic Roundabout Carousel**, 1972-74, red/yellow/blue working roundabout with Swiss musical movement playing the TV theme. Dylan, Paul, Rosalie, Florence and Basil figures. Blue/yellow pictorial card box........ **£200-250**

H853 **Magic Roundabout Playground**, contains a modified H852, H851 (with the figures), plus Zebedee, Dylan, four kids, see-saw, park bench, 3 blue and 3 orange shrubs and 2 flowers. Operating carousel and track. Theme music plays when Dylan is wound up........ **£300-400**

H859 **Mr McHenry's Trike**, 1972-74, red/yellow trike and trailer, Mr McHenry and Zebedee figures, blue and yellow pictorial 'window' box with blue towing cord and instruction sheet........ **£75-100**

H860-H868 **Magic Roundabout figures**, 1972-74, packed in individual clear plastic tubs.
Magic Roundabout figures, 860 Dougal, 861 Florence, 862 Zebedee, 863 Mr Rusty, 864 Brian the Snail, 865 Basil, 866 Ermintrude the Cow, 868 Dylan the Rabbit each........ **£20-30**

925 **Batcopter**, 1976-81, black body, red 'Bat' rotors, Batman figure, operable winch........ **£65-75**

926 **Stromberg Helicopter**, 1978-80, (from 'The Spy Who Loved Me')........ **£**
Stromberg Helicopter, black body/rotors, ten spare rockets, black/yellow 'window' box........ **£60-70**

927 **Chopper Squad Helicopter**, 1978-80, white/metallic blue Jet Ranger helicopter, operating winch, black/yellow pictorial 'window' box........ **£25-35**

928 **Spidercopter**, 1981-82, blue/red body, 'spider legs' black/yellow pictorial 'window' box........ **£40-50**

929 **'DAILY PLANET' Jetcopter**, 1979-80, red/white body, rocket launchers, black/yellow pictorial 'window' box contains 10 spare rockets........ **£30-50**

930 **'Drax' Helicopter**, 1972-80, (from the film 'Moonraker').
'Drax' Helicopter, white body, 'Drax' logo, ten spare rockets. Black/yellow 'window' box........ **£70-100**

9004 **'The World of Wooster' Bentley**, 1967-69, green 9002 Bentley with figures of Jeeves and Wooster, plated wheels. Bubble-packed in display base........ **£90-100**

MAJOR MODELS TV & Film

1121 **'CHIPPERFIELDS' Crane Truck**, 1960-62, red body, raised blue log and wheels, operable grey tinplate jib and hook, instruction leaflet. blue/yellow lidded box with packing........ **£150-175**
'CHIPPERFIELDS' Crane Truck, 1963-69, red body, raised blue logo and wheels, operable chrome tinplate jib/hook, leaflet. blue/yellow card box with end flaps........ **£150-175**

1123 **'CHIPPERFIELDS' Circus Cage**, 1961-62, red body, yellow chassis, smooth hubs, red diecast end and middle sliding doors, 2 plastic Lions (in stapled bags), animal name decals, instructions. Blue/yellow lidded box with packing........ **£100-110**
'CHIPPERFIELDS' Circus Cage, 1963-68, red body, yellow chassis, smooth or spun hubs, blue plastic end and middle sliding doors, 4 animals (Lions, Tigers or Polar Bears in stapled bags), animal name decals. blue/yellow card box with end flaps........ **£75-100**

1130 **'CHIPPERFIELDS' Horse Transporter**, 1962-70, Bedford TK truck, red/blue, green or red 'horse-head' design at rear, cast or spun hubs, 6 brown or grey horses, blue/yellow card box with card packing around horses........ **£100-150**
'CHIPPERFIELDS' Horse Transporter, 1970-72, as previous model but with larger 'truck' wheels........ **£100-150**

1139 **'CHIPPERFIELDS' Menagerie Transporter**, 1968-72, Scammell Handyman MkIII, blue/red cab, blue trailer with 3 plastic cages, 2 Lions, 2 Tigers and 2 Bears, blue and yellow pictorial 'window' box with packing to hold animals, plus spare self-adhesive securing tape for animals........ **£200-300**

1144 **'CHIPPERFIELDS' Crane & Cage with Rhino**, 1969-72, red/blue Scammell Handyman MkIII, 'COME TO THE CIRCUS' on n/s, silver jib/hook, stepped 'truck' front wheels on some, grey Rhinoceros in plastic cage. Blue/yellow 'window' box with pre-formed blister-pack around animals........ **£250-300**

1163 **Human Cannon Truck**, 1978-82, red and blue body, 'MARVO' figure........ **£30-40**

1164 **Berliet 'DOLPHINARIUM'**, 1980-83, yellow cab, blue trailer, clear plastic tank, two dolphins, girl trainer, black/yellow 'window' box with header card on some........ **£80-100**
Berliet 'DOLPHINARIUM', yellow cab, yellow trailer, 'window' box with header card on some........ **£100-125**

TV/FILM DUO PACKS

1360 **Batmobile**, 1982, 267 plus a Corgi juniors version, black/red/yellow 'window' box........ **£150-200**

1361 **James Bond Aston-Martin**, 1982, 271 plus a Corgi Juniors version, black/red/yellow 'window' box........ **£100-150**

1362 **James Bond Lotus Esprit**, 1982, 269 plus a Corgi Juniors version, black/red/yellow 'window' box........ **£100-150**

1363 **Buck Rogers Set**, 1982, 647 and a smaller version, black/yellow pictorial 'window' box........ **£40-50**

1376 **Starsky & Hutch Ford Torino**, 1982, 292 plus a Corgi Juniors version........ **£25-35**

1372 **'Magnum PI' Ferrari**, 1982, red standard model (298) plus a smaller version........ **£80-100**

THE 'EXPLORATION' RANGE

A range of fantasy toys introduced in 1980.

D2022 **'SCANOTRON'**, green/black........ **£10-15**
D2023 **'ROCKETRON'**, blue/yellow........ **£10-15**
D2024 **'LASERTRON'**, orange/black........ **£10-15**
D2025 **'MAGNETRON'**, red/black........ **£10-15**

'THE MUPPETS SHOW'

D2030 **Kermit's Car**, 1979, yellow car with a famous green frog, bubble-packed........ **£40-45**
Kermit's Car, same model but in red/yellow pictorial 'window' box........ **£35-40**

D2031 **Fozzie Bear's Truck**, 1979, red/brown/white truck, silver or black hooter, bubble-packed........ **£35-40**
Fozzie Bear's Truck, same model but in red/yellow pictorial 'window' box........ **£30-35**

D2032 **Miss Piggy's Sport Coupé**, 1979, pink sports car, red or pink dress, bubble-packed........ **£40-45**
Miss Piggy's Sport Coupé, same model but in red/yellow pictorial 'window' box........ **£35-40**

D2033 **Animal's Percussionmobile**, 1979, red traction-engine, yellow or red wheels, yellow or black chimney, yellow or silver cymbal. Bubble-packed........ **£35-40**
Animal's Percussionmobile, same model but in red/yellow pictorial 'window' box........ **£30-35**

MARKS & SPENCER ISSUES

In 1978 a special series of models and sets were produced for sale through selected M & S stores. They were packed in attractive non-standard boxes and had unique liveries. They were issued in small quantities.

Small sets

8000 **F1 Racing Set**, 1978, 162 'ELF' Tyrrell (dark blue) and 160 Hesketh F1 (white)........ **£30-50**

8001 **Wings Flying Team**, 1978, 301 Lotus Elite (green), Nipper aircraft (white), grey trailer........ **£100-150**

8002 **Motorway Police Patrol**, 1978, C429 'POLICE' Jaguar (green) and blue Fiat X1-9........ **£60-80**

8003 **Spindrift Power Boat Team**, 1979, 301 Ferrari Daytona (yellow) and yellow power boat on trailer........ **£50-75**

Medium sets

8101 **Wings Flying School**, 1978, C421 Land Rover (grey with 'WINGS' logo) grey helicopter, Nipper aircraft on grey trailer........ **£150-200**

8102 **Motorway Breakdown**, 1978, C429 'POLICE' Jaguar, 293 Renault 5 (yellow) plus Berliet Wrecker with 'RESCUE BREAKDOWN SERVICES'........ **£100-150**

8103 **Spindrift Power Boat Team**, 1979, includes Spindrift 301 Ferrari, Helicopter and Dinghy........ **£150-200**

Large sets

8400 **GP 'Formula 1 Racing Team'**, 1978, 160 Hesketh (white), 162 'ELF' Tyrrell (dark blue), Fiat X1-9 (blue) and Land Rover (white)........ **£200-250**

8401 **Wings Flying Club**, 1978, Land Rover, Helicopter, Tipsy Nipper aircraft on trailer, Lotus Elite........ **£200-250**

8402 **Motorway Rescue**, 1978, 'POLICE' Jaguar, Berliet Wrecker, Renault 5 and Fiat X1-9........ **£200-250**

8403 **Spindrift Power Boat Team**, 1979, Ferrari Daytona (yellow), yellow power boat on trailer, yellow/black helicopter, plus MF Tractor and 'RESCUE' dinghy........ **£200-250**

Single models

8800 **Custom Van**, 1979, no details........ **£25-35**

8801	**Spindrift Helicopter**, 1979, black body with yellow chassis, floats and rotor blades.......................................£25-35
8802	**Massey Ferguson Tractor**, 1979, red/black body with white arms and red shovel.....................................£40-50
8803	**Buick 'FIRE CHIEF' Car**, 1979, red body with 'City Fire Department' logo on bonnet.........................£50-75
198100	**Racing Team**, 1978, C421 Land Rover (white with 'FORMULA' logo), 338 Rover, and 301 Lotus on trailer.......£150-200

TROPHY MODELS

The models were specially produced in 1961 to be sold by Marks & Spencer. The set consisted of five vacuum-plated 'gold' models taken from the existing Corgi product range, each mounted on a detachable black moulded base with a gold name label. The models were packaged in white boxes with red/grey design plus 'St Michael Trophy Models' in red. They did not sell well at the time of issue but are keenly sought after by present day collectors. All have gold vacuum-plated body and red wheels and radiator grille.

150 S	**Vanwall Racing Car**......................................£100-150
152	**BRM Racing Car**...£100-150
300	**Austin-Healey Sports Car**...........................£100-150
301	**Triumph TR2 Sports Car**.............................£100-150
302	**MG 'MGA' Sports Car**...................................£100-150

QUALITOYS

A range of sturdy toys made up from the same basic parts. First issued in 1969, they were aimed at the pre-school age group. They were publicized as being from the 'makers of Corgi Toys' and did not form part of the Corgi range as such. Sold in bubble packs.

701	**Pick Up Truck**...£10-15
702	**Side Tipper**, white cab, red chassis , blue back.......£15-20
703	**Breakdown Truck**..NGPP
704	**Tower Wagon**, red cab, blue chassis yellow tower......£15-20
705	**Horse Box**, white cab, yellow chassis turquoise back £10-15
706	**Giraffe Transporter**, white cab, yellow chassis dark red back, with giraffe.................................£10-15
707	**Fire Engine**...NGPP
708	**Pick Up Trailer**, blue and white......................£10-15
712	**Water Sprinkler Truck**, white cab, yellow chassis green tank......£10-15
714	**Jumbo Loader**, orange, yellow cab and fork lift.......£20-25
715	**Jumbo Dozer**, orange, red blade, blue drivers seat......£25-30
750	**Fire Egine with Tender**, red with yellow ladders.......£20-15

CORGITRONICS, CORGIMATICS

These models are generally of plastic construction and feature a device called 'Battery-operated Micro-Chip Action'.

1001	**HCB Angus Firestreak**, 1982, red/yellow/white, 'RESCUE', electronic siren, on/off switch................£60-70
1002	**Sonic Corgi Truck Set**, 1981, yellow/white/black/red, remote control, SHELL SUPER OIL', 'BP OIL'.......£25-30
1002	**'YORKIE' Truck Set**, 1981, white/yellow/blue/orange, remote control, 'MILK CHOCOLATE YORKIE'.......£25-30
1003	**Ford Road Hog**, 1981, black, yellow/white twirls, 2-tone horn, press-down start...........................£15-20

1004	**'Beep Beep Bus'**, 1981, red, 'BTA WELCOME TO BRITAIN', 2-tone horn, press-down start................£20-25
	'Beep Beep Bus', red body with 'WELCOME TO HAMLEYS'....................£20-25
1005	**Police Land Rover**, 1982, white/red/blue, 'POLICE', electronic siren, press-down start......................£15-20
1006	**'RADIO WEST' Roadshow**, 1982, 'Your Local Radio 605', AM radio, advertised but not issued............NPP
1006	**'RADIO LUXEMBOURG'**, 1982, red/white, 'RTL 208', AM radio, 3 loud-speakers...........................£25-30
1007	**Road Repair Unit**, 1982, Land Rover and Trailer yellow/red/silver, 'ROADWORKS', press start, road drill and sound...£25-35
1008	**Fire Chief's Car**, 1982, red/white/yellow/silver, 'FIRE DEPARTMENT', press-down start, siren.......£15-20
1009	**MG Maestro 1600**, 1983, yellow/black, press start, working front and rear lights..............................£15-20
	Red/black body. Sold in Austin-Rover Group box......£20-25
1024	**'Beep Beep Bus'**, 1983, red, 'BTA', supplied exclusively to Mothercare shops........................£20-25
1121	**Ford Transit Tipper Lorry**, 1983, orange/black, flashing light and working tipper.......................£20-25

ROUTEMASTER BUSES

Only models thought to have been totally produced by Corgi have been included in these listings.

Routemaster Buses, 1964–1975 (1st casting)

468	**'NATURALLY CORGI'**, 1964, red, London Transport, 'CORGI CLASSICS' adverts............................£60-70
468	**'NATURALLY CORGI'**, (Australian), 1964, green/cream/brown, 'NEW SOUTH WALES GOVERNMENT TRANSPORT', 'CORGI CLASSICS' adverts.................£400-600
	'NATURALLY CORGI', (Australian), pre-production: as above but with silver uper detaiing inclding middle band......£500-600
	'NATURALLY CORGI', (Australian), empty box for above: blue & yellow box with original "New South Wales" label attached to front and side..............£75-100
468	**'RED ROSE TEA/COFFEE'**, 1966, (Canadian promotional), red body, driver and clippie, 1st type box.......£250-350
468	**'OUTSPAN ORANGES'**, 1967, (Australian issue) 'NEW SOUTH WALES GOVERNMENT TRANSPORT', green/cream/brown body..........£1,000-1,250
468	**'OUTSPAN ORANGES'**, 1967, red, London Transport, '10', (diecast or Whizz Wheels)..............£50-75
468	**'GAMAGES'**, 1968, red, London Transport, '10'.......£200-250
468	**'CHURCH'S SHOES'**, 1969, red, London Transport, '10', Union Jacks................................£15-200
468	**'MADAME TUSSAUDS'**, 1970, red, London Transport, '10'.......£100-175
468	**'THE DESIGN CENTRE'**, 1975, red, London Transport, '10'.......£80-100
468	**'Cokerchu'**, 1969, '2d', red, London Transport.......£150-200

Routemaster Buses 1975–1983 (2nd casting)

C467	**'SELFRIDGES'**, 1977, red, London Transport, '12'. Box 1 – standard; Box 2 – 'SELFRIDGES' own.......£20-25
C469	**'BTA WELCOME TO BRITAIN'**, 1975, red, London Transport, '11', driver, clippie..........£15-20
C469	**'THE DESIGN CENTRE'**, 1976, red, LT, '11', driver, clippie, 'Visit

	The Design Centre' in black or red......................£125-150
C469	**'CADBURYS DOUBLE DECKER'**, 1977, orange, on-pack offer, special box..............................£12-18
C469	**'METTOY Welcomes Swiss Buyers to Swansea'**, 1977£300-400
C469	**'SELFRIDGES'**, 1979, red, London Transport, '12'. Re-issue of C467 (see above)..........................£15-20
C469	**'LEEDS PERMANENT' BUILDING SOCIETY'**, 1979, 'LEEDS', '22'..£15-20
C469	**'SWAN & EDGAR'**, 1979, red, London Transport, '11'.......£15-20
C469	**'HAMLEYS'**, 1979, red, London Transport, '11'.......£15-20
C469	**'HAMLEYS'**, 1980, five clowns advert., '6'.......£10-15
C469	**'BTA'**, 1978, red, London Transport, ('7', '11' or '12')........£10-15
C469	**'BLACKPOOL ILLUMINATIONS'**, 1982, cream/green, '21'.......£30-40
C469	**'CORGI COLLECTORS VISIT'**, 1983.......£300-400
C469	**'GAMLEYS'**, 1983, red, 'Toyshop Of The South'.......£10-15
C469	**'EAGLE STAR'**, 1983, white/black, '1 Threadneedle Street'£10-15
C469	**'REDGATES'**, 1983, cream/brown (red seats) '25'.......£30-40
C469	**'L.T. GOLDEN JUBILEE'**, 1983, (1,000) red/white/silver, 21, 1933-1983...........................£30-40
C469	**'BLACKPOOL PLEASURE BEACH'**, 1983, cream/green, blackpool Transport, '23', 'Britain's No.1 Tourist Attraction'.......£35-45
C469	**'BLACKPOOL PLEASURE BEACH'**, as previous model but open top..................................£50-55
C469	**'NORBROOK MOTORS'**, 1983, dark blue (white seats), '57'.......£12-18
C469	**'NORBROOK MOTORS'**, as previous model but red version.......£12-18
C469	**'DION DION'**, 1983, dark blue, 'Saves You More'.......£10-15
	'DION DION', S. African issue: incorrect label 'Saves You Money'.......£15-20
C469	**'THORNTONS'**, 1983, brown/cream, route '14'.......£10-15
C469	**'MANCHESTER LIONS'**, 1983, cream, '105BN Manchester'.......£15-20
C469	**'NEW CORGI COMPANY'**, 1984, (2,000) red, '29th March 84', 'South Wales - De Cymru'.......£15-20
C469	**'BRITISH MEAT'**, 1984, red..............£10-15
C469	**'COBHAM BUS MUSEUM'**....................£25-35
C469	**'MARKS AND SPENCERS'**, Visit to Factory.......£15-20
C469	**LONDON TRANSPORT ROUTEMASTER BUS**, "Qualitoys visit to Northampton March 1977" - silver, redupper and lower decks.......£100-150
C470	**'DISNEYLAND'**, 1977, yellow open top.......£10-15
C471	**'SEE MORE LONDON'**, 1977, silver, '25','The Queen's silver Jubilee London Celebrations 1977'.......£10-15
C471	**'WOOLWORTHS'**, 1977, silver, '25', 'Woolworths Welcome The World', 'Queens silver Jubilee 1977'.......£20-30
C471	**'ARC Making More of our Natural Resources'**, silver, red interior, silver striped box.......£35-50
C523	**'BRITISH DIECAST MODEL TOYS CATALOGUE'**, 1986, red.......£10-15
C638	**'Great Book of CORGI'**, 1989, yellow/blue, '1956-1983'. Originally only available with book.......£25-35
C469	**'BLACKPOOL PLEASURE BEACH'**, 1983, cream/green, Blackpool Transport, '23', 'Britain's No.1 Tourist Attraction'.......£35-45
C469	**'BLACKPOOL PLEASURE BEACH'**, as previous model but open top..................................£50-55
C469	**'BLACKPOOL PLEASURE BEACH'**, 'Lincoln City Transport'.......£30-50
C469	**'The Last Corgi Collectors Visit to Swansea, 1990, September 26 1990'** only 12 produced in standard issue blue and yellow window box.......£75-100
C470	**'DISNEYLAND'**, 1977, yellow open top.......£10-15
C523	**'BRITISH DIECAST MODEL TOYS CATALOGUE'**, 1986, red.......£10-15
	"SKYRIDER BUS COLLECTORS SOCIETY", white, red upper and lower decks, "South Wales" with destination board "Mumbles".......£100-£120

CORGI TOYS ACCESSORIES

Corgi Kits

601	Batley 'LEOFRIC' Garage, 61-68	£40-60
602	'A.A.' and 'RAC' Telephone Boxes, 61-66	£50-60
603	Silverstone Pits, 61-66	£30-40
604	Silverstone Press Box, 61-66	£50-60
605	Silverstone Club House and Timekeepers Box, 63-67	£60-70
606	Lamp Standards (2), 61-66	£5-10
607	Circus Elephant and Cage, 63-67	£45-55
608	'SHELL' Filling Station, 63-66	£40-60
609	'SHELL' Filling Station Forecourt Accessories, 63-66	£25-35
610	Metropolitan Police Box and Public Telephone Kiosk, 63-66	£60-70
611	Motel Chalet, 63-66	£25-35

Self-adhesive accessories

1460	'A' Pack, 1959, (66 items) including tax discs, number plates, 'GB' and 'Running-In' labels, etc	£10-15
1461	'B' Pack, 1959, (36 items) including white-wall tyre trim, 'Styla Sports Discs', number plates, etc	£10-15
1462	'C' Pack, 1959, (69 items) including number plates, commercial and road fund licences (A, B and C), 20 and 30mph speed limit and trailer plates, etc	£10-15
1463	'D' Pack, 1959, (100 items) including number plates, 'Corps Diplomatique' and 'L' Plates, touring pennants, etc	£10-15
1464	'E' Pack, 1961, (86 items) including assorted badges, 'Take-Off Wheels', trade and licence plates, etc	£10-15

Spare wheels

For 'Take-off Wheels' models; bubble-packed on card.

1341	For 344 Ferrari Dino Sport, 1970, shown in 1969 catalogue but model issued with Whizz Wheels	£10-15
1342	For 300 Chevrolet Corvette, 1968	£10-15
1351	For 275 Rover 2000 TC, 1968	£10-15
1352	For 276 Oldsmobile Toronado, 1968	£10-15
	For 338 Chevrolet Camaro	£10-15
	For 343 Pontiac Firebird, shown in 1969 catalogue but model issued without 'Take-off Wheels'	£10-15
1353	For 342 Lamborghini P400, 1970	£10-15
	For 302 Hillman Hunter Rally	£10-15
1354	273 Rolls silver Shadow, 1970	£10-15
1361	341 Mini Marcos GT 850, 1968, (the first 'Take-Off Wheels' model)	£10-15

Figures

1501	Racing Drivers and Pit Mechanics (6), 63-69	£10-15
1502	Silverstone Spectators (6), 63-69	£10-15
1503	Race Track Officials (6), 63-69	£10-15
1504	Press Officials (6), 63-69	£10-15
1505	Garage Attendants (6), 63-69	£10-15

CORGI 'CARGOES'

Bubble-packed on card

1485	Lorry Load - Planks, 1960	£10-15
1486	Lorry Load - Bricks, 1960	£10-15
1487	Lorry Load - Milk Churns, 1960	£10-15
1488	Lorry Load - Cement, 1960	£10-15
1490	Skip and 3 Churns, 1960	£10-15

Spare tyre packs

1449	New Standard 15 mm, 70-71	£10-15
1450	Standard 15 mm, 58-70	£10-15
1451	Utility Vehicles 17 mm, 61-70	£10-15
1452	Major Models 19 mm, 61-70	£8-10
1453	Mini Cars 13 mm, 65-70	£10-15
1454	Tractor wheels (Rear) 33 mm, 67-70	£10-15
1455	Tractor wheels (Front) 19 mm, 67-70	£10-15
1456	Racing wheels (Rear) 16 mm, 67-70	£10-15
1457	Racing wheels (Front) 14 mm, 67-70	£10-15
1458	Commercial (Large) 24 mm, 67-70	£10-15
1459	Commercial (Medium) 19 mm, 67-70	£10-15

Miscellaneous

1401	Service Ramp (operable), 58-60	£15-20
1445	Red bulb for 437 Ambulance, 1962	£2-3
1441	Blue bulb for 464 Police Van, 1963	£2-3
1443	Red flashing bulb, 437 Ambulance, 1967	£2-3
1444	Blue flashing bulb, 464 Police, 1967	£2-3
1445	Bulb for 'TV' in 262 Lincoln, 1967	£2-3
1446	Tyres for 1150 Snowplough, 1970	£2-3
1480	Nose cone, Corporal Missile, 1959	£2-3
1497	James Bond Spares 2 Bandits + lapel badge (261), 1967	£15-25
1498	James Bond Spares Missiles for 336 Toyota, 1967	£10-15
1499	Green Hornet Spares Missiles & scanners (268), 1967	£10-15
	Corgi Club Badge Gold Corgi dog, red backing, 1960s	£20-25
	'SHELL' Filling Station and Garage, blue/red/white, single floor, plastic 'SHELL' logo, 62-64	£300-400
	'CENTRAL PARK GARAGE', blue/yellow/red/white, three floors, 'SKYPARK' logo, 62-64	£300-400
24205	Batmobile Accessory Pack (sprue of missiles), 1967	£25-35

Empty Boxes

51	Massey Ferguson 65 Trailer and Tipper	£10-15
53	Massey Ferguson 65 Tractor with Shovel	£15-25
57	Massey Ferguson 65 Tractor with Fork	£10-15
62	"For Your Eyes Only" Empty Trade Counter Box	£175-200
64	Plough	£10-15
101	Platform Trailer	£10-12
161	Santa Pod Raceway Commuter Dragster	£3-5
205	Rover 90 Saloon	£75-100
205	Riley Pathfinder Saloon	£15-20
207	Standard Vanguard (Blue)	£35-45
211	Studebaker Golden Hawk	£15-20
214	Ford Thunderbird	£5-8
217	Fiat	£8-12
218	Aston Martin DB4	£15-20
220	Chevrolet Impala	£10-12
223	Chevrolet Impala 'State Patrol'	£15-20
224	Bentley	£8-12
225	Austin 7	£8-12
226	Morris Mini Minor	£15-20
231	Triumph Herald Coupe	£10-12
238	Jaguar Mk.X	£15-20
241	Ghia L.6.4	£15-20
247	Mercedes Pullman 600	£15-20
252	Rover	£8-12
258	Saints Volvo	£20-30
260	Renault	£15-20
261	James Bond's Aston Martin DB5	£20-30

269	Lotus Esprit	£25-30
275	Rover 2000TC	£15-20
300	Austin Healey Sports Car (Blue)	£40-60
301	Triumph TR2 Sports Car (Blue)	£40-60
302	Hillman Hunter 'London to Sydney Marathon Winner'	£25-30
	MGA Sports Car (Blue)	£35-45
305	Triumph TR3 Sports Car	£15-20
310	Chevrolet Corvette Stingray	£10-12
312	Marcos Mantis window box	£15-20
314	Ferrari Berlinetta	£15-20
317	Monte Carlo BMC Mini Cooper S	£35-50
320	Ford Mustang	£15-25
332	Lancia Fulvia	£10-15
336	James Bond Toyota 2000 GT	£20-30
337	Chevrolet Corvette Stingray	£20-30
339	BMC Mini Cooper S 'Rallye Monte Carlo', blue and yellow carded picture box	£50-75
343	Pontiac Firebird	£3-5
344	Ferrari	£5-10
394	Datsun 240Z	£3-5
403	Ford Thunderbird 'Taxi Bermuda'	£20-30
404	Bedford Dormobile Minibus	£30-40
416	Land Rover 'RAC Radio Rescue'	£10-15
417 S	Land Rover Breakdown	£15-25
419	Ford Zephyr 'Motorway Patrol'	£15-20
422	Bedford 12 CWT Van Corgi Van	£40-75
440	Ford Consul Cortina Super Estate Car	£25-30
441	Volkswagen Toblerone Van	£5-10
448	BMC Mini Police Van	£15-25
454	Commer Platform Lorry	£5-10
464	Commer Police Van	£5-10
464	Citroen Le Dandy Coupe	£5-10
468	Blue and Yellow Routemaster Bus Box with original 'New South Wales' label	£75-100
497	Thrushbuster outer box	£20-30
499	Citroen Safari Winter Olympics	£20-30
500	"US Army" Land Rover	£10-12
503	Bedford "Chipperfields Circus"	£25-30
607	Circus Elephant Transport Cage	£20-30
801	'Noddy's Car' with 'Noddy, Big Ears & Golly' figures	£75-100
808	'Basil Brush'	£25-30
1108	Bristol Bloodhound Guided Missile	£20-30
1121	'Chipperfield Circus' Crane Truck	£20-30
1123	Animal Cage	£10-15
1129	Articulated Milk Tanker	£10-15
GS17	Land Rover with Ferrari Racing Car	£17-100
GS21	ERF Dropside and Platform Trailer	£25-30
GS26	Tarzan	£20-30
	Bedford Articulated Tanker 'Benzene Shell', promotional box complete with correct colour folded leaflet	£750-1,000

GIFT SETS

Original internal packaging for securing models and accessories must all be present before sets can be considered complete and therefore achieve the best price. See Corgi Toys model identification page.

1	Transporter and 4 Cars, 1957-62, 1101 blue/yellow Bedford Carrimore Transporter plus 201 Austin Cambridge, 208 Jaguar 24, 301 Triumph TR2 (or 300 Austin-Healey) and 302 MGA, plus two yellow/black 'Corgi Toys' dummy boxes	£700-900
1a	Transporter and 4 Cars, 1957-62, 1101 red/two-tone blue Transporter, 200 Ford Consul, 201 Austin Cambridge, 204 Rover 90, 205 Riley, 2 yellow 'Corgi Toys' dummy boxes	£350-450
1b	Transporter and 4 Cars, 1959-62, 1101 red/two-tone blue Transporter, 214 Thunderbird Hardtop, 215 Thunderbird Convertible, 219 Plymouth Suburban, 220 Chevrolet Impala. (US set)	£500-750
1101	Yellow/blue Transporter	£750-1000
1b	Car Transporter and 4 Cars, 1101 Bedford Carrimore Car Transporter, red cab, blue/off white trailer 216 Austin A40 Saloon, No.226 Morris Mini Minor, light blue, red interior, spun hubs, No.234 Ford Consul Classic, cream, pink roof, yellow interior, spun hubs, No.305 Triumph TR3 Sports Car	£800-900
1c	Transporter and 4 Cars, 1961-62, 1101 red/two-tone blue Transporter, 210s Citroën (or 217 Fiat 1800), 219 Plymouth Suburban, 226 Mini, 305 Triumph TR3. (US issue set)	£400-500
1	Farm Set, 1966-72, Ford 5000 Tractor + 58 Beast Carrier, pictorial stand	£200-250
1	Ford Sierra Set, 1983, Ford Sierra 299 with blue body, blue/cream caravan	£20-30
2	Land Rover and Pony Trailer, 1958-68, 438 Land Rover (green, beige tin tilt) and 102 Rice Pony Trailer (red/black)	£100-150
	Same set but all red Land Rover.	£175-225
	Lt. brown Land Rover (Apricot plastic tilt), light brown/cream trailer	£100-150
2	Unimog Dumper and Shovel, 1971-73, 1128 Mercedes Tipper and 1145 Unimog Goose. Yellow/blue 'window' box	£60-70
2	Construction Set, 1980-81, 54 Tractor, 440 Mazda, tool-box and cement mixer	£30-35
	1980-80 French export: 1110 and 1156 plus cement mixer.	£30-40
3	Thunderbird Missile Set, 1959-63, 350 Thunderbird Missile and	

351 Land Rover. Blue/yellow card box ***£175-220***

3 **Batmobile and Batboat**, 1967-69, 1st issue: 267 Batmobile with 'Bat' wheels, plus 107 Batboat, in plain blue 1st issue 'window' box with inner tray and 4 figures, instruction sheet ***£500-700***
2nd issue: 267 Batmobile with red wheels (without 'Bat' design), plus 107 Batboat. Yellow/blue 'window' box should also have unopened instruction pack ***£900-1,100***
3rd issue: 1980, 267 Batmobile (plain cast wheels), and 107 Batboat (WW), two figures. Striped 'window' box should also contain instructions in unopened packet ***£250-350***

4 **Bristol Ferranti Bloodhound Guided Missile Set**, 1958-60, Contains: 351, 1115, 1116, 1117. Blue/yellow card box ***£250-350***

4 **Country Farm Set**, 1974-75, models 50 and 62 plus hay load, boy and girl. Striped 'window' box ***£100-125***

5 **Racing Car Set**, 1959-60, 150 (red), 151 (blue), 152 (green). Smooth hubs. Yellow/blue lift-off lid box, vac-formed inner ***£300-400***
1960-61, 150 (red), 151 (blue with red bonnet stripe), 152 (green). Flat or cast spoked wheels. Yellow/blue box, polystyrene tray ***£300-350***

5S **Racing Car Set**, 1962-63, 150s (red), 151a (blue), 152s (turquoise). Yellow/blue box with 'Gift Set 5s' stickers, inner polystyrene tray ***£350-450***

5 **Agricultural Set**, 1967-72, 484 Livestock Transporter and pigs, 438 Land Rover (no hood) 62, 69, 71, accessories 1490 skip and churns, 4 calves, farmhand and dog, 6 sacks. Box has inner pictorial stand ***£500-750***

5 **Country Farm Set**, 1976-77, as Farm Set 4, but minus boy, girl and hay load ***£100-150***

6 **'Rocket Age' Set**, 1959-60, contains: 350, 351, 352, 353, 1106, 1108, 1117 ***£1,500-2,500***

6 **Cooper-Maserati Set**, 1967-69, contains 490 VW Breakdown Truck plus 156 Maserati on trailer. 'Window'/flap box ***£180-220***

7 **Tractor and Trailer Set**, 1959-64, 50 Massey-Ferguson 65 Tractor and 51 Trailer. Yellow/blue card box ***£300-400***

7 **'DAKTARI' Set**, 1968-76, 438 Land Rover in green with black Zebra stripes, spun or cast hubs. 5 figures: Paula, Dr Marsh Tracy with chimp Judy on his lap, a Tiger on the bonnet, and Clarence The Short-Sighted Lion (with spectacles!), yellow/blue 'window' box ***£175-200***
With WhizzWheels. Striped box ***£100-125***

8 **Combine Harvester**, tractor and trailer set, 1959-62, contains 1111, 50 and 51. Tractor has copper seat, red metal hubs ***£250-300***

8 **'Lions of Longleat' Set**, 1968-74, Land Rover with shaped hubs, keeper, 3 lions, plastic den, 3 joints of meat. Yellow/blue 'window' box with header card and inner packing ***£100-150***
Same but WW. Striped 'window' box ***£100-125***

9 **Corporal Guided Missile Set**, contains: 1112, 1113, 1118 ***£300-400***

9 **Tractor, Trailer and Shovel Set**, 1968-72, contains 66 Ferguson 165 Tractor with 69 Shovel and 62 Tipper Trailer with detachable raves. Yellow/blue all-card box, inner pictorial stand ***£250-275***

9 **'RNLI' Rescue Set**, 1979-82, Land Rover 'Mumbles' on door, Dinghy on trailer. White, blue, red, black. Striped 'window' box ***£75-95***

9 **Three Racing Minis Set**, yellow, white and blue, numbers/stripes and adverts, special 'Hamleys' box ***£90-110***

10 **Marlin Rambler Set**, 1968-69, blue/white 319 with Trailer, 2 canoes (1 with figure). Yellow/blue box, inner packing, pictorial tray ***£200-250***

10 **Tank Transporter Set**, 1973-78, contains 901 Centurion Mk.I Tank and 1100 Mack articulated transporter. Picture card box ***£100-120***

10 **Jeep Set**, 1982, Red 441 plus motorcycle on trailer ***£20-25***

10 **Sierra and Caravan Set**, 1985, C299 Sierra + pale brown caravan ***£25-35***

11 **ERF Dropside and Trailer**, 1960-64, 456 and 101 with cement and planks load. Yellow/blue picture box, inner card stand ***£150-200***

12 **'Chipperfields Circus' Set**, 1961-64, 1121 Crane Truck, 'CHIPPERFIELDS' and 1123 Circus Cage, plus instructions. Yellow/blue all-card picture box ***£250-350***

12 **Grand Prix Racing Set**, 1968-71, 155, 156 and 330 with 490 VW tender, 3 mechanics, 16 bollards and hay bales. Yellow/blue 'window' box also contains cones in bag, instructions, 'Mr Retailer' card and inner polystyrene tray ***£250-350***
1971-72, 158, 159 and 330 (or 371) with 490 Volkswagen tender, 3 mechanics, 16 bollards and hay bales. The artwork on the box and the vac-formed base are different from previous issue ***£450-550***

12 **Glider and Trailer Set**, 1981-, 345 with trailer and glider ***£50-60***

13 **Fordson Tractor and Plough Set**, 1964-66, contains 60 Fordson Power Major Tractor and 61 four furrow plough in blue, orange plastic front and rear hubs. Yellow/blue box with inner tray ***£250-350***

13 **Renault 16 Film Unit**, 1968-72, white/black, 'TOUR DE FRANCE', 'PARAMOUNT', cameraman, cyclist. Yellow/blue box with inner tray plus plain orange card backdrop ***£200-250***

13 **Tour de France 'RALEIGH' Team Car**, 1981-82, 373 Peugeot, white body, red/yellow 'RALEIGH'/'TOTAL' logos, racing cycles, Manager with loudhailer ***£150-175***

14 **Tower Wagon Set**, 1961-64, 409 Jeep, yellow cradle, lamp standard, electrician. Yellow/blue card box ***£100-120***

14 **Giant 'DAKTARI' Set**, gift set and items plus 503 and 484 transporters (spun hubs), large and small elephants. Blue/yellow window box with pictorial header card, inner tray ***£300-400***
Version with WhizzWheels. Striped 'window' box with pictorial header card and inner tray ***£150-200***

15 **Silverstone Set**, 1963-64, 150s, 151a, 152s, 215s, 304s, 309, 417s, three buildings, plain box (no picture) ***£2,000-2,500***
1964-66, 150s, 154, 152s, 215s, 304s, 309, 417s, three buildings, layout on box ***£2,000-2,500***

15 **Land Rover and Horsebox Set**, 1968-77, contains 438, 112, spun hubs, mare and foal. Yellow/blue box contains inner polystyrene tray ***£100-150***
Version with WhizzWheels, striped 'window' box has inner card packing ***£55-75***

15 **'TARMAC' Motorway Set**, 1986, 'Motorway Maintenance' green/black 1128 Mercedes Tipper, Mazda Pickup and a compressor ***£20-30***

16 **'ECURIE ECOSSE' Set**, 1961-65, 1126 Transporter with 3 individually boxed racing cars in all-card lift-off lid box with instruction leaflet and internal packing. Metallic dark blue 1126 Transporter (with orange lettering), 150 Vanwall (red, '25'), 151 Lotus XI (blue, RN '3'), 152 BRM (turquoise, RN '3') ***£400-500***
Met. Dk. blue 1126 Transporter (with yellow lettering), 1965, 150s Vanwall, 151a Lotus XI (blue, '7'), 152s BRM ***£400-500***
Met. Light blue 1126 Transporter (with red Lettering), 150s Vanwall, 152s BRM, 154 Ferrari (RN '36') ***£750-1,000***
Met. Dk. blue 1126 Transporter (with light blue lettering and ridges), 150s Vanwall, 152s BRM, 154 Ferrari ***£300-350***

17 **Ferrari Racing Set**, 1963-67, 438 Land Rover in red with green or Tan tilte, red 154 Ferrari F1 on yellow trailer. Yellow/blue box has inner tray ***£200-240***

17 **Military Set**, 1977-80, contains 904, 906, 920 ***£40-50***

18 **Ford Tractor and Plough Set**, 1961-63, 55 Fordson Power Major Tractor and 56 four furrow plough in blue/red/yellow. Drab orange hubs. Yellow/blue box with inner tray ***£200-250***

18 **Emergency Gift Set**, 1975-80, contains 402, 481, C921 ***£60-70***

18 **3 Mini Racers Set**, CHELSEA', 'PARK LANE' and 'PICADILLY' logos ***£20-30***

18 **Mini Special Editions Set**, with 'RED HOT', 'RITZ' & 'JET BLACK' logos ***£20-30***
NB C18/1 and C18/2 were sold (in long 'window' boxes) exclusively by Woolworths.

19 **'CHIPPERFIELDS' Cage Set**, 1962-68, 1st issue: 438 Land Rover (metal tilt) and 607 elephant and cage on trailer. Blue/yellow picture box has inner card tray + additional packing ***£250-300***
2nd issue: as before but 438 Land Rover has a plastic tilt ***£130-175***

19 **Land Rover and Nipper Aircraft**, 1972-77, 438 Land-Rover (blue/orange, tinplate tilt) + trailer. blue/orange/yellow plane '23' or blue/ orange/white plane '23', yellow/blue 'window' box ***£60-70***

19 **'CORGI FLYING CLUB'**, 1973-77, as previous set but Land-Rover has a plastic tilt ***£45-60***

19 **Emergency Gift Set**, 1979-82, C339 and C921. Striped 'window' box ***£40-60***

19 **Emergency Gift Set**, 1980-82, C339 & C931 in red/white. Striped 'window' box ***£40-60***

20 **'Golden Guinea' Set**, 1961-64, gold-plated 224 Bentley Continental, 234 Ford Consul, 229 Chevrolet Corvair, Catalogue, 2 Accessory Packs. Inner card tray with lower card packing, outer dark green sleeve with window some sets have Simca 1000 sports in place of the Corvair ***£400-500***

20 **Tri-Deck Transporter Set**, 1970-73, (Scammell Handyman Mk.III), 1st issue contains 1146 Transporter with six 'WhizzWheels' cars: 210 'Saint's' Volvo, 311 Ford Capri, 343 Pontiac, 372 Lancia, 377 Marcos, 378 MGC GT (red body). Instruction sheet, 'Mr Retailer' transit card protector ***£600-700***
NB GS 20 may be found with widely differing contents as Corgi used up excess stock in this Set.
Harrods set: late issue set with: 1146 T Transporter, 382 Porsche Targa (silver blue), 313 Ford Cortina GXL (Bronze/black), 201 Volvo (orange 'Saint' label), 334 Mini (orange) and 377 Marcos (silver green). Box also has instruction sheet and 'Mr Retailer' transit card protector ***£600-700***

20 **Emergency Gift Set**, 1978-80, C429, C482, C921. Box has inner tray ***£35-45***

21 **ERF Dropside and Trailer**, 1962-66, 456 and 101 with milk churns and self-adhesive accessories. Yellow/blue box with inner card stand ***£225-275***

21 **'Chipperfields' Circus Set**, 1969-71, contains 1144 Crane and Cage, and 1139 Menagerie Transporter. Yellow/blue window box with internal packaging and 'Mr Dealer' box protector card ***£1,000-1,600***

21 **Superman Set**, 1980-82, contains 260, 265 and 925, plus inner tray and plastic rockets on sprue ***£500-600***

22 **Farming Set**, 1962-65, contains 1111 M-F Combine Harvester, 406 Land-Rover &Trailer, 51 Tipping Trailer, 101 Platform Trailer, 53 M-F 65 Tractor with Shovel, 1487 Milk Churns, 1490 Skip & 3 churns, plus models in Gift Set 18. Lift-off lid all-card picture box with inner polystyrene tray ***£1,750-2,000***

22 **James Bond Set**, 1980-82, 269 Lotus Esprit, 271 Aston-Martin DB5 and 649 Space Shuttle + rockets, 2 spare bandit figures. Box has inner tray ***£400-475***

23 **'CHIPPERFIELDS' Set**, 1962-66, 1st issue: 1121 Crane Truck, 2 x 1123 Animal Cages (2 lions, 2 polar bears), plus Gift Set 19 and 426 Booking Office. All-card lift-off lid picture box with inner polystyrene tray ***£400-500***
1964, 2nd issue: as 1st issue but 503 'TK Giraffe Truck' replaces 426 Booking Office, inner polystyrene tray ***£300-400***

23 **Spiderman Set**, 1980-82, 261 Spiderbuggy, 266 Spiderbike, 928 Spider-copter with figures, missiles on sprue. In striped 'window' box ***£250-300***

24 **Commer Constructor Set**, 1963-68, 2 cab/chassis units, 4 interchangeable bodies plus milkman and accessories, yellow/blue picture box with lift-off lid and inner polystyrene tray ***£100-130***

24 **Mercedes and Caravan**, 1976-78, 285 in metallic blue plus 490 caravan in white. Striped 'window' box ***£30-40***
1979, 285 in metallic brown plus 490 caravan in bronze. Striped 'window' box ***£30-40***

25 **BP or Shell Garage Set**, 1963-66, Contains 224 Bentley Continental, 225 Austin Seven 229 Chevrolet Corvair, 234 Ford Consul, 419 Ford Zephyr, Motorway Patrol, 601 Bentley, Garage x 3, 606 Lamp Standards x 2, 608 Shell filling station, 609 Shell filling station accessories, 1505 Garage Attendants ***£1,000-1,500***

25 **Racing Car and Tender**, 1969-71, 159 and VW Tender, 2 sets of decals in stapled bags. Blue/yellow window box, inner plastic tray ***£120-150***

25 **Talbot Rancho Set**, 1980-81, 457 plus two motorcycles on trailer ***£25-30***
26 **Beach Buggy Set**, 1971-76, 381 plus red Sailing Boat with blue sail, orange/yellow 'window' box........ ***£40-50***
26 **Corgi Racing Set**, 1981-83, 457 Talbot Matra Rancho, 160 Hesketh (yellow), 'Corgi Racing Team' trailer........ ***£35-45***
27 **Priestman Shovel on Machinery Carrier**, 1963-72, 1128 and 1131 (Bedford). Blue/yellow box with inner tray........ ***£175-225***
28 **Transporter and 4 Cars**, 1963-65, 1105 Bedford TK Transporter with 222 Renault Floride, 230 Mercedes-Benz, 232 Fiat, 234 Ford Classic, 2 dummy 'Corgi Toys' boxes, instructions. Pictorial box, internal card packing........ ***£400-500***
28 **Mazda B1600 Dinghy Set**, 1975-78, 493 Mazda + dinghy and trailer. Striped 'window' box........ ***£35-40***
29 **Massey-Ferguson Set**, 1963-65, contains 50 Massey-Ferguson Tractor with driver and 51 Tipper Trailer - cream/yellow, red plastic rear hubs. Yellow/blue all-card box with inner tray........ ***£150-200***
29 **'CORGI' Pony Club**, 1981-82, contains 441 Jeep, 112 trailer, girl on pony, 3 jumps, 3 hay bales. Striped 'window' box........ ***£55-65***
29 **'DUCKHAMS' FI Racing Set**, 1975-76, Surtees Racing Set with 323 Ferrari Daytona and 150 Ferrari in blue/yellow 'DUCKHAMS RACING TEAM' livery. Striped 'window' box........ ***£35-40***
30 **Grand Prix Gift Set**, 1973-73, 'Kit' versions of 151 Yardley (1501), 154 JPS (1504), 152 Surtees (1502) plus 153 Surtees (1503)? in unique Norris livery. Picture 'window' box. Mail order only........ ***£100-120***
30 **Circus Gift Set**, 1979-80, Land Rover and Trailer........ ***£60-75***
31 **Buick Riviera Boat Set**, 1964-68, 245 Buick, red boat trailer, and Dolphin Cabin Cruiser towing lady water-skier. Pictorial sleeve box with internal packing display tray around models.. ***£250-350***
31 **Safari Land Rover Set**, 1976-80, C341 Land Rover with animal trailer, warden and lion. Box has inner polystyrene tray... ***£35-45***
32 **Tractor, Shovel and Trailer Set**, 1965-68, 54 Massey-Ferguson 65 Tractor, 69 Shovel, 62 Tipping Trailer with detachable raves - red/cream/yellow. Yellow/blue picture box with inner pictorial stand........ ***£250-300***
32 **Lotus Racing Set**, 1976-79, C301 Lotus Elite, and C154 JPS Lotus on trailer........ ***£100-125***
C301 Lotus Elite, and C154 Texaco Lotus on trailer, 1979-83........ ***£35-45***
33 **Tractor and Beast Carrier**, 1965-68, Contains 55 and 58........ ***£300-450***
Contains 67 and 58, 1968-72........ ***£80-100***
33 **'DLRG' Rescue Set**, 1980-82, white/red 421 Land Rover and boat on trailer........ ***£50-70***
34 **Tractor & Tipping Trailer**, 1976-79, contains 55 and 56.***£55-65***
35 **London Traffic Set**, 1964-68, 418 Taxi with 468 'Corgi Toys' or 'Outspan' Bus, policeman on stand, yellow/blue box, inner tray........ ***£200-300***
35 **'CHOPPER SQUAD' Surf Boat**, 1978-79, contains 927, 419, trailer, rescue boat........ ***£30-40***
36 **Marlin Rambler Set**, 1967-70, contains 263 and Boat.... ***£75-100***
36 **Oldsmobile Toronado Set**, 1967-71, 276 (greenish-blue), chrome trailer, yellow/blue 'SWORDFISH' boat, 3 figures. Yellow/blue box........ ***£150-200***
36 **Off-Road Set**, 1983, 447 (dark blue/cream, RN '5') plus power-boat on trailer........ ***£25-35***
36 **Tarzan Set**, 1976-78, light green 421 Land Rover and trailer, paler green 'zebra' stripes, Tarzan, Jane, Cheetah (chimp), boy, dinghy with hunter, elephant, snake, vines, etc. yellow/blue 'window' box with inner pictorial backing display........ ***£250-350***
37 **'Lotus Racing Team'**, 1966-69, 490 VW Breakdown Truck, red trailer with cars 318, 319, 155, plus 2 sets of spare racing numbers ('5' and '9' or '4' and '8'), a 1966 illustrated checklist, a sealed pack of cones, set of bollards and a spare Lotus chassis unit. Yellow/blue 'window' box has inner polystyrene tray........ ***£400-500***
37 **Fiat X-19 Set**, 1979-80, Fiat X-19 and boat 'Carlsberg'........ ***£30-40***
38 **Mini 1000 Camping Set**, 1977-78, cream Mini with 2 figures, tent, barbecue, in inner display stand........ ***£125-50***
38 **'1965 Monte Carlo Rally'**, 1965-67, 318 Mini Cooper 'S', 322 Rover 2000, and 326 Citroën DS19. Monte Carlo Rally emblem on each bonnet. Yellow/blue all-card box contains pictorial stand and inner card packing........ ***£1,000-1,250***
38 **Jaguar XJS Set**, 1980-, 319 with Powerboat on Trailer........ ***£20-30***
40 **'The Avengers' Set**, 1966-69, John Steed's Bentley (green body, red wire wheels), Emma Peel's Lotus Elan (black/white body), Steed and Emma Peel figures, 3 black umbrellas. Yellow/blue picture box with inner pictorial stand........ ***£500-600***
With red/black Bentley with silver wire wheels........ ***£350-450***
40 **'Batman' Gift Set**, Contains modified 107 Trailer plus 267 Batmobile (WW) and 925 Helicopter. 12 missiles on a sprue. Striped box also has inner tray with card packing........ ***£850-950***
41 **Carrimore Car Transporter**, 1966-68, (with Ford Tilt Cab), 1138 Transporter (red/Two-tone blue), 252 Rover 2000 (Metallic Plum), 251 Hillman Imp (Metallic Bronze), 440 Ford Cortina Estate (Metallic blue), 226 Morris Mini-Minor (Light blue), 321 Austin Mini Cooper 'S' (red, RN '2', '1966 Monte Carlo Rally', with roof signatures), 249 Morris Mini Cooper DeLuxe (black/red, 'wickerwork' panels). Pictorial lift-off lid box with inner polystyrene tray. Only sold by mail order........ ***£550-750***
41 **Carrimore Car Transporter**, 1969-69, (with Scammell Cab), 1148 Transporter (red/two-tone blue), 226 Morris Mini-Minor (metallic maroon), 345 MGC GT (orange in earliest sets, yellow/black later), 340 Sunbeam Imp (1967 Monte Carlo, Metallic blue, RN '77'), 258 Saint's Volvo P1800 (white with orange label), 249 Morris Mini Cooper DeLuxe (black/red with 'wicker-work' panels), 339 Mini Cooper 'S' ('1967 Monte Carlo Rally', RN '177'), plus sealed bag of cones and leaflet. Pictorial lift-off lid box with inner polystyrene tray. Only sold by mail order........ ***£750-850***
41 **Silver Jubilee Set**, 1977-81, The State Landau, HRH Queen Elizabeth and Prince Phillip (+ a Corgi!)........ ***£15-20***
42 **Agricultural Set**, 1978-79, Contains 55 David brown Tractor plus 56 Trailer, Silo and Elevator........ ***£100-125***
43 **Silo and Conveyor Set**, 1979-80, 'CORGI HARVESTING COMPANY Ltd'........ ***£40-50***
44 **Metropolitan Police Set**, 1978-80, 421 Land Rover, 112 Horsebox, Policeman on horse. Striped 'window' box........ ***£40-50***
44 **Mounted Police Set**, 1978-80, French issue, policeman on horse........ ***£50-75***
45 **'All Winners' Set**, 1966, 261 James Bond's Aston-Martin, 310 Chevrolet Stingray, 324 Marcos Volvo, 325 Ford Mustang Competition, 314 Ferrari Berlinetta. Yellow/blue 'window' box........ ***£350-450***
45 **Royal Canadian Police Set**, 1978-79, Land Rover (421), Trailer (102), 'Mountie' on horse........ ***£125-150***
46 **'All Winners' Set**, 1966-69, 264 Oldsmobile Toronado (Metallic blue), 307 Jaguar 'E'-type (Chrome finish, RN '2', driver), 314 Ferrari Berlinetta (red, RN '4'), 337 Chevrolet Stingray (yellow, RN '13'), 327 MGB GT (red/black, suitcase). Box should contain unopened bag of cones and decal sheets........ ***£500-660***
46 **Super Karts Set**, 1982, red Kart, Purple Kart, with silver/red driver in each........ ***NGPP***

47 **Ford 5000 Tractor & Conveyor Set**, 1966-71, Contains 67, trailer with conveyor belt, figure & accessories. Box has inner display card........ ***£200-250***
47 **Pony Club Set**, 1978-80, 421 Land Rover and Horsebox in metallic bronze, girl on pony figure........ ***£35-40***
48 **Carrimore Car Transporter**, 1967-68, (with Ford Tilt Cab), 1138 Transporter (orange/silver/two-tone blue) with 252 Rover 2000 (metallic plum), 251 Hillman Imp (metallic maroon), 440 Ford Cortina Estate (metallic blue), 249 Morris Mini Cooper DeLuxe (with wickerwork' panels), 226 Morris Mini-Minor (metallic maroon), 321 Mini Cooper 'S' ('1966 Monte Carlo Rally'), red/white, RN '2'. blue/yellow 'window' box with inner polystyrene packing........ ***£600-800***
1968, 'SUN/RAC' variation: as previous set but 321 Mini Cooper is replaced by 333 SUN/RAC Rally Mini. 251 Hillman Imp is changed to metallic gold with white stripe and the 226 Austin 7 Mini is now metallic blue with RN '21'........ ***£700-900***
48 **Carrimore Car Transporter**, 1969, (with Scammell Cab), 1148 Transporter (red/white) with 345 MGB (orange), 340 Sunbeam Imp (1967 Monte Carlo, Metallic blue, '77'), 258 Saint's Volvo P1800 (white with orange label), 249 Morris Mini Cooper DeLuxe (with 'wickerwork' panels), 339 Mini Cooper 'S' ('1967 Monte Carlo Rally', RN '177'), 226 Morris Mini-Minor (metallic maroon), plus sealed bag of cones and leaflet. Blue/yellow 'window' box, inner polystyrene packing........ ***£800-900***
48 **'PINDER' Circus Set**, 1978-80, contains C426, C1163, C30, ringmaster, artistes, animals, seating, and cardboard cut-out 'Jean Richard Pinder' 'Big-Top' circus tent. Striped 'window' box......... ***£100-110***
48 **"KNIE" Circus Gift Set**, Land Rover, Booking Office, 2 x Trailers, Human Cannon plus various accessories including Big Top diorama........ ***£125-175***
49 **'CORGI FLYING CLUB'**, 1978-80, metallic green/white Jeep (419) with blue/white Tipsy Nipper Aircraft........ ***£30-50***
51 **'100 Years of the Car' Set**, 19??, 3 Mercedes: C805 (white), C806 (black), C811 (red), originally for Germany........ ***£20-25***
'The Jaguar Collection', 1978-80, C804 (cream), C816 (red), C318 (Mobil green/white). ('UNIPART' stores)........ ***£30-35***
53 **Land Rover & Thunderbirds Missile Set**, models as listed........ ***£500-750***
54 **Swiss Rega Set**, 1978-80, Bonna Ambulance and Helicopter........ ***£30-35***
55 **Norway Emergency Set**, 1978-80, Police Car, Breakdown Truck, Ford Transit Ambulance, 'UTRYKKNINGUSSETT'........ ***£20-30***
56 **Swedish Set**, 1978-80, Ford 'POLIS', Bonna Ambulance.... ***£12-18***
57 **Swedish Set**, 1978-80, red Volvo, white/red/blue caravan. Swedish export........ ***£15-20***
61 **Swiss 'FEUERWEHR' Set**, 1978-80, 1120 Dennis Fire Engine, Sierra 'POLITZEI', Escort Van 'NOTRUF'........ ***£30-35***
64 **FC Jeep 150 and Conveyor Belt**, 1965-69, Jeep (409) yellow/white Conveyor........ ***£100-130***
65 **Norway Set**, 1978-80, Ford Transit Ambulance plus Helicopter........ ***£20-30***
67 **Cyclists Sets**, 1978-80, sold in France, 2 Cars, 2 Bicycles. Three sets: 67/1, 67/2, 67/3 Each set:........ ***£20-30***
70 **Danish 'FALCK' Set**, 1978-80, Bonna Ambulance and Ford Breakdown Truck........ ***£20-30***
72 **Norway Set**, 1978-80, With C542 plus Helicopter 'LN OSH'***£20-30***
1151, Scammell 'Co-op' Set, 1970, blue/white 1147, 466 and 462. Promo in brown box........ ***£300-400***

Monte Carlo Game Set, 1967, (Scandinavian set), Fernel Developments game with two Lavender 226 Minis, '1967 Rallye Monte Carlo' bonnet labels, RNs '1' and '4', plastic/paper winding roads, cards, dice shakers, blue/white/red box........ ***£150-200***

Construction Site Set, 1980, contains 54 with 440 (Mazda Pick-Up)........ ***£30-35***

US EXPORT SETS

Made exclusively for FAO Schwarz of America

FAO-012 **'BEST IN SHOW' Animal Gift Set**, 1966, Contains: GS2 Land-Rover with Rice's Pony Trailer, 484 Dodge Kew Fargo and 486 Chevrolet Impala 'Kennel Club'. Blue/yellow individual card boxes, blue/yellow presentation box........ ***£1,500-2,000***
FAO-804 **'CIRCUS' Set**, 1968, Contains: GS7 'Daktari' Set, 470 Forward Control Jeep, 1123 'Chipperfields' Circus Animal Cage and GS19 'Chipperfields Circus' Land-Rover and Elephant Cage on Trailer. Blue/yellow individual boxes, blue/yellow presentation box........ ***£1,750-2,250***

'The Italian Job', 1995, Produced by TMC Marketing for Rover MG to celebrate shipment of real Minis. Finished in red, white and blue with 'Longbridge Channel Tunnel Crossing 1965' decal on roof. 1:36 scale, on wooden plinth and in presentation box. Only100 sets issued..... ***£100-175***

'HUSKY' MODELS 1964-1969 AND CORGI 'JUNIORS' 1970-1983

1 **Jaguar Mk.10**, 65-69, all have yellow interior........ ***£***
1-a1 **Met. blue**, GPW, 65-66, (small),........ ***£20-25***
1-a2 **Red body**, GPW, 1966, (small)........ ***£50-60***
1-b1 **Light Metallic blue**, GPW, 1967,........ ***£20-25***
1-b2 **Blue body**, GPW, 1967........ ***£25-30***
1-b3 **Light Met. blue body**, tyres, 1968........ ***£25-30***
1-b4 **Cream body**, tyres, 1968,........ ***£45-55***

1-b5 **Dark blue body**, tyres, 1969 ***£25-30***
1-b6 **Dark maroon body**, tyres, 1969 ***£30-35***
1-a1 **Reliant TW9 Pick Up**, 1970, beige body, black WW ***£20-25***
1-a2 **Orange body**, black WW, 70-72, ***£15-20***
2 **Citroën Safari with Boat**, 65-69
2-a1 **Pale yellow body**, tan boat, GPW, 65-66, (small casting) ***£20-25***
2-b1 **Metallic green body**, brown boat, GPW, 1967 ***£35-50***
2-b2 **Metallic gold body**, blue boat, GPW, 1967, ***£40-45***
2-b3 **Met. gold**, blue boat, tyres, 68-69 ***£20-25***
2-a1 **Citroën Safari with (white) Boat**, 1970, blue body, tyres ***£30-40***
2-a2 **With black WhizzWheels**, 1970 ***£20-25***
2-a3 **Yellow body**, BWW, 71-72, ***£20-25***
2-a4 **Purple body**, BWW, 71-72, ***£20-25***
3-a1 **Mercedes 220**, 65-67, pale blue, opening boot GPW ***£20-25***
3-bt **Volkswagen Police Car**, 67-68, white/black doors, smooth hubs with tyres ***£25-30***
3-b2 **With detailed hubs/tyres**, 1969 ***£25-30***
3-a1 **Volkswagen 1300 Police**, 1970, car white body, tyres ***£30-35***
3-a2 **With black WhizzWheels**, 1970, ***£20-25***
3-a3/4 **With chrome WhizzWheels**, 71-72, ***£20-25***
4 **Jaguar Fire Chief**, 65-69
4-a1 **Red body**, chrome siren, 'Fire', GPW, 65-66, (small casting) ***£25-30***
4-bl **As previous model**, 1967, ***£25-30***
4-b2 **Same but with tyres**, 68-69 ***£30-35***
4-a1 **Zeteor 5511 Tractor**, 70-72, orange, red base, BPW ***£10-15***
5-a1 **Lancia Flaminia**, 1965, red, GPW ***£20-25***
5-a2 **Blue**, GPW, 65-66 ***£20-25***
5-b1 **Willys Jeep**, 67-69, metallic green, grey windshield ***£15-20***
5-b2 **With yellow windshield**, 67-69 ***£25-30***
5-a1 **Tan body**, brown int., tyres, 1970 ***£15-20***
5-a2 **With black WhizzWheels**, 1970 ***£10-15***
5-a3 **With chrome WhizzWheels**, 1971 ***£10-15***
5-a4 **Orange**, brown int., BWW, 1970 ***£10-15***
5-a5 **Same**, chrome Whizzwheels, 1971 ***£10-15***
5-a6 **Red body**, yellow int., CWW, 71-72 ***£10-15***
5c **NASA Space Shuttle 70mm**, 80-83, black and white with US Flag and U.S.A logos. Packaged either as 'Columbia' or 'Enterprise' ***£25-30***
6-a1 **De Tomaso Mangusta**, 1970, lime green, BWW ***£10-15***
6-a2 **Metallic purple**, black WW, 1970 ***£10-15***
6-a3 **Metallic purple**, CWW, 71-72, ***£10-15***
6-a1 **Citroën Safari Ambulance**, 65-67, white, red cross, GPW ***£25-40***
6-b1 **Ferrari Berlinetta**, 68-69, red body, tyres ***£25-30***
6-b2 **Maroon body**, tyres, 68-69 ***£25-30***
7-a1 **Buick Electra**, 65-66, orange-red, GPW ***£15-20***
7-b1 **Duple Vista 25 Coach**, 67, green/white, GPW ***£30-35***
7-b2 **Same but with tyres**, 68-69 ***£20-25***
7-a1 **Duple Vista 25 Coach**, 1970, red body/white roof, tyres ***£20-25***
7-a2 **Yellow/white**, black WW, 1970, ***£12-15***
7-a3 **Purple/white**, chrome WW, 71-72, ***£12-15***
7-a4 **Orange/white**, chrome WW, 71-72, ***£12-15***
8 **Ford Thunderbird Convertible**, 65-66, pink, black open body, GPW ***£30-35***
8-b1 **Ford Thunderbird Hardtop**, 1967, yellow, blue top, GPW ***£45-55***
8-c1 **Tipping Farm Trailer**, 67-69, yellow, red back, tyres ***£10-15***
8 **Rover 3500 Saloon**, 79-83, dark metallic blue WW ***£8-12***
80-81 **Light Metallic blue** ***£8-12***
Other colours, yellow, blue, maroon red & silver ***£8-12***
9-a1 **Buick 'Police' Patrol**, 65-67, dark blue, GPW ***£20-25***
9-b1 **Vigilant Range Rover**, 71-72, white body, chrome WW ***£12-15***
9-b1 **Cadillac Eldorado**, 68-69, light blue, tyres ***£20-25***
9-c **Police Range Rover**, 73-80, white Dome lights 'Police' WW ***£10-12***
9-a1 **Cadillac Eldorado**, 1970, met. green, red int., tyres ***£25-30***
9-a2 **With black WhizzWheels**, 1970 ***£15-20***
9-a3 **White/black**, BWW, 1970 ***£15-20***
9-a4 **White/black**, chrome WW, 1971, ***£15-20***
9-b1 **Vigilant Range Rover**, 71-72, white body, chrome WW ***£12-15***
10-a1 **Guy Warrior Coal Truck**, 64-69, red, GPW ***£15-20***
10-a2 **Orange**, tyres, 1970 ***£25-30***
10-b1 **Ford GT7O**, orange, CWW, 73-7, ***£20-25***
10c **Triumph TR7 77mm**, 77/83, white/blue, silver/red, silver. No.3 'TR7' on bonnet ***£10-15***
Red/dark blue flash, red, No.7 'British Airways' logo ***£10-15***
Red, orange, yellow, green, black, brown, blue, metallic copper, cream no labels ***£10-15***
Gold plated, display plinth, gold presentation box promotional model for British Leyland at launch of real car ***NGPP***
11-a1 **Forward Control Land Rover 66mm**, 65-67, green body (shades), metal or plastic base, rear corner windows, GPW ***£10-15***
11-a2 **Same**, but metallic green, no corner windows, GPW, 68-69, ***£15-20***
11-af **Austin Healey Sprite Le Mans**, 1970, red body, blue interior, grey base, '50', sticker pack, black WW ***£30-35***
11-a2 **Yellow interior**, chrome WW,1971, ***£30-35***
11-a3 **Red body**, yellow interior, black base, CWW, 71-72, ***£30-35***
11c **Supermobile**, 79/83, blue, striking fists Logo ***£20-30***
12-a1 **Reliant-Ogle Scimitar GTE**, 1970, white body, black WW ***£20-25***
12-a2 **Metallic blue**, chrome WW, 1970 ***£20-25***
12-a3 **Matt blue**, chrome WW, 71-72, ***£20-25***
12-a1 **Volkswagen Tower Wagon**, 65-66, yellow/red, GPW ***£20-25***

12-b1 **Ford Tower Truck**, 1967, yellow, red tower, GPW ***£30-35***
12-b2 **White**, red tower, GPW, 1967, ***£30-35***
12-b3 **White**, red tower, tyres, 68-69 ***£20-25***
12d **Ford FT 70 73mm**, 75-76, orange, metallic green ***£10-15***
12e **Golden Eagle Jeep 68mm**, 79-81, metallic brown, white or tan top ***£10-15***
13-a1 **Guy Warrior Sand Truck**, 65-66, yellow, GPW ***£15-20***
13-a2 **Blue**, GPW, 67-68, ***£15-20***
13-a3 **Blue**, tyres, 1969, ***£20-25***
13-b **Rough Terrain Truck 66mm**, 76-78, red or blue tow hook ***£8-12***
13c **Buck Rogers Starfighter 72mm**, 80-83, white, yellow retracting wings no wheels ***£10-12***
14-a1 **Guy Warrior Tanker 'Shell'**, 65-66, yellow, round tank, GPW ***£20-25***
14-b1 **Same but square tank**, 1967, ***£20-25***
14-b2 **Guy Warrior Tanker 'Esso'**, 1967, white, square tank, GPW ***£20-25***
14-b3 **Same but with tyres**, 68-69 ***£20-25***
14d **Buick Regal Taxi 70mm**, 77-80, white black base WW ***£10-15***
15-a1 **VW Pick Up**, turquoise, GPW, 67-71 ***£15-20***
15-b1 **Studebaker Wagonaire TV Car**, 67-68, yellow body, GPW ***£20-25***
15-b2 **Metallic blue body**, GPW, 1968 ***£25-30***
15-b3 **Metallic blue body**, tyres, 1969 ***£25-30***
15-a1 **Studebaker Wagonaire TV Car**, 1970, metallic turquoise, tyres ***£35-40***
15-a2 **Yellow body**, black WW, 1970 ***£25-30***
15-a3 **Met. Lime green**, BWW, 1970, ***£25-30***
15-a4 **Met. Lime green**, CWW, 71-72, ***£25-30***
15c **Mercedes-Benz Bus 74mm**, 73-83, various colours, black base WW 'School Bus' logo ***£8-12***
16-a1 **Dump Truck/Dozer**, 65-66, yellow, red back, GPW ***£15-20***
16-a2 **Dump Truck/Dozer**, 1966, red, grey back, GPW ***£20-25***
16-a **Land Rover Pick Up**, 70-72, metallic green, blue, purple non metallic olive, green, CWW ***£20-25***
17c **Rover 3500 Police Car 77mm**, 80-83, white blue roof bar 'Police'on side and Hatch WW ***£10-15***
17 **Guy Warrior 'Milk' Tanker**, 65-69.
17-a1 **White**, round tank, GPW, 65-66 ***£20-25***
17-b1 **White**, square tank, GPW, 1967 ***£20-25***
17-b2 **Cream**, round tank, GPW,1968 ***£20-25***
17-b3 **Cream**, round tank, tyres,1969 ***£20-25***
17-af **Volkswagen 1300 Beetle**, 1970, met. blue, 'flower' decals ***£45-50***
17-a2 **Metallic green body**, 70-72 ***£20-25***
17d **Buick City of Metropolis Police Car**, 79-83, red roof light, 'City of Metropolis on bonnet. Police on side, WW metallic dark blue, non metallic light blue ***£15-20***

18-a1 **Plated Jaguar (small casting 66mm)**, 65-66, gold plated, GPW ***£20-25***
Large casting 71mm tyres silver or gold plated ***£20-25***
18c **Wigwam Camper Van 77mm**, 77-??, red, dark blue, Lt blue WW ***£15-20***
19-a1 **Commer Walk Thro' Van**, 65-69, red body, GPW ***£40-45***
19-a2 **Green body**, GPW, 66-67, ***£25-30***
19-b1 **Speedboat on Trailer**, 68-69, gold trailer, red, white and blue boat, tyres ***£15-20***
19-a1 **Blue trailer**, red, white and blue boat, tyres, 70-73, ***£20-30***
19-a2 **With black WhizzWheels**, 1970 ***£20-30***
19-a3 **With chrome WhizzWheels**, 71-72 ***£10-15***
19c **Pink Panther Motorcycle 68mm**, 80-82, unpainted metal and plastic bike, black plastic spoked wheels, pink Panther figure ***£20-25***
20-a1 **Ford Thames Van**, 65-66, red, yellow ladder, GPW ***£20-25***
20-b1 **VW 1300 with Luggage**, 1967, tan body, tyres ***£35-45***
20-b2 **With blue body**, 67-69 ***£20-25***
Red or yellow VW, 70-71 ***£20-25***
20c **Cement Mixer Trailer 45mm**, 79-81, gold engine, red plastic barrel black plastic wheels ***£8-12***
20d **Penguinmobile 73mm**, 79-81, white, Penguin driver, 'Penguin' logo on spoiler, umbrella lable on bonnet WW ***£20-25***
21-a1 **Forward Control Military**, 66-67, Land Rover, olive green, white star on roof, GPW ***£15-20***
21-a1 **BVRT Vita-Min Mini Cooper S**, 71-72, metallic purple, Race No. on side WW ***£30-40***
21-b1 **Jaguar 'E'-type 2+2**, 68-69, maroon body, tyres ***£20-25***
21d **Chevrolet Charlie's Angels Van 68mm**, 77-81, pink, 'Charlie's Angels' logo 'Chevrolet Van' on base ***£15-25***
As above with 'US Van' on base WW on both ***£15-25***
22-a1 **Citroën Safari Military Ambulance**, GPW ***£20-25***
22-b1 **Aston-Martin DB6**, 67-68, metallic bronze body, GPW ***£30-50***
22-b2 **Purple body**, tyres, 68-69 ***£30-35***
22-a2 **Metallic olive body**, tyres, 1970 ***£45-50***
22-b1 **Formula 1 GP Racing Car**, 73-78, yellow body, Union flag Race No. 3. WW ***£15-20***
Promotional model 'Weetabix' ***NGPP***
22d **Paramedic Emergency Unit 68mm**, 81-83, white Chevrolet van, red & black graphics on side, tinted windows 'US' or 'Chevrolet' van on base ***£5-8***
23-a1 **Guy Army Tanker**, 66-67, white star and US Army transfers, GPW ***£15-20***
23-b1 **Loadmaster Shovel**, 1968, orange body, BPW ***£25-30***
23-b2 **Yellow body**, BPW, 68-69, ***£15-20***
70-74 **Yellow body**, BPW ***£10-12***
23c **Batbike 68mm**, 79-83, unpainted and black plastic bike, black/yellow Bat label, Batman figure, black plastic 5 spoke wheels ***£20-25***
24-a1 **Ford Zephyr Estate**, 66-69, red or blue metallic body, GPW ***£20-25***
24-a1 **Aston-Martin DBS**, 71-73, light green body, chrome WW ***£30-40***
24c **Shazam Thunderbolt 77mm**, 79-81, yellow, red/yellow/black labels ***£20-25***
25-a1 **SD Refuse Van**, blue, GPW, 66-67 ***£15-20***
25-a2 **Red body**, GPW, 1968 ***£40-50***
25-a3 **Red body**, tyres, 68-69 ***£40-45***
26-a1 **Sunbeam Alpine 61mm**, 66-67, metallic bronze body, blue hard top, GPW ***£20-25***
26-a2 **Same but red body**, GPW, 1967 ***£45-55***
26-a3 **Red body**, blue top, tyres, 68-69 ***£50-55***
26b **ERF Fire Tender 76mm**, 70-74, red body, yellow ladder, chrome WW ***£12-15***
As above with opaque black windows, 82-83, ***£10-15***
27-a1 **Bedford Skip Lorry**, 66-67, maroon, unpainted skip,GPW ***£20-25***
27-a2 **Dark green unpainted skip**, GPW, 1967 ***£50-60***
27-a3 **Orange silver skip**, GPW, 1967 ***£20-25***
27-a4 **Orange body**, tyres, 68-69 ***£20-25***
Red, silver skip, tyres, 70, ***£20-25***
Red, yellow skip, diecast wheels with black tyres, 71, ***£15-20***
28b **Formula 5000 Racing Car 74mm**, 73-81, black, white driver, Race No.4 blue & white stripe,WW ***£10-15***
Red, yellow driver, No.4 blue & white stripe WW ***£10-15***
Red, yellow driver, No.8 yellow & silver stripe WW ***£10-15***
28-a1 **Ford Breakdown Truck**, 66-67, blue, metal jib, GPW ***£15-20***
28-a2 **Blue**, gold jib, tyres, 68-69, ***£20-25***
70-71 **Dark blue**, BPW ***£25-30***
Pale green, WW ***£20-25***
28b **Hot Rodder 77mm**, 73-76, yellow, tinted windshield, red & blue stripe, WW ***£15-20***
28c **Buick Regal Police Car 76mm**, 77-78, white, black roof, red roof light, white & black POLICE labels, WW ***£8-12***
29d **Buick Regal Sheriff's Car 76mm**, 80-81, black, white roof, tinted or clear windows, black & white 'Sheriff' labels ***£8-12***
29-a1 **ERF Cement Mixer**, yellow, red barrel, GPW, 66-67, ***£15-20***
29-a2 **Yellow**, red barrel, BPW, 68-69, ***£20-25***
29b **ERF Simon Snorkel Fire Engine 79mm**, 70-71, dark red BPW or WW ***£15-25***
29c **New casting with longer cab**, and deeper basket WW, 72-73, ***£10-15***
29d **Bright red**, various tinted windows 1970 WW, 74-83, ***£5-10***
30-a1 **Studebaker Wagonaire Ambulance White**, red Cross, on roof,

stretcher, GPW, 66-67 ....£25-30
30-a2 **Same**, but with BPW £25-30
30-a3 **Pale green body**, tyres, 1969 ....£35-40
30-a3 **With non-removable stretcher**, black WW, 1970 ....£15-20
30-a4/5 **Fixed stretcher**, small CWW, 71-72 ....£15-20
30d **Ford Mobile Cement Mixer 73mm**, 76-83, 76-79 metallic or non metallic olive green, yellow barrel, WW £8-12
80-83 **Mixture of various colours for body and Barrel** £8-12
31-a1 **Oldsmobile Starfire Coupé 76mm**, 66-67, metallic olive green or blue body, yellow interior GPW £15-20
31-a1 **Same but with BPW**, 68-69, ...£20-25
31-a1 **Land Rover Breakdown**, 70-80, red or purple body 'Wrecker Truck' decals
31-a2 **Metallic or non metallic blue**, '24 Hour Crash Service'..£12-15
Red, no label £10-15
Matt olive green 'Recovery' label WW £8-10
Metallic dark blue 'Motor Trader' Promotional for magazine £20-25
Red, 'M1 Breakdown' £15-20
32-a1 **Volkswagen Luggage Elevator**, 66-67, white body, with red or yellow conveyor, GPW £25-30
Red, red conveyor GPW £25-30
32-a2 **With blue conveyor**, GPW, 1967, ...£35-45
32-a3 **Red with blue conveyor**, GPW, 68-69, ...£35-40
32-a1 **Lotus Europa 71mm**, 70-71, metallic green, Union Jack label on one side opening rear hatch WW £20-30
32-a2 **Light green as above**, 1972, ...£15-20
32c **The Saint's Jaguar XJS 76mm**, 78-81, white, red or yellow interior, black Saint figure label on bonnet £20-25
33-a1 **Farm Trailer and Calves**, 67-70, four tan plastic calves, yellow plastic wheels 'Husky' or 'Juniors' on base £10-15
33-b1 **Jaguar 'E'-type 2+2 71mm**, 70-75, yellow, red or blue body CWW £20-30
33c **Chevrolet Ambulance Van** ....NPP
33d **Wonder Woman's Wonder Car 62mm**, 79-80, orange, 'Wonder Woman' label on bonnet, WW £25-30
34-a1 **B.M. Volvo 400 Tractor**, 67-69, red, yellow wheels, tyres 'Husky' base £15-20
70-74 **As above 'Juniors' base** £15-20
34b **Stinger Army Helicopter 70mm**, 75-78, olive body, white 'Army' label £10-15
White body, 'Search' labels £10-15
White body no labels £8-12
35-a1 **Ford Camper**, 67-72, 1967 yellow, GPW £20-25
Metallic blue, GPW, 1967 ....£30-40
Metallic blue, tyres, 68-69, ...£25-30
Turquoise, tyres £30-35
35-a2 **Same but black WW**, 70-2, ...£25-30
35-a3 **Red with cream back**, BWW, 70-2, ...£25-30
35b **Air Bus Helicopter 70mm**, 1983, orange or metallic blue body, white 'A', with black 'Airbus' label £8-12
35c **Tipper Truck 71mm**, 1983, silver with blue tipper WW £20-25
Red with tan or white tipper £20-25
36-a1 **Simon Snorkel Fire Engine**, 1967, red, GPW ..£20-25
36-a2 **Red with tyres**, 68-69 ....£20-25
36b **Healer Wheeler 76mm**, 73-77, 'Healer Wheeler' on base, WW white, Red Cross and Ambulance labels £15-20
36c **Chevrolet Coca-Cola Van 68mm**, 79-80, red, red and white 'Coca-Cola' label 'US Van' or Chevrolet Van' on base £15-20
37-a1 **NSU Ro80 Metallic blue body**, tyres, 68-69, ..£25-30
37-a2 **Metallic Mauve body**, BWW, 1970 ....£15-20
37-a3 **Purple body**, BWW, 1970 ....£15-20
37-a4 **Purple body**, CWW, 71-72 ....£15-20
37-a5 **Metallic Copper body**, CWW, 71-72 ....£15-20
Pink Body WW £15-20
37b **Porsche Carrera Police Car 74mm**, 76-80, white, 'Police' label over red stripe WW £10-15
White with green top 'Polizei' label (German Issue)......£15-20
38-a1 **Rices Beaufort Single Horse Box**, 1968, Turquoise, tyres£10-15
38-a2 **Metallic green body**, tyres £20-25
38-a2 **Red body**, tyres, 1970 ....£20-30
38-a3 **Red body**, black WW, 1970 ....£20-25
38-a4 **Metallic Copper**, CWW, 71-72 ....£20-25
38b **Jerry's Banger 75mm**, 80-83, orange body, short fat green plastic cannon, red cannonball, brown figure £15-20
As above with blue cannonball £15-20
39-a1 **Jaguar XJ6 4.2**, 1969, yellow, red interior, tyres £45-55
39-a2 **Silver with red interior**, BWW, 1970 ....£25-35
39-a3 **Silver with red interior**, CWW, 71-72 ....£25-30
39-a4 **Met. red**, yellow int., CWW, 71-72 ....£25-30
39-a5 **Red body**, yellow int., CWW, 71-72 ....£25-30
39b **Jaguar E type 2+2 71mm**, 75-77, As 33B, WW brick red, or metallic purple £12-15
39c **Chevrolet Pepsi-Cola Van 68mm**, 79-80, no interior, black plastic base WW white, red/white/lt blue/dk blue 'Pepsi-Cola' label on sides with either 'US Van' or Chevrolet Van' on base £15-20
40-a1 **Ford Transit Caravan**, 1969, red body, tyres £25-35
40-a1 **Lime green body**, tyres, 1969 ....£25-35
40-a1 **Ford Transit Caravan**, 1970, yellow body, blue interior, silver rear door, tyres £25-30
40-a2 **Yellow, cream int.**, BWW, 1970, ...£20-25

40-a3 **Blue body**, cream int., BWW, 1970 ....£20-25
40-a4 **Blue body**, cream int., CWW 71-72 ....£20-25
40-a5 **Metallic pale blue body**, cream interior, CWW, 71-72 ....£15-20
40-a6 **Metallic pale blue body**, cream int., black plastic base, CWW, 1972 ....£15-20
40b **Metallic Grey**, CWW £10-15
40b **Army Red Cross Helicopter 70mm**, 77-78, same casting as 35B, olive green, Army' red cross labels £10-15
40c **James Bond Aston Martin 72mm**, 79-83, metallic silver body, red interior, 2 figures, WW £25-35
41-a1 **Porsche Carrera 6**, 70-73, white with red 19 decal on bonnet 'Corgi Junior' BPW on base £15-20
White with red 19 decal on bonnet 'Corgi Junior Whizzwheels' on base WW £6-10
41b **James Bond Space Shuttle 70mm**, 79-81, same as 5c with yellow labels with No.5 and 'Drax logo £20-25

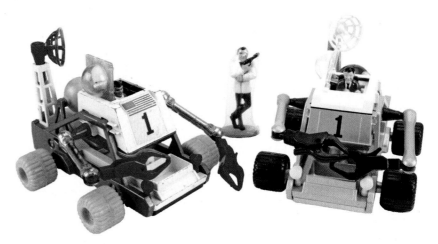

42-a **Euclid Truck 35 Ton Rear Dump Truck 70mm**, 69-71, yellow cab, red back, dark grey base, black wheels £20-25
42-a2 **Red cab**, yellow back, unpainted base, CWW, 1970 ....£10-15
42-a3 **Yellow cab**, red back, dark grey base, BWW, 71-72 ..£10-15
42-a4 **Blue cab**, silver back, dark grey base, CWW, 71-72, ...£10-15
42-a5 **Blue cab**, yellow back, dark grey base, CWW, 71-72 ..£10-15
42-b **Terex R35 Rear Dump Truck 70mm**, 72-75, red, yellow tipper WW £10-15
Blue with yellow, blue or beige tipper £10-15
42c **Rescue Range Rover 69mm**, 77-80, red, various interior colours, pale yellow stripe, 'Rescue Team' WW £10-15
Red, white stripe, 'Crash Tender WW £15-20
Red or orange, yellow label 'Rescue' WW £15-20
Light blue, white labels 'Coastguard' WW £20-25
43-a **Massey-Ferguson 3003 with Blade**, 69-80, yellow body/blade 'Husky' base £10-15
'Junior Base' £10-12
44-a1 **Raygo Rascal Road Roller**, 70-72, blue/orange, BPW ..£10-12
45-a1 **Mercedes 280SL**, 1970, met. silver, red int., tyres ..£30-35
45-a2 **Metallic blue body**, red interior, black WW, 1970 ..£20-25
45-a3 **Yellow body**, red interior, unpainted base, BWW, 1970 ..£15-20
45-a4 **Yellow body**, red interior, white base, BWW, 1970 ....£15-20

45-a5 **Red body**, cream interior, BWW, 1970 ....£25-30
45-a6 **Red body**, cream interior, CWW, 71-72, ...£25-30
45-a7 **Blue body**, cream interior, unpainted base, CWW, 71-72, £20-25
46-a1 **Jensen Interceptor**, 1970, maroon body, yellow interior, unpainted base, tyres £35-40
46-a2 **Maroon body**, black WW, 1970 ....£25-30
46-a4 **Orange body**, CWW, 1971 ....£30-50
46-a4 **Metallic green body**, CWW, 1972 ....£25-30
47-a1 **Scammell Concrete Mixer**, 71-72, white/red, CWW......£10-15
48-a1 **ERF Tipper Truck**, 71-72, red cab, silver back, unpainted or grey base, CWW £15-20
48-a1 **Blue cab**, orange back, 71-72 ....£15-20
48-a1 **Blue cab**, yellow back, 71-72 ....£15-20
49-a1 **Pininfarina Modulo**, 71-72, yellow, red stripe, CWW ..£15-20
50-a1 **Ferrari 512s**, 71-72, metallic red, CWW £15-20
51-a1 **Porsche 917**, 71-72, gold, RN '23', CWW £15-20

52-a1 **Adams Probe 16**, 71-72, metallic pink, CWW £15-20
54-a1 **Ford Container Wagon**, 71-72, red, yellow skip, CWW....£15-20
55-a1 **Daimler Fleetline Bus**, 70-72, red, 'Uniflo', CWW £15-20
56-a1 **Ford Capri Fire Chief** red/white, 'Fire' decal on door, white interior, CWW, 70-72 ....£25-30
56-a2 **With 'Fire Chief' decal**, 70-72 ....£25-30
56-a3 **All-red**, 'Fire Chief' on door, yellow interior, CWW, 70-72£25-30
57-a1 **Caddy Hot Rodder**, 70-72, metallic blue, 'Caddy Hot Roddy' on doors, sticker pack, CWW £12-15
57-a2 **Metallic pink body**, CWW, 70-72 ....£12-15
58-a1 **G.P. Beach Buggy**, 71-72, Met. red, cream int., CWW £10-12
58-a2 **Same but yellow interior**, 71-72 ....£10-12
59-a1 **The Futura**, 71-72, orange, black base, sheet of stickers, CWW....£15-20
60-a1 **VW Double Trouble Hot Rod**, 71-72, metallic pink, CWW....£15-20
61-a1 **Mercury Cougar Police Car**, 70-72 ....£15-20
62-a1 **Volvo P1800**, 1970, red, yellow interior, CWW £35-40
62-a2 **Red**, blue interior, CWW, 71-72 ....£25-30
62-a3 **Red**, cream interior, CWW, 1972 ....£45-50
63-a1 **Ford Escort Monte Carlo Rally Car**, 70-72, met. blue, RN '32', CWW ....
Red interior, stickers sheet, CWW £40-50

63-a2 **With yellow interior**, CWW, 1972 ... *£50-60*
63-a3 **With cream interior**, CWW, 1972 ... *£50-60*
64-a1 **Morgan Plus 8**, 71-72, yellow, CWW ... *£25-35*
64-a2 **Red**, RN '20', CWW, 71-72 ... *£25-35*
65-a1 **Bertone Carabo**, 71-72, met. purple, white int, CWW ... *£12-15*
65-a2 **Orange interior**, CWW, 71-72 ... *£10-12*
67-a1 **Ford Capri 'Hot Pants' Dragster**, 71-72, yellow body, CWW ... *£35-40*
70-a1 **US Racing Buggy**, blue, 71-72 ... *£15-20*
71-a1 **Marcos XP**, orange, CWW, 71-72 ... *£15-20*
72-a1 **Mercedes-Benz C111**, red, ... *£15-20*
73-a1 **Pininfarina Alfa Romeo P33**, 71-72, blue body, chrome WW ... *£15-20*
74-a1 **Bertone Barchetta**, orange, 71-72, ... *£15-20*
75-a1 **Superstock Car**, 71-72, silver, Union Jack, stickers ... *£20-25*
76-a1 **Chevrolet Astro**, metallic red, 71-72, ... *£15-20*
77-a1 **Bizzarrini Manta**, pink, 71-72, ... *£15-20*
78-a1 **Old MacDonald's Truck**, 71-72, ... *£30-40*
1017 **Holmes Wrecker and Towing Cradle**, 71-72, yellow cab, red back, 'Auto Rescue' ... *£100-120*

Husky Accessories

1550 **Playmat**, 67-69, vinyl mat with printed play scene ... *£25-35*
1561/2 **Traffic Signs**, 68-69 ... *£20-30*
1571 **Pedestrians**, 68-69 ... *£15-20*
1572 **Workmen**, 68-69 ... *£15-20*
1573 **Garage Personnel**, 68-69 ... *£10-15*
1574 **Public Servants**, 68-69 ... *£10-15*
1580 **Husky Collector Case**, 68-69, storage for 48 models ... *£15-25*
1585 **Husky Traveller Case**, 68-69, opens to form Service Station (this item never seen) ... *NPP*
2001 **'HUSKY' Multi Garage**, 68-69, a set of four garages, (no cars), 'Husky' on base ... *£25-35*
As previous but with 'CORGI' logo, 'Juniors' on base, 70-75 ... *£10-15*
1970s USA Dealer display unit, A wooden revolving unit with lighting, brown/black, 'Collect Husky Models' ... *£200-300*

HUSKY MAJORS 1964-69/SUPER CORGI JUNIORS MODELS 1970-83

2001 **'HUSKY' Multi Garage**, a set of four garages yellow or red framework (no cars), 'Husky' on base ... *£35-50*
Corgi Juniors issue as previous model but with 'CORGI' logo, 'Juniors' on base, 70-75 ... *£10-15*
2002 **'HUSKY' Car Transporter Hoynor MkII**, white/blue/orange, cab, 'Husky' on base ... *£30-40*
Corgi Juniors issue as previous model but with 'CORGI' logo, 'Juniors' on base ... *£25-35*
2003a **Ford Machinery Low-Loader**, red/blue/yellow, cab, drop-down ramp, 'Husky' base ... *£20-25*
2003b **Corgi Juniors issue** as previous model with metal wheels or WW, 'Juniors' on base ... *£20-25*
2004a **Removals Delivery Van**, red or blue cab, plated box, 'HUSKY REMOVALS', metal wheels, 'Husky' on base ... *£40-50*
2004b **Corgi Juniors issue**, 'CORGI REMOVALS', WW, 'Juniors' base ... *£30-35*
2006 **Mack 'ESSO' Tanker**, white body and tank, WW, 'Juniors' on base ... *£30-35*
2007 **Ford Low Loader with Shovel Loader 140mm WW**, same casting as 2003, yellow cab, blue semi-trailer, red & yellow shovel loader (48b) ... *£30-40*
Red cab, blue semi-trailer, orange & yellow shovel loader (48b) ... *£30-40*
2008 **Greyhound Bus 169mm**, white, red/white/blue Greyhound American cruiser labels ... *£25-35*
2009 **Aerocar 150mm**, yellow car with black propeller, red & yellow stripe with white N846 labels WW ... *£45-50*
2010 **Mack Exxon Tanker** ... *NPP*
2011 **Mack U.S. Army Tanker 180mm**, same casting as 2006 drab olive cab chassis. U.S. Army and white star logo ... *£35-45*
2012 **Ford U.S, Army Low loader & Armored Car 140mm**, olive cab and trailer, white star labels, Commando Armoured Car BWW ... *£35-45*
2014 **Mercedes Benz Car Transporter**, white cab body, red cab chassis lower deck and tailgate WW ... *£25-35*
2015 **Mercedes Benz Car Transporter & Trailer 415mm**, Transporter as above. Trailer with white cab, red chassis, yellow upper deck, red lower deck WW ... *£35-45*
2017 **Scamoa Dump Truck 147mm**, yellow cab, chassis red plastic tipper WW ... *£15-20*
2018 **Scania Container Truck 138mm**, red cab, chassis, grey flatbed, white plastic container with blue/black 'Seatrain' labels WW ... *£20-25*
Pre-production: burnt orange cab and back, brown roof deflector and container with "WH Smith" to one side only ... *£75-100*
2019 **Scania Silo Truck 144mm**, orange cab, chassis, brown, tan & white containers, 'British Grain' logo WW ... *£15-20*
2020 **Mercedes Benz Refrigerator Van**, white cab, blue or metallic blue chassis, red & white 'Birdseye' logo WW ... *£25-35*
2025 **Swiss P.T.T. Bus 169mm**, yellow, white roof, red/yellow/black P.T.T. logo WW ... *£45-55*
2027 **Mack Ryder Rentals Van**, 1979-?, yellow Cab, trailer, black chassis 'Ryder Truck Rental' logo WW ... *£25-35*
2028 **Mercedes Refrigerator Truck 125mm**, 1977-78, White cab, and trailer, blue chassis 'Gervais' & 'Danone' Logos WW ... *£20-25*
2029 **Mack Fire Engine 143 mm**, 1979-83, red, white roof, yellow ladders, 'No.3 Hammond Fire Dept.' logo chrome wheels. *£20-30*

Husky Film and TV-related Models, 1967–1969

1001-a1 **James Bond Aston Martin DB6**, 1967, silver, red or brown interior, 2 ejector figures, GPW ... *£180-200*
1001-a2 **James Bond Aston Martin DB6**, 1968-69, same but with tyres ... *£180-200*
1002-a1 **Batmobile**, 1967-69, black, Batman and Robin figures, tow hook, GPW ... *£150-160*
1003-a1 **Batboat**, 1967-69, black boat, red fin, Batman and Robin figures, GPW ... *£150-160*
1004-a1 **Monkeemobile**, 1968-69, red, white roof, 4 figures, 'Monkees' on doors, tyres ... *£160-180*
1005-a1 **Man From UNCLE Car**, 1968-69, blue, 3 Missiles on sprue, 2 figures, tyres ... *£160-175*
1006-a1 **Chitty Chitty Bang Bang**, 1969, chrome, dark Grey base, red wings, yellow fins, 4 figures, tyres ... *£140-180*

Husky and Corgi Juniors Gift Sets 1968-83

3001 **Four Garage Set**, 1968-69, contains 23, 27, 29, or 9, 30 or 36 ... *£75-130*
3002 **Batmobile Set**, 1968-69, 1002 Batmobile and 1003 Batboat on trailer ... *£250-320*
3002 **'Club Racing' Set**, 1970, Juniors set of 8 racing cars including Mini Cooper 'S' in Metallic Mauve, Ford Capri, Morgan, etc ... *£150-250*
3003 **Car Transporter Set**, 1968-69, 2002 Husky Car Transporter plus 16, 26, 6-2, 21-2, 22-2, 26 ... *£260-360*
3004 **Four Garage Set**, 68-69, contains 23-2, 29 ... *£100-125*
3004 **James Bond 'OHMSS' Set**, 19??, contains 1004, 1001, 1011, 1012 plus un-numbered VW Beetle in red with black No '5' on white circle on sides. (Film 'On Her Majesty's Secret Service') ... *£4,000-5,000*
3004 **Bond OHMSS Set**, "James Bond 007" 3-piece gift set taken from the film "On Her Majesty's Secret Service" "007" Bobsleigh, "Spectre" Bobsleigh and Volkswagen Saloon ... *£6,000-7,000*
3005 **Holiday Time/Leisure Time**, 68-69, contains 2-2, 5-2, 7-2, 15-2, 19-2, 20-2, 21-2, 35-1 ... *£150-200*
3006 **Service Station**, 68-69, contains 14-c, 22-2, 28 ... *£75-100*
3007 **'Husky Multipark'**, 68-69, in 1968 catalogue but not issued *NPP*
3008 **Crime Busters Set**, 68-69, contains 1001, 1002, 1003, 1005 ... *£600-800*
Corgi Juniors 3008 set, 1970 ... *£750-1,000*
3009 **Service Station Set**, 70-71, Station building, three vehicles, gas pumps. Ford F-350 Wrecker, Guy Esso Tanker, Aston-Martin DBS. Land Rover Wrecker, Guy Esso Tanker, NSU RO-BO ... *£75-100*
3010 **Farm Buildings and Six Vehicles**, 70-71, two brown plastic farm buildings, yellow Jaguar XJ6, metallic green Horse Trailer, red Tractor, red & yellow Tipping Trailer, mint green Livestock Trailer, metallic green Willys Jeep (only one example known) ... *NGPP*
3011 **Road Construction Set**, 70-7?, Flatbed 2003 with red cab, five construction vehicles in standard colours ... *£60-75*
3013 **Emergency Rescue Set**, 77-80, building with three vehicles ... *£25-35*
3015 **Transporter Set**, 80-83, Transporter 2014 & four vehicles *£40-50*
3015B **Off-Road Set**, 80-83, maroon open Range Rover with white interior, tan Volvo 245DL with tan caravan trailer, blue Renault 5 Turbo with red base, red Mercedes-Benz 500SL coupe with tan interior, yellow open top Jeep with red roll cage ... *£10-20*
3019 **Argicultural Set**, 77-77, Two buildings with six vehicles in standard colours ... *£40-50*
3019 **James Bond Octopussy Set**, 83-83, maroon open Range Rover with tan interior, tan horsebox trailer, white aircraft with dark cockpit cover and red and blue wing stripes ... *£200-300*
Maroon open Range Rover with white interior, tan horsebox trailer, white aircraft with dark cockpit cover and red and blue wing stripes ... *£200-300*
Red open Range Rover with white interior, tan horsebox trailer, white aircraft with dark cockpit cover and red and blue wing stripes ... *£200-250*
3020 **Club Racing Set**, 71-7?, Non-standard dark blue Escort Mk I with "B" labels, non-standard dark blue car trailer, yellow Morgan Plus-B, purple Land Rover Breakdown, red Austin-Healey Sprite maroon Ferrari 312, white Porsche Carrera 6, purple BVRT Mini, figures and traffic cones ... *£100-130*
Non-standard metallic teal Capri with white base and No. 8 labels, non-standard dark blue car trailer, red Morgan Plus-8 with 'No. 20' labels, red Land Rover Breakdown, red Austin-Healey Sprite, maroon Ferrari 312, white Porsche Cerrera 6, purple BVRT Mini, figures and traffic cones ... *£100-130*
Non-standard red Capri with white base and "B" labels, non-standard dark blue car trailer, red Morgan Plus-B with "20" labels, red Land Rover Breakdown, red Austin-Healey Sprite, maroon Ferrarl 312, white Porsche Carrera 6, purple BVRT Mini, figures and traffic cones ... *£100-130*
3021 **Emergency 999 Set**, 72-74, Non-standard Duple-Vista or Mercedes bus with added flat black scorch marks on body and roof, Wrecker, white Studebaker ambulance, red and white Ford Capri Fire Chief, VW Police, fire engine, figures, trafflc signs, traffic cones. Red and yellow Ford Holmes wrecker, purple and white Duple-Vista ... *£175-200*
Red and yellow Ford Holmes wrecker, orange and white Duple-Vista ... *£175-200*
Purple Land Rover wrecker, orange and white Duple-Vista ... *£50-75*
Red Land Rover wrecker, metallic blue Mercedes bus without labels ... *£50-75*
3021 **Trucking Set**, 83-83, five vehicles ... *£40-50*
3021 **Crime Fighters Set**, "Kojak's" Buick; "James Bond" Lotus Esprit; "Starsky & Hutch" Ford Torino; "Batman's" Batmobile, Batcopter and "Spiderman" Spidercopter ... *£300-400*
3022 **Rescue Set**, 77-71, building, playmat, standard Porsche police car, nonstandard Land Rover, Range Rover ambulance, Coast Guard Range Rover, rough terrain truck and dinghy on trailer ... *£50-75*
3023 **Transporter Set**, 71-79, Transporter and four vehicles. Vehicles and colours vary per production date ... *£40-60*
3024 **Road Construction Set**, 77-71, Flatbed 2003 Road Roller, Scammell Cement Truck, Massey Ferguson Tractor, Terex Dumper, Ford Container truck, Front Loader. All in Standard Colors with Figures and Accessories ... *£50-75*
3024 **Road Construction Set**, 78-79, revised version of above (six different vehicles) ... *£50-75*
3025 **Transporter Set**, 77-78, Transporter 2002 and five vehicles. Vehicles and colours vary per production date and may be without standard labels or other graphics ... *£60-75*
3026 **Leisure Time Set**, 71-72, Eight vehicles & accessories, standard colors and trim ... *£100-125*

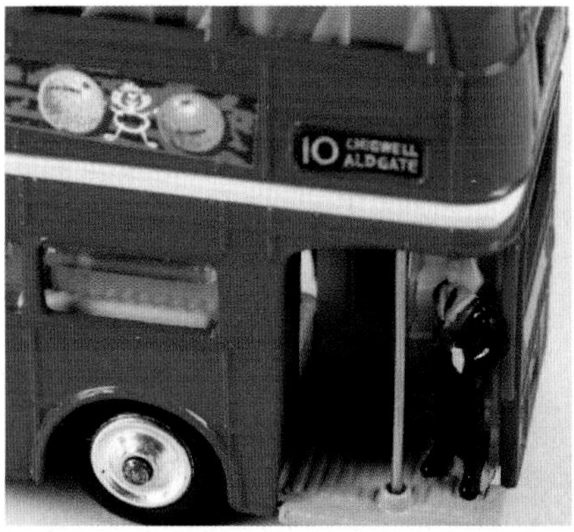

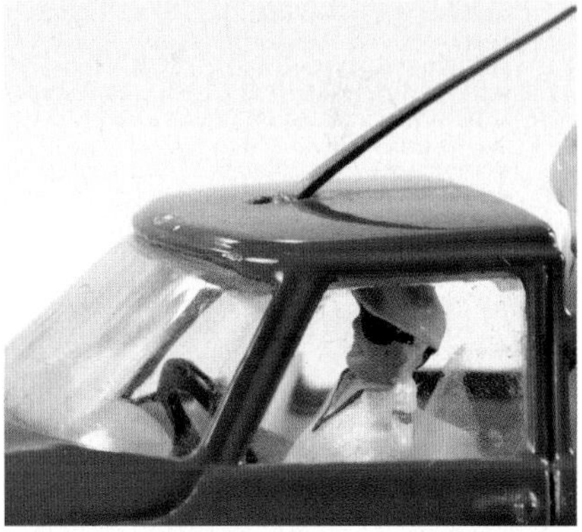

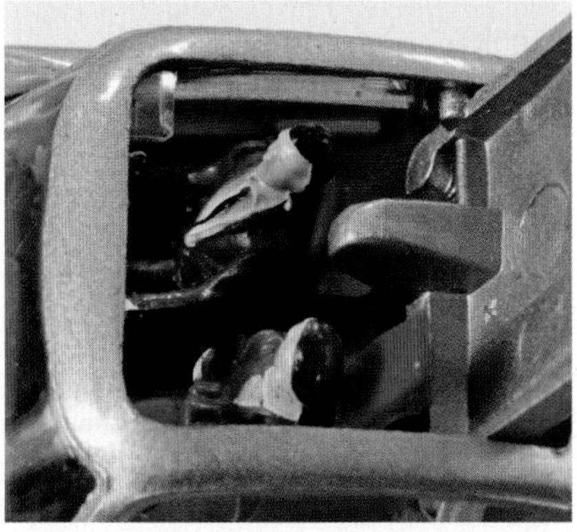

3026 **Emergency Set**, 76-79, Snorkel, ERF Fire Tender, Ambulance, Mercury Fire Chief, Range Rover Ambulance, Police Helicopter, signs and figures *£40-50*
3029 **Race Track Special Set**, 77-79, Seven vehicles including non-standard red Range Rover........ *£50-75*
3029 **Military Set**, 78-71, Seven vehicles including non standard Army Land Rover Wrecker, Stinger Helicopter, Armored Car, Land Rover Military Ambulance, Commando Car, Military Jeep, Field Gun and figures........ *£35-50*
3030 **James Bond 'Spy Who Loved Me' Set**, 78-79, Five vehicles including non standard Jaws Telephone Van, Stromberg's black Mercedes 2400 with gray paint splatter, and Speedboat on Trailer *£200-250*
3036 **Garage and Four Car Set**, 83-83, red 2001 garage with blue doors, four vehicles. Vehicles in various colours *£20-35*
3050 **Concorde Set**, 78-77, 650 Concorde, building, non standard Mercedes Bus, Leyland Van and Helicopter........ *£25-35*
3051 **Filling Station Set**, 71-80, building and three vehicles..... *£20-25*
3052 **Police Station Set**, 71-80, building, police Range Rover, police Porsche 911, police helicopter *£20-25*
3053 **Fire Station Set**, 71-80, building and three fire vehicles including Torino "FIRE DEPT model *£20-25*
3071 **Growler Set**, 75-76, six Growler vehicles, standard colors and trim........ *£25-35*
3073 **Steer Geer-Single Peck**, 77-7?........ *NPP*
3074 **Steer Geer-Double Peck**, 77-7?........ *NPP*
3080 **Batmen Set**, 80-81, five Batman vehicles with standard graphics *£200-300*
3081 **Superman Set**, 80-81, Super mobile, Metropolis Police car, Supervan, red Metropolis Newspaper Van, Police Helicopter, all with standard graphics. Silver or red Supervan........ *£200-300*
3082 **Bond Set**, 80-81, James Bond Aston Martin DB6, Lotus Esprit, white and yellow Helicopter, Space Shuttle, and non-standard Jaws telephone van *£200-300*
3084 **Cartoon Characters**, 80-81, Pink Panther, Tom & Jerry, Popeye and Olive Oyl vehicles *£150-200*
3100 **Construction Set**, 80-83, orange Ford Cement Truck with black barrel, yellow Tipper Truck with black tipper, yellow Crane with vacuum plated boom, orange Front Loader with vacuum plated scoop, yellow Digger with green base and vacuum plated scoop, orange Massey Ferguson Tractor with black scoop, green Skip Dumper with yellow tipper. Colours may vary........ *£25-30*
3101 **Fire Set**, 80-8?, Six vehicles and figures including non-standard orange Range Rover with yellow "RESCUE" door label, Rover 3500 "POLICE" car, Ford Torino "FIRE CHIEF" car, Simon Snorkel, ERF Fire Tender and Helicopter........ *£30-40*
3103 **Emergency Set**, 80-8?, Six vehicles including non-standard yellow Chevrolet "AA" van, non-standard gold VW Polo, blue Land Rover Wrecker, Range Rover, white Mercedes ambulance, Porsche 911, with unpainted figures white Range Rover Police, white Porsche 911 Police. Red Range Rover with non-standard yellow 'RESCUE' door label, white and red Porsche 911 'Rijkspolitie' *£25-30*
3105 **Transporter Set**, 82-83, Transporter 2014 and four various vehicles........ *£20-30*
3107 **Sports Car Set**, 82-83, metallic blue Jaguar XJS, red 1957 Thunderbird, metallic green Mercedes-Benz 350SL, black Porsche 911, yellow-green Fiat XI/9 .... *£20-25*
3108 **Flintstone's Set**, 82-83, five Flintstone's vehicles........ *£175-225*
3109 **Best of British Set**, 1983, seven British vehicles *£25-35*
3110 **Emergency Set**, 82-83, Ford Transit tow truck, Airport Fire Tender, Helicopter, Mercedes Ambulance, Buick police car *£20-30*
Ford Transit tow truck, Airport Fire Tender, Paramedic Van, Mercedes Ambulance, Snorkel fire truck........ *£20-30*
3111 **Wild West Railroad Set**, 82-83, three vehicles and buildings........ *£20-25*
3112 **Wild West Frontier Set**, 82-83, three vehicles, including non standard horse-drawn flat wagon, and buildings *£20-25*
3113 **Wild West Set**, 82-83, Locomotive, Union Pacific Coach, Stage Coach, Covered Wagon, River Boat *£25-30*
3114 **Superheroes Set**, 82-83, standard trim on Batmobile, Batbike, Batboat, Supermobile and Metropolis Buick Police Car........ *£75-100*
3115 **Off-Road Set**, 82-83, yellow Jeep with red interior and roll bar, blue Jeep with white interior, yellow Baja Van, Safari Park Matra Rancho, yellow Renault R5-T16 without labels, maroon open top Range Rover, orange Mustang Cobra, black and red Dinghy on black trailer........ *£30-40*
3118 **Crime Fighter Set**, 82-83, Star Trek Enterprise, Buck Rogers Starship, Spiderbike, James Bond Lotus Esprit. Buick Police car........ *£75-100*
NASA Enterprise, Buck Rogers Starship, Dan Tanna T-Bird, James Bond Lotus Esprit, James Bond Aston-Martin....... *£75-100*
3118 **Commando Set**, 82-83, olive green buildings, Commando vehicle, Army Jeep, and tank........ *£20-25*
3121 **Super Sports Car Set**, 1983, Triplex Rover, Alitalia Capri, Datapost Mini Metro, cream and red VW Polo, orange Fiat XI/9, black Porsche Carrera, Elf Renault 5-T16 .... *£30-40*
3122 **Turbochargers Set**, 1983, three vehicles, pit, Dunlop bridge........ *£20-25*
3123 **Truckers Set**, 1983, three vehicles and buildings. *£20-30*

Corgi Juniors Film and TV-related models, 1970–1972

1001-a1 **James Bond Aston-Martin DB6**, 1970, silver, red interior, 2 ejector figures, grey plastic wheels........ *£150-175*
1001-a2 **James Bond Aston-Martin DB6**, 1970, silver, red interior, 2 ejector figures, black WhizzWheels........ *£150-175*
1001-a3 **James Bond Aston-Martin DB6**, 71-72, silver, red interior, 2 ejector figures, chrome WhizzWheels *£150-175*
1002-a1 **Batmobile**, 1970, black, Batman and Robin figures, tow hook, GPW, 'Corgi Junior' base........ *£125-150*
1002-a2 **Batmobile**, 1970, black, Batman and Robin figures, tow hook, black WhizzWheels........ *£125-150*
1002-a3 **Batmobile**, 71-72, black, Batman and Robin figures, tow hook, chrome WhizzWheels *£125-150*
1003-a1 **Batboat**, 1970, black boat, red fin, Batman and Robin figures, GPW, 'Junior' base *£125-150*
1003-a2 **Batboat**, 1970, black boat, red fin, Batman and Robin figures, black WhizzWheels........ *£125-150*
1003-a3 **Batboat**, 71-72, Black boat, red fin, Batman and Robin figures, chrome WhizzWheels........ *£125-150*
1004-a1 **Monkeemobile**, 1970, red, white roof, 4 figures, 'Monkees' on doors, tyres, 'Junior' base........ *£75-100*
1004-a3 **Monkeemobile**, 1971, red, white roof, 4 figures, 'Monkees' on doors, tyres, black WW........ *£125-150*
1005-a1 **Man From U.N.C.L.E. Car**, 1970, blue, 3 missiles on sprue, 2 figures, tyres, 'Junior' label on base *£150-175*
1006-a1 **Chitty Chitty Bang Bang**, 1970, chrome body, 4 figures, tyres........ *£100-125*
1006-a2 **Chitty Chitty Bang Bang**, 1971, chrome body, 4 figures, BWW........ *£100-125*
1007-a1 **Ironsides Police Van**, 71-72, blue, 'San Francisco' logo, Ironside in back, chrome WhizzWheels........ *£100-125*
1008-a1 **Popeye's Paddle Wagon**, 71-72, yellow, blue, Popeye with Olive and Sweet Pea, chrome WW *£75-100*
1010-a1 **James Bond Volkswagen**, 1972, orange, green stripe/'Corgi Toys' on roof, RN '5', yellow interior, chrome WhizzWheels.... *£700-900*
1011-a1 **James Bond Bobsleigh**, 71-72, yellow, '007' decal, Grey plastic bumper, George Lazenby figure, BWW *£400-600*
1012-a1 **S.P.E.C.T.R.E. Bobsleigh**, 71-72, orange, 'Boars Head' decal, grey plastic bumper, Blofleld figure, black WhizzWheels....... *£600-700*
1013-a1 **Tom's Go Cart**, 71-72, yellow, Tom figure, chrome WW ... *£50-60*
1014-a1 **Jerry's Banger**, 71-72, red, Jerry figure, CWW........ *£50-60*

HUSKY AND CORGI JUNIORS CATALOGUES AND LISTINGS

Husky Catalogues

Leaflet (single fold), Mettoy Playcraft (Sales) Ltd 1966. Red, illustrating No.1 Jaguar Mk.10 on cover and Nos.1-29 inside. '1/9 each'........ *£20-25*
Leaflet (Belgian issue), Mettoy Playcraft (Sales) Ltd 1966. As previous leaflet but Nos.1-32 shown, printed in French........ *£20-25*
Booklet (10 pages), Mettoy Playcraft (Sales) Ltd 1966. Front/rear covers feature a row of garages and cars. 1002 Batmobile and 1001 JB's Aston Martin featured, plus Nos.1-36........ *NGPP*
Catalogue (24 pages) no ref. 1967, cover shows boy with Husky vehicles and sets. Good pictures of all the rare models and Gift Sets plus accessories and models 1-41........ *£30-40*

Corgi Junior Catalogues

Catalogue (16 pages), Mettoy Playcraft 1970. Blue cover with 10 models featured. Fine pictures of all the rare early models including GS 3004 Bond 'O.H.M.S.S.' Set etc........ *£30-40*
Corgi Juniors Collectors Album, no ref. 1970. 28 pages. To hold cards cut from Corgi Junior bubble packs. Has details of featured models below space for card. Centre two pages have 'Corgi Toys' adverts plus articles, etc *£10-15*

CORGI JUNIORS 1975–1983

Market Price Range - scarcer items as shown, otherwise

E2	**Blake's Seven Liberator**, 80-81	*£75-100*
E3	**Stromberg's Helicopter**, 77-81	*£25-35*
E6	**'Daily Planet' Helicopter**, 79-80	*£15-20*
E11	**Supermobile**, 79-85	*£20-30*
E17-2	**Metropolis 'POLICE' Car**, 79-81	*£25-35*
E19	**Pink Panther Motorcycle**, 80-82	*£15-20*
E20-2	**Penguinmobile**, 79-81	*£20-30*
E21	**Charlie's Angels Van**, 77-80	*£15-20*
E23	**Batbike**, 79-81	*£75-100*
E24	**'SHAZAM' Thunderbolt**, 79-80	*£40-50*
E25	**'Capt. America' Porsche**, 79-80	*£40-50*
E32	**The Saint's Jaguar XJS**, 70-74	*£65-85*
E33	**'Wonderwoman's Car**, 79-80	*£30-40*
E38	**Jerry's Banger**, 80-83	*£15-20*
E40-2	**James Bond's Aston-Martin**, 79-81	*£100-125*
E41	**James Bond Space Shuttle**, 79-81	*£15-20*
E44-2	**Starship Liberator**, 79-80	*£50-75*
E45	**Starsky & Hutch Ford Torino**, 77-81	*£15-20*
E49-2	**Woody Woodpecker's Car**, 81-83	*£15-20*
E50	**'Daily Planet' (Leyland) Van**, 79-80, red or silver	*£15-20*
E52-2	**Scooby Doo's Vehicle**, 82-83	*£20-25*

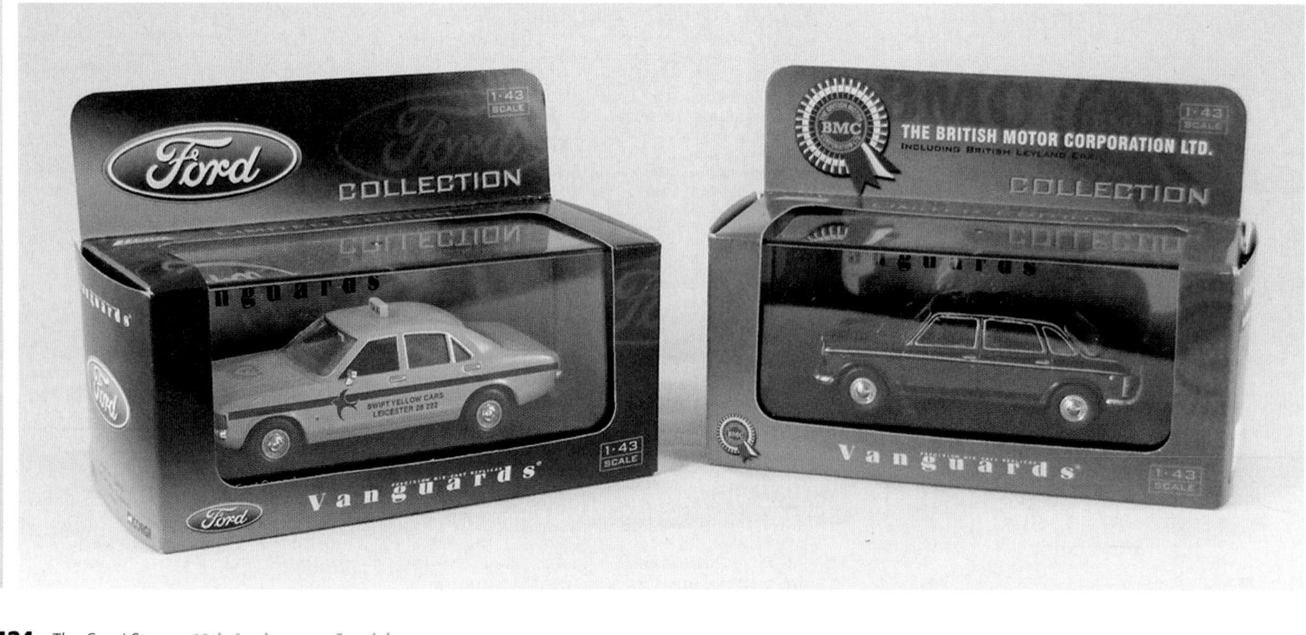

E56	Chevrolet 'SPIDERVAN', 79-80	£20-25
E57-2	Spiderbike, 79-80	£20-25
E59-1	Tom's Cart, 80-83	£15-20
E60	James Bond Lotus Esprit, 77-79, 1: with side & rear wings	£100-125
	2: without wings; some have 'TURBO' side design	£100-125
E64	'The Professionals' Ford Capri, 80-82	£15-20
E67-2	Popeye's Tugboat, 80-83	£15-20
E68	Kojak's Buick Regal, 77-79	£20-25
E69	Batmobile, 76-80	£75-100
E72-2	Jaguar XJS, 79-83, blue or red	NGPP
	Jaguar XJS, red with white 'MOTOR SHOW' logo	£20-30
E73	'DRAX' Helicopter, 80	£20-25
E75	Spidercopter, 77-80	£20-30
E78	Batcopter, 76-81	£60-70
E79-2	Olive Oyl's Aeroplane, 80-83	£15-20
E80	'MARVEL COMICS' Van, 79-80	£20-25
E82-2	Yogi Bear's Jeep, 81-82	£20-30
E84-2	Bugs Bunny Vehicle, 80-83	£15-20

99	Jokermobile, 79-81	£30-40
100	Hulk Cycle, 81-83	£30-40
E115	James Bond 2cv Citroën, 81-83	£40-50
128	Fred's Flyer, 82-83	£25-35
131	Ferrari 308, 'Magnum PI', 82-83	£25-35
133	Buick Regal 'POLICE' Car, 'Magnum PI', 82-83	£25-35
134	Barney's Buggy, red/orange, (The Flintstones), 82-83	£25-35
E148	USS Enterprise, 83-84	£15-20
E149	Klingon Warship, 83	£15-20
E151	Wilma's Coupé, 83	£25-35
198	James Bond Citroën 2cv, 83	£50-75
E2009	James Bond 'Aerocar', ?, 'The Man With the golden Gun'. NB: Not a licensed product	£160-190
	Empty box for the above set	£900-1,100

GERMAN ISSUES

E119	'FLUGHAFEN-FEURWEHR', 83, Fire Engine	£15-20
120	Leyland Van, 'Eiszeit', ?	£15-20
120	Ice cream Van, 'FRESHLICHE', 83	£15-20
121	Chevrolet Van, 'TECHNISCHER', 83	£15-20
126	Ford Transit Breakdown, 'ABSCHIEPPDIENST', 82-83	£15-20
127	'ADAC' Car, 82-83	£20-25

Miscellaneous Items

Wooden Prototype Morris Minor Estate Car, Model with wooden detail added, pencil line detail, smooth cast hubs with black tyres, "Morris 1000 Estate Car" (1958) in pencil to base ...£750-850
'BOAC' Concorde, Chrome plated finish complete with display stand. Made in Spain by Aero Pilen using old Corgi Toys castings ...£50-75
Original Marcel Van Cleemput drawing showing a 269 'James Bond' Lotus Esprit featured in the 'The Great Book of Corgi' ...£450-550
Grand Prix Soap and Car Set, McLaren Racing Car Set Promotional for 'Yardley' Soap white with black and orange stripes, Race No. 55, mounted in plastic tray with bar of unused soap ...£30-50
Corgi 'Rocket Age', original operating instruction leaflet for Corporal Guided Missile Launcher ...£15-20
Volkswagen Van, believed to preproduction, finished in pale blue 'Toblerone Colour' lemon interior, spun hubs with 'Ecurie Corgi' side decals. Its understood that the model was going to be used in the GS17 Gift Set but was never released ...£235-275

CORGI SUPER JUNIORS AND SUPERHAULERS
Mercedes tractor units, car transporter (issued 1976)

2014/15	White cab and deck, blue chassis	£20-25
2015	White cab, yellow deck, red chassis	£20-25
	NB. Transporter Sets 3023, 3015, 3105	£30-35

Mercedes Tankers (1983-84)

1130	'CORGI CHEMCO', red or white	£10-15
1130	'SHELL', yellow or white cab	£10-15
1166	'GUINNESS'	£10-15
1167	'DUCKHAMS'	£10-15
1167	'7 UP'	£20-30

Mercedes Box Trailers (1978-85)

1111	'SAFEWAY'	£15-20
1129	'ASG SP EDITION'	£10-15
1129	'CORGI', black or white cab	£10-15
1131	'CHRISTIAN SALVESON'	£10-15
1137	'SOUKS SUPERMARKET', (Saudi issue)	£25-30
1139	'HALLS FOOD'	£10-15
1144	'ROYAL MAIL PARCELS',	£10-15
1145	'YORKIE'	£10-15
1146	'DUNLOP'	£10-15
1166	'ARIA DAIRY'	£10-15

1175	'INTERNATIONAL'	£60-70
1175	'TI RALEIGH'	£10-15
1176	'ZANUSSI'	£10-15
1177	'WEETABIX'	£10-15
1178	'MAYNARDS'	£10-15
1202	'PICKFORDS HOMESPEED'	£60-70
2028	'GERVALS DANONE'	£10-15
2020	'BIRDS EYE'	£10-15
	'B. H. S.'	£20-30
	'CARTERS Lemonade'	£25-35

Mercedes Sets

1200	'DUCKHAMS' & 'GUINNESS', tanker plus 3 Scammells	£40-50
1403	'CORGI CHEMCO', plus Junior Van	£25-30
3128	'DUCKHAMS' & 'YORKIE', plus 10 Juniors	£40-50

CORGI JUNIORS TWIN-PACKS
Corgi Juniors bubble-packed in pairs from 1977 (approx)

2501	London Bus and Taxi	£20-30
2502	Land Rover Breakdown/Jaguar XJS	£30-40
2503	Land Rover and Horse Box	£20-30
2504	Land Rover Breakdown plus AMC Pace Car	£30-40
2505	'DAILY PLANET' Van + Helicopter	£20-30
2506	Supermobile and Superman Van	£50-60
2507	Tom's Cart and Jerry's Banger	£30-50
2508	Popeye's Tugboat plus Olive Oyl's Aeroplane	£30-50
2510	F1 and F5000 Racing Cars	£30-40
2511	Sting Helicopter and Scout Car	£20-30
2512	Space Shuttle + Star Ship 'Liberator'	£40-50
2513	Fire Tender and Ambulance	£20-30
2514	Building Set	£25-35
2515	Citroën and Speedboat	£25-35
2516	Tractor and Tipping Trailer	£25-35
2518	Mercedes and Caravan	£25-35
2519	Batmobile and Batboat	£75-100
2520	Rescue Set	£30-40
2521	James Bond Lotus plus Aston-Martin DB5	£100-125
2522	Army Attack Set	£30-40
2523	Police Car and Helicopter	£25-35
2524	Custom Van Twin	£25-35
2525	Triumph TR7 + Dinghy on Trailer	£40-50
2526	Dumper Truck + Shovel Loader	£25-35
2527	'Kojak' and Police Helicopter	£50-60

2528	Starsky and Hutch Twin Pack	£50-60
2529	James Bond Lotus and Helicopter	£75-125
2530	Rescue Range Rover and Helicopter	£30-40
2506	AMF 'Ski-daddler' Snowmobile and trailer	£50-75
2538	Buck Rogers Starfighter and NASA Columbia Shuttle	£40-50

CORGI ROCKETS

This model range was issued between 1970 and 1972 to compete against Mattel Hot Wheels and similar products. The models had WhizzWheels and featured a special 'Tune-Up' system which increased the play value and speed of the virtually frictionless wheels. They were very robust, being advertised as 'four times stronger' than most other diecast racers. To begin with, seven Corgi Juniors were adapted as Rockets and five of those received a vacuum metallised finish. A range of accessories was also issued in the form of 'Speed Circuits' etc, and each car was provided with a special 'golden Tune-Up Key' which released the base. The bubble-packed models are difficult to find in top condition and prices reflect their scarcity.

D 901	Aston-Martin DB-6, 1970-72, met. deep gold, green int	£60-70
	Orange, yellow interior	£75-100
D 902	Jaguar XJ-6, 1970-72, metallic green, cream interior	£80-90
D 903	Mercedes-Benz 280 SL, 1970-72, met. orange body, white interior.	£60-70
D 904	Porsche Carrera 6, 1970-72, orange-yellow body, black '19'	£60-70
D 905	'The Saint's' Volvo P1800, 1970-72, white body, blue/white 'Saint' label on bonnet	£80-90
D 906	Jensen Interceptor, 1970-72, metallic red, yellow int	£50-60
	Pink/cream body	£70-90
D 907	Cadillac Eldorado, 1970-72, metallic copper, white int	£60-70
D 908	Chevrolet Astro, 1970-72, metallic red/black body	£40-50
D 909	Mercedes-Benz C111, 1970-72, red or blue, white int	£40-50
D 910	Beach Buggy, 1970-72, orange body, black interior	£30-40
D 911	Marcos XP, 1970-72, gold body, chrome interior	£30-40
D 912	Ford Capri, 1970-72, purple body	£40-50
D 913	Aston-Martin DBS, 1970-72, metallic blue, yellow int	£70-90
D 916	Carabo Bertone, 1970-72, met. green/blue, orange int	£20-30
D 917	Pininfarina Alfa-Romeo, 1970-72, met. purple/white	£20-30
D 918	Bitzzarini Manta, 1970-72, met. dark blue, white int	£20-30
D 919	'Todd Sweeney' Stock Car, 1970-72, red/purple/yellow/black, '531'	£75-100
D 920	'Derek Fiske' Stock Car, 1970-72, white/red, silver bonnet, red logo, RN '304'	£75-100
D 921	Morgan Open Sports, 1970-72, metallic red body, black seats	£60-75
D 922	Rally Ford Capri, 1970-72, yellow, orange/black stripe, '8'	£75-100
	Green, black bonnet, (GS 2 model)	£60-75
D 923	'James Bond' Ford Escort, 1970-72, white, pale blue stripes, '7', 'JAMES BOND' and 'SPECIAL AGENT' logos (from film 'On Her Majesty's Secret Service')	£500-700
D 924	Mercury Cougar XR7, 1970-72, red body, black roof, yellow int	£30-40
D 924	'James Bond' issue: red/black with yellow side flash, interior and skis on roof rack, from film 'On Her Majesty's Secret Service'	£500-700
D 925	'James Bond' Ford Capri, 1970-72, white body, black/white check design, 2 bonnet stripes, RN '6', (film'On Her Majesty's Secret Service')	£500-700

D 926 **Jaguar 'Control Car'**, 1970-72, metallic brown body, red roof blade, blue/white figures.......... *£200-250*
D 927 **Ford Escort Rally**, 1970-72, white, red '18', 'DAILY MIRROR' labels on doors, '1970 Mexico World Cup Rally Winner' *£250-300*
D 928 **Mercedes 280 SL 'SPECTRE'**, 1970-7 2, black body with red 'SPECTRE' logo, plus boar's head design.......... *£250-300*
D 930 **Bertone Barchetta**, 1970-72, met. green over white, red int.......... *£40-50*
D 931 **'Old MacDonald's Truck'**, 1970-72, yellow cab, brown rear.......... *£50-75*
D 933 **'Holmes Wrecker'**, 1970-72, white or blue cab, white back, 'AUTO RESCUE'.......... *£125-150*
D 937 **Mercury Cougar**, 1970-72, met. dark green body, yellow int.......... *£20-30*

Rockets Gift Sets
D 975 **Super Stock Gift Set 1**, 1970, D 905, D 919, Trailer, 3 figures.......... *£200-250*
D 976 **Super Stock Gift Set 2**, 1970, D 922, D 920, Trailer, 3 figures.......... *£200-250*
D 977 **Super Stock Gift Set 3**, 1970, D 926, D 919, D 920, 5 figures.......... *£400-450*
D 978 **'OHMSS' Gift Set**, Models of cars in the James Bond film 'On Her Majesty's Secret Service': D 923 and D 925 (as driven in the ice-racing scene), D 924 (as driven by 'Tracey'), D 928 (as driven by the Chief of 'SPECTRE').......... *£4,500-5,500*
NB Male skier has red metal base, red/yellow skis, yellow poles.

Rockets Catalogues
1969 **8-page booklet**, listing the first 7 issues, green model on cover.......... *£20-25*
1970 **16-page booklet**, most issues, good pictures of rare models, sets, etc.......... *£30-35*

Rockets Accessories
(Introduced in 1970. All NGPP)
D2051 **Action Speedset**, One car, 'Autostart', 12 ft of track
D2052 **Super Autobatics Speedset**, One car, 'Autostart', 16 ft of track plus 'leaps' etc
D2053 **Clover Leaf Special**, Speedset, a car, 'Autostart', track, 'clover-leaf leaps' etc
D2058 **Race-Abatic Speedset**, 2 cars, 'Autostart', 32' of track plus 'leaps' etc
D2060 **Skypark Tower Garage Set**, light grey, blue, orange, yellow.......... *£30-50*
D2071 **Jetspeed Circuit, One car**, 'Superbooster', 16 ft of track + 'leaps' etc
D2074 **Triple-Leap Speed Circuit**, one car, 19 ft, 6 in of track
D2075 **Grand Canyon Circuit**, one car, 12 ft of track
D2079 **World Champion Speedset**
D1928 **Rocketlube Tune-up Kit**
D1931 **Superleap**
D1934 **Autofinish**
D1935 **Connections (3)**
D1936 **Space Leap**
D1937 **Autostart**
D1938 **Super Crossover**
D1945 **Adaptors (3)**
D1963 **Track (16ft)**
D1970 **Super Booster**
D1971 **Hairpin Tunnel**
D1976 **Quickfire Start**
D1977 **Lap Counter**
D1978 **Pitstop**
D1979 **Spacehanger Bend**

CATALOGUES (UK EDITIONS)
Information taken from the Cecil Gibson Archives and previous compiler's own collection of reference material. Note: 'Concertina' leaflets were issued with models sold in the early blue boxes.

Concertina leaflet, 1956, no ref. blue cover, famous Corgi dog, shows first 14 models, no prices.......... *£25-30*
Concertina leaflet, 1956, no ref. blue coverwith red/gold Corgi dog. Depicts first 14 models; shows prices of both normal and mechanical models.......... *£25-30*
Concertina leaflet 50/157/K1, 1957, blue cover with red/gold Corgi dog. Depicts ten models and lists mechanical models in red.......... *£25-30*
Concertina leaflet 40/257/K1, 1957, as previous item, but no mechanical models.......... *£25-30*
Concertina leaflet 40/257/K2, 1957, as previous leaflet but with the addition of 208.......... *£25-30*
Concertina leaflet 50/557/K3, 1957, as 40/257/K2 plus 100,150, 408, 454, 'WOW! CORGI TOYS' logo.......... *£25-30*
Catalogue Leaflet 20/657/C2, 1957, unfolded size (11" x 8 3/4"). Cover shows 1st type blue box for 208 Jaguar.......... *£25-30*
Concertina leaflet 100/1057/K3, 1957, blue cover showing 100, 150, 207, 208, 302, 405, 408, 453, 455.......... *£25-30*
Concertina leaflet 50/1057/K4, 1957, blue cover, 'WOW! CORGI TOYS' logo. First 'MAJOR' toy (1101) within.......... *£25-30*

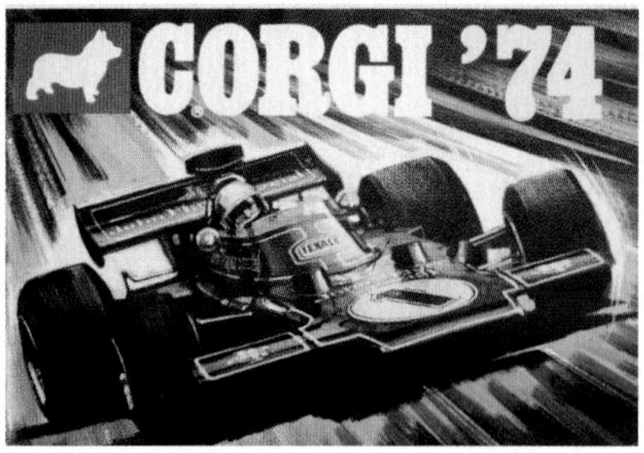

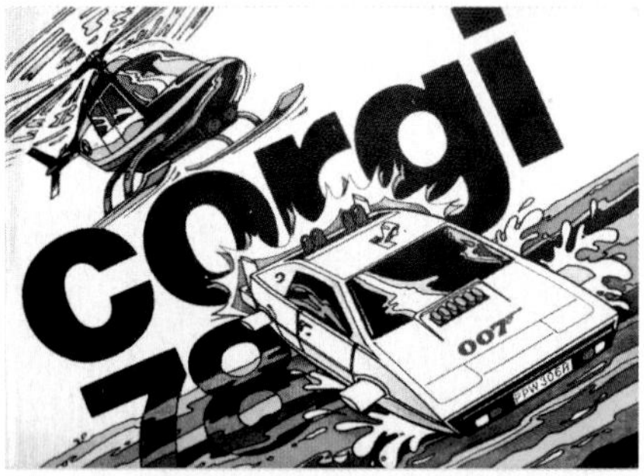

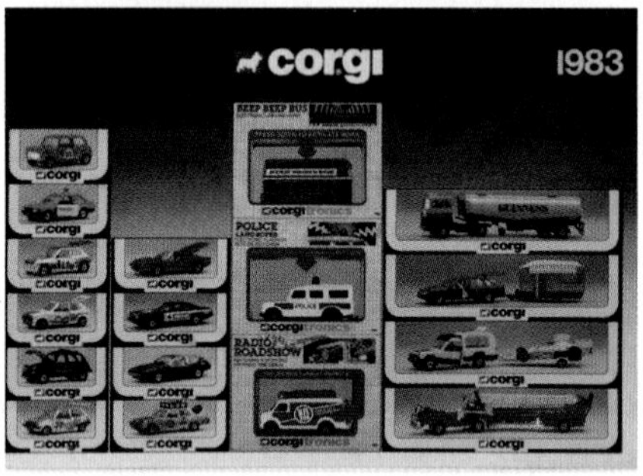

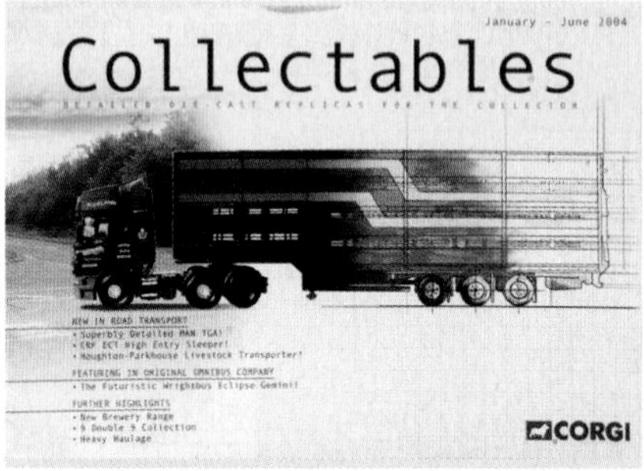

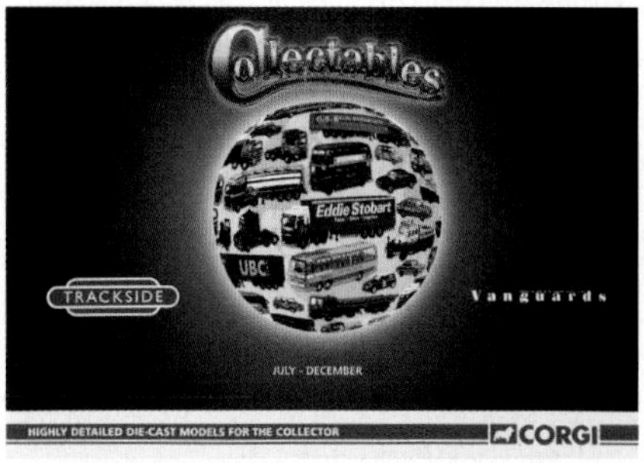

Concertina leaflet 50/1157/K4, 1957, cover shows 102, 210, 406, 407, 412, 1101, 'WOW! CORGI TOYS' logo.......... *£25-30*
Four-fold leaflet 25/257/C1/UK, 1957, 'Blue box' 208 Jaguar on cover, 15 model pictures inside.......... *£25-35*
Four-fold leaflet 25/257/C2/UK, 1957, as previous item but 24 model pictures.......... *£25-35*
Four-fold leaflet 50/1057/C3/UK, 1957, shows GS 1 Bedford Transporter and six cars on blue/yellow cover.......... *£25-35*
Four-fold leaflet 25/1157/C4/UK, 1957, as previous leaflet plus 101 and 102.......... *£25-35*
Catalogue Leaflet 15/158/C4, 1958, unfolded size (1' x 11"). 1101 Transporter on cover.......... *£20-25*
Catalogue Leaflet 10/258/C5, 1958, unfolded size (1' x 11"). 1101 Transporter on cover.......... *£20-25*
Catalogue Leaflet 40/258/C5, 1958, same.......... *£20-25*
Concertina leaflet 52/258/K5, 1958, cover shows GS 1 and 2, 101, 211, 302, 457, 459, 1100, 1401, 1450.......... *£20-25*
Box Insert 52/258/K5, 1958, 1401 Corgi Service Ramp on cover... *£15-20*
Box Insert 52/258/K6, 1958, 350 'Thunderbird' Missile on cover... *£15-20*
Concertina leaflet 52/258/K6, 1958, cover has GS 1 and 2, 101, 211, 302, 457, 459, 1100, 1401, 1450, + 350, 351.......... *£20-25*
Concertina leaflet 300/658/K7, 1958, shows GS 3, 151, 209, 458, 'NEW CORGI TOYS' logo + prices.......... *£20-25*
Box Insert 3.350/658/K7, 1958, 1401 Corgi Service Ramp on cover *£15-20*
Four-fold leaflet, 1958, No ref. shows GS 1 Bedford Transporter and 6 cars on blue/yellow cover, plus 211. No prices or car listing.......... *£25-35*
Box Insert 5/658/K7, 1958, 458 E.R.F. Truck and 209 Police Car on cover.......... *£15-20*
Catalogue 650/858/C8, 1958, First 'book' catalogue. Cover depicts boy playing with Bloodhound Missile + other vehicles.......... *£40-50*
Box Insert 10/658/K7, 1958, 458 E.R.F. Truck and 209 Police Car on cover.......... *£15-20*
16 page Catalogue 40/1058/C8, 1958, boy and large collection on cover.......... *£20-25*
Box Insert 120/1058/K8. 458 E.R.F, 1958, Truck and 209 Police Car on cover.......... *£15-20*
Four-fold leaflet, 1959, No ref. blue cover with 'THE ROCKET AGE WITH CORGI TOYS' (issued with Rocket Age models).......... *£20-30*
Interim leaflet, 1959, No ref. September 1959. Lists 152, 50 Tractor, 350 Thunderbird, new Ford TT van and accessories.......... *£20-30*
16 page Catalogue UK 9/59, 1959, M-F Tractor No. 50 and BRM No. 152 on cover. Farming + 'MAJOR' issues.......... *£35-45*
20 page Catalogue, 1959, No ref. Racing Car and Tractor design on cover.......... *£30-35*
Single page leaflet, 1959, No ref. Features Renault Floride plus 'STRAIGHT FROM THE MOTOR SHOW' logo.......... *£20-30*
Two fold leaflet, 1959, No ref. 'AUTHENTIC ROCKET AGE MODELS' models.......... *£20-30*
Interim leaflet, 1960, No ref. Depicts M1 Motorway scene.......... *£20-30*
20 page Catalogue, 1960, No ref. otherwise as next item.......... *£25-35*
20 page Catalogue UK 9/60, 1960, Cover has motorway bridge scene and Corgi models. First 'CHIPPERFIELDS' issues.......... *£30-40*
Interim Leaflet, 1960, No ref. 1119 Hovercraft, etc. on cover.......... *£20-25*
24 page Catalogue, 1961, No ref. otherwise as next item.......... *£30-40*
24 page Catalogue UK 9/61, 1961, racetrack scene on cover. Listings/pictures include new sports cars, Express Coach and kits.......... *£30-40*
Price List, 1961, No ref. Single double-sided sheet (size as catalogue), 'Revised price list as from August 1961'. 'UK' on back.......... *£10-15*
Interim Leaflet, 1961, No ref. 231 Triumph Herald, etc. on cover.. *£20-25*
Two-fold Checklist, 1962, No ref. front depicts blue/yellow 'CORGI TOYS' + 7 models. red/grey interior plus first check list.......... *£20-30*
Interim Leaflet, 1962, No ref. 224 Bentley plus 304s Mercedes on cover.......... *£20-25*
32 page Catalogue C/100/62, 1963, cover depicts schoolboy (in red cap and blazer) crossing road with Corgi dog. No date shown.......... *£40-50*
32 page Catalogue, 1963, No ref. Same cover as C/100/62 but boy's cap and blazer are blue. '1963-64' shown on cover.......... *£30-40*
40 page Catalogue, 1963, as previous item, but expanded to 40 pages.......... *£30-40*
Interim Leaflet - Playcraft Toys Ltd 1964, 1964, 251 Hillman Imp, etc. on cover.......... *NGPP*
40 page Catalogue - Playcraft Toys Ltd 1964, 1964, '1965', 'CORGI TOYS', 'CORGI CLASSICS'. First Routemaster listed.......... *£25-35*
Two-fold Checklist - Playcraft Toys Ltd 1964, 1964, leaflet featuring 241 Ghia.......... *£25-35*
Interim Leaflet - Playcraft Toys Ltd 1965, 1965, 155 Lotus Climax Racing Car, etc.......... *£20-25*
40 page Catalogue, 1965, No reference number or text, otherwise as next item.......... *£25-35*
40 page Catalogue - Playcraft Toys Ltd 1965, 1965, 261 JB's Aston Martin DB5 on cover. Rallye Monte Carlo issues. 'Price 3d'.......... *£25-35*
Two-fold Checklist - Mettoy Playcraft (Sales) Ltd, 1965, leaflet with 6 model cars from 6 nations on cover.......... *£20-25*
48 page Catalogue C2017/9/66, 1966, Features 'BATMAN' and 'THE AVENGERS' etc. Includes price list. 190 x 78mm.'4d'.......... *£25-35*
Leaflet C2038/66, 1966, 'MODEL CAR MAKERS TO JAMES BOND' *£20-25*
Four-fold Checklist C2039/4/66, 1966, leaflet similar to previous with 'MODEL CAR MAKERS TO JAMES BOND'. 1127 Simon Snorkel featured.......... *£20-25*
Three-fold Checklist - Mettoy Playcraft (Sales), 1967, front shows 'NEW' in five languages + 1142 Holmes Wrecker.......... *£20-25*
48 page Catalogue C/2017/7/67, 1967, Lincoln Continental (262) on both covers. 'Price 6d'. Unissued 9022 Daimler and 9014 'Lyons Tea' shown.......... *£30-35*
Interim Leaflet, 1967, No ref. 1142 'Holmes' Wrecker on cover.......... *£20-25*
48 page Catalogue C2017/9/68, 1968, cover has 268 'Chitty Chitty Bang

Bang'. 'Take-off Wheels' issues listed £30-35
Seven-fold Checklist - Mettoy Playcraft (Sales) Ltd, 1969, unfolds to 2'6" x 8 3/4". 'Concorde' model on cover + 302 Hillman Hunter. Listings include 'Corgi Comics', 'CHIPPERFIELDS' and Set No. 48..................£30-35
48 page Catalogue - The Mettoy Co Ltd, 1970, 388 Mercedes-Benz C111 on cover, first 'WhizzWheels' models listed...£30-35
Two-fold Checklist - 1970 Mettoy Co Ltd., 1971, 6 WhizzWheels models on the cover. The final 'Take-Off Wheels' issues listed......................£15-20
48 page Catalogue C2017 Petty 7/71/LOI7b, 1972, cover shows 1972 Car models. 'CORGI COMICS' inside..£20-25
48 page Catalogue, 1972, C2017 Petty 7/71/LOI7B (2nd). Cars across both covers £20-25
4-page Brochure (A4) No ref., 1972, 'Corgi Juniors with WhizzWheels' 'Juniors Extra' section of TV models..£10-15
40 page Catalogue 1973 Mettoy Co Ltd, 1973, F1 Racing Cars featured on the cover..£10-15
40 page Catalogue C2107, 1974, 'Corgi '74' on cover..........................£10-15
40 page Catalogue C2111, 1974, same..£10-15
40 page Catalogue 1974 Mettoy Co Ltd, 1974, **'John Player' Lotus on cover** £10-15
Catalogue Leaflet, 1975, No ref. Unfolded size 2' x 8½". 'Corgi 75' on cover £10-15
Three-fold leaflet - 1975 Mettoy Co Ltd, 1975, Helicopters, Noddy's Car, etc on the cover. Numbers given 'C' prefix..£10-15
Three-fold leaflet - 1976 Mettoy Co Ltd, 1976, 'KOJAK' on first page. Roadmaking and Public Services listings...£10-15
48 page Catalogue C2210, 1977, Silver Jubilee Coach on cover. Large section listing Corgi 'Juniors'..£10-15
48 page Catalogue C2211, 1977, 'Corgi 77' on cover...........................£10-15
32 page Catalogue C2222, 1977, 'Corgi 77' on cover...........................£10-15
48 page Catalogue The Mettoy Co Ltd, 1978, James Bond's Lotus on cover, 'JEAN RICHARD PINDER' models within......................................£10-15
48 page Catalogue C2250, 1979, James Bond's Space Shuttle on the cover. 'SUPERMAN' and 'THE MUPPETS' listed inside.......................£10-15
48 page Catalogue C2270, 1980, C339 Rover 'Police' and C1001 HCB ANGUS on cover. Foreign 'POLICE' issues listed...................................£10-15
48 page Catalogue C2275, 1980, RESCUE' Vehicle plus '1980/81' on cover £10-15
32 page Catalogue C2282, 1980, as previous, but no Juniors included....... ....£10-15
32 page Catalogue C2283, 1980, same..£10-15
32 page Catalogue C2285, 1981, 'CORGI' container on cover..........£10-15
32 page Catalogue C2290, 1981, same..£10-15
32 page Catalogue C2292, 1981, same..£10-15
32 page Catalogue C2337, 1982, C802 Mercedes on cover, 'Corgitronics' within £10-15
36 page Catalogue - Mettoy Co PLC, 1983, boxed models on cover, new Mercedes and Scania trucks inside..£10-15
32 page Catalogue, 1984, No ref. 'CORGI ` 84' and boxed models on cover. The last catalogue with the Corgi Dog emblem...........................£5-10
48 page Catalogue, 1985, No ref. Cover shows new 'CORGI' trade name logo. The new 'CLASSICS' Commercials listed £5-10

TRADE CATALOGUES METTOY DEALERS TRADE CATALOGUES

A range of models (produced between 1951 and 1954) based on just two vehicles - the Standard Vanguard and a Rolls Royce. They came in attractive window boxes and featured a clockwork motor plus brake, adjustable steering (controlled by moving the central fog lamp) and moulded grey plastic wheels. Both diecast and plastic bodies have been observed. This listing has been taken from the 1951 Mettoy Catalogue and the editor would welcome any additional information

36 pages 1948, diecast mechanical vehicles, tinplate air craft, cars, lorries, motorcycles, domestic appliances, train Sets....................£150-200
36 pages 1949, diecast vehicles, aircraft, tinplate cars, lorries, motorcycles, tractors, train sets and family games, with string binding............. £150-200
36 pages 1951, novelty toys, boats, miniature clockwork models, cars & caravans, fire engines and stations, commercial vehicles and motorcycles, diecast vehicles, farm equipment, train sets, games and others. Also 1951 supplementary list of mechanical novelties for export only two sided flyer..£80-120
32 pages 1952, train sets, household toys, boats, aircraft, farm equipment, fire engines, cars, lorries, diecast & tinplate, action toys and novel ties. Plus 1952 wholesale price list, four sided list with three type written amendments dated January 1952..£100-130
28 pages 1953, tanks and military toys, emergency vehicles, tinplate, diecast, plastic toys, Rolls Royce, farm vehicles and crane, boats, nursery toys, aircraft, kitchen range, Eagle rocket space ship, train sets £120-150
30 pages 1961, Diecast vehicles, Kitchen toys, guns and fort, Wembley series of footballs and rugby balls, plastic nursery toys & others...£60-80

Newsletters and club magazines

Mettoy Corgi Newsletters £5-6
Corgi Club Magazines, 1950s £20-25
Corgi Club Magazines, 1960s £15-18

CATALOGUES, LEAFLETS AND BOX INSERTS (OVERSEAS EDITIONS)

African issues, English text - local currency

British East Africa

16 page Catalogue '8/59', 1959, 'British East Africa 8/59' on cover, along with a tractor and racing car £70-80
20 page Catalogue '9/60', 1960, 'British East Africa 9/60' on cover£50-60
Interim Leaflet, 62/63, No ref. 'British East Africa' on checklist.....£25-35
Interim Leaflet, 61/62, No ref. 'British East Africa' on top of page 2.....£25-35

East Africa

Box Insert '52/258/K5 East Africa', 1958, 'East Africa' on checklist........... ....£25-35
Interim Leaflet, 1965, No ref. 'East Africa' plus 'Mettoy 1965' on checklist £20-25
40 page Catalogue, 64/65, No ref. 'East Africa 8/64' on checklist ..£35-45

Kenya, Uganda and Tanganyika

Catalogue Leaflet '15/158/C3 KUT', 1958, 'Kenya, Uganda and Tanganyika'...£30-35
Box Insert, 1958, '3.350/658/K7/KEN.-UG.-TAN'.................................£30-35

Rhodesia

Early Distributors: Coombe & Dewar Pty Ltd. P.O. Box 1572, Bulawayo and P.O. Box 663, Salisbury.

Interim Leaflet, 61/62, No ref. 'Rhodesia' top of page two £25-35

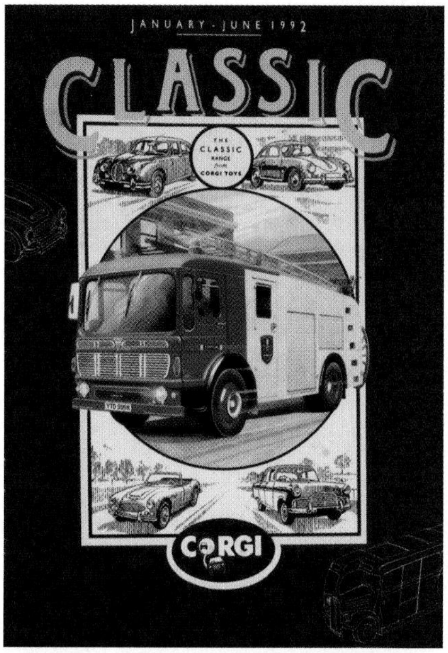

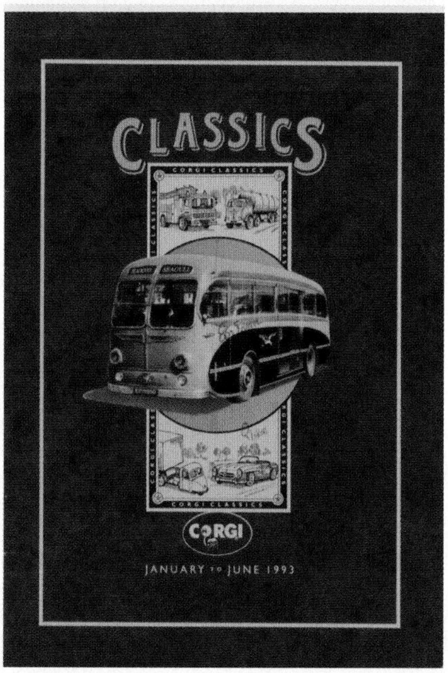

Interim Leaflet, 62/3, No ref. 'Rhodesia' on checklist.........................£25-35
32 page Catalogue 'C/100/62'., 1962, 'Rhodesia 1/63' on checklist. red suited boy on cover...£50-60
Interim Leaflet, 1964, No ref. 'Rhodesia' plus 'Playcraft 1964' on checklist £20-30
Interim Leaflet, 1965, No ref. 'Rhodesia' + 'Mettoy 1965' on checklist......... ....£20-30

Rhodesia, Zambia and Malawi

40 page Catalogue, 65/66, No ref. 'Rhodesia/Zambia/Malawi 8/65' on checklist, + '1965' on cover..£50-60

South Africa and Rhodesia

Box Insert '52/258/K5, 1958, South Africa/Rhodesia' on checklist£25-35
Box Insert '52/258/K6, 1958, 'South Africa/Rhodesia' on checklist£25-35
Catalogue, 1959, Illustrated catalogue "South Africa/Rhodesia 8/59" to cover, with Johannesburg shop stamp neatly printed to front cover £40-50

South Africa

Box Insert '10/658/K7/S. Africa', 1958, 'S. Africa' on checklist page............ ....£25-35
16 page Catalogue '40/1058/C8/S. Africa', 58/59, 'S. Africa' on back......... ....£50-60
Interim Leaflet, 61/62, No ref. 'South Africa' on page two...............£25-35
Interim Leaflet, 62/63, No ref. 'South Africa' on checklist £25-35
Interim Leaflet, 1964, No ref. 'S. Africa' and 'Playcraft Toys Ltd. 1964' checklist...£25-35
Interim Leaflet, 1965, No ref. 'South Africa' plus 'Mettoy 1965' on checklist...£25-35
48 page Catalogue 'C/2017/9/66', 1966, 'South Africa' on checklist and cover £30-40
Interim Leaflet, 1967, No ref, 'South Africa' on cover, plus 'Mettoy, etc. 1967' on last page...£25-35
2-fold checklist '© 1970 Mettoy Co Ltd', 1971, 'Corgi Toys with WhizzWheels' plus 'Australia', 'S.Africa' and 'USA' on cover, Checklist prices in all 3 currencies..£15-20
NB As listed under CANADA, a catalogue was issued in 1970 with a combined CANADA and SOUTH AFRICAN checklist

Australia

Address of Corgi Club in 1959: The Secretary, Corgi Model Club (Australian Section), P.O. Box 1607, M. Melbourne C1

Catalogue Leaflet '20/657/C2/AUS', 1957, checklist dated 1.6.57. Cover shows early 'blue Box' with model 208...£25-35
Box Insert '52/258/K5/Australia', 1958, cover shows model 350 £25-35
Box Insert '52/258/K6/Australia', 1958, 1401 Service Ramp on cover £25-35
Box Insert '10/658/K7/Australia', 1958, cover shows models 209 & 458...... ....£25-35
16 page catalogue, 1959, No ref. 'Australia 8/59' on cover..............£70-80
Leaflet, 61/62, No ref. 'Australia' on top of page two..........................£25-35
Leaflet, 62/63, No ref. 'Australia' checklist..£25-35
Leaflet, 1967, No ref. 'Australia' on cover...£20-25
2-fold Checklist '© 1970 Mettoy Co Ltd', 1971, 'Corgi Toys with WhizzWheels' plus 'Australia', 'S.Africa' and 'USA' on cover. Checklist prices in all 3 currencies..£10-15

Austria

German Text. 'Kontrolliste fur den sammler'

Leaflet '20/657/C2/A', 1957, 'Austria' on checklist..............................£30-35
Interim Leaflet, 61/62, No ref. 'Austria' on top of page two £20-25
Interim Leaflet, 1964, No ref. 'Austria' on checklist...............................£20-25
40 page catalogue, 64/65, No ref. 'Austria 9/64' on checklist..........£35-45
Interim Leaflet, 1965, No ref. 'Austria' on checklist..............................£20-25

Belgium

Early distribution: Joets Eisenmann, S.A., 111/113 Rui Masui, Bruxelles, Tel: (02) 15.48.50.

Belgian Corgi Club: 1958, M. Le Secretaire du Club Corgi, Jouets Eisenmann, 20 BD M. Lemonnier, Bruxelles.

English Text - French Checklist: 'Liste de Contrôlle pour le Collectionneur'

Box Insert '52/258/K6/Belgium', 1958, 'Belgium' on checklist.....£30-35
Box Insert '5/658/K7/Belg.', 1958, 'Belg' on checklist........................£30-35
Leaflet, 1967, No ref. 'Belgium' on cover...£20-25

English Text - Flemish Checklist:

'Kontroleer zo de Verzameling', 48 page Catalogue 'C/2017/9/66', 1966, 'Belgium' on cover and on checklist...£35-45
Leaflet, 1967, No ref. 'Belgium (Flemish)' on cover...............................£20-25

English Text - separate French and Flemish checklists:

Interim Leaflet, 61/62, No ref. 'Belgium' on top of page two...........£20-25
Interim Leaflet, 62/63, No ref. 'Belgium' on checklist £20-25
40 page Catalogue, 63/64, No ref. 'Belgium 8/63' on checklist £40-50
Interim Leaflet, 64, No ref. 'Belgium' and 'Playcraft 1964' checklist£20-25
Interim Leaflet, 65, No ref. 'Belgium' and 'Mettoy 1965' on checklist.......... ....£20-25
Leaflet, 1967, No ref. 'Belgium' on cover £20-25
48 page Catalogue 'C/2017/7/67',67/68, 'Belgium (French) 1967' on checklist..£35-45

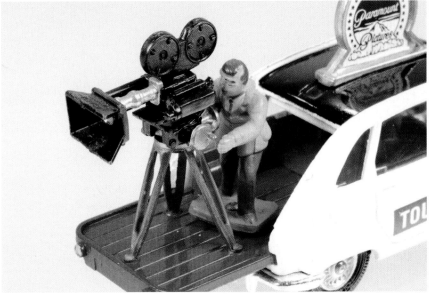

France

English Text - French checklist

Interim Leaflet, 61/62, No ref. 'France' on page two..........................£30-40
Interim Leaflet, 62/63, No ref. 'France' on checklist..........................£30-40
40 page Catalogue, 63/64, No ref. 'France 8/63' on checklist plus '1963-64'
on cover £60-70
Interim Leaflet, 64/65, No ref. 'France' and 'Playcraft 1964' on checklist ...
....£30-40
Interim Leaflet, 1965, No ref. 'France' and 'Mettoy 1965' on checklist........
....£30-40

French Text and checklist
'Liste de Controle pour le Collectioneur'

40 page Catalogue, 1965, No ref. 'France 8/65' on checklist plus 'Playcraft
Toys Ltd. 1965' on rear cover £50-60
48 page Catalogue 'C2017/8/67', 1968, French text '1968' on cover ....
....£30-40
48 page Catalogue 'C2017/9/68', 1969, French text '1969' on cover ....
....£20-30
40 page Catalogue, 1973, No ref. French text '1973' on cover £15-20
40 page Catalogue 'C2107 1974', 1974, French text '1974' on cover...........
....£15-20
Catalogue Leaflet, 1975, No ref. French text 'Corgi '75' on cover £10-15
16 page Catalogue 'C2222', 1977, French text 'Corgi '77' on cover ..£20-30
48 page Catalogue 'C2275'. 80/81, French text plus '1980/81' on cover
(includes Juniors) £15-20
32 page Catalogue 'C2282', 80/81, French text plus '1980/81' on cover.....
....£15-20
32 page Catalogue 'C2290', 81/82, French text plus '1981 Mettoy' on rear
cover £15-20

Holland

Agent for Holland: N.V.S/O, Herengracht 25, Amsterdam.
Dutch Text throughout

20 page Catalogue, 1959, No ref. 'Holland 8/59' plus 'FL.O.10' on cover
plus Dutch text £70-80
24 page Catalogue, 1961, No ref. 'Holland 9/61' plus 'F.O.10' on cover
plus Dutch text £50-60

French Text - Dutch checklist:
'Kontroleer zo de Verzameling'.

48 page Catalogue 'C2281', 80/81, '1980 Mettoy' on rear cover.....£20-30
30 page Catalogue 'C2291', 81/82, French text, Dutch checklist, plus
'1981 Mettoy' on rear cover £20-30

English Text with French and Dutch checklists

40 page Catalogue, 1974, No ref. 'C2107 1974' on French checklist. 'C2103
1974' on Dutch checklist..£20-30

English text - Dutch checklist

Catalogue Leaflet '20/657C2/NL', 1957, 'Holland' on checklist £20-30
Catalogue Leaflet '15/158/C4/H', 1958, 'Holland' on checklist £25-30
Box Insert '52/258/K5/HOLLAND', 1958, 'Holland' on checklist £25-30
Box Insert '52/258/K6/HOLLAND', 1958, 'Holland' on checklist .£25-30
Box Insert '5/658/K7/HOL.', 1958, 'HOL' on checklist................£25-30
Interim Leaflet, 60/6, No ref. 'Holland' on checklist.......................£25-30
Interim Leaflet, 61/62, No ref. 'Holland' top of page two...............£25-30
Interim Leaflet, 62/63, No ref. 'Holland' on checklist £25-30
40 page Catalogue, 63/64, No ref. 'Holland 8/63' on checklist.......£60-80
Interim Leaflet, 1964, No ref. 'Holland' on checklist £25-30
40 page Catalogue, 64/65, No ref. 'Holland 9/64' on checklist.......£25-30
Interim Leaflet, 1965, No ref. 'Holland' on checklist £25-30
48 page Catalogue 'C2017/9/66', 1966, 'Holland' on cover and checklist...
....£40-50

---

48 page Catalogue 'C2017/7/67', 67/68, 'Belgium 8/67' on Flemish
checklist and 'Belgium (French) 8/67' on French checklist................£35-45
40 page Catalogue, 1974, No ref. 'C2103 Belgium' on Flemish checklist
plus '2107' on French checklist...£15-25

English Text - French/Flemish combined checklist:
Catalogue Leaflet '20/657/C2/B'.,1957, 'Belgium' on checklist £25-35
Catalogue Leaflet '20/258/C5/B'., 1958, 'Belgium' on checklist £25-35

French Text - French checklist:
Box Insert '120/1058/K8/Belg'., 1958, No. 458 E.R.F. on cover £25-35
20 page Catalogue, 1960, No ref. 'Belgium 9/60' and 'Frs.3.' on cover.........
....£40-50
24 page Catalogue, 1961, No ref. 'Belgium 9/61' and 'Frs.3.' on cover.........
....£40-50
40 page Catalogue, 65/66, No ref. 'Belgium 8/65' on checklist £30-40

Canada
English text - local currency

Catalogue Leaflet '40/258/C5/CA', 1958, 'Canada' on checklist £30-35
Box Insert '52/258/K5/Canada', 1958, 'Canada' on checklist £30-35
Box Insert '52/258/K6/Canada', 1958, 'Canada' on checklist £30-35
Box Insert '5/658/K7/CAN', 1958, 'CAN' on checklist.....................£30-35
20 page Catalogue 'Canada 9/60'., 1960, 'Canada 9/60' on cover £40-50
Interim Leaflet 'Canada'., 60/61, 'Canada' on checklist £30-35
24 page Catalogue 'Canada 9/61', 61/62, 'Canada 9/61' on cover£60-70
Interim Leaflet 'Canada'., 61/62, 'Canada' on checklist...................£30-35
32 page Catalogue 'C/100/62', 1963, 'Canada 1/63' on checklist..£50-60
Interim Leaflet 'Canada'.,1964, 'Canada' and 'Playcraft Toys Ltd. 1964'
checklist...£30-35
Interim Leaflet 'Canada'., 1965, 'Canada' and 'Mettoy etc. 1965' on
checklist...£30-35
40 page Catalogue 'Canada 9/64', 64/65, 'Canada 9/64' on checklist plus
'1965' on cover..£40-50
40 page Catalogue 'Canada 8/65'., 65/66, 'Canada 8/65' on checklist
plus '1966' on cover...£40-50
48 page Catalogue 'C2017/9/60'., 1966, 'Canada' on cover and checklist.
....£40-50
Interim Leaflet 'Canada', 1967, 'Canada' on cover plus 'Mettoy 1967' on
last page..£25-35
7-fold Leaflet 'Canada'., 1969, Concorde featured on cover; '8/69' on
checklist..£50-60

French Text Issue
48 page Catalogue 'C/2017/9/66'., 1966, 'Canadian (French)' on cover....
....£50-60

Combined Canadian and South African checklist
48 page Catalogue,, 1970, No ref. 'Canada, South Africa' on checklist. 'The
Mettoy Co. Ltd. 1970' on rear cover...................................£50-60

Denmark
All the text in Danish
20 page Catalogue, 1960, No ref. 'Denmark 9/60' and '25 re' on cover ....
....£40-50
24 page Catalogue, 1961/62, No ref. 'Denmark 9/61' and '25 re' on cover......
....£40-50
48 page Catalogue 'C2214'., 1977, 'Katalog' and 'Corgi '77' on cover.........
....£10-15

English text - Danish checklist.
'Samlerers Kontrolliste'

Interim Leaflet, 60/61, No ref. 'Denmark' £20-25
Interim Leaflet, 61/62, No ref. 'Denmark' on page two................£20-25
40 page Catalogue, 63/64, No ref. '1963-64' on cover, 'Denmark 8/63' on
checklist..£50-60
Interim Leaflet, 1964 I, No ref. 'Denmark' and 'Playcraft 1964' on
checklist..£20-25
40 page Catalogue, 64/65, No ref. '1965' on cover, 'Denmark 9/64' on
checklist..£40-50
40 page catalogue, 65/66, No ref. 'Denmark 8/65' on checklist plus '1966'
on cover...£30-40
48 page Catalogue 'C2017/9/66', 1966, 'Denmark' on cover and
checklist..£30-40
40 page Catalogue 'C2105 1974'., 1974, Danish checklist, 'Corgi 74' on
cover..£10-15
48 page Catalogue 'C2271', 80/81, Checklist '1980/81' on cover ..£10-15
30 page Catalogue 'C2292', 81/82, Checklist 1981-82' on cover ..£10-15

Eire
Box Insert '52/258/K6/EIRE', 1958, 'Eire' on checklist £20-25
Box Insert '5/658/K7/EIRE', 1958, 'Eire' on checklist £20-25
Interim Leaflet, 60/61, No ref. 'Eire' on checklist £20-25
Interim Leaflet, 62/63, No ref. 'Eire' on checklist £15-20
Interim Leaflet, 64/65, No ref. 'Eire' plus 'Playcraft 1964' on checklist.......
....£15-20

Finland
English Text - local currency
40 page Catalogue, 63/64, No ref. 'Finland 8/63' on checklist plus '1963-
64' on cover...£30-40
Interim Leaflet, 1965, No ref. 'Finland 6/65' and 'Mettoy 1965' on
checklist..£20-25

Interim Leaflet, 1967, No ref. 'Holland' on cover..................£20-25
48 page Catalogue 'C2017/7/67', 67/68, 'Holland 8/67' on checklist ....
....£50-60
48 page Catalogue 'C2017/9/68', 1969, 'Holland 10/68' on checklist........
....£30-40
40 page Catalogue 'C2211 1974', 1974, Dutch text in checklist £20-25
40 page Catalogue, 1974, No ref. C2107 on French checklist plus C2103 on Dutch checklist...£20-25

Hong Kong
Catalogue, 1961, No ref. 24 pages, 'Hong Kong 9/61' on cover £70-80
Interim Leaflet, 61/62, No ref. 'Hong Kong' on page two £20-25
Catalogue 'C/100/62', 1963, 24 pages, 'Hong Kong 3/63' on checklist ....
....£60-80
Interim Leaflet, 1963, No ref. 'Hong Kong' on checklist £20-25
Interim Leaflet, 1964, No ref. 'Hong Kong' on checklist £20-25
0 pages, 65/66 4, No ref. 'Hong Kong 8/65' on checklist.................£60-80
Catalogue 'C2017/9/66'., 1966, 48 pages, 'Hong Kong' on cover and checklist..£60-80

Italy
1963 Concessionaria per l'Italia: Ditta 'Guimar' via Disciplini 7, Milano (303). 'Distinta di Controllo per i Collezzionisti'
Box Insert '52/258/K5 ITALY', 1958, 'Italy' on checklist £25-35
Box Insert '52/258/K6 ITALY', 1958, 'Italy' on checklist £25-35
Box Insert '5/658/K7 ITALY', 1958, 'Italy' on checklist £25-35
Catalogue, 1959, No ref. 20 pages, 'Italy 8/59' on cover £50-75
Interim Leaflet, 60/61, No ref. 'Italy' on checklist £20-25
Catalogue, 1961, No ref. 24 pages, 'Italy 9/61' on cover £40-50
Interim Leaflet, 61/62, No ref. 'Italy' on page two £20-25
Interim Leaflet, 62/63, No ref. 'Italy' on checklist £20-25
Catalogue, 63/64, No ref. 40 pages, 'Italy 8/63' on checklist..........£70-80
Interim Leaflet, 1964, No ref. 'Italy' on checklist £20-25
Catalogue, 64/65, No ref. 40 pages, 'Italy 9/64' on checklist..........£30-40
Interim Leaflet, 1965, No ref. 'Italy' on checklist £20-25
Interim Leaflet, 1967, No ref. 'Italy' on cover. 'ATTENDETE OGNIMESE LE NOVITA 'CORGI'...£20-25

Concessionaria per l'Italia:
1974   Toyuro s.n.c., Via S. Vittore 45, Milano (20123)
Catalogue 'C2112 1974'., 1974, 40 pages, 'Italia' reference on checklist .....
....£15-20
Catalogue 'C2278', 80/81, 48 pages, Italian text throughout £10-15
Catalogue 'C2293', 81/82, 32 pages, Italian text throughout £10-15

Japan
Folded Leaflet, 1968...£40-50
Catalogue, 1973, No ref. 40 pages, Japanese text throughout........£20-30

Malta
Leaflet, 1964, No ref. 'Malta' on checklist...................................£25-35
Catalogue, 64/65, No ref. 40 pages, 'Malta 8/64' on checklist........£50-60
Leaflet, 1965, No ref. 'Malta' on checklist...................................£25-35

New Zealand
Catalogue, 64/65, No ref. 40 pages, 'New Zealand 8/64' on checklist ....
....£50-60
Leaflet, 1965, No ref. 'New Zealand' on checklist £25-35
Catalogue, 65/66, No ref. 40 pages, 'New Zealand 8/65' on checklist ....
....£50-60

Norway
'Se dem alle 1 den nye Katalogen, Samlers Liste'. English Text - Norwegian checklist
Leaflet, 61/62, No ref. 'Norway' on page 2 ....£25-30

Leaflet, 62/63, No ref. 'Norway' checklist....................................£25-30
Leaflet, 1964, No ref. 'Norway' checklist.....................................£20-25
Catalogue, 64/65, No ref. 40 pages, 'Norway 9/64' on checklist £30-40
Leaflet, 1965, No ref. 'Norway' checklist.....................................£20-25
Catalogue, 1966, No ref. 40 pages, 'Norway 8/65' on checklist £30-40
Catalogue 'C2017/9/66', 1966, 48 pages, 'Norway' on cover and checklist....
....£35-45
Catalogue 'C2017/7/67', 67/68, 48 pages, 'Norway 8/67' on checklist ....
....£35-45
Catalogue, 1970, No ref. 48 pages, 'Norway' on checklist £25-30
Catalogue 'C2113', 1974, 40 pages, Norwegian checklist £15-20
Catalogue 'C2272', 80/81, 48 pages, Norwegian checklist £10-15
Catalogue Leaflet, 1975, No ref. Norwegian text throughout, plus '1975 Mettoy'...£10-15

Portugal
'Lista de controle para o colecionador'
English Text - Portuguese checklist.
Catalogue Leaflet '25/257/C2/P', 1957, 'Portugal' on checklist....£25-35
Leaflet, 1960, No ref. 'Portugal' checklist....................................£20-25
Leaflet, 61/62, No ref. 'Portugal' on page 2 ....£20-25
Leaflet, 62/63, No ref. 'Portugal' checklist £20-25
Catalogue, 63/64, No ref. 40 pages, 'Portugal 8/63' on checklist ...£35-45
Leaflet, 1964, No ref. 'Portugal' checklist £20-25
Catalogue 'C2017/7/67', 67/68, 48 pages, 'Portugal 8/67' on checklist ......
....£35-45

Singapore/Malaya
Box Insert '52/258/K5, 1958, SINGAPORE/MALAYA, 'Singapore/Malaya' on checklist...£25-35
Catalogue Leaflet '10/258/C5/SM', 1958, 'Singapore/Malaya' on checklist..£25-35
Box Insert '3.350/658/K7 SING.-MAL', 1958, 'Sing-Mal' on checklist ....
....£25-35
Catalogue, 1960, No ref. 20 pages, 'Singapore Malaya 9/60' on cover..........
....£70-80
Leaflet, 1960, No ref. 'Singapore/Malaya' on checklist £25-35
Catalogue, 1961, No ref. 24 pages, 'Singapore/Malaya 9/61' on checklist ...
....£60-70
Leaflet, 62/63, No ref. 'Singapore/Malaya' on checklist £25-30
Catalogue 'C/100/62', 62/63, 32 pages, 'Singapore/Malaya 2/63' on checklist..£50-60
Leaflet, 1965, No ref. 'Singapore/Malaya' on checklist £20-25

Spain
Spanish Text and checklist. 'Lista de Coleccionistas'.
Checklist., 1961, 24 pages, 'Spanish 9/61' on cover £30-40

English Text - Spanish checklist. 'Lista de Precios para Coleccionistas'
Checklist 'C/100/62', 1962, 'Spanish' on checklist £25-30
Checklist 'C2273'., 80/81, Spanish text in checklist £10-15

Sweden
'Kontrollista för Samlaren'. English text - Swedish checklist
Box Insert '52/258/K5/SWEDEN', 1958, 'Sweden' on checklist £25-35
Box Insert '52/258/K6/SWEDEN', 1958, 'Sweden' on checklist £25-35
Box Insert '5/658/K7/SWEDEN', 1958, 'Sweden' on checklist......£25-35
Catalogue, 1959, No ref. 16 pages, 'Sweden 8/59' on cover...........£40-50
Leaflet, 60/61, No ref. 'Sweden' checklist.....................................£20-25
Catalogue, 1961, No ref. 24 pages, 'Sweden 9/61' on cover...........£40-50
Leaflet, 61/62, No ref. 'Sweden' on page 2 ....£20-25
Leaflet, 62/63, No ref. 'Sweden' checklist.....................................£20-25
Catalogue, 63/64, No ref. 40 pages, 'Sweden 8/63' on checklist.....£50-60
Catalogue, 64/65, No ref. 40 pages, 'Sweden 9/64' on checklist.....£40-50
Leaflet, 1965, No ref. 'Sweden' checklist......................................£20-25
Catalogue, 1966, No ref. 40 pages, 'Sweden 6/65' on checklist £35-45
Catalogue 'C2017/9/66', 1966, 40 pages, 'Sweden' on cover and checklist ..
....£35-45
Leaflet 1967, No ref. 'Sweden' on cover.......................................£20-25
Catalogue 'C2106 1974', 1974, 40 pages, Swedish text on checklist £15-20
Leaflet, 1975, No ref. All Swedish text...£10-15
Catalogue 'C2277', 80/81, 48 pages, Swedish text throughout £10-15

Swedish text - Norwegian checklist
Catalogue 'C2287', 81/82, 32 pages, Swedish text + Norwegian checklist..
....£10-15

Switzerland
English Text - English/Swiss checklist
Catalogue Leaflet '20/657/C2/CH', 1957, 'Switzerland' on checklist.........
....£70-80
Box Insert '52/258/K5/Switzerland', 1958, Reference on checklist...........
....£25-35
Box Insert '52/258/K6/Switzerland', 1958, Reference on checklist...........
....£25-35
Box Insert '5/658/K7/SWITZ', 1958, Reference on checklist £25-35
Catalogue '25/1058/C8/SWITZ', 1958, 16 pages, 'Switz' on checklist. New issues in French £70-80
Catalogue Leaflet '5/658/C5/CH', 1958, 'Switzerland' on checklist ....
....£25-35
Leaflet, 1960/61, No ref. 'Switzerland' on checklist £25-30

Catalogue, 1961, No ref. 24 pages, 'Switzerland 9/61' on cover.......£40-50
Leaflet, 61/62, No ref. 'Switzerland' on page 2..................................£20-25
Catalogue 'C100/62'., 62/63, 32 pages, 'Switzerland 1/63' on checklist......
....£40-50
Leaflet, 62/63, No ref. 'Switzerland' on checklist...............................£20-25
Leaflet, 1964, No ref. 'Switzerland' on checklist.................................£20-25
Catalogue, 64/65, No ref. 40 pages, 'Switzerland' on checklist.......£25-35
Leaflet, 1965, No ref. 'Switzerland' on checklist.................................£20-25
Catalogue, 1966, No ref. 40 pages, 'Switzerland 8/65' on checklist ...£30-40
Catalogue 'C/2017/9/66', 1966, 48 pages, 'Switzerland' on cover and
checklist..£30-40
Leaflet, 1967, No ref. 'Switzerland' on cover £20-25
Catalogue 'C2017/9/68', 1969, 48 pages, 'Switzerland 10/68' on checklist
....£30-40

USA
Sole Distributor for U.S.A.:
1958, Reeves International Incorp., 1107 Broadway, New York 10, N.Y.,
Catalogue Leaflet '20/458/C5/U.S.A.', 1958, 'U.S.A.' on checklist £30-40
Box Insert '20/658/K7/U.S.A.', 1958, 'U.S.A.' on checklist................£30-40
Catalogue 'USA 8/59', 1959, 16 pages, pictures of tractor and racing car
on cover...£70-80
Catalogue 'USA 9/61', 1961, 24 pages, 'U.S.A. 9/61' on cover £50-60
Leaflet, 1961/62, 'U.S.A.' on page two..£25-30
Catalogue 'C/100/62', 1962/63, 32 pages, Cover shows boy in red with
corgi dog. 'U.S.A. 5/63' on checklist..£70-80
Leaflet 'USA 8/65', 1962/63, 'USA' on checklist.............................£25-30
2-fold Checklist, 1964, No ref. Ghia L 6.4 featured on cover. 'USA' and '©
Playcraft Toys 1964' £25-30
Catalogue, 1964/65, No ref. 40 pages, green 9001 Bentley and Ghia L6.4 on
cover. 'USA 8/64' on checklist...£55-65
Catalogue, 1965/66, No ref. 40 pages, 'U.S.A. 8/65' on checklist.....£55-65
Leaflet, 1967, No ref. 'U.S.A.' on cover...£20-25
Catalogue 'C2017/9/68', 1968/69, 48 pages, Chitty-Chitty-Bang-Bang on
cover 'USA 10/68' on checklist..£30-40
2-fold Checklist '© 1970 Mettoy Co Ltd', 1971, 'Corgi Toys with
WhizzWheels' plus 'Australia', 'S.Africa' and 'USA' on cover. Checklist
prices in all three currencies...£25-30

International issues 1981–1985
The catalogue listings are printed in English, French and
German. Catalogue 'C2293' was issued as a miniature booklet.

Shop Display and 'Point-of-Sale' Items
1950s Display Card sign, Corgi Major Toys 'Major', 'Bedford', 'Carrimore'
Car Transporter', 'Now with Hydraulic Feel'. An authentic model it looks
right it feels right Ask to see it work' £120-180
1950s Carded 3-D display Stand, red, yellow, blue black 'CORGI TOYS'
plus 'NEW' in various languages...£250-350
57-59 Display stand, wooden. Ten cream 'corrugated' hardboard shelves,
pale blue display background with yellow and blue plastic 'CORGI TOYS'
sign screwed to top of display, (30 x 29 x 12 inches)..................£200-300
57-59 Display card/sign, tin/cardboard, yellow/blue with gold 'dog'
logo, 'Wow! Corgi Toys-The Ones with Windows' £100-150
57-59 Display card/sign, as previous item but with 'New Corgi Major
Toys The Ones With Windows'...£100-150
57-59 Wooden display unit, two shelf stand with blue backing logo
'CORGI TOYS', 'THE ONES WITH WINDOWS', 'MODEL PERFECTION'
and 'NEW' plus the early gold Corgi Dog on red background...£200-300
57-59 Counter display unit, cardboard, single model display card with
dark blue inner display area, 'new - CORGI TOYS'............................£75-125
57-59 Counter display unit, cardboard, 2 tiers with 'New - CORGI MAJOR
TOYS' in yellow/blue..£200-300
57-59 Counter display unit, cardboard, 2 tier unit, 'COLLECT CORGI
TOYS' and 'New MODELS EVERY MONTH' logos in yellow/blue. £200-300
57-59 Counter display unit, cardboard, Renault Floride (222) pictorial
display card with '1959 MOTOR SHOW' and 'EARLS COURT' logos ....
....£300-400
57-59 Counter display unit, cardboard, Citroën (475) pictorial display
card with 'new - THE CITROEN' and 'OLYMPIC WINTER SPORTS' logos...
....£200-300
1959 Display unit, shows picture of GS8 'Combine Harvester Set'. 'At work
in the field' logo £150-200
57-67 Metal display stand, tiered stand 75cm x 30cm x 45cm high, three
'CORGI TOYS' and black logos, + 3 early gold Corgi dog emblems................
....£175-225
1950? Shop Display Stand, Three dimensional carded shop display
stand with "Corgi Toys New" to top and "That's More Like It" to bottom ...
....£450-550
1960 Counter display box, stand for GS1 Bedford Carrimore (1101) and
4 cars £300-400
1960 Window display sign, yellow background with 'Naturally Corgi
Toys' in red and blue, illuminated. 27" long x 8" high. (Belgian market?) ....
....£500-700
60-61 Window sticker, 'NEW MODELS EVERY MONTH' £30-40
1960s Metal display stand, has 'Corgi Display C2034' on the back.............
....£100-150
66-69 Window sticker, advertising new releases...............................£20-30
60-69 Oblong window sign, glass or plastic with 'CORGI TOYS' and
'PRECISION DIE-CAST SCALE MODELS' logos plus gold Corgi Dog logo

in blue/yellow/red design..£200-300
1960s Tinplate stand, five grey tiers topped by 'CORGI TOYS'/gold dog
header £200-300
60-69 Glass display sign, square sign, gold corgi dog on red panel within
blue lined glass surround...£150-200
1961 Moulded Corgi Dog, on hind feet holding a 'CORGI CHRISTMAS
CARD' £200-300
68-83 Metal display stand, tiered stand 75 cm x 3.5 cm x 45 cm high,
with three 'CORGI TOYS' black/yellow logos, plus 3 white/red late Corgi
dog emblems..£150-200
71-73 Oblong sign, plastic, with 'CORGI' and 'TESTED BY THE CORGI
TECHNOCRATS' plus white Corgi 'dog' logo on red square, yellow
background plus three 'Technocrats' faces...£100-150
63-65 Display stand, rotary, C2001/2 for self-selection, 7 tray unit, large
'CORGI TOYS' header sign...£200-300
63-65 Display stand. Rotary, C2003. Self-selection, 4 columns, 4
compartments (45 x 30 in.), large 'CORGI TOYS' header boards **£200-300**
63-65 Display stand. Rotary C2004 Self-selection, 4 column, 72

compartments (72 x 30 in.) £200-300
63-65 Display stand. Rotary, C2005 Self-selection, 2 column, 36
compartments (72 x 30 in.)..£150-200
63-65 Display stand, Rotary, C2006 Self-selection, 2 column, 36
compartments (55 x 30 in.)...£100-150
63-65 Display stand, Plastic, C2007 large moulded plastic counter
display to house up to 50 models, large black header display board with
'NATURALLY CORGI TOYS' on yellow/blue background, and 'JOIN THE
CORGI MODEL CLUB' on display front £200-300
1960s Electric Display stand, revolving, C2008 glass fronted, to house
100-120 models with light and dark simulated wood panels with four
'CORGI' logos, (38 x 24 x 24 in.)..£350-450
57-66 Showcase. Glass, C2009 3 glass shelves, 3 'CORGI TOYS' logos
(black/blue) plus gold Corgi 'dog' logo on red background, (20x15x9 in.)....
....£200-300
1970s Corgi Juniors unit, E9051. Yellow plastic (21.75 x 21.75 in.), for 48
models, 'LOOK FOR WHIZZWHEELS' £100-150
1970 Retailers Shop Display Cabinet, illuminated 'Corgi Toys', 172cms
high, 121cms wide, 50cms deep, 3 drawers, upper glass fronted display
cabinet, 8 glass shelves...£900-1000
1975 Army diorama, plastic vacuum formed to hold various models
from Corgi Military Range green, grey and brown...............................£300-380
1976 Kojak's Buick, Card counter-top £100-125
1979 'Corgi Toys' display unit, metal, approx. 3' x 2' with 4 shelves/
racks £250-300
Shop display card, 'Mr Softee Ice cream free with this Corgi Toy' **£300-400**
Shop display stand, 'New! Chrysler Imperial' £100-130
Shop Display Stand, With 'New! The Bentley Continental' brown and
cream fold out cardboard counter display unit...................................£400-500
'Corgi Toys' Hanging Tin Sign, 'Corgi Dog and 'Corgi Kits' (52cm x
20cm) £400-500
Corgi Toys Shop Counter Display. Four Motorway Spaghetti Junctions,
wooden base, card back, plastic three lane motor-ways with metal pillars
and supports, 75cm tall, 60 x 40cm base...£500-650
1979 'CORGI TOYS' Metal Stand, Approx. 3ft x 2ft with 4 shelves/racks .....
....£250-300
Magic Roundabout display stand, cardboard................................£400-500

CORGI TOYS WINDOW POSTERS
485   **Mini Countryman with Surfer**, 'New This Month', 245mm x
200mm...£100-120
428   **Karrier Bantam Ice cream Van**, 'Mister Softee' 'New This
Month', 245mm x 200mm...£100-150
      Citroën Safari 'Wildlife Preservation', 'New This Month'
      245mm x 200mm...£150-200
428   **Karrier Bantam Ice cream Van**, 'Mister Softee'. 'Each box end
worth 6d for any Mister Softee Van', 270mm x 140mm..................£100-150
270   **Aston-Martin DB5**, 'James Bond' - 'Now with Revolving Number
Plates and Tyre Slashers', 400mm x 120mm..................................£100-130
261   **Aston-Martin DB5**, 'James Bond' and 'goldfinger', 300mm x
200mm...£200-250
268   **'The Green Hornet'**, Black Beauty original 1960s window
advertising poster £120-150